EX LIBRIS

VINTAGE **CLASSICS**

W. SOMERSET MAUGHAM

William Somerset Maugham was born in 1874 and lived in Paris until he was ten. He was educated at King's School, Canterbury, and at Heidelberg University. He spent some time at St. Thomas' Hospital with the idea of practising medicine, but the success of his first novel, *Liza of Lambeth*, published in 1897, won him over to letters. Of *Human Bondage*, the first of his masterpieces, came out in 1915, and with the publication in 1919 of *The Moon and Sixpence* his reputation as a novelist was established. At the same time his fame as a successful playwright and short story writer was being consolidated with acclaimed productions of various plays and the publication of *The Trembling of a Leaf*, subtitled *Little Stories of the South Sea Islands*, in 1921, which was followed by seven more collections. His other works include travel books, essays, criticism and the autobiographical *The Summing Up* and *A Writer's Notebook*.

In 1927 Somerset Maugham settled in the South of France and lived there until his death in 1965

OTHER WORKS BY W. SOMERSET MAUGHAM

Novels
The Moon and Sixpence
Of Human Bondage
The Narrow Corner
The Razor's Edge
Cakes and Ale
The Merry-Go-Round
The Painted Veil
Catalina
Up at the Villa
Mrs Craddock
Christmas Holiday
The Magician
Theatre
Liza of Lambeth
Then and Now

Collected Short Stories
Collected Short Stories Vol. 1
Collected Short Stories Vol. 2
Collected Short Stories Vol. 3
Collected Short Stories Vol. 4
Short Stories
Ashenden
Far Eastern Tales
More Far Eastern Tales

Travel Writing
The Gentleman in the Parlour
On a Chinese Screen
Don Fernando

Literary Criticism
Ten Novels and their Authors
Points of View
The Vagrant Mood

Autobiography
A Writer's Notebook
The Summing Up

W. SOMERSET MAUGHAM

Plays: Volume One

VINTAGE

1 3 5 7 9 10 8 6 4 2

Vintage
20 Vauxhall Bridge Road,
London SW1V 2SA

Vintage Classics is part of the Penguin Random House group of companies
whose addresses can be found at global.penguinrandomhouse.com.

Penguin
Random House
UK

Copyright © The Royal Literary Fund

W. Somerset Maugham has asserted his right to be identified as the author of this
Work in accordance with the Copyright, Designs and Patents Act 1988

penguin.co.uk/vintage

A CIP catalogue record for this book is available from the British Library

ISBN 9781784872120

Printed and bound by Clays Ltd, St Ives plc

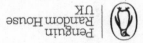

CONTENTS

Sheppey

A PLAY IN THREE ACTS

Characters

Albert
Two Customers
Miss Grange
Sheppey
Bradley
Mr Bolton
A Hairdresser
Miss James
A Reporter
Bessie Legros
Mrs Miller
Florrie
Ernest Turner
Dr Jervis
Cooper

The action takes place in Bradley's Hairdressing and Barber's saloon in Jermyn Street and in Sheppey's house in Camberwell.

Act One

The scene is Bradley's Hairdressing and Barber's Saloon in Jermyn Street.

At the back is the front shop in which the cashier sits, and the door from the street leads into it. From this a doorway, closed by a curtain, gives entrance to the saloon. This is lined with mirrors, with basins, and in front of each basin is a barber's chair. In the middle of the room is a table on which are papers and magazines, two or three chairs for customers to sit on if they have to wait, and a round coat-and-hat rack and umbrella stand. A door in one of the side-walls leads to the room where the assistants sit when they are not occupied.

[*When the curtain rises* **Two Customers** *are being served. One of them has just had his hair cut by* **Albert**, *and* **Miss Grange**, *the manicurist, is finishing his nails. The other customer is in process of being shaved by* **Sheppey**. **Sheppey** *is a stoutish, middle-aged man, with a red face and twinkling eyes. He has a fine head of black wavy hair. He has a jovial, well-fed look. He is a bit of a character and knows it.* **Miss Grange** *is very refined.*]

Albert: Anything on the 'air, sir?

Customer: As long as it's not greasy.

Albert: Number three, sir?

Customer: All right.

[**Albert** *sprinkles some hair wash on the customer's head. During the next few speeches he brushes and combs the hair.*]

Albert: Anything you're wanting today, sir?

Customer: No.

Albert: 'Air's very dry, sir.

Customer: That's how I like it.

3

Sheppey

Albert: Getting a bit thin on top, sir.

Customer: I think it's rather becoming.

Albert: Matter of taste, sir. I can thoroughly recommend our number three. We sell a rare lot of it.

Customer: You're not going to sell any to me.

Albert: Very good, sir. All I meant to say is, it can't 'elp but do the 'air good. Mr Bradley makes it 'imself. It's made of the very best materials. I can guarantee that.

Customer: Shut up!

Miss Grange: You don't want a high polish on them, do you?

Customer: Just ordinary.

Miss Grange: I'll put a high polish on them if you like.

Customer: I don't want to see my face in them, you know.

Miss Grange: I never like to see a gentleman's nails too highly polished.

Customer: I dare say you're right.

Miss Grange: I mean to say, I always think it makes one look like a foreigner.

Customer: Oh, do you think it does?

Miss Grange: I'm positive of it. And one doesn't want to look like one of them Argentines, does he?

Customer: They look terribly rich, you know.

Miss Grange: I can put as much polish on your nails as you like, you know.

Customer: Oh no, don't trouble.

Miss Grange: Oh, it's no trouble. I mean, you've only got to say the word.

Customer: As long as they're neat and clean that'll do me.

Miss Grange: That's what I always say, neat but not gaudy.

Sheppey [*to the customer he is shaving*]: Razor all right, sir?

Second Customer: Yes.

Sheppey: Very mild today, sir.

Second Customer: Yes.

4

Sheppey: I shouldn't be surprised if we 'ad a bit of rain tonight, sir.

Second Customer: Yes?

Sheppey: I 'ear the French 'orse won the three-thirty, sir.

Second Customer: Yes.

Sheppey: 'Ave anything on, sir?

Second Customer: Yes.

Sheppey: Bit of luck for you, sir.

Second Customer: Yes.

Sheppey: I backed Varsity Boy meself, sir. Shilling each way.

Second Customer: Yes?

Sheppey: 'E 'ad a pretty good chance.

Second Customer: Yes.

Sheppey: You 'ave to be pretty smart to spot a winner every time.

Second Customer: Yes.

Sheppey: It's a mug's game, backing 'orses.

Second Customer: Yes.

Sheppey: That's what I say. But one must 'ave a bit of excitement. Sport of Kings, they call it.

Second Customer: Yes.

Sheppey: Pity so many owners giving up.

Second Customer: Yes.

Sheppey: 'Ard times for all of us.

Second Customer: Yes.

[**Mr Bolton** *comes in. He is a smart-looking, middle-aged man.* **Bradley**, *the proprietor, precedes him through the curtains.*]

Bradley: This way, sir.

Bolton: I'm not too late, am I?

Bradley: No, sir, we don't shut till seven. I told my other young lady she might go, but Miss Grange is here. [*Calling*] Number Three.

Bolton: I'll wait for Sheppey.

Bradley: Just as you like, sir.

Sheppey: I shan't be above two minutes, sir.

[*No. 3 comes through the door.*]

Bradley: All right, Victor. Mr Bolton's going to wait for Sheppey.

[*No. 3 nods and goes back again.* **Bradley** *takes* **Mr Bolton's** *hat and stick.*]

Evening paper, sir?

Bolton: Afternoon, Miss Grange.

Miss Grange: Afternoon, sir. You're quite a stranger. I'm just finished.

Bolton: I don't know that I want a manicure today.

Miss Grange: It's nearly a fortnight since you had them done last, Mr Bolton.

Bolton: I'm only going to have a shave.

Miss Grange: That'll give me plenty of time. I can finish by the time Sheppey does.

Sheppey: Don't you put me on my mettle, Miss Grange. I can shave a customer in four and a 'alf minutes if I want to.

Bolton: You needn't try to make any records on me, Sheppey.

Miss Grange: I don't say I can make an absolutely first-rate job of it in the time it takes you to give a gentleman a shave, but I *can* make his nails look decent.

Bradley: That's right, Mr Bolton. I've 'ad to do with a good many young ladies in my time. I can't off' and remember one as was quicker than Miss Grange.

Miss Grange: Well, practice makes perfect, they say. I like a gentleman's hands to look as if they were a gentleman's hands, and I don't mind who knows it. [*To the customer she is serving*] There, sir, I think that's all right.

Customer: Grand.

[*He gets up.* **Albert** *removes his gown, and takes up a brush and gives him a rapid brush down.*]

Albert: Allow me, sir.

Customer: Oh, that's all right.

Miss Grange [*archly*]: We must send you out of the shop nice and tidy, you know.

Customer: How much do I owe?

6

Albert: Pay at the desk, sir.

[**The Customer** *takes a shilling out of his pocket and gives it to* **Miss Grange**.]

Customer: Here you are.

Miss Grange: Thank you, sir.

Bradley [*helping him on with his coat*]: Allow me, Sir.

Albert [*producing a bottle of hair wash*]: This is our number three, sir.

Customer: Very pretty.

Bradley: We sell a rare lot of it, sir.

Customer: So the gentleman who was cutting my hair said. The information left me speechless.

Bradley: There isn't a preparation on the market to come up to it. And it's not because I make it myself that I say that.

Albert: You'd be surprised what it would do for your 'air, sir.

Customer: I hate surprises. [*He nods.*] Afternoon.

[*The* **Customer** *is ushered out by* **Albert**.]

Sheppey: A little off the ears, sir?

Second Customer: No.

Sheppey: Very good, sir. Shall you be wanting any 'air wash today, sir?

Second Customer: No.

Sheppey: Razor blades?

Second Customer: No.

Sheppey: There's a new safety razor just been put on the market. Beautiful bit of work. I suppose you wouldn't like just to 'ave a look at it.

Second Customer: No.

Sheppey: Very good, sir. Shall I just give the 'air a brush, sir?

Second Customer: No.

Sheppey: Very good, sir. Then I think that'll be all, sir.

[*The* **Customer** *gets up and* **Sheppey** *takes his gown off him. The* **Customer** *tips him.*]

Thank you, sir. [*To* **Mr Bolton**] Now I'm ready for you, sir.

Bradley: I'll just give you a brush, sir.

[**Mr Bolton** *sits down in* **Sheppey's** *chair and* **Miss Grange** *brings up her little stool.* **Sheppey** *fetches a clean gown. Meanwhile* **Bradley** *brushes down the second customer and gives him his hat.*]

Miss Grange: Now let me have a look at those nails of yours, Mr Bolton. Oh, Mr Bolton. I do believe you've been unfaithful to me.

Bolton: What makes you think that, Miss Grange?

Miss Grange: Well, I can see with half an eye that someone has been messing about with your hands. Oh, Mr Bolton, that is too bad of you.

Bolton: I broke a nail playing golf down in the country. I had to do something about it.

Miss Grange: Well, I am disappointed. I never thought you'd do a thing like that. I shall have no end of a job getting your nails nice again. The fact is you can't trust anyone in this world.

Bolton: I apologize, Miss Grange.

Miss Grange: Oh, I didn't mean you, sir. You're a gentleman and that nobody can deny. I meant that girl that done your nails. Well, I ask you.

[**Sheppey** *comes back with a gown and puts it on* **Mr Bolton.**]

Bolton: Sheppey, I regret to inform you that Miss Grange is upset.

Miss Grange: I am and I'm not going to deny it.

Sheppey: Why, what's the trouble?

Miss Grange: Mr Bolton's been unfaithful to me.

Sheppey: You know what men are, Miss Grange. You can't trust them out of your sight.

Miss Grange: And no one knows that better than me, Sheppey.

[**Sheppey** *begins to lather* **Mr Bolton's** *face.* **Albert** *comes in again.*]

Bolton: You didn't seem to be doing very well with your last customer, Sheppey.

Sheppey: Not what you'd call a brilliant conversation-

alist, was he? I knew there was nothing doing the
moment he sat down. I only asked 'im if he was wanting anything today so as he shouldn't feel slighted.

Bolton [*to* **Albert**]: You didn't have much luck with your
number three either, Albert.

Albert: You're right there, sir. He was one of them tight
ones and no mistake.

Miss Grange: I'll say this for you, Albert. You had a good
try.

Sheppey: I was listening to you. You didn't try the right
way.

Albert: When a gent says he likes being bald – well, I ask
you.

Miss Grange: He was aggravating, I must say. He had an
answer to everything.

Sheppey: When a customer tries to be funny 'e's easy.

Miss Grange: Well, Sheppey, I don't believe even you
could have got him to buy anything.

Bolton: Is Sheppey a good salesman?

Miss Grange: You ask Mr Bradley.

Bradley: Best I've ever had.

Bolton: How d'you do it, Sheppey?

Sheppey: Oh, it's just a knack, sir. Of course you want a
lot of tact.

Bolton: You needn't mind telling me, you know. You'll
never catch me if you try till doomsday. All these preparations of yours. A lot of damned nonsense. I wouldn't
take one of them as a gift.

[**Sheppey**, *unseen by* **Bolton**, *gives* **Bradley** *and* **Albert**
a wink. **Bradley** *presently goes out*.]

Sheppey: I know I couldn't sell you anything, not in a
hundred years. You 'ave to be a judge of character in
my business and I know it would be just a waste of
time to try.

Bolton: Thank you for those kind words.

Sheppey: You see, we make our money out of the vanity
of the 'uman race. And I don't mind telling you that
men are every bit as vain as women.

9

Miss Grange: Vainer, if you ask me.

Sheppey: Now don't think I'm wrong in stating that you 'aven't got a spark of vanity in your composition.

Bolton: I daresay you're right.

Sheppey: I know I'm right. I mean, if you was vain you wouldn't want to look any older than you need, would you?

Bolton: I'm only just over forty, you know.

Sheppey: Is that a fact, sir? Of course, being so grey over the temples makes you look more.

Miss Grange: Oh, I like the grey over the temples, Sheppey. I always think it makes a gentleman look so distingay.

Sheppey: I don't say it don't look distingay. I only say it adds a good five years to one's age. If Mr Bolton 'adn't got that grey 'e wouldn't look a day over thirty-five.

Miss Grange: He wouldn't look that, Sheppey.

Bolton: I'm not going to dye my hair to please you, Sheppey.

Sheppey: I don't blame you. I'd never recommend a gentleman to dye his hair. It seems unnatural somehow.

Miss Grange: I always think it makes a face look so hard.

Sheppey: What I mean to say is, I don't suppose you mind if you look thirty-five or forty-eight. Why should you?

Bolton: I don't know that I want to look as though I had one foot in the grave, you know.

Sheppey: You know what I'm thinking of, Miss Grange?

Miss Grange: That German stuff.

Sheppey: Mind you, sir, I'm not trying to sell it to you.

Bolton: That's a good job because you won't succeed.

Sheppey: I'm all for British goods. I don't 'old with foreigners or their doings. When the traveller come in with it I was all against it meself, but 'e persuaded Mr Bradley to give it a trial. And you'd be surprised at the amount we've sold of it.

Miss Grange: Especially when you think what it costs.

Sheppey: What with the duty and one thing and another we can't sell it for less than twenty-five shillings a bottle.

Bolton: What is it, a dye?

Sheppey: No, that's what it isn't. It just makes the 'air grow its natural colour. The result is so gradual that nobody notices. I can tell you this, if you give it a trial, at the end of three weeks you wouldn't 'ave a grey 'air on your 'ead.

Bolton: You don't really expect me to believe that?

Sheppey: What reason 'ave I got for saying it? I know you're not going to try it, sir. Why should you? I know you're not the sort of gentleman as minds what 'e looks like.

Bolton: You're not pulling my leg, are you?

Sheppey: How d'you mean, sir?

Bolton: I thought you might be up to some hanky-panky.

Sheppey: Trying to sell you that stuff? That's not the way I'd go about it. Look here, sir, I don't mind telling you a secret. If you want to sell something to a customer you've got to keep your eye on 'im all the time. You've got to watch 'im like as if you was a boxer in the ring. Now, 'ave I been looking at you?

Bolton: I haven't noticed it.

Sheppey: Well, then. A funny thing 'appened the other day. I expect you know the Marquess of Twickenham, sir.

Bolton: No, I don't.

Sheppey: 'E's one of our customers and so's 'is brother, Lord John. He absolutely insisted on trying this preparation. He was getting terribly grey and it upset 'im like. Well, one morning a gentleman come in and sat down in my chair. Good morning, Lord John, I said to 'im. He began to laugh. I'm not Lord John, 'e said, I'm the Marquess of Twickenham. Would you believe it, I'd taken 'im for 'is younger brother. 'E 'adn't got a grey 'air in 'is 'ead.

Miss Grange: I couldn't help laughing at the sight of Sheppey's face.

Sheppey: Well, his lordship told me there was fifteen years between them.

Miss Grange: Almost a miracle, I call it.

Bolton: What's the stuff called?

Sheppey: Get a bottle, Albert, and let Mr Bolton 'ave a look at it.

Bolton: Don't bother. It doesn't matter at all.

Sheppey [*with a wink at* **Albert**]: Just as a matter of curiosity.

'Ave anything on the race today, sir?

Bolton: No, I didn't.

Sheppey: I wish I 'adn't.

[**Albert** *goes into the front shop.*]

Bolton: Mug's game, betting.

Miss Grange: Sheppey doesn't think so. You'd be surprised the winners he picks.

Sheppey: Of course I never 'ave more than a shilling each way. With a wife and daughter to provide for I can't afford to take risks. I must say I like to 'ave a bit on.

Bolton: You must be pretty smart if you don't lose more than you win.

Sheppey: Well, I'll tell you, I'm lucky. I always 'ave been.

Miss Grange: They say it's better to be born lucky than rich, don't they?

Bolton: Did you have a ticket for the Irish Sweep?

Sheppey: Yes, I wouldn't miss that for anything. I've always 'ad one, ever since they started.

Bolton: You've never won anything, I suppose?

Sheppey: Not yet, but I'm in 'opes.

Bolton: The draw was yesterday, wasn't it?

Sheppey: Yes. They're drawing the consolation prizes today. I might win one of them.

Miss Grange: It would be a nice thing if you opened your paper tomorrow morning and saw your name there.

Sheppey: I shouldn't be surprised.

[**Albert** *comes in.*]

Albert: Captain Fortescue's on the phone, Sheppey. He wants to know if you're free tomorrow morning at eleven-thirty.

Sheppey: Yes. I'm free. Book him, will you?

Albert: All right.

[*He goes out.*]

Miss Grange: He was in this morning, Sheppey. He *was* in a way when he found you wasn't here.

Sheppey: Well, it wasn't my fault, was it?

Miss Grange: Cursing and swearing all over the place, he was.

Sheppey: I know. Only a captain and thinks 'imself a colonel.

[**Albert** *comes in again.*]

Albert: He says, he ain't going to put up with any of your damned impudence again, and if you're not ready and waiting at eleven-thirty sharp he won't be responsible for the consequences.

Sheppey: I suppose they've made 'im commander-in-chief all of a sudden.

Bolton: How is it that you weren't here this morning? I thought you'd never missed a day for fourteen years.

Sheppey: No more I 'ave. Except for me fortnight's 'oliday in the summer. I was at Lambeth Police Court all the morning.

Bolton: Drunk or disorderly?

Sheppey: Not me. 'Alf a pint of bitter to my dinner, and 'alf a pint when I go off work in the evening, that's all the liquor that ever passes my lips.

Miss Grange: He was witness in a case.

Sheppey: I caught a chap stealing the doctor's overcoat out of 'is car. It was standing outside the next 'ouse to mine and I come out of my front door just in the nick of time.

Bolton: You can't leave a thing in your car now. It's rotten. You gave him in charge?

Sheppey: Yes. I almost wished I 'adn't afterwards. Out of work. Told the magistrate 'e 'adn't 'ad a bite for two days. You couldn't 'ardly 'elp feeling sorry for him really.

Miss Grange: You're too soft-hearted, Sheppey. All this

unemployment. I believe if you really want a job you can always find one.

Sheppey: You wouldn't say that if you'd 'eard all I did this morning. My case didn't come on till near the end and I sat there and listened. It made me quite uncomfortable.

Bolton: Why?

Sheppey: Well, you know, I'd 'ad a good breakfast before I left 'ome, and I was enjoying meself. It was a bit of a treat for me not 'aving to come to the shop for once in a way. A lot of cases there was.

Bolton: Anything interesting?

Sheppey: Well, I don't know if you'd call 'em interesting. There was one woman who'd been caught stealing a bit of steak off a barrer. She 'ad eighteen bob a week to keep 'erself and three children. A respectable-looking woman she was too.

Bolton: Of course there's a good deal of distress about nowadays, but there's nothing to do about it.

Miss Grange: That's what I say, there always have been rich and poor in the world and there always will be.

Sheppey: It seems funny in a country like this there should be a lot of people starving.

Miss Grange: If you have three good meals a day and a roof over your head, be thankful, I say, and don't worry about anybody else.

Sheppey: Well, I don't, not as a rule. Only you see, 'aving it brought 'ome to me all of a sudden, like it was this morning, it did give me a bit of a turn. There they was standing in the dock. They didn't look any different to anybody else. They looked just like you and me, if you understand what I mean. I couldn't 'elp saying to meself, not one of them'd be 'ere if they earned what I do.

Bolton: You earn good money because you're steady and industrious.

Sheppey: I know that. But p'raps if they'd 'ad my chances they'd 'ave been just as good as me.

Miss Grange: You are morbid today, Sheppey. You can't be well.

Bolton: Well, it's just on seven. You'll feel better after you've had your glass of beer.

Sheppey: Perhaps I shall. I generally 'ave a steak and veg for my dinner, but some'ow today I didn't fancy it.

Miss Grange: I hope you haven't caught something sitting with all those dirty, unhealthy people.

Sheppey: You don't 'ave much 'eart to keep yourself clean when you don't know where your next meal is coming from and I don't expect it's so easy to keep 'ealthy when you don't get 'ardly enough nourishment to keep body and soul together.

Miss Grange: Oh, don't harp so. Why, you might be a Socialist to hear you talk. I always thought you were a good Conservative.

Sheppey: I'm a Conservative all right. I'll tell you what, Miss Grange, you let me take you to a police court one morning when we're slack and you see for yourself.

Miss Grange: Not me. I'm not going to upset myself. What the eye doesn't see the heart doesn't grieve over, I say. We've all got troubles enough of our own without bothering about other people's.

Bolton: That's the only sensible way to look at it, you know, Sheppey. Everyone knows there's a lot of poverty in this world, but it can't be helped. It's just one of those things that you have to accept, like influenza or a run of bad luck at cards. And the fact remains that no one need starve to death in this country. There are institutions where he can always get a meal and there are shelters where he can always get a bed.

Miss Grange: My belief is that a lot of those people who sleep out on the Embankment sleep there because they really like it.

Bolton: What did your fellow get?

Sheppey: Remanded for a week, sir.

Bolton: Well, I wouldn't mind betting they'll find out

that's not the only thing he's done. A man doesn't steal because he's hungry, he steals because he's a thief.

Miss Grange: And if he's hungry I should have thought he was better off in prison than outside.

Bolton: It's no good fashing oneself about things one can't help. Better brains than yours have tried to find a way out, and if they haven't it's not likely you will.

Miss Grange: Everyone for himself and the devil take the hindmost, I say.

Sheppey: I'm a very ignorant man, I know that. All the same it does make me a bit uncomfortable to think it was me as gave the poor devil in charge.

Bolton: You did quite right. Society must be protected, and it's a citizen's duty to uphold the law. A pretty state of things it would be if a fellow was justified in helping himself to whatever he fancied.

[**Albert** *comes through the curtains.*]

Albert: You're wanted on the phone, Sheppey.

Sheppey: Say I'm busy and ask 'em to leave a message.

Albert: It's your wife and she says it's urgent.

Sheppey: I don't care who it is. My wife knows very well I won't 'ave 'er ringing me up when I'm working.

Bolton: Never mind about me, Sheppey. You go to the telephone. I don't mind waiting.

Sheppey: I wouldn't think of it. You know what women are, sir, give 'em an inch and they'll take an ell.

Miss Grange: Perhaps it's important, Sheppey. She's never rung you up before all the time I've been here.

Sheppey: I should think not indeed. When I'm at 'ome I'm at 'er beck and call, within reason, you know, but when I'm at the shop I'm me own master, as far as she's concerned.

[**Albert** *comes in again.*]

Albert: She says she can't leave a message and you've got to go to the phone yourself.

Sheppey: You tell 'er if it was the King of England ringing up from Buckingham Palace to give me the Order of the Garter I wouldn't go, not while I was in the middle of shaving a customer.

[**Albert** *goes out.*]

Bolton: How long have you been married, Sheppey?

Sheppey: Twenty-three years, sir, and if I may quote the words of our national bard it don't seem a day too much.

Bolton [*smiling*]: Well, if this is the first time your wife has ever rung you up in working hours I don't think it would hurt you to see what she wants.

Sheppey: When you've been at the job as long as I 'ave, sir, you'll know there's one thing you must never do in married life, and that's create a precedent.

Miss Grange: The way you talk, Sheppey. A nicer woman than Mrs Miller I never did know.

Bolton: Who's Mrs Miller?

Sheppey: That's my old lady. My name's Miller really.

Bolton: Is it? I never knew that.

Sheppey: They call me Sheppey because I was born there. Isle of Sheppey. Kent, you know. They kid me because they say I've got Sheppey on the brain.

Miss Grange: To hear him talk you'd think there was no place like it.

Sheppey: No more there is. I always go there for me 'olidays and when I retire I'm going to settle down there.

Miss Grange: I went there one bank holiday. I didn't think so much of it.

Sheppey: The garden of England, that's what it is. I know the very 'ouse I'm going to buy when my ship comes home. Two acres of land. View of the sea. Just the place for me and my old woman.

[**Bradley** *comes in followed by* **Albert** *and the young lady who acts as cashier,* **Miss James** *by name.*]

Bradley: Put that razor down, Sheppey.

Sheppey: Why, what's the trouble?

Bradley: You've won a prize in the Sweep.

Sheppey

Sheppey: Is that all? That's no reason to leave a job unfinished.

[*He is about to go on with his shaving when* **Mr Bolton** *holds his arm.*]

Bolton: No, you don't. I don't want my throat cut.

Sheppey: A little thing like that's not going to affect my 'and. Is that what you're frightened of? Why, I could shave a gentleman if they was dropping bombs over St James's Palace and Jermyn Street was burning like a load of straw.

Bolton: I don't mind telling you I'm not a gentleman who'd be wanting a shave just at that moment.

Bradley: I'll finish Mr Bolton myself. Give me your razor.

Bolton [*passing his hand over his chin*]: No, that's all right. That'll do.

[*Bradley sponges and wipes his face.*]

Albert: There's a wire for you from Dublin, and they've rung up your house from the *Daily Echo*. They wanted your business address.

Bradley: You haven't lost the ticket, Sheppey?

Sheppey: Not me. I've got it on me now. [*He takes out his pocket book and produces the ticket.*]

Miss Grange: How much is it, Mr Bradley?

Albert: Mrs Miller didn't say. She was all excited. Crying and laughing she was. The consolation prizes are a hundred pounds.

Bolton: Well, even that's worth having.

Sheppey: I can do with it.

Miss Grange: You don't seem a bit excited, Sheppey.

Sheppey: Well, to tell you the truth I've been sort of expecting it. I was born lucky.

Miss Grange: If it was me I'd be doing Catherine-wheels all over the shop.

Sheppey: I don't believe Mr Bradley would like that, Miss Grange. Besides, it might put ideas in Albert's 'ead. 'Im not being a married man and all that.

Miss Grange: Oh, don't be so coarse, Sheppey. You know I don't like that sort of joke.

[**Mr Bolton**, *now ready, gets up from his chair.*]

Bolton: You'd better ring up the *Echo* and ask how much it is.

Bradley: A hundred pounds.

Bolton: What about the ten residuary prizes? How do you know it's not one of them?

Sheppey: I never thought of that.

Bradley: Couldn't be.

Albert: There'll be a special edition. Perhaps it's out by now.

Bradley: You nip along round the corner, Albert, and see if it is.

Albert: All right, sir.

[*He goes out.*]

Bolton [*giving* **Sheppey** *a tip*]: Here you are, Sheppey, my best congratulations.

Sheppey: Thank you very much, sir.

Bolton: Whatever it is don't blue it.

Sheppey: Not me, sir. I've made up my mind exactly what I'm going to do with it.

Miss Grange: How can you when you don't know how much it is yet? I mean, supposing it is one of the residuary prizes? [*Pocketing* **Bolton's** *tip*] Thank you, sir.

Sheppey: Anything up to thirty thousand pounds I've got all fixed up.

Bolton: I'll tell you what I'll do, Sheppey: to celebrate the occasion I'll have a bottle of that German stuff you were talking about.

Sheppey: Very good, sir. Shall I send it or will you take it with you?

Bolton: Mind you, I don't believe in it, but to oblige you I'll try it.

Sheppey: Well, sir, I'm sure you'll be surprised.

Bolton: I may just as well take it with me.

Sheppey: A bottle of Grayline for Mr Bolton, please, Mr Bradley.

Bradley: I'll just do it up for you, sir. Cash, please.

Bolton: Good night.

Sheppey

The others: Good night, sir.

> [**Miss James** *steps out and* **Bolton** *follows.* **Bradley** *has held open the curtain for him and goes out after him.*]

Miss Grange: You are a caution, Sheppey.

Sheppey: I know I am. I don't believe there's another man in the business could 'ave sold Mr Bolton a bottle of 'air-dye. They can say what they like, that's all it is. If it's anything at all, that's to say.

Miss Grange: Oh, I wasn't thinking of that.

Sheppey: You wasn't? But it was a masterpiece the way I kidded him. 'E put me on my mettle, saying I'd never sell 'im anything not if I tried till doomsday. 'E's no fool either. Not like some of these young fellows as'll believe anything you tell them. You know, I was listening myself to what I was saying and I said to myself, you're a wonder, Sheppey, there's no doubt about it, you're a little wonder.

Miss Grange: Oh, you make me sick, Sheppey, patting yourself on the back because you sell a mug a bottle of hair restorer, when you've just won a prize in the Irish Sweep.

Sheppey [*taking off his long white working coat*]: Well, I'll tell you, Miss Grange, seeing's believing. I don't ever believe anything till I see it in the papers.

Miss Grange: There's Albert.

> [**Albert** *comes in.*]

Albert: The papers 'aven't come yet.

Miss Grange: Oh, bother.

Bradley [*coming in*]: I've told Miss James to try and get the *Echo*. It's just on seven. Draw the blind down, Albert.

Albert: Right you are, sir.

Bradley: I expect you'll be glad to be getting along home, Sheppey.

Miss Grange: Mrs Miller and your daughter will be in a state.

> [*The bell rings as the door opens.*]

Bradley: Hulloa, who's that?

Miss Grange: My word, people think they can come at any old time.

Bradley: Oh, that's all right. Albert'll say we're closed.
    [**Albert** *re-enters*.]

Albert [*in a whisper*]: It's a fellow from the *Echo*. Wants to see Sheppey.

Miss Grange [*overwhelmed*]: No!

Bradley: Tell him to come along.

Miss Grange: Gracious! And me all anyhow.
    [*She takes out her powder and begins to make up*.]

Sheppey: Where do you come in?

Miss Grange: I don't want to disgrace the shop.

Albert [*through the curtains*]: Step this way, sir.
    [*A young pasty-faced man with a camera enters*.]

Reporter: Mr Miller?

Sheppey: That's my name. Sheppey for short.

Reporter [*shaking hands with him*]: Best congratulations.

Sheppey: Don't mention it.

Reporter: Paper sent me along to get a brief interview.

Sheppey: You've just come in time. Another five minutes and you'd have found us all gone.

Reporter: Feeling pretty good, I suppose?

Sheppey: Not so bad.

Reporter: Ever won anything before?

Sheppey: Never.

Reporter: I suppose you've had tickets?

Sheppey: Never missed since they started.

Reporter: Well, you don't mind if I say it's the first time you ever had one. I mean, it makes a better story.

Sheppey: No, I don't object to that.

Bradley: We were just trying to get on to your paper when you came in.

Reporter: Oh, what about?

Miss Grange: It's one of the hundred-pound prizes, I suppose?

Reporter: D'you mean to say you didn't know? It's one

of the residuary prizes. Eight thousand five hundred pounds.

Sheppey: Is that what it is? That's real money that is.

[**Miss James**, *who has followed the reporter in, suddenly bursts into tears.*]

Bradley: Hulloa, what's the matter with you, Miss James?

Miss James [*sobbing*]: I do apologize. I can't help it. Eight thousand five hundred pounds. It makes me feel quite sick.

Miss Grange: If you're going to be sick you'd better go to the lavatory, I think.

Miss James: Oh, it's all right. Excitement always takes me like that.

Sheppey: It's 'er stomach, poor girl.

Reporter: What'll you do with the money? I suppose you've hardly had time to decide yet.

Sheppey: What makes you think a silly thing like that? I decided that when I bought the ticket. I'm going to pay off the rest of the money on my 'ouse. And there's a little place on the Isle of Sheppey I've got my eye on, two acres of land and just the sort of dinky little 'ouse I've always thought would suit me.

Miss Grange: Fancy you a landed proprietor, Sheppey. We shall have to call you squire.

Sheppey: Then there's my daughter wants to get married. I'll give her a slap-up wedding. Champagne and caviare. And I'll keep a girl to 'elp my wife. No more rough work for that old lady.

Albert: I'd buy a baby Austin if I was in your place.

Sheppey: And who says I won't buy a baby Austin? It would save me a lot of expense getting down to my property in the country.

Reporter: You won't go on working, then?

Sheppey: Me? I wouldn't know what to do with myself if I stopped working. I'm what you might call an artist. Isn't that right, Governor?

Bradley: I wouldn't swear you weren't, not in a court of law.

Sheppey: No, young fellow, I'm not one to waste the gifts the Almighty has given me.

Reporter: What about a photograph of you at work? I think the paper'd like that. Pity it's so late and no customers.

Miss Grange: Mr Bradley can pretend he's a customer.

Bradley: That's right. Give me a gown, Albert.

Albert: Here you are, Governor.

Bradley: You put on your coat, Sheppey.

Sheppey: Half a tick. Shave or hair-cut?

Reporter: Shave, I think. Looks more natural.

Bradley: I'll just put a bit of lather on my face.

Miss Grange: I'll get my stool and pretend I'm doing your nails.

Sheppey: 'Ere, who's being photographed, Miss Grange, you or me?

Miss Grange: Don't be a dog in the manger, Sheppey. I only want it to make a good picture.

Sheppey: You might be one of them Society beauties shoving yourself in like that. Albert'll be wanting to come in next.

Reporter: She's all right. I like that.

[*They all get into attitudes. The* **Reporter** *looks through his camera.*]

Bradley: Don't stand like that, Sheppey. They won't see anything but my legs.

Sheppey: They want to see my face, don't they?

Reporter: Get on the other side of him.

Sheppey: You won't be able to see me.

Reporter: Yes, I shall. That's a good position. Let me see the razor.

Bradley: Not too near my face, Sheppey.

Reporter: Hold it right out.

[**Sheppey** *stretches out his arm.*]

Reporter: That's right. Fine.

Bradley [*noticing that* **Albert** *has edged in*]: What are you doing there, Albert? You get the hell out of there, see?

Sheppey: You don't want to break the camera, do you?

Sheppey

Albert [*sulkily*]: All right. One'd think you'd never been photoed before. Fuss you make of it.

Reporter: Now look at me. Pleasant, now. This isn't a funeral. He's just won a prize in the Irish Sweep. Smile. That's right. Hold it. Thank you.

[*They put on frozen smiles, and when he says thank you return to their natural state.* **Bradley** *wipes the soap off his face and gets out of the chair.* **Miss Grange** *gathers up her stool and her box of utensils.*]

Miss Grange: Will it be in the paper tomorrow?

Reporter: It should be.

Miss Grange: I shall be excited.

Sheppey: It'll be in the papers tonight, won't it? I mean about the draw, the names and all that?

Reporter: Yes. Haven't you seen a paper yet? I've got one on me. For the address, you know.

Sheppey: Mind letting me 'ave a squint? You know, I've never seen my name in print before. Fact is, I can't quite believe it's all true till I see it in black and white.

Reporter [*taking the newspaper out of his pocket*]: Here you are. Front page.

[**Sheppey** *takes the paper and looks at it.*]

Sheppey: That's right. Eight thousand five hundred pounds, Isle of Sheppey. That's my synonym. Joseph Miller, The Rosary, Moore Street, Camberwell, SE17. Well, well, well, who'd 'ave thought it. [*Without thinking he takes off his wig and discloses a very bald head. He meditatively scratches it.*]

Reporter [*taken aback*]: Is that a wig you're wearing?

Sheppey [*coming down to earth*]: Me? Yes. I 'ave to in working hours. Customers are that funny. If you try and sell them a 'air tonic and you're bald like I am, they say it don't seem to 'ave done you much good.

Reporter: It gave me quite a turn to see you take it off all of a sudden.

Sheppey: 'Ere, you're not going to say anything about it in the paper?

Reporter [*with a smile*]: That's asking something.

Sheppey: You wouldn't do that. I mean, you and me are in the same trade, so to speak. I mean, we 'ave to kid the public a bit, don't we? And you know what the public is, it wants to be kidded.

Reporter [*good-naturedly*]: All right. I'll forget about it. Thank you very much. Good evening.

Bradley: Good evening, sir. Give us a look in when you want a hair-cut. Sheppey'll attend to you himself.

Sheppey: I will with pleasure.

Reporter: But I tell you what, you'll never sell me a hair restorer.

Sheppey: I wouldn't be too sure, sir.

Reporter: Good night.

All: Good night, sir.

[*He goes out.* **Albert** *accompanies him to the door and soon after comes back.*]

Miss Grange: Well, that's what I call luck.

Sheppey: Yes, I'll admit that.

Miss James: And you so calm about it all. That's what I can't get over.

Sheppey: Well, I'm used to it, as you might say. I been lucky all my life.

Bradley: I wish I knew how it was done.

Sheppey: I'll tell you. You must believe in it. When I was a young fellow I was a rare one for the girls. And d'you know how I used to get 'em? Bounce. It's the same with luck, you've got to bounce it.

Miss Grange [*with a toss of her head*]: I like that. No one will get me with bounce. The fellow who gets me has got to have a good situation and a bit put by in the savings bank.

Miss James: Men are not what they were. There's no denying that.

Sheppey: That's your poor stomach again, Miss James.

Bradley: Well I'll be getting off. *Tempus fugit*, as they say.

Sheppey: 'Alf a mo, Governor. You must all drink my

'ealth first. I tell you what, I'll pop over to the Bunch of Keys and get a bottle of champagne.

Miss Grange: Oh, Sheppey, if there's anything I like it's a glass of fizz.

Sheppey: I shan't be a minute.

[*He hurries out.*]

Miss Grange: It's funny when you think about it; I'm almost as excited as if I'd won something myself.

Bradley: That shows you have a nice nature, Miss Grange.

Miss Grange: One has to have a nice nature in this business or you couldn't listen to the silly things gentlemen say to one all day long.

Albert: I never pay any attention. It just goes in at one ear and out at the other with me.

Miss Grange: It's easy for you. Gentlemen expect a manicurist to be bright and snappy. And you've got to laugh at their silly jokes or else they say you've got no sense of humour.

Bradley: That's all part of the job.

Miss Grange: I know it is. I'm not complaining. And of course you get a dinner and a theatre out of it now and again.

Albert: To say nothing of a kiss and cuddle in the taxi on the way home.

Miss James: You are vulgar, Albert.

Miss Grange: Well, if a girl won't give a gentleman a kiss in return for dinner and a theatre more fool her, I say. I mean she must know when to stop, of course. But if you're a lady you can always keep a gentleman in his place.

Albert: I suppose they take you to the stalls, don't they?

Miss Grange: Well, it all depends. If they're bachelors, yes. But if they're married it's generally dress circles. They don't think it's so conspicuous.

Bradley: Of course we have a lot of tip-top swells coming to this establishment and naturally they have to be careful.

Miss Grange: Oh, I'm not blaming them. If they mention it, I always say I quite understand. *Noblesse oblige*, if you know what I mean.

[*The whole staff is gathered in the shop when* **Sheppey** *comes in with a bottle of champagne in his hand. He is accompanied by a pretty, painted woman, no longer very young, and flashily dressed in rather shabby clothes. This is* **Bessie Legros**.]

Sheppey: Here I am and here's the champagne. I got the best. Fourteen and nine.

Albert: Whew! It ought to be good at the price.

Bradley: Who's the lady, Sheppey?

Sheppey: A friend of mine. Well, not exactly a friend, but I know 'er, see? I always go in to the Bunch of Keys to 'ave my beer when I shut up of an evening and she's generally 'aving one at the same time.

Bradley [*with a nod to* **Bessie**]: Pleased to meet you.

Bessie: The pleasure's mine.

Sheppey: So we got talking like. And so when I saw 'er just now, I said to 'er, no beer for you today, miss. You come along with me and 'ave a glass of fizz.

Bessie: I didn't say yes and I didn't say no. You know the song, don't you?

Bradley: But you came along, I see.

Bessie: I didn't want to, not really. I said to Mr Miller, Oh, they won't want me, I shall only be in the way. But he said, Get along with you, it's months since you tasted fizz, I lay. And he was right there.

Bradley: Well, you're welcome as far as I'm concerned, and it's Sheppey that's standing the champagne.

Albert: Better let me open it, Sheppey. I'm more used to it than you are.

Sheppey: 'Ark at 'im. All right, only be careful. Now then, you girls, what about glasses?

Miss James: We can manage.

Miss Grange: There's a glass in the lavatory, Victor.

[**Victor** *goes out and comes in again in a moment with a glass.* **Miss James** *goes round the shop and*

Sheppey

collects whatever there is that can be used to drink out of.]

Bessie [*to* **Bradley**]: You have got a beautiful place here.

Bradley: You have to have these days. Lots of competition, you know.

Bessie: It's the same in everything. There ought to be a law against it, I think.

Bradley: You'd be surprised the amount of stuff we have to carry. You come and have a look at my show-cases. [*They walk into the front shop.*]

Miss Grange: Come over here a minute, Sheppey. I want to say something to you.

Sheppey [*going over to her*]: What is it?

Miss Grange: She's a tart.

Sheppey: I know that.

Miss Grange: You didn't ought to have brought her in here, Sheppey.

Sheppey: Why?

Miss Grange: You ought to have more respect for me and Miss James.

Sheppey: Now look 'ere, my dear, you may be in the ladies' 'air-dressing yourself one day. If you think a ladies' salon can get along without tarts you're crazy.

Miss Grange: I don't say I've got any objection to them in business; it's meeting them socially I object to.

Sheppey: Oh, be a sport, Miss Grange. After all one doesn't win eight thousand five 'undred pounds in a sweep every day of one's life. To oblige me.

Miss Grange: Well, as long as you know, I don't mind so much. And they do say, to the pure all things are pure. [*By this time* **Albert** *has opened the bottle, and* **Bradley** *and* **Bessie** *stroll in again.*]

Albert: Come on, all of you. First come first served. [*They gather round and take the tumblers he fills.*]

Bradley: Well, Sheppey, here's your very good health. If I couldn't win a prize myself there's no one I'd rather see win it than you.

Albert: And so say all of us.

28

All [*chanting*]: And so say all of us. For he's a jolly good fellow. For he's a jolly good fellow.

Sheppey: I'm very much obliged to you, ladies and gentlemen. This spontaneous effusion of good will has touched me to the bottom of me 'eart. Ladies and gentlemen, I drink your very good 'ealth.

Miss Grange: I must say, I like a glass of champagne.

Bessie: It's class. That's what it is.

Miss Grange: Mind you, I wouldn't want it every day.

Bessie: Oh, no, I mean if you drunk it every day it wouldn't be a treat, would it?

Albert: A1, Sheppey. Reminds me of the fizz we 'ad at my sister's wedding.

Sheppey: It ought to be good for the money. They 'ad some at twelve and six, but I said, No, on a day like this I want the best.

Bradley: Now, Sheppey, just because you've won a nice bit of money, don't you go wasting it on a lot of foolishness.

Sheppey: Not me. I've got me 'ead screwed on me shoulders all right.

Bradley: I'm very glad to hear you say it. Now I must be getting along home or my wife'll think I'm up to some hanky-panky. You'll shut up all right, Sheppey, won't you?

Sheppey: You can trust me.

Albert: I'll be going too. I'm taking my young lady to the pictures.

[*He and* **Victor** *go out to take off their white coats.*]

Miss Grange: Are you coming, Miss James?

Miss James: I'm quite ready.

Bradley: Good night all. See you tomorrow.

All: Good night, sir.

[**Bradley** *goes out.*]

Miss Grange: Are you going anywhere tonight, dear?

Miss James: No, I'm going to run up that *crêpe de Chine* I bought yesterday.

[**Miss Grange** *and* **Miss James** *go out.*]

29

Sheppey

Bessie: I'll be getting along too.

Sheppey: Don't you hurry. Here, there's a drop more in the bottle. Pity to waste it.

Bessie: I won't say no.

[**Albert** *and* **Victor** *come through.*]

Albert: Good night.

Sheppey: Good night.

Bessie: Hope you have a nice time with your young lady.

Albert: Trust me.

[**Albert** *and* **Victor** *go out as* **Miss James** *and* **Miss Grange** *come in with their hats on.*]

Sheppey: You ain't been long.

Miss Grange: I haven't got too much time. It's partnership evening at my bridge club and I don't want to keep them waiting.

Sheppey: Well, good night.

Miss Grange: Night, Sheppey. [*She gives* **Bessie** *a stiff bow.*] Good night.

Bessie: Good night, miss.

[*The two girls go out.*]

Sheppey: I'll just put the catch on the door.

[*He goes out. When* **Bessie** *is left alone she crumples wearily on her chair. Her face is screwed up into a grimace and a sob is wrung from her. She clenches her hands in the effort to control herself, but the tears come and she takes her handkerchief out of her bag.* **Sheppey** *returns.*]

Sheppey: 'Ulloa, what are you crying for?

Bessie: I'm not crying. It's only tears running out of me eyes.

Sheppey: What's the trouble?

Bessie: Nothing. Only it's cosy here. And you all being so friendly. I shall be all right in a minute.

Sheppey: Here, drink your champagne.

Bessie: No, I daren't. Not on an empty stomach. I expect that's what upset me.

Sheppey: Didn't you have no tea?

Bessie: No, nor dinner either. I'm banting.

30

Sheppey: Well, that's a silly thing to do.

Bessie: Not if you've got no money. I only had tenpence. I spent threepence on my bus up west and I must keep threepence for me bus home if I don't click tonight. And I was going to spend the other fourpence on a beer when you come in.

Sheppey: Well, I saved you that anyway.

Bessie: I felt I just couldn't walk up and down and round and round for hours if I didn't have my beer.

Sheppey: You must be pretty peckish, aren't you?

Bessie: Oh, I don't mind that. I'm getting used to it by now. It's me room I'm worrying about. I'm three weeks behind with me rent and if I don't get a job tonight she'll turn me out.

Sheppey: Oh, I say.

Bessie: Oh, well, the night's young yet. Never say die, that's my motto. It's fine and dry, that's something. It's when it's wet I don't like it.

Sheppey: It ain't exactly my idea of a life of pleasure, I must say.

Bessie: Pleasure? Believe me or not, it's no pleasure to me.

Sheppey: What'll you do if you're turned out of your room?

Bessie: I don't know. Salvation Army Shelter. But you have to sing hymns there. If it don't rain you're better off on the Embankment, they tell me, and the river's nice and close if you happen to feel like jumping in.

Sheppey: Ain't you got any family?

Bessie: Not in London. And then they think I'm doing well. I wouldn't humiliate myself by going to them.

Sheppey: I don't want to hurt your feelings, and of course I never mentioned it when we 'ad our little chats at the Bunch of Keys, but you've always seemed a very respectable woman to me, it surprised me that you was, well, as you might say, on the streets.

Bessie: And well you might be. It's a rare come-down for me, I can tell you. If you'd told me eighteen months ago I'd come to this, I'd have said, Why, you're dreaming.

Sheppey: I knew I was right. The very first time we 'ad a talk, afterwards I said to myself, That's a superior class of woman. I mean, you're not silly. You can talk sensibly. The dogs and football and politics.

Bessie: I'm no fool. I know that.

Sheppey: Seems funny you should be doing this, if you understand what I mean.

Bessie: It's the slump done it. I was all right before that come. I had a nice little flat in Kennington. And I had three or four gentlemen used to visit me regular. Respectable tradesmen, you know, with wives and families, one was a J.P., nice class of men. I used to make my seven or eight pounds a week. And they liked me because they knew they could trust me. If you're a married man and in a good position, you have to be careful, don't you?

Sheppey: Yes, I suppose so. Speaking for myself, from the day I married me wife I've never looked this way or that way.

Bessie: I don't blame you. But you don't find many like that. My experience is, most men want a little bit of fun now and again and somehow they don't want to have it with their wives.

Sheppey: Well, what 'appened then?

Bessie: I had a bit of bad luck. I got double pneumonia and I had to go away for a bit. And when I come back one of my gentlemen had been sold up and another said he couldn't afford luxuries any more. I dare say I wasn't as good-looking as I had been. Well, to cut a long story short, things just went from bad to worse, and the end of it was I had to put me pride in me pocket and come up west.

Sheppey: I say, what's your name? You never told me.

Bessie: Bessie Legros.

Sheppey: Oh, French.

Bessie: Not really. But gentlemen think it is and when

they ask me and I tell them Bessie Legros, they get all
excited. Paris and all that. That's why I took the name.
When I had my little flat in Kennington I used to call
myself Mrs Gloucester, because my first situation
when I come to London was in Gloucester Place. Very
nice lady, she was, not like some I could name, and I
thought I owed her something.

Sheppey: Sort of compliment you paid her, as you might
say.

Bessie [*getting up*]: Well, I must be getting on the job if
I want to earn my rent. No rest for the weary. My God,
what a life.

Sheppey: It's slavery, that's what it is.

Bessie: So's domestic service for the matter of that. And
in my business, well, it is a bit of a gamble, you know.

Sheppey: That 'elps, of course.

Bessie: You may click and you may not. And that keeps
you going.

Sheppey: Look 'ere. I don't 'alf like the idea of you walking about on an empty stomach. It can't be good for
you. 'Ere's five bob. You can get a good meal on that
and there'll be something over in case you want it. [*He
takes two half-crowns out of his pocket and gives them
to her.*]

Bessie: I scarcely like to take it.

Sheppey: Why not?

Bessie: Well, from a friend. I mean, it's not like as if it
was from a gentleman. I'll pay it back as soon as ever
I can. I promise you. I always have paid my way and
except the rent I've never owed sixpence to nobody.

Sheppey: D'you know what I recommend? A nice bit of
steak: with a baked potato.

Bessie: I'll have that, Mr Miller, and thank you for the
idea.

Sheppey: I'll come out with you. I expect my old woman's
terribly excited. Crying and laughing, they said she was.
Good old Ada. [*He gets up. He puts his hand to his
forehead.*] Oh, my 'ead. I do feel funny.

Sheppey

Bessie: Aren't you well, Mr Miller? Sit down, do.

Sheppey: All muzzy.

[*He sinks down on the chair and immediately falls over on the ground.*]

Bessie: My God! [*She sinks down on her knees beside him and shakes him.*] Mr Miller. Mr Miller. Sheppey. Pull yourself together. Don't be silly. Oh, my God, I believe he's fainted. Sheppey. Come on now. Wake up. Oh dear! Oh dear!

Sheppey [*coming to*]: I'm choking.

Bessie: Half a mo'. I'll loosen your collar. My word, it is tight. The things men wear.

Sheppey: Where am I?

Bessie: My God, you did give me a turn. I thought you was dead and I'd be had up for murder. How are you feeling?

Sheppey: Like a bit of fish that's gone wonky.

Bessie: Well, lie still a minute.

Sheppey: I must have fainted. Thing I never done in my life before.

Bessie: Looked more like a fit to me.

Sheppey: Never been fits in my family.

Bessie: I expect it was the champagne.

Sheppey: Fourteen and nine a bottle. Couldn't've been that. You saw me pay for it yourself.

Bessie: You not being used to it and all.

Sheppey: I'm feeling better now. I'll just 'ave a set down for a minute.

Bessie: I'll help you.

[*He gets up on his feet and sits down again in the chair.*]

Sheppey: I'll be all right in two shakes now. Don't you bother about me. I can look after myself.

Bessie: How are you going to get home?

Sheppey: Bus from Piccadilly Circus.

Bessie: You're not fit to go by bus. You ought to take a taxi.

34

Sheppey: My old woman'll think me off me nut if she sees me driving up in a taxi.

Bessie: Well, a taxi you'll take, my boy. I don't think you're fit to go alone either. Like me to come with you?

Sheppey: I shall be all right. I don't want you to neglect your work for my sake.

Bessie: Oh, that's all right. Trade's slack at this sort of time anyhow. I shall get back before things get busy.

Sheppey: Well, I don't mind telling you I do feel a bit queer.

Bessie: The sooner you get home the better. Where's your hat?

Sheppey: Through that door, and me coat's with it.

[*She goes out and comes in again immediately with his hat and coat.*]

That's very good of you, I'm sure.

Bessie: I'll just help you on. [*She helps him on with his coat.*]

What about shutting up?

Sheppey: Only got to slam the gate behind us. There's the lights.

Bessie: I'll put them out.

[*They go to the door,* **Sheppey** *leaning on her arm.*]

Feeling all right?

Sheppey: Feeling fine. All light inside. And 'appy.

Bessie: That's a good thing. There ain't too much happiness in the world, I always say.

Sheppey: I'd like everybody to be happy.

Bessie: Well, they can't be. There ain't enough happiness to go round.

Sheppey [*pointing*]: There are the switches.

Bessie: Which do I turn? All of them?

Sheppey: That's right.

[*As he says this she switches off the lights and they disappear through the curtains into the front shop.*]

Act Two

The scene represents the living-room of Sheppey's house at Camberwell. It is furnished with a suite in fumed oak bought many years ago on the hire-purchase system. There is a shabby old cottage piano with yellow keys and a large grandfather's chair covered with faded twill. On an overmantel above the fireplace are china ornaments. In the place of honour in the middle of the mantelshelf is an old silver-gilt snuff-box. The curtains are of plush. The walls are decorated with hand-painted plates, photogravures in gilt frames, and enlarged photographs of family groups. It is stuffy and overcrowded.

It is latish on Saturday afternoon. Just over a week has passed since the events shown in the preceding act.

*[***Mrs Miller*** *is sitting on a chair, darning socks, and her daughter* ***Florrie*** *is at the dining-table, studying a French grammar and writing an exercise.*

Mrs Miller *is a stout, middle-aged woman, with a good natured, homely face. She has kind eyes and a pleasant smile. She is neat enough in her person, but she has been married too long to bother much how she looks.* ***Florrie*** *is rather smart. She wears a frock bought at the sales, artificial silk stockings, and very high-heeled shoes. Her short hair is permanently waved. She is pretty, alert, and self-assured. She has been a typist in the city, and is confident that there is little worth knowing that she doesn't know.]*

Mrs Miller: I shall 'ave to be thinking about getting supper on the way soon.

Florrie: Oh, Mum, how can I be expected to work if you keep on talking?

Mrs Miller: Sorry. It's a bit of a change 'aving you 'ome on a Saturday afternoon.

Florrie: Ernie had to umpire. The first eleven are playing Cricklewood.

Mrs Miller: Teaching in the Council School all the week, it seems a shame 'e shouldn't 'ave 'is Saturday afternoons.

Florrie: Oh, dry up, Mother.

Mrs Miller: Sorry. You'll strain your eyes reading too much.

Florrie: I'm not reading. I'm writing. Don't say anything to Ernie.

Mrs Miller: How can I? I don't know what you're writing any more than the man in the moon.

Florrie: Exercises. I'm learning French. Only it's a secret.

Mrs Miller: Whatever are you learning French for, Florrie? I don't believe any good can come of that.

Florrie: Now Dad's got this money, me and Ernie have made up our minds to spend our honeymoon in Paris.

Mrs Miller: Oh, 'ave you? Well, it remains to be seen what your dad and me 'ave got to say to that. Paris, indeed. A nice place for a young married couple to go to.

Florrie [*with a grin*]: You mean it's a nice place for a young unmarried couple to go to.

Mrs Miller: Don't be common, Florrie. You know I can't abide anything common.

Florrie: You're so old-fashioned, Mum. Why, it's an education to go to Paris. You know how keen Ernie is on culture.

Mrs Miller: I know he's an educated man. I mean, he wouldn't 'ave got a job as master in one of the County Council Schools if he wasn't.

Florrie: You see, I want to surprise him. You look such a fool if you can't say a word. I can see his face when I start jabbering away at *parlez-vous français, garçong, apportez-moi une café-au-lait, a quelle heuere parti le traing, oui, oui.*

Mrs Miller: Wonders will never cease.

Florrie: I've got a gift for languages. I know that. D'you remember the gipsy last summer on the pier? That's one of the things she said, that I had a gift for languages.

Mrs Miller: I wasn't thinking of that. What amuses me is, you was always going to the pictures and flattening your nose against the shop windows, thinking of nothing but dress, and now you read Ernie's books and you're studying French and I don't know what all.

Florrie: Well, it's natural, isn't it? I don't want Ernie to think I'm just an ignoramus.

Mrs Miller: A what?

Florrie: An ignoramus. He says he knows I've got a good brain, but I haven't had the chance to develop it that he has; he says he's quite ready to make allowances.

Mrs Miller: That's very kind of 'im, to be sure, I think a young fellow's very lucky if 'e can find a girl as can make her own clothes and cook his dinner for him and not spend more money than 'e gives 'er. I know it was in my time.

Florrie: Oh, well, things are different now. Now a girl's got to be educated same as a fellow. Education's everything. I mean, it's only by having education that we can make the world what it ought to be.

Mrs Miller: Who's going to do that? You and Ernie?

Florrie: You see, I know Ernie looks upon it as a bit of a come-down marrying me. Of course he hasn't said so, but I know he feels it, Dad being only a hairdresser and not even having a saloon of his own. Being an employee.

Mrs Miller: Your dad earns better money than many as are their own masters and 'e 'asn't got the responsibility.

Florrie: It's not the money, it's the position. Ernie's father was a clerk in the City. Quite a gentleman by all accounts and naturally that means a lot to Ernie. Mum, you won't ever let on that before you married Dad you were in service, will you?

Mrs Miller: I'm not ashamed of it. If Ernie thinks I learnt to make them meat pies he likes so much without being a professional cook he's a bigger fool than I take 'im for.

Florrie: He never notices what he's eating. I mean, he knows it's good, but his mind is busy with his thoughts. What you don't understand is that Ernie's got a wonderful brain.

Mrs Miller [*with a fond smile*]: Perhaps not. But what I do understand is that you're more in love with 'im than I ever thought to see you with anybody.

Florrie [*charmingly*]: I know, Mum, I can't help it, I'm just silly about him.

Mrs Miller: I don't blame you, my girl. It only comes once in a lifetime, love like that. I daresay 'e's all right. You love 'im all you can. You've been a good daughter to me and a good daughter to your dad. I 'ope you'll be as 'appy together as your dad and me 'ave been and I can't say more than that.

Florrie: Dear old mum.

[*There is a knock at the front door.*]

Mrs Miller: There's Ernie, I expect.

Florrie [*getting up and going to the window*]: No, it isn't. I'd know his knock in a thousand. It's more masterful than that. [*Looking out*] It's a gentleman. He's come in a car.

Mrs Miller: Go and see who it is.

Florrie: All right.

[*She goes out.* **Mrs Miller** *goes to the window and looks out.* **Florrie** *comes in again.*]

Florrie: It's Mr Bradley, Mum. He's asking for Dad. Seems quite surprised he's out.

Mrs Miller: Ask 'im to come in.

[**Florrie** *goes to the door and opens it and speaks.*]

Florrie: Will you come in, sir?

[**Bradley** *enters.*]

Bradley: My name's Bradley. I just came to see how your husband was getting on, Mrs Miller.

Mrs Miller: Won't you sit down, sir?

Bradley: I don't mind if I do.

Mrs Miller: He's out just at the minute.

Bradley: Seems to be out a lot.

Mrs Miller: I 'ad the doctor to 'im and the doctor said 'e ought to stay in bed. I tried to make 'im, but would 'e listen to me? Seems as though 'e couldn't sit still. Out all day long.

Bradley: Where does he go?

Mrs Miller: Well, that's just what I don't know. 'E 'ardly seems to know 'imself.

Bradley: If he's well enough to go gadding about all over the place, I should have thought he was well enough to do a job of work.

Mrs Miller: The doctor wouldn't 'ear of 'im working. 'E's not 'imself. Friday, not yesterday, Friday a week ago, the day we 'eard about the Sweep 'e comes 'ome in a taxi. 'E said 'e'd fainted in the shop.

Bradley: I know. He told me when he came on the Saturday morning.

Mrs Miller: I didn't want 'im to go to work that morning. But 'e would go. Said 'e 'ad an appointment with the Commander-in-Chief.

Bradley [*with a smile*]: That's right. Captain Fortescue. Sheppey calls him that because of the side he puts on.

Mrs Miller: Well, on the Saturday afternoon, after dinner, I could see 'e wasn't well and suddenly 'e came all over queer. 'E just fell like a stone. My word, I was frightened. Fortunately Florrie was 'ere.

Bradley: Your daughter, I suppose?

Florrie: That's right.

Bradley: Pleased to meet you.

Mrs Miller: She phoned for the doctor. The doctor said it looked more like a stroke to 'im than a faint.

Bradley: Lucky he's not paralysed if that's the case.

Mrs Miller: The doctor says the shock and the excitement of winning all that money and Sheppey 'aving such a 'igh blood pressure and all, 'e's convinced it wasn't just an ordinary faint in the shop, but that was a sort of stroke too.

Bradley: I don't wonder you're anxious. If he's had two strokes. They always say three's fatal.

Mrs Miller: The doctor says not to worry. 'E's only got to get 'is blood pressure down and 'e'll be good for another twenty years.

Bradley: Doctors don't know everything.

Mrs Miller: 'E's going back to work on Monday morning.
Bradley: Oh, is he? That's just what I wanted to see him about.

Mrs Miller: It would break 'is 'eart if 'e couldn't' go on working. He takes such a pride in his profession.

Bradley [*with a shrewd look at her*]: He wrote me a letter last night.

Mrs Miller: Did 'e? 'E never told me.

Bradley: He must have left it himself. It hadn't got a stamp on.

Florrie: What did he say?

Bradley: I don't know that I'm quite at liberty to divulge the contents. Perhaps I ought to have a talk to him about it first.

Mrs Miller: 'E's bound to be in soon. 'E knows we're 'aving supper early because Florrie and the gentleman she's engaged to are going to the pictures.

Bradley [*to Florrie*]: Oh, yes. Sheppey told me you were engaged to be married. And when is the happy event going to take place, may I ask?

Florrie [*becoming very refined*]: July. My fiancé's in the scholastic profession and of course we've got to wait till the boys break up for the summer holidays.

Bradley: Almost the first thing Sheppey said when he knew he'd won a prize was, Now I shall be able to give my daughter a slap-up wedding.

Florrie: My fiancé's father was on the Stock Exchange, you know, and sometimes my fiancé' says he wonders if he didn't make a mistake not going into the City, on account of the money, you know, but I say to him, Money isn't everything, if you're in the scholastic profession you do have decent hols.

Mrs Miller [*to* **Bradley**]: 'Olidays, you know. Well, if it wasn't for the money your dad's getting for the Sweep I don't know when you'd 'ave married. In them County Council schools the pay's terrible.

Bradley: Oh? Teacher in a board school, is he?

Florrie: Of course, if you're a professional man you don't expect to make the money you do in trade.

Mrs Miller: How they expect a fellow to keep a wife and two or three children on it, I don't know, especially when you consider the position they have to keep up.

[*There is a tat-tat-tat on the door.*]

Florrie: There's Ernie.

[*She bolts out of the room.*]

Bradley: Bit of luck Sheppey winning all that money, Mrs Miller.

Mrs Miller: I know. Florrie was crazy to get married. She was in the City, you know, typewriting. She didn't take long to give in her notice, I can tell you.

Bradley: It'll make a difference to you too.

Mrs Miller: I expect it will. I shan't be sorry to 'ave a girl to do the rough work for me. Funny thing, you know, I never 'ave liked washing-up, and God knows I've done enough of it. But when you've been in the 'ouses I 'ave, with always a kitchen-maid to do the rough work, it goes against the grain to do it yourself, and that nobody can deny.

[**Florrie** *comes in with* **Ernest Turner**. *He is a very young man, twenty-two or twenty-three, and extremely good-looking in a somewhat romantic way, with long wavy hair, fine eyes and the profile of a film-star. He is dressed in grey flannel trousers and a brown tweed coat, loose, easy, and shabby, because it is his pose not to pay any attention to the minor matter of clothes. He is alert, vibrant, as they say, and charming.*]

Ernie: Hulloa, Mrs Miller.

Mrs Miller: Come in, Ernie. This is Mr Bradley, Dad's employer.

Ernie [*shaking hands with him cordially*]: I'm very glad to meet you.

Bradley: Same here. I hear I've got to congratulate you on being engaged to this young lady.

Ernie: We've been engaged for two years. What you can congratulate me on is that I'm going to make a blushing bride of her now.

Bradley: Send me an invite and I'll roll up with a wedding present.

Mrs Miller: Of course we'll send you an invite, Mr Bradley. It'll be an honour to 'ave you come.

Bradley: Well, Sheppey's been in my employment for fifteen years and I look upon him as a friend. I really do. You know we all call him Sheppey at the shop?

Ernie: Yes, I know. I call him Sheppey too. Seems to suit him somehow.

Mrs Miller: I've got in the 'abit of it meself now.

Bradley: He's wonderfully popular with my customers. Lot of them won't let anybody touch them but him, and if he's busy they'll wait or come another day.

Mrs Miller: I never asked you if you'd like a cup of tea, Mr Bradley.

Bradley: No, thank you. I wouldn't trouble you.

Mrs Miller: It's no trouble. I've got to go into the kitchen anyway to get my supper going.

Florrie: If you want to please Mum you'll ask her to show you the kitchen. She's as proud of that.

Mrs Miller: Sheppey give me one of them new Eagle Stoves for my birthday. You wouldn't believe the difference it makes.

Bradley: I know. He was talking about it in the shop. I should like to see that, I must admit. If all I hear is true, I've half a mind to buy one myself.

Mrs Miller: I'll show it you with pleasure.

Bradley [*to* **Florrie**]: You'll excuse me, won't you?

[*They go out.* **Florrie** *turns and faces* **Ernie**, *smiling.*]

Ernie: You've got a nerve, shooing him off like that.

Florrie: I saw at a glance that he was that sort of man, interested in contraptions.

Ernie: Wonderful eye for character you've got.

[*He goes up to her and leans his face forward. She leans hers forward too and gradually their lips meet. Then he takes her in his arms and a long kiss is exchanged. She breaks away with a sigh.*]

Florrie: Oh! I feel all the better for that.

Ernie: I don't think it's done me any harm either.

Florrie: Did you win your match?

Ernie: What do you think? With me umpiring. As a matter of fact I had a few words with their umpire. But I wasn't going to let my boys be licked by any Cricklewood chaps. You can't blame me.

Florrie: I don't. You'd do anything for your boys, wouldn't you?

Ernie: Well, I like them, I don't deny that, and they like me. They're getting up a subscription, a penny each, to give me a wedding present.

Florrie: That is nice of them.

Ernie: It's voluntary, of course, but I shouldn't like to be in any boy's shoes who didn't subscribe. It's a grand thing, teaching. Getting a hold on all those young minds and training them. I mean, it must mean something to a man when he sees the way they look up to him.

Florrie: I should be very much surprised if they didn't look up to you.

Ernie: That's as it may be, but it does give one a sort of sense of responsibility. After all, they're citizens of the future. And what sort of citizens they'll be depends on me. You might almost say that what I think today Camberwell'll think tomorrow.

Florrie: It is a responsibility, I see that.

Ernie: Kiss me.

[*They kiss again.*]

Florrie: Oh, Ernie, I do love you so.

Ernie: I'm not going to blame you for that.

Florrie: I wish you loved me as much as I love you.

Ernie: I love you more than anyone in the world. I can't say more than that. But you mustn't forget that man's love is of man's life a thing apart; 'tis woman's whole existence.

Florrie: You're so ambitious.

Ernie: Well, don't you want me to be?

Florrie: Yes. I won't stand in your way, Ernie. I know you want to get on.

Ernie: There's no reason why I shouldn't, that I can see. I mean, think of the advantages I've got. And this money you'll have now. That'll make a difference. I don't see why I shouldn't stand for Parliament.

Florrie: Oh, Ernie, that would be lovely.

Ernie: It's a chance in a lifetime. The old men are finished. Youth is the only thing that counts now. The world's in a mess and who's going to put it right? Youth. It's people like you and me who've got to get busy if we don't want to see civilization crumbling under our feet. What the people want is a leader.

Florrie: You couldn't expect to be a leader right away, Ernie.

Ernie: Perhaps not, but just as a matter of historical information I don't mind telling you that Pitt was Prime Minister at twenty-four. You wouldn't mind living in Downing Street, would you? Convenient, you know.

Florrie: Ernie.

Ernie: Well, why not? Look at Snowden and Ramsay Mac-Donald. If they could do it, why can't I? With my brains and your beauty we can do anything.

Florrie: With the light behind you're not bad looking yourself, Ernie.

Ernie: Looks don't matter for a man. What a man wants is personality. That's one of the reasons I'd like to go to Paris for our honeymoon. One's got to develop one's personality.

Florrie: I was telling Mum just now. She doesn't like the idea much. I think Dad's going to give us a hundred pounds, and I don't see why we shouldn't do what we like with it.

Ernie: We could go to Switzerland on that.

Florrie: Oh, Ernie, I'd simply love to climb Mont Blanc.

Ernie: I wouldn't mind myself. And Switzerland does seem the right place for a schoolmaster to go to in August. We'd meet lots of my colleagues.

Florrie: And then there's lovely Lucerne.

Ernie: There's only one thing; it seems a bit thick doing all that on your money.

Florrie: That's silly. It won't be my money, it'll be our money.

Ernie: Of course it's really an investment. It's not as if we were going just for pleasure. We're going to enlarge our minds. What can they know of England that only England know?

Florrie: That's right.

Ernie: We've got to train ourselves so that when the opportunity comes we shall be ready to take it. We don't want to live for ourselves. We want to live for others. A life of service, that's what I look forward to.

Florrie: Well, I'll do all I can, Ernie.

Ernie: I know you will. But look here, I think we ought to begin as we mean to go on. It's struck me, when we're in a big position, it'll sound silly you calling me Ernie and me calling you Florrie. I think we ought to stop it before it gets so much of a habit we can't break it.

Florrie: Whatever do you mean, Ernie?

Ernie: Well, I think I ought to call you Florence and you ought to call me Ernest.

Florrie: It would make me laugh.

Ernie: Well, try. To oblige me. You couldn't call a Prime Minister Ernie. People wouldn't have any respect for him.

Florrie: All right. I don't mind trying. But not till after the honeymoon. As long as we're on our honeymoon I want you to be just Ernie.

Ernie: Have it your own way.

Florrie: Oh, isn't life lovely?

Ernie: Of course it's lovely. I'm an optimist, I am. I mean, what's the good of taking a gloomy view of things? I know the world isn't perfect. But you can't have everything all at once. I believe in life and I believe in my fellow-men. You must believe.

Florrie: Kiss me.

[*Just as he is about to kiss her* **Bradley** *comes in.*]

Bradley: Your ma wants you a minute, Miss Florrie.

Florrie: Oh, does she? All right.

[*She goes out.*]

Bradley: Well, aren't you going to say thank you?

Ernie: What for?

Bradley: Leaving you alone with your young lady. I saw you couldn't get rid of me fast enough. I've been a young fellow myself, you know.

Ernie: I see you've got tact.

Bradley: You want it in my business. A hairdresser that hasn't got tact is no more use than a canary that can't sing. I just wanted to have a word or two with you.

Ernie: Fire away.

Bradley: I flatter myself I'm not a bad judge of character, and the moment I saw you I said to myself that young fellow's got his head screwed on his shoulders all right.

Ernie: I know how many beans make five, if that's what you mean.

Bradley: You'll never guess why I've come here today. Now Sheppey's got all this money it's all wrong that he should only be an assistant. [*Impressively*] I've come here today to offer him a partnership in my business.

Ernie: You haven't?

Bradley: I have. And mind you, it's a fine business. The accounts are in apple-pie order, and anyone can see them who wants to. I'll give him ten per cent on his money and a share of the profits.

Ernie: That sounds pretty good to me.

Bradley: I expect he'll jump at it, but he's a funny fellow,

Sheppey; he may not like the idea of the responsibility. I want you to back me up.

Ernie: I certainly will. I don't think anyone can call me a snob, but there is a difference between having a father-in-law who's a hairdresser and a father-in-law who runs a high-class saloon in Jermyn Street.

Bradley: All the difference in the world. Then that's settled. But there's something else I wanted to say to you.

Ernie: Yes?

Bradley: Sheppey was up in the West End last night. He left a letter at my place. There's a pub just opposite. The Bunch of Keys it's called. He always has his dinner there.

Ernie: I know. A cut off the joint, veg, and half a pint of bitter. Every day of his life as regular as clockwork.

Bradley: And every night after shutting up he goes there and has another half-pint. A creature of habit, that's what he is. You can always depend on him. Well, I just happened to hear that he was in there last night.

Ernie: Nothing strange in that.

Bradley: No. Only he's got to know a tart there. He brought her in to my place to have a drink the evening he heard about the Sweep. Well, to cut a long story short, he went off with her last night.

Ernie: You don't mean to tell me that.

Bradley: Of course it's no business of mine. All I mean to say is, if he's coming into partnership with me, he can't go about with common tarts, can he? It would be a pity if just because he's got a bit of money he went off the rails.

Ernie: You do surprise me. That's the last thing I should ever have thought he'd do.

Bradley: You know what these women are.

Ernie: He's so steady.

Bradley: I know he is. Mind you, I'm not accusing him. I only say it looks fishy.

Ernie: What do you expect me to do about it?

Bradley: I thought if you gave your young lady a hint – girls know a lot nowadays – she'll understand, and if she gave her ma a hint to keep an eye on him . . . A good woman's influence can do a lot, and my experience is, if a fellow's wife once gets suspicious he has to be pretty smart to put anything over on her.

[**Sheppey** *comes in. His cheeks are flushed and his eyes are shining, but otherwise he looks just as he did when we last saw him. Of course, he does not wear the official wig of his business hours.*]

Sheppey: Good evening, gentlemen.

Bradley: There you are.

Sheppey: Mrs Miller told me you was 'ere, sir. Sorry I've kept you waiting.

Bradley: That's all right. I'm glad to see you looking so fit.

Sheppey: I'm fine. The doctor says I've made a wonderful recovery.

Ernie: You'd better not let him find out you've been out and about when he said you were to stay in and keep quiet.

Bradley: Now, young fellow, if you wouldn't mind I'd just like to have a talk with Sheppey.

Ernie: I'll hop it. See you later.

[*He goes out.*]

Bradley: I wasn't a bit surprised to get your letter, Sheppey.

Sheppey: Won't you sit down, sir?

Bradley: No, I'll stand if you don't mind. You sit down.

Sheppey: I think I will. I'm a bit tired. I been doing a lot today.

Bradley: Naturally it was a bit of a shock to me when you said you were leaving. After fifteen years. But in a manner of speaking I was expecting it. I said to myself at once, now Sheppey's got all this money he won't want to go on being an assistant. I mean, it's not in human nature.

Sheppey: I've always been very 'appy with you, sir. You'd

49

been a good master. And I know I've tried to give satisfaction.

Bradley: You're the best assistant I've ever had, Sheppey, and I don't mind who knows it. No one's got the way you have with a customer. And they like you. You've got a sense of humour.

Sheppey: I suppose I 'ave. Sometimes the things I say almost make me laugh myself.

Bradley: I suppose it's no good offering you more wages.

Sheppey: No, sir, it isn't. When I wrote that letter resigning my position it wasn't because I wanted a rise. I've always been satisfied with what I got.

Bradley: It's no good beating about the bush. Fair and square's my motto. I'm prepared to put my cards on the table. I don't want to lose you, Sheppey.

Sheppey: They say the best of friends must part.

Bradley: I know what you want, Sheppey, and I'm prepared to give it to you.

Sheppey: What do you mean by that, sir?

Bradley: Oh, go on. I wasn't born yesterday. And look here, you needn't go on calling me sir. From now on I'm Jim to you. The moment I read your letter I saw what the game was. Well, all right. I'm on.

Sheppey: I give you my word I don't know what you're talking about.

Bradley: Oh, yes, you do. And I'm quite agreeable. I'll take you in. Of course we shall have to discuss terms. We must keep the old name. The public's used to it and it's worth something.

Sheppey: You're not offering me a partnership in Bradley's?

Bradley: Yes, I am.

[**Sheppey** *gives him a little startled look, hesitates for a moment, and then speaks in a low, harsh voice.*]

Sheppey: Get thee behind me, Satan.

Bradley [*startled*]: Sheppey! What d'you mean?

Sheppey: You know there's nothing I wanted more than to be a partner at Bradley's. It's been the ambition of my life. I never shut up the shop, not a night, without saying to meself, I'd give a lot to be Jim Bradley's partner.

Bradley: Well, now you can be.

Sheppey: No, I can't. It's come too late. I've got other fish to fry.

Bradley: You haven't fixed up with another firm? Sheppey, you wouldn't play me a dirty trick like that, without saying a word to me about it? Not after fifteen years. Look here, Sheppey, I tell you what I'll do. I'll put your name up beside mine. Bradley and Miller it'll be. What do you say to that? It'll be a wonderful moment for you when you see it over the window.

Sheppey: It's not that, Mr Bradley. I'm giving up the 'air-dressing.

Bradley: You're not going to lead an evil life, Sheppey?

Sheppey [*smiling*]: I 'ope not. It would be rather late in the day for that.

Bradley: They say there's no fool like an old fool. You've got money now, I know. But it won't last for ever. Wine, women and song, and you'll run through it in no time.

Sheppey: I'm going to invest it.

Bradley: You'll never find a better investment than what I offer you.

Sheppey: That's a matter of opinion.

Bradley: A man that's got a real gift for hairdressing. I mean, it's such a waste. What do you expect to get for your money?

Sheppey [*casually*]: Treasure in 'eaven.

Bradley: Now, my boy, don't you go into any wild-cat schemes. You talk to your wife about it. She's a sensible woman. I know this offer of mine comes sudden. I'm not going to take no for an answer now. You think it over.

Sheppey: Thanks. But I've quite made up my mind.

Bradley: My experience is that no married man's ever made up his mind till he's heard what his wife has got

to say about it. I'll tell you what I'll do. I'll be off now.
You'll be working next week, I suppose?

Sheppey: Yes. I must work out my notice.

Bradley: I'll give you the week to think it over. Say good-
bye to Mrs Miller for me, won't you?

Sheppey: I will. I'll just see you to the door.

Bradley: I'll find my way out all right. Don't trouble.

Sheppey: O.K. Good evening, sir. Thank you for coming.
[**Bradley** *goes out.* **Sheppey** *goes over to the window
and looks out into the street.* **Mrs Miller, Florrie,** *and*
Ernie *come in.*]

Ernie: We heard him go.

Sheppey: Nice-looking car, that is. My word, the Governor's proud of it.

Florrie: You'll be having one just as good yourself now,
Dad.

Mrs Miller: Ernie's told us, Dad.

Sheppey: Told you what?

Florrie: Oh, Dad, don't try and make a secret of it.

Mrs Miller: I'm so glad for your sake, dear. I know there's
nothing you wanted so much. I almost feel like crying.

Sheppey: Now what are you all talking about?

Ernie: It's like this, Sheppey, Bradley gave me a hint. In
fact he told me in so many words that he was going to
offer you partnership.

Sheppey: Oh, that?

Florrie: Don't take it so calm, Dad. Aren't you excited?

Mrs Miller: It'll be a grand day for me when I walk up
Jermyn Street and see your name in great big letters
alongside of Mr Bradley's.

Florrie: Whoops, dearie.

Mrs Miller: And of course there's the position too. I must
'ave a girl to do the rough work now.

Florrie: You don't want a girl. You must have a general
and a char in twice a week to do the scrubbing.

Mrs Miller [*with a happy little grin*]: I shall be quite the
lady before I'm finished.

Ernie: And why not?

Sheppey [*quietly*]: I'll tell you why not. Because I've declined the governor's invitation with thanks.

Florrie: Dad.

Mrs Miller: Whatever for? Your 'eart's been set on being your own master.

Sheppey: I know it 'as.

Ernie: You haven't turned it down flat?

Sheppey: I 'ave.

Ernie: Naturally he wasn't going to make his final offer straight away. He said to me terms would have to be discussed.

Mrs Miller: It's not the responsibility you're afraid of, Sheppey?

Sheppey: No.

Ernie: But it's a chance in a thousand.

Florrie: You don't want to be ordered about when you can order other people about, surely.

Sheppey: I gave in my notice last night. Of course I shall 'ave to work out the week. Then I'm through.

Mrs Miller: D'you mean you're giving up work altogether? You'd never be 'appy without something to do, Dad.

Ernie: You can't get more than three and a half per cent on your money now, you know. What with income tax and one thing and another you won't find you'll have so much. I mean, it'll be a tight squeeze to make both ends meet.

Florrie: Especially with me and Ernie getting married so soon. We counted on your being able to help us a bit at first.

Sheppey: I'm not going to invest my money at three and a half per cent. I'm not going to invest it to bring that sort of return at all.

Ernie: What's the idea?

Sheppey: Well, you know, I been worried lately. You know that day I had to go to the police court. The prisoners, you know, they was just the same as you and me, I mean, if you'd passed them in the street you'd 'ave thought them exactly like anybody else, and d'you know what put them in the dock, three out of four? Just that they 'adn't enough to eat. It give me quite a turn.

Ernie: The Government's to blame.

Mrs Miller: Quiet, Ernie.

Sheppey: And that same evening I met a woman I know up west, and I discovered accidentally that she 'adn't 'ad a bite of food in twenty-four hours.

Ernie: Times are bad, of course.

Sheppey: Now, this money I've got. I could do with it of course, but I don't really need it, not in comparison, I mean, with the people 'as 'aven't got enough to eat and, no coal to put in their grates.

Ernie: Perhaps not. But you've got it and they haven't. That's the luck of the game. You were born lucky. I've heard you say that dozens of times.

Sheppey: I know it. And perhaps the luckiest thing that's ever 'appened to me is 'aving the chance I've got now.

Mrs Miller: What d'you mean exactly, Dad?

Sheppey: Well, I don't feel justified some'ow in keeping this money.

Florrie: Then give it to Ernie and me. We'll be glad to take it.

Sheppey [*with a smile*]: You don't want it either.

Ernie: What are you going to do with it then?

Sheppey: Ever read the Gospel, Ernie?

Ernie: Of course I have. It's got some damned good lines in it. And the style's fine. Of course you wouldn't want to write like that now.

Sheppey: I been reading it a lot this last week. Not being able to go to the shop, you know. But I'm not an educated man like you, Ernie. I read it for the story.

Ernie: It's a good story. I don't think anyone would deny that.

Sheppey: I came across one bit that knocked me all of a heap. It seemed as if it 'ad been written for me.

Ernie: What was that?

Sheppey: Sell all that thou 'ast, and distribute it to the poor, and thou shalt 'ave treasure in 'eaven: and come and follow me.

Ernie: I know. And it goes on: it's easier for a camel to go through the eye of a needle than for a rich man to enter the Kingdom of Heaven. The rich have been trying to get round that for the last two thousand years.

Sheppey: It was like a great white light. I saw my way plain before me. I'm going to give this money of mine away to them as needs it more than I do.

[*They are thunderstruck. They speak on each other's words.*]

Mrs Miller: Sheppey, what do you mean?

Ernie: You're crazy. You can't do a thing like that.

Florrie: I should think Mum would have something to say to that.

Mrs Miller: You don't mean it, Dad?

Sheppey: Yes, I do.

Ernie: It's ridiculous.

Florrie: Criminal, I call it.

Ernie: After all, what's eight thousand pounds? A drop in the ocean. You might as well throw the money down a drain-pipe for all the good it will do.

Mrs Miller: But, Sheppey, you can't afford to do a thing like that. It would be all very well for some of them rich people in the West End.

Sheppey: They can't do anything. They 'aven't got more money than they know what to do with.

Ernie: Never heard that before.

Sheppey: That's why I'm telling you. Now I do know what I'm talking about. We've always 'ad a tip-top trade at Bradley's. Some of the most important men in the country. Why, only the other day I 'ad a gentleman in as said if things didn't look up soon 'e'd 'ave to give up either his yacht or 'is racing stable.

Ernie: He isn't obliged to have a racing stable, is he?

Sheppey: It's not for 'imself 'e 'as it. 'E's told me over and over again. It's for the good of the country.

Sheppey

Ernie: And do you believe that?

Sheppey: 'E's a gentleman. There's no reason for 'im to tell me a lie, is there? And you wouldn't believe 'ow much it costs to run a pack of 'ounds. I was shaving Lord Mereston one day last week and 'e said to me, Sheppey, 'e said, you wouldn't believe 'ow expensive life is, my daughter's coming out and I've got to give a ball, seven 'undred people and champagne at eighteen bob a bottle. My boy's nursing a constituency and it's costing me fifteen 'undred a year, and to put the lid on, Sheppey, 'e says, I've 'ad to fork out a couple of thousand quid for a diamond bracelet to give my wife for our silver wedding. I tell you what, Sheppey, 'e says, if things don't take a turn for the better soon I'll 'ave to give up being shaved and damned well shave meself. The rich ain't got more money than they can spend on themselves. I know that for a fact. And besides, they don't know about the poor.

Ernie: They can find out, can't they? They can read the papers.

Sheppey: Well, by the time they've read the court and society news, the divorces and the sporting intelligence, they've read enough. They don't want to be depressed by reading about unpleasant things. You can't 'ardly blame them. It's the poor as must help the poor.

Ernie: And they do, don't they? Everyone knows that the poor are splendid to one another. Everyone who writes about them says that. But when all's said and done charity begins at home.

Florrie: That's right. I mean, one must think of those who are near and dear to one first.

Ernie: Mind you, I don't deny that things are pretty rotten in the state of Denmark. But it's no job for an individual. It's a problem and a very grave one, but it's a problem for the community. And the community's tackling it. I don't say charity doesn't want organizing. It does. But there's one thing I'm quite sure about, that the indiscriminate charity of private individuals does more harm than good. That's been proved over and over again. I mean, there's not a charity organization in England that won't tell you that to give a penny to a beggar in the street is a crime.

Sheppey: You may be right. But when you see an old fellow with one leg selling matches in the bitter cold it seems almost against 'uman nature not to give 'im a copper.

Ernie: Well, one ought not to. One's only encouraging them. One's got to take a broad view of things. The law of life is simple as ABC. Get on or get under. If a man can't earn his own living he's no good, to the state or anybody else, and he must be eliminated. That's natural selection. If you molly-coddle the unfit you only make it harder for the rest of us.

Sheppey: I'm not an educated man, but I 'ave got two eyes in my 'ead. And I can't see much difference between the fit and the unfit. It seems to me that good and bad are pretty much alike. I think it's just a toss-up which you are. You remember that story about the seed that was thrown on stony ground and the seed that was thrown on good rich ground.

Ernie: You've got that all wrong, Sheppey. That seed never did any good because it couldn't adapt itself to its surroundings. That's the struggle for life and the survival of the fittest. It just proves what I say.

Sheppey: I read it different. I thought perhaps if it'd been watered a bit and given a bit of shade it might 'ave been all right. You see, these organizations are all very well, but there's a lot of red-tape about them, you know that, and they don't realize a lot of people are proud and don't like asking, and some of them ain't got the nerve to, and there's a lot as are downright stupid, you can't deny that.

Ernie: Well, what can you do about it?

Sheppey: I'll tell you. I'll just keep my eyes open and talk to people, and I'll give 'alf a crown 'ere and five bob there, just as man to man, you know, and a sack of coals to someone as 'asn't got any, and if I see a kid wants a pair of boots I'll buy him a pair.

Ernie: Of course you know you'll have every rotter and sponger after you. And those half crowns and five bobs, where do you think they'll go? On drink.

Sheppey: I dare say I shall make mistakes sometimes. I don't think that matters. Besides, if a chap's down and out and he'd rather spend 'alf a crown on beer than on food and lodging, that's 'is look out.

Ernie: And what do you expect to get out of it for yourself?

Sheppey: Oh, I don't know. Peace of mind. The Kingdom of Heaven, perhaps.

Ernie: And what'll be the result? In a year or two your money'll be gone. D'you think anything'll be different?

Sheppey: You never can tell. Perhaps someone'll come and take my place. If I can only get people to see what I mean. I might be an example to others. Someone's got to start a thing like this.

Ernie: D'you think a hairdresser's the right man to start it?

Sheppey: I don't know why not. Jesus was only a carpenter, wasn't he?

Florrie: I think it's awful comparing yourself to Jesus, Dad. I wonder you're not afraid a thunderbolt'll come down from Heaven and smite you.

Ernie [*sulkily*]: Well, it's not my money, and it's no business of mine what you do with it, but if you'll take my advice you'll look before you leap.

Sheppey [*with a twinkle in his eye*]: I'm always glad to take advice from those younger than myself.

Florrie: What about me and Ernie getting married? We're going to wait, but when you won that Sweep, we settled to marry now. I've given notice at the office and everything.

Sheppey: There's no reason I can see why you shouldn't get married. You'll 'ave as much as Mum and me 'ad when we married.

Florrie: Things are different now. And besides, Ernie's got to keep up a position that you didn't have to. We were counting on your paying the rent of our flat.

Sheppey: You can live here.

Florrie: Can I? Well, I'm marrying to have a home of my own. Say something, Mum, do. You can't let him play ducks and drakes with our money like that.

Mrs Miller: I don't know if I'm standing on me 'ead or me 'eels.

Ernie [*crossly*]: Well, it's not the first time a man has loved the human race so much, he's left his own family to starve.

Florrie: Don't blame me, Ernie.

Sheppey: I knew it would be a sort of disappointment to you.

Ernie: The mistake you make, Sheppey, is taking things too literally. The New Testament must be looked upon as fiction, a beautiful fiction if you like, but a fiction. No educated man accepts the Gospel narrative as sober fact. In fact a great many people believe that Jesus never existed at all.

Sheppey: I don't know that that matters so much.

Ernie: Just now, when I asked you what you expected to get out of it, you said the Kingdom of Heaven.

Sheppey: I know I did. But sometimes I think the Kingdom of 'Eaven's in me own 'eart.

Florrie: You're barmy.

Sheppey [*smiling*]: Because I want to live like Jesus?

Florrie: Well, who ever heard of anyone wanting to live like Jesus at this time of day? I think it's just blasphemous.

Ernie: And there's another thing you must remember. Everyone knows the Gospels were written by ignorant men. I mean they were just ordinary working chaps. And the parables and all that were addressed to the same sort of crowd you might see at Woolworth's of a Saturday night.

Sheppey: Well, perhaps that's why it all come 'ome to me so much, because I'm an ignorant working man meself.

Ernie: Yes, but don't you see, they've got to be explained. Why do you suppose they have professors of theology and doctors of divinity? They're there to explain to people that whatever Jesus said he didn't really mean it, but something quite different.

Sheppey: You may be right, of course. But I don't see why 'e shouldn't 'ave.

Ernie: It stands to reason. Those precepts, the sermon on the Mount and all that, may have been very well for a small peasant community, but they're just not applicable to our great world states. They're impracticable.

Sheppey: I don't know so much about that. Personally I don't know anyone as 'as tried to put them in practice.

Florrie: Well, that's a proof they're impracticable, Dad. I mean, if they were, clergymen and ministers and that like, would do them.

Sheppey: Perhaps they don't believe in them.

Florrie: I don't know why they shouldn't. I believe in them. But there's all the difference in believing a thing just as a thing you believe . . .

Ernie: Theoretically, she means.

Florrie: Yes, and believing it so that you act on it. I mean, when you believe a horse can't lose, you don't believe it in the same way as you believe that if you go out in the rain you'll get wet.

Ernie [*to* **Sheppey**]: I see what you mean, of course. It's an ideal. But you've always got to remember this, an ideal's something you aim at; as soon as you reach it, it stops being an ideal.

Sheppey: It don't seem like an ideal to me. It seems to me like plain common sense.

Ernie: Well, I think it's the damndest nonsense I ever heard.

Sheppey: I'm not quite sure that what you think is gospel truth either.

Florrie: Ernie's an educated man, Dad, and you're not.

[*A knock at the door is heard.*]

Mrs Miller: See who that is, Florrie. Who ever can be coming here at this hour?

[**Florrie** *goes to the window.*]

Florrie: Oh, Mum, it's a lady. She's got a silk dress on. Her shoes don't look none too good.

Sheppey: I know who it is. It's someone I was expecting. I'll go.

[*He goes out.*]

Florrie: Did you know anything about this, Mum?

Mrs Miller: Not a word. It's come as a complete surprise to me.

Ernie [*to* **Florrie**]: You got it in one, Florrie. You hit the nail on the head.

Florrie: How do you mean?

Ernie: He's barmy.

Mrs Miller: Oh, Ernie, that's a horrible thing to say.

Ernie: I don't say it's permanent. But he's barmy. I mean, that's obvious. Look here, what do you say to me running for the doctor?

Florrie: That's a good idea, Ernie.

Mrs Miller: I don't know what to say. I mean it's so unlike him.

Florrie: Go on, Ernie. Here's my key.

Ernie [*taking it*]: I shan't be two ticks.

[*He goes out.*]

Mrs Miller: And him that's always been so sensible. He's never been near, that's not in 'is nature, but 'e's never been one to throw money about neither.

Florrie: Ernie's upset.

Mrs Miller: I don't know what he's got to be upset for.

Florrie: Oh, don't you? Mum, this has got to be stopped. I won't lose Ernie. I won't.

Mrs Miller: Oh, don't be so silly, Florrie. Why should you lose Ernie?

Florrie: You don't know men like I do.

Mrs Miller: I like that. I suppose I didn't know men before you were born.

Sheppey

Florrie: When a woman's been married a year or two she forgets. I can see Ernie's upset.

[**Sheppey** *comes in with* **Bessie Legros.**]

Sheppey: Come in, my dear. Mum, I've brought a friend to see you. This is my wife and that's my daughter Florrie.

Mrs Miller: Oh, Sheppey, and me not dressed or anything. [*To* **Bessie**] Good evening. Won't you sit down?

Bessie: Pleased to meet you. [*To* **Florrie** *with a smile*] Good evening.

Florrie: Good evening. [*She looks her up and down and with her cockney sharpness sums her up and purses her lips.*]

Sheppey: She's going to stay and 'ave a bit of supper with us.

Mrs Miller: Oh, Dad, you might 'ave warned me.

Sheppey: You don't mind pot-luck, do you?

Bessie: Me? A pleasure, I'm sure.

Sheppey: There's always plenty and my wife's a wonderful good cook. You'd be surprised 'ow tasty she makes things.

Florrie [*to* **Bessie**]: You known Dad long?

Bessie: Well, in a manner of speaking I have and in a manner of speaking I haven't.

Sheppey: I knew 'er by sight first. She was always at the Bunch of Keys when I went in to 'ave my beer after I'd shut up. And so we got talking, see? And then last week when I fainted she brought me round. She came in the taxi with me as far as the door.

Bessie: I thought he wasn't fit to take a taxi by himself.

Mrs Miller: That was very kind of you, I'm sure. I'll give you a nice supper. I'm very glad Sheppey asked you to drop in.

Florrie [*suspiciously*]: But I thought you fainted *after* the shop shut.

Sheppey: So I did. We'd just been 'aving a bottle of fizz to celebrate the occasion and the others 'ad gone.

Florrie [*acidly*]: Oh, I see.

Sheppey: Now look 'ere, Florrie, I want you and 'er to be friends. I want you to be a sister to 'er. And I want Mum to be a mother to 'er.

Florrie: The acquaintance is a bit short for that, isn't it?

Sheppey: She's in trouble, Mum, and I want you to 'elp 'er. That evening when I fainted she 'adn't 'ad a bit of food all day and I don't believe she's 'ad much today either. She ain't got a place to sleep tonight, so I said we'd give 'er a shake-down here.

Mrs Miller: Sheppey, we 'aven't got room.

Sheppey: Yes, we 'ave. There's the attic and we can rig up that old bed you said you was going to sell.

Mrs Miller: I wouldn't like to ask anybody to sleep in that.

Bessie: Didn't I tell you? I knew they wouldn't like it. It's all right. I'll manage somehow.

Sheppey [*to his wife*]: To oblige me, my dear. If you say no, it means the Embankment or the streets.

Florrie: Well, she'd be at home there, wouldn't she?

Sheppey: You speak when you're spoken to, Florrie. [*To wife*] She's a nice woman and a good woman. You can't deny me. It's not often I ask you to do me a favour.

Mrs Miller [*giving in*]: I'll be glad to 'ave you to stay the night, miss.

Bessie: That is kind of you. It's a relief to me. I tell you that straight. I didn't know which way to turn.

[**Ernie** *comes in. He gives* **Florrie** *a little nod to indicate that he has executed his commission.*]

Sheppey: 'Ullo, Ernie, where 'ave you been?

Ernie: I just went out to get a packet of fags.

Sheppey: There are some in the snuff-box.

Ernie: I thought they were only for show. [*Seeing* **Bessie**] Got a visitor?

Sheppey: This is Ernie, our Florrie's intended. And this is Bessie.

Ernie: Bessie what?

Bessie: Legros.

Sheppey: She ain't really French.

Sheppey

Bessie: No, it's the name I go by for business purposes.

Florrie: Dad met her at the Bunch of Keys.

Ernie [*remembering what* **Bradley** *had said to him*]: Oh, did he? I see.

Mrs Miller: Well, I'll just go and 'ave a look and see 'ow my supper's getting on.

[*She goes out.*]

Florrie: I'll be getting the table laid.

Bessie: If I can lend a hand I'll be glad to, I'm sure.

Florrie [*with a little sniff*]: I can manage.

Sheppey [*to Bessie*]: I'd like to show you my snuff-box. [*He goes over to the chimney-piece and takes it up.*] One of my customers left it me in 'is will. A very nice gentleman 'e was. I shaved 'im when 'e was dead.

Bessie: It's lovely.

Sheppey: 'E told me it was given to 'is grandfather by King George the Fourth.

Bessie: It must be worth a packet.

Sheppey: It's not that so much. It's the sentiment. I mean, 'aving it left me, see? I wouldn't sell it for a thousand pounds.

Florrie [*getting out the tablecloth*]: I suppose you haven't asked anyone else to drop in, Dad?

Sheppey: Well, now you come to mention it' I 'ave.

Florrie: Oh, you haven't, Dad?

Sheppey: Yes, you know that chap what I caught sneaking the doctor's overcoat. I told 'im to come round.

Florrie: Dad!

Ernie: Isn't he in gaol?

Sheppey: No, the magistrate said 'ed give 'im another chance this time, 'im 'aving been out of work so long, and not 'aving 'ad anything to eat for two days.

Ernie: But the copper told you he'd been in jug two or three times before.

Sheppey: Yes, 'e's 'ad bad luck. That's right. 'E's never 'ad a chance really.

Florrie: Oh, and are you going to give him one?

Sheppey: That's the idea.

[*The door is opened and the* **Doctor** *comes in. He is a middle-aged red-faced man, and very hearty.*]

Doctor: May I come in?

Sheppey: Why, doctor, where 'ave you sprung from?

Doctor: I was just passing and I thought I'd look in and see how you were getting along.

Sheppey: I've never been better in my life. I'm going back to work next Monday.

Doctor: You musn't try and do too much. When are they going to pay you your Sweep money?

Sheppey: In a week or two, I believe.

Doctor: Why don't you go down to the Isle of Sheppey for a bit, and have another look at that cottage you've had your eye on?

Sheppey: I'm not going to buy that now.

Doctor: Oh, why not? I thought your heart was set on it.

Sheppey [*with a sigh*]: I know. I can't. Not now. I should never 'ave a moment's peace.

Doctor: You'll have to be looking out for a nice safe investment then. Don't put too many eggs in one basket, that's all.

Sheppey: I've just been talking about that to my family. I'd be very much obliged if you'd tell them I'm in full possession of my senses.

Doctor: Why? What's the trouble?

Sheppey: Well, you see, it's my money, isn't it? I don't see why I shouldn't do what I like with it.

Doctor: And what do you want to do with it?

Sheppey: Clothe the naked and visit the sick, give food to 'im that is a'ungered and drink to 'im that is athirst.

Doctor: Very praiseworthy of course, within reason. What put the idea into your head?

Sheppey: It came. A great white light.

Doctor: Oh, yes. I see. Of course it's a thing to think over. What we've got to do before we go any further is to get you fit and strong. At your age one can't take liberties with one's constitution. I don't mind telling you I don't like this high blood pressure of yours. Often has funny effects. D'you see things?

Sheppey: I see you.

Doctor: Yes, of course. I mean, do you see things other people don't see?

Sheppey: I see wickedness and vice beating the land with their wings.

[*The* **Doctor** *looks at him meditatively, wondering what he shall ask him next, when* **Mrs Miller** *comes in.*]

Mrs Miller: Sheppey, there's a man at the door says you told him to come here.

Sheppey: That's right.

[**Cooper** *appears at the open door. He is a ragged-looking fellow in a cap, with a scarf round his neck.*]

Sheppey: Come in, old man. Pleased to see you. Found your way all right?

Cooper: I 'ave good reason to remember.

Sheppey: You'll stay to supper, won't you?

Cooper: I don't mind if I do.

Mrs Miller: Who is 'e', Dad?

Sheppey: He's your brother.

Mrs Miller: That! That's no brother of mine. I 'aven't got a brother and no one knows that better than what you do.

Sheppey: 'E's your brother and my brother.

Mrs Miller: I never 'ad but one brother. 'Is name was Percy, and 'e died of meningitis when 'e was seven years of age. [*To* **Cooper**] What's your name?

Cooper: Cooper, mum. Jim Cooper.

Mrs Miller: I never even known a Cooper. [*To* **Sheppey**] What are you going to do with him?

Sheppey: 'E's 'ungry and I'm going to give 'im food. 'E's 'omeless and I'm going to give 'im shelter.

Mrs Miller: Shelter? Where?

Sheppey: 'Ere. In my 'ouse. In my bed.

Mrs Miller: In my bed? And where am I to sleep, then?

Sheppey: You can sleep with Florrie.

Florrie: I can tell you who he is, Mum. He's the chap Dad caught sneaking the doctor's coat and he's been in and out of prison half a dozen times. He's a thief.

Cooper: 'Ere, who are you a'calling a thief?

Florrie: Well, you are, aren't you?

Cooper: I may be. But if you was a man I'd like to see you say it.

Florrie [to **Bessie**]: And as for you. You're a tart.

Bessie: You can call me that if you like, but when I had my little flat in Kennington I described myself as an actress.

Mrs Miller: Supper's ready. If you don't want it to spoil you'd better finish laying the cloth, Florrie.

[**Florrie** *sinks down on a chair and gives a sob.*]

Florrie: What a humiliation! What a humiliation for people in our position!

Mrs Miller: I thought this Sweep money was going to bring us all peace and 'appiness. It don't look much like that now.

Sheppey: Peace and 'appiness, that's what we're all looking for, but where are we going to find it?

Act Three

The scene is the same as in the preceding act.

[**Florrie** *is at the window, looking out.* **Bessie** *comes in. She has an exercise book in her hand.*]

Bessie: Your ma says, what's this doing in the kitchen? She very nearly throwed it away.

Florrie: I shouldn't have cared if she had. It's my exercise book. Fat chance I've got of going to France now.

Bessie: It's a long lane that has no turning.

Florrie: What's the time? [*She looks out of window again.*]

Bessie: Getting on for six. Expecting somebody?

Florrie: Yes and no.

Sheppey

Bessie: Dead-and-alive street this. You never see anything going on.

Florrie: It's a very good class of street, that's why.

Bessie: I don't say it isn't.

Florrie: How much longer are you going to stay here?

Bessie: It depends on your pa. I mean, as far as I'm concerned, I'm sure I don't want to stay where I'm not wanted. You don't like me, do you?

Florrie: Oh, I don't mind you. After the first shock, I mean you being an immoral woman and me being virtuous, I can't see you're any different from anybody else.

Bessie: I don't feel different.

Florrie: Of course at first I thought you were after Dad.

Bessie: Me? I like your pa as a friend. But that's all.

Florrie: Ernie says he wouldn't be surprised if it hadn't been going on ever so long.

Bessie: He doesn't know what he's talking about.

Florrie: Ernie's very respectable. And when you're very respectable you always believe the worst of people.

Bessie: You're worried about Ernie, aren't you?

Florrie: Well, all this has been an upset to him.

Bessie: I can quite understand that. Men don't like surprises. They always want things to go on in the same old way. They're not like women. Anything for a change. Men are awfully conventional, you know.

Florrie: You see, we were going to be married next month, and now I don't know when it'll be.

Bessie: Oh, I say. I know what it is when you've made all your plans and then something happens.

Florrie: He wants to break it off.

Bessie: He hasn't said so?

Florrie: No. But I know he's got it in his mind. Only he's got his self-respect to think of, he's got to find an excuse. Mum says if he wants to break it off it shows he doesn't really love me. But she doesn't know men like I do.

Bessie: They want knowing. There's no mistake about that.

Florrie: I wish you'd give me some advice. You ought to know more about men than most people.

Bessie: Well, I'll tell you. They're near, they'll spend money if they can make a splash, but if they think no one'll know, they're as mean as cat's meat. They're timid, you know, make a scene in public and they'll just go all to pieces. Some of them don't like to see a woman cry. But you have to be careful not to cry too much, you may drive them away, and my experience is, if a man once goes, he don't come back. It'd be a tough job dealing with them if they didn't like flattery. You can't lay it on too thick, my dear, they can never have enough of it. Flattery's meat and drink to them. They'll listen to it for hours. You get sick and tired, but there they are, as fresh as a daisy, just eating it.

Florrie: It's easy for you. I'm so much in love with Ernie. I'd forgive him anything.

Bessie: It's bad when it takes you like that. It makes you so helpless.

Florrie: When you're in love with a man like I am with Ernie he does aggravate you so.

Bessie: I know. It does seem as if they've got no sense sometimes.

Florrie: Ernie's stuck on politics for some reason.

Bessie: You have to put up with a man's ideas. My experience is they don't amount to anything, really, but you must never let on you think that.

[*There is a knock at the door.*]

Florrie: That's his knock. Oh, my heart. It's thumping so I can hardly bear it.

Bessie: I'll go and open the door for him. You stay here.

Florrie: Thanks. My knees are wobbling so I'd have a job to get to the door.

Bessie: Pull yourself together, dear. If you let a man see he means all that to you, he'll lead you a dog's life.

[*She goes out. In a moment* **Ernie** *comes in. He has an evening paper in his hand.*]

Florrie [*bright and eager*]: Ernie! I never recognized your knock. This is a surprise.

Ernie [*on the surly side*]: I told you I was coming along about now.

Florrie: I didn't know it was so late. Time slips by so quickly when you're busy.

Ernie: I see that woman's here still. What about the fellow?

Florrie: Cooper? Oh, he's here. I wonder we haven't all been murdered in our beds by now.

Ernie: Where's your dad?

Florrie: Out somewhere. I don't know. [*She can't keep it up any longer.*] Haven't you forgotten something, Ernie?

Ernie: Me?

Florrie: You haven't kissed me.

Ernie: Sorry. [*He goes towards her.*]

Florrie: You need not if you don't want to.

Ernie: Don't be so silly. [*He kisses her.*]

Florrie [*clinging to him*]: Oh, Ernie, I'm so miserable.

Ernie: Of course you're worried. That's only natural. You can't expect anyone to like seeing their father make a fool of himself.

Florrie: I wish he'd never won that beastly money. We were all as happy as could be.

Ernie: I should have thought your mum could have done something.

Florrie: That's what I tell her. She says he won't listen.

Ernie: It seems almost a pity you should have given up your job.

Florrie [*with a quick look at him*]: I suppose the best thing I can do is to look out for another.

Ernie: It's no good not looking facts in the face. I don't see how we can marry just yet, Florrie.

Florrie: Of course it's for you to say.

Ernie: Naturally it's a disappointment. But we were prepared to wait before and I suppose we can wait now.

Florrie [*clutching her hands in her wretchedness*]: If you want to break it off you've only got to say so.

Ernie: Me? Whatever put an idea like that in your head?

Florrie: Only that I saw it was in yours.

Ernie: I wouldn't let you down, Florrie. Not for anything in the world.

Florrie: It's not much good being engaged if nothing's ever going to come of it.

Ernie: Who says nothing's ever going to come of it?

Florrie: You don't love me like you did a month ago.

Ernie: That's a lie.

Florrie: Listen, Ernie, I love you so much, I've got to know one way or the other. This uncertainty's killing me.

Ernie: My dear, you must be reasonable. We decided we wouldn't be married till I was in a position to provide for you. I didn't want you to have to work. You'd have enough to do looking after the home. And you ought to have a kid or two.

Florrie: Oh, don't, Ernie. It makes me feel awful, hearing you talk like that.

Ernie: You must look at my side of it too.

Florrie: What d'you mean?

Ernie: Well, I'm ambitious. I know I've got ability. I've got a good brain.

Florrie: No one's ever denied that, Ernie.

Ernie: If I've got exceptional powers I ought to use them. I don't want to stick in the common rut. They say you can't keep a good man down, but it's no use hanging a millstone round your neck.

Florrie: Meaning me?

Ernie: Of course not. I wasn't thinking of you. I love you no end, Florrie. I've never seen a girl I could think of marrying except you and my firm conviction is that I never shall.

Florrie: You're not just saying that to please me?

Ernie: No, I swear I'm not. And you mustn't think that what I'm going to say now doesn't mean I don't love you as much as ever I did. If things come right and we could be married tomorrow there wouldn't be a happier chap in London.

Florrie: Well, what is it you're going to say?

Ernie: It's just this: what your father does is his business, and he can do what he likes with his own money. But I'm not going to be made to look a fool by any man.

Florrie: What's going to make you look a fool?

Ernie: If I have a father-in-law who lives like Jesus of course I shall look a fool. How do you expect me to keep my authority over the boys I teach when they know my father-in-law's a funny old buffer mixing with the lowest of the low, and giving his money away? They'd rot the life out of me.

Florrie: It's not very nice for Mum or me.

Ernie: I think it's awful for your poor mother. Of course it won't really be so bad for you, having your work in the City, and naturally, people there won't know anything about it.

Florrie: All the same, I don't see how I can help feeling the disgrace of it.

Ernie: There you are, you see. Now, put yourself in my place.

Florrie: What do you propose?

Ernie: Well, I'd rather leave it to you.

Florrie: I see.

[**Mrs Miller** *comes in.*]

Florrie: Here's Mum.

Ernie: Oh, good evening.

Mrs Miller: Why, Ernie, you're quite a stranger.

Ernie: I've had a lot of school work to do yesterday and the day before.

Mrs Miller: The place 'as been all upside-down with Bessie and that there Cooper being 'ere.

Ernie: A shame, I call it.

Mrs Miller: The extra work keeps me from thinking and that's something.

Florrie: It isn't our house any more. It's a home for waifs and strays.

Ernie: Where's Sheppey, now?

Mrs Miller: 'E 'ad an appointment to see the doctor at four. I'm surprised 'e's not back. It's gone six.

Florrie: You never told me he was going to the doctor's, Mum.

Mrs Miller: I thought I'd better not say anything about it. It's not very pleasant.

Ernie: Why, what's up?

Mrs Miller: I'd rather not speak about it.

Florrie: Oh, go on, Mum. We shall have to know sooner or later.

Mrs Miller: Well, the fact is, Dr Jervis is making an examination as to the state of his mind. I didn't like the idea myself, but 'e said 'e thought 'e ought to. It seems so under'and somehow.

Ernie: How do you mean?

Mrs Miller: Well, Dr Jervis got Sheppey up there pretending 'e wanted to make a thorough examination of 'is 'eart. Said 'e could do it better in 'is consulting-room, where 'e 'ad all 'is instruments, than what he could 'ere.

Ernie: Well, Sheppey's got a high blood pressure, we know that, I mean I shouldn't be surprised if his heart wasn't a bit wonky.

Mrs Miller: Dr Jervis 'as got a friend of 'is to come up. 'E's a specialist it seems, and 'e's coming as a great favour to Dr Jervis. 'E's one of the 'eads at Bethlehem.

Ernie: The lunatic asylum!

[**Florrie** *with clasped hands begins to move her lips, speaking with soundless words.*]

Mrs Miller: 'E's going to pretend 'e's just dropped in for a cup of tea, and then Dr Jervis is going to ask Sheppey to stay and 'ave a cup. And they're going to get 'im in conversation. Dr Jervis said it might take an hour or more before they come to a decision. I tell you I can't bear it. I can't bear the idea of letting my poor old man walk into a trap like that.

Ernie: It's for his own good, isn't it?

Mrs Miller [*noticing Florrie*]: Florrie, whatever are you doing of?

Florrie: Praying to God.

Mrs Miller: Not in the sitting-room, Florrie. I'm sure that's not right.

Florrie: O God, make them say he's potty. O God, make them say he's potty. O God, make them say he's potty.

Mrs Miller: Oh, Florrie, how can you ask God to do a thing like that?

Florrie: If God makes them say he's potty he'll be shut up. Then he can't throw all that money away and he can't make an exhibition of himself. [*Going on in a whisper*] O God, make them say he's potty. O God, make them say he's potty.

Mrs Miller: They won't shut him up. I shouldn't like them to do that. Oh, do stop it, Florrie.

Florrie: I won't stop it. It means life and happiness to me. O God, make them say he's potty, and I'll give up sugar in my tea all through Lent.

Mrs Miller: That's not giving up very much. You're trying to break yourself of sugar as it is because you think it's fattening.

Florrie: Well, it's giving up something you like, isn't it? O God, make them say he's potty, and I promise I won't go to the pictures all next month. [*She goes on muttering to herself with her hands clasped and her eyes turned to the ceiling.*]

Mrs Miller: I wish I 'adn't let Dr Jervis persuade me. I never thought they might want to shut 'im up.

Ernie: It's quite evident he can't manage his own affairs.

Mrs Miller: 'Ow do you know?

Ernie: Well, it's obvious, isn't it? Wanting to give his money away.

Florrie [*interrupting herself for a moment*]: And filling the house with riff-raff. O God, make them say he's ... [*Her voice dwindles away, but her lips keep on moving.*]

Ernie: It's not the behaviour of a sane man. Nobody can deny that.

Mrs Miller: 'Ow do you know 'e's not sane, and it ain't all the rest of us as are potty?

Ernie: That's absurd. Sanity means doing what everybody else does, and thinking what everybody else thinks. That's the whole foundation of democracy. If the individual isn't prepared to act the same way as everybody else there's only one place for him and that's the lunatic asylum.

Florrie: Don't argue with her, Ernie. O God, make them say . . .

Mrs Miller: Jesus didn't do what everybody else did.

Florrie: Oh, Mum, don't talk about Jesus. It's blasphemous, it really is. Can't you see I'm praying?

Ernie: All that was a long time ago. As I was saying to Sheppey only the other day, circumstances alter cases. We're civilized now. Besides – mind you, I don't want to say anything offensive, live and let live is my motto, and I'm all for toleration – but looking at the facts impartially I can't help seeing there was a lot to be said on the other side and if I'd been in Pontius Pilate's position I dare say I'd have done just what he did.

Mrs Miller: I was brought up different from you. Living in the country and all, I never 'ad the opportunity to get the education girls get now. I began to earn my own living when I was fifteen.

Florrie [*sharply*]: Mum. We don't want to go into ancient history. [*Her lips go on moving as she repeats and repeats her prayer.*]

Mrs Miller: But we was church-going people, and I used to go to Sunday school. Nothing of what Sheppey says was new to me, as you might say.

Florrie [*aghast*]: Whatever do you mean by that, Mum?

Mrs Miller: Well, I knew it all, I mean. I'd 'eard it all over and over again when I was a girl. I never paid any attention to it of course, but when Sheppey brought it up again it all come back to me.

Sheppey

Ernie: I may be dense, but really I don't follow.

Mrs Miller: Sheppey's right about what Jesus said. About giving to the poor and all that. And loving your neighbour as yourself. I remember all that.

Ernie: I dare say you do. But you never knew anyone that acted on it, did you?

Mrs Miller: They was young ladies as took Sunday school at 'ome, and I don't think they'd 'ave liked it if one acted on it. They'd 'ave thought it presuming.

Ernie: And so it is presuming. It's always presumption to think you know better than other people.

Mrs Miller: I'm sure Sheppey doesn't mean it like that. No one knows 'is place better than what he does. Why, I've 'eard 'im say twenty times, I like a joke as well as any man, but I wouldn't take a liberty with one of my customers any more than I'd like 'im to take a liberty with me.

Florrie [*almost with agony*]: You're not going to take Dad's side? You can't do that, Mum. I mean, think of Ernie and me.

Mrs Miller: It's not a matter of taking sides. I want to do what's best for everybody. But it's like this, if the doctors say e's not quite right in 'is 'ead, well, that settles it. But if they say 'e is, then I don't feel justified in preventing 'im from doing what 'e thinks is right.

Florrie: Mum. Mum. I think that's awful. [*Almost in tears*] O God, make them say he's potty. O God make them say he's potty.

Mrs Miller: I don't say that I don't think the idea's peculiar. And I know it won't be very pleasant for any of us. But 'ow do I know 'e's not right?

Ernie: I should have thought your common sense would have told you that.

Mrs Miller: I'm not clever like you, Ernie. I feel a lot that I can't exactly say. There's something in my 'eart that says, Dear old Sheppey, 'e always was a character.

Ernie: D'you mean to say you're going to sit there twiddling your thumbs and watch him throwing all that money down the drain?

Mrs Miller: I shan't like it, of course. I mean, I should 'ave liked to own this 'ouse and it would 'ave been a 'elp to 'ave a girl in to do the rough work. But there's something inside me that says, All that don't matter really; if Sheppey wants to do what Jesus said – well' that's only what you was taught when you was a girl.

Florrie: And what's to happen to you when the money's gone? You don't suppose they'd have Dad back at the shop after making such an exhibition of himself?

Ernie: And jobs aren't easy to get these days. Especially for a man of Sheppey's age.

Mrs Miller: Well, 'e's been a good 'usband to me. Never a 'arsh word. 'E's worked for me a good many years. I can earn my own living and 'is too.

Ernie: Easier said than done.

Mrs Miller: When one's as good a cook as what I am, and honest, it's not 'ard to get a job. Why, there's not one of these girls that's a patch on me. I'm not one for praising myself, God knows, but I do know my own value. Put me in front of a decent stove and give me the materials and not even the Queen of England can turn out a better dinner than me. And now, my girl, you'd better come and peel the potatoes.

Florrie: All right, Mum. Are you coming, Ernie?

Ernie: Yes, I will in a minute. I just want to take a look at the paper.

[**Florrie** *quickly bites her finger to choke down the tears that have sprung to her eyes. The two women go out.* **Ernie** *opens the paper, but he does not read it, he looks sullenly in front of him.* **Bessie** *comes in. He gives her a look, but does not speak. He starts reading.*]

Bessie: Anything in the paper?

Ernie: No.

Bessie: What are you reading then?

Ernie: The news.

Bessie: Racing?

Ernie: No, political.

Bessie: Florrie tells me you want to be a Member of Parliament.

Ernie: Fat chance I have now.

Bessie: I suppose you was counting on Sheppey doing something for you.

Ernie: Wouldn't you have in my place?

Bessie: Well, whatever happens you're lucky to have got Florrie. She's a nice girl. And with her looks she could marry almost anybody.

Ernie: I suppose you think she's throwing herself away on me?

Bessie: There's no accounting for tastes. Working in the City like she does I wonder she hasn't been snapped up by one of them rich men long ago.

Ernie: I'll thank you not to put ideas in Florrie's head. Her future's settled and if I hear of another fellow running after her I shall have something to say to him.

[**Bessie** *smiles quietly to herself. The door is opened softly and* **Cooper** *slinks in.*]

Cooper: 'Afternoon all.

Bessie: Hulloa! How did you get in? I never heard you knock.

Cooper: The lock's got one of them safety catches. I don't ave to 'ave anybody open a door like that for me.

Bessie: That's good news, I must say.

Cooper: Any fags around?

Bessie: I haven't got any.

Cooper: Suppose I shall 'ave to smoke me own then.
[*He takes a packet out of his pocket and lights a cigarette.*]

Bessie: You aren't going to offer me one, I suppose?

Cooper: No, I don't approve of ladies smoking.

Ernie [*taking out a packet and offering it to* **Bessie**]: Here's one if you want it.

Bessie: Thanks.

Cooper: What won the three-thirty?

Ernie: I haven't looked.

Cooper: What'd you buy a paper for then? Wanton waste, I call that.

Ernie: If you two are going to have a little chat I'll ask you to excuse me.

Bessie [*mincing*]: Oh, don't mention it.

    [**Ernie** *goes out.*]

Cooper: Quite the gentleman, eh?

Bessie: He's all right. He's only a kid. Swallowed the multiplication table when he was at school and it won't go up or down. Makes him kind of uneasy like.

Cooper: Where's Sheppey?

Bessie: Out somewhere.

Cooper: What's he after? I can't make 'im out.

Bessie: He's a puzzle to me too.

Cooper: Religion, I suppose it is, at the back of it.

Bessie: I'm not so sure. I know a lot about religion. When I had my little flat in Kennington one of my regulars was a religious man. He was a draper in a very good way of business. A prominent Baptist he was. Used to come every Tuesday and Friday. After he'd had his little bit of fun he used to love a good old talk about religion. But he didn't give much away. He used to say there wasn't a draper in the South of London as could squeeze more profit out of a reel of cotton than what he could.

Cooper: You have to be pretty smart with all the competition there is nowadays.

Bessie: D'you find that in your business?

Cooper: There's always room at the top.

Bessie: Swank.

Cooper: Besides, what is my business?

Bessie: Petty thieving, ain't it?

Cooper: Oh, and who do you think you are? You've got no cause to despise me.

Bessie: I don't despise you. I shouldn't have thought it was worth it, that's all. I mean, in and out of quod all the time. It can't be pleasant.

Cooper: Well, I'll tell you, it's the excitement. And then again, when you've done a job you feel all keyed up, if you know what I mean. You can't hardly help laughing when you think how blasted clever you are. But it's the excitement that's the chief thing.

Bessie: I can understand that. You'd think after all I've been through, turned out of my room and everything, now I've got a good bed to sleep in and plenty to eat, I'd be satisfied. But if the truth was only known, when it gets about time for me to get all dolled up and go up west – oh, I feel simply terrible.

Cooper: Do you really?

Bessie: D'you know what I did last night? I put my dress on and I made up the old face and I put on my usual perfume, and I just stood in my room and fancied myself walking down Jermyn Street.

Cooper: Why didn't you go?

Bessie: Oh, well, on account of poor old Sheppey, I suppose.

Cooper: It don't look as if he was going to show up.

Bessie: What d'you want to see him about?

Cooper: Well, if you must know, I get sort of restless when the pubs open. I could do with a bob to get a drop of beer.

Bessie: Oh, well, I don't blame you.

Cooper [*going*]: If he asks for me, say I've gone up the street. I'll be back presently.

[**Bessie** *gives a quick look round and sees the snuff-box is missing. She gets between* **Cooper** *and the door.*]

Bessie: Where's that snuff-box?

Cooper: What snuff-box?

Bessie: You know. The one Sheppey had left him.

Cooper: How should I know?

Bessie: Sheppey sets a rare store on that. He wouldn't lose it for the world.

Cooper: Perhaps the old girl put it away when you come 'ere. Thought it safer.

Bessie: It was here a minute ago. I saw it.

Cooper: I can't help that. I don't even know what you're talking about.

Bessie: Yes, you do. You give it up now.

Cooper: 'Ere, who are you talking to?

Bessie: I thought you was in a great hurry to get out all of a sudden.

Cooper: Look 'ere, my girl. You mind your own business or something unpleasant will 'appen to you.

Bessie: I'm not frightened of a dirty little tyke like you.

Cooper: Get out of my way. D'you think I'm going to demean myself by arguing with a common prostitute?

Bessie: You give up that snuff-box.

Cooper: I tell you I 'aven't got it.

Bessie: Yes, you have. It's in your pocket. Why, I can see it.

Cooper [*with an instinctive gesture of his hand towards his hip pocket*]: That's a lie.

Bessie [*with a hoarse chuckle of triumph*]: Ah. I've caught you. I knew you had it.

Cooper [*trying to push past her*]: Oh, shut your mug.

Bessie: You're not going out of this room till you give that back.

Cooper: What's it got to do with you, anyway?

Bessie: He may be a silly old fathead, but he means well, and I'm not going to stand by and see you sneak his bits and pieces.

Cooper: I tell you I've got to 'ave a drink.

Bessie: What you do outside's got nothing to do with me. But not here you don't do anything.

Cooper: If you don't get out of my way I'll give you such a swipe over the jaw.

Bessie [*peering right into his face*]: You dare to hit me. You filthy little sneak-thief. You snivelling little mongrel cur. You dirty son of a . . . [*With a quick movement she tries to snatch the snuffbox out of his pocket.*]

Cooper: No, you don't.

Bessie: Damn you.

Sheppey

[*There is a short struggle in the middle of which* **Sheppey** *comes in.*]

Sheppey: Hulloa, what's this?

[*They separate. They are both a trifle out of breath.*]

Bessie: He's got that snuff-box of yours.

Sheppey: What about it?

Bessie: He was just going out to pawn it.

Sheppey: What d'you want to do that for, Jim?

Cooper: It's a bleeding lie.

Sheppey: It ain't in its usual place.

Cooper: If anyone took it she did. You know what them women are. Just trying to put the blame on me.

Bessie: You look in his hip pocket.

Sheppey: Empty out your pockets, old man.

Cooper: I won't. I won't be treated like this by any man. D'you think you've got the right to insult me just because I'm your guest?

Bessie: Oh, dear, 'ark at you.

Sheppey: It's no good, old man, I'm afraid you've got to empty them pockets of yours.

Cooper: Who says so?

Sheppey: I do and if necessary I can make you.

Cooper: I've 'ad enough of this. I'm going.

[*He tries to push past* **Sheppey**, *but* **Sheppey**, *with surprising quickness, seizes him and trips him up, and with his knee on his chest to hold him down gets the snuffbox out of his pocket.*]

Sheppey: Get up now. Why didn't you give it quietly?

Cooper: 'Ere, you nearly broke my arm.

Bessie: Why, Sheppey, I am surprised. I didn't know you was as nippy as that.

Sheppey: I was a bit of a wrestler when I was a young feller.

Bessie: Shall I get a cop?

Cooper [*springing to his feet*]: You ain't going to give me in charge, governor? I didn't really mean to take it. It was a sudden temptation. I didn't know what I was doing really.

82

Bessie: Whine. Go on. Whine.

Sheppey: No, I'm not going to give you in charge. The judge said 'e'd give you the maximum if you ever come before 'im again.

Bessie: You ain't going to let him go? After all you done for him.

Sheppey: I ain't done anything for 'im. What I done I done for meself. Sorry if I 'urt you, old man. I'm stronger than you'd think for, and sometimes I put more strength into a thing than I should.

Cooper: No one's got a right to leave things like that about.

Sheppey: It's not gold, you know, it's only silver-gilt. It's not the worth I value it for, it's the sentiment. It was left me by a gentleman I'd attended for years and all through 'is last illness 'e would 'ave me go to his 'ouse and shave 'im every day. 'E said to 'is daughter only the day before 'e died, if I appear before my Maker looking like a gentleman it'll be to Sheppey I owe it. 'Ere take it. [*He hands the snuff-box to* **Cooper**.]

Cooper: What d'you mean?

Sheppey: I'm giving it you.

Cooper: Why?

Sheppey: You want it, don't you?

Cooper: No.

Sheppey: Why did you pinch it, then?

Cooper: That's quite another matter. I didn't mind pinching it. I'm not going to take it as a present. I only pinched it because I wanted a bob or two for a few beers. I'd 'ave give you back the ticket. Straight, I would.

Sheppey: If you wanted a bob why didn't you say so? [*Putting his hand in his pocket and taking out a shilling*] 'Ere you are.

[**Cooper** *looks at the shilling in his hand and then at* **Sheppey**. *He is full of suspicion.*]

Cooper: 'Ere, what's the meaning of this?

Sheppey: If a chap can only see God in a pint of beer 'e may as well look there as not see 'im at all.

Cooper: Is it a trap?

Sheppey: Don't talk so silly.

[**Cooper** *is puzzled and uneasy. He looks at the shilling, and he looks at* **Sheppey**.]

Cooper: I don't like this. There's something funny about it all. What are you getting at? What's the idea? 'Ere, take your bob. I won't 'ave it. It'll bring me bad luck. I'm off. I've 'ad enough of this place. I like to know where I am with people. This gives me the creeps. I wish I'd never come 'ere.

[*He goes out quickly.*]

Bessie: Well, that's a good riddance to bad rubbish.

Sheppey: Whoever would 'a thought it'd 'ave taken 'im like that?

Bessie: What did you want to give him that there box for?

Sheppey: Well, I just couldn't 'elp meself.

Bessie: You know, you ought to be a bit more careful. You're going to get a nasty knock one of these days if you go on treating good and bad alike.

Sheppey: The fact is, I can't see there's much to choose between them.

Bessie: Come off it, Sheppey. Why, that Cooper, he's just a dirty tyke.

Sheppey: I know 'e is. Some'ow I don't mind.

Bessie: Fact is, Sheppey, you've got no moral sense.

Sheppey: I suppose that's it. Lucky I was born lucky.

Bessie: You're a caution and no mistake.

Sheppey: Sorry 'e's gone. I'd got quite used to seeing 'im about the 'ouse.

Bessie: I'm going too, Sheppey.

Sheppey: Why? Ain't you getting on with Mum and Florrie?

Bessie: It's not that, I want to get back to the West End. I've been glad to have a bit of a rest here. It's done me no end of good. I miss the girls and I miss the street. When you've been used to meeting a lot of people you do come to depend on it somehow. And then, you never

know what's going to happen to you. It's not the going
with men I like, it's the getting off. I mean, you can't
help feeling, well, that's one up to me. And besides –
oh, well, I don't know, it's the whole thing. It's got its
ups and downs, I don't say it hasn't, but it's exciting;
even if you don't get off it's exciting. That's what I
mean, see?

Sheppey: I thought you was fed up with it.

Bessie: So I was. I was run down and out of sorts. But now
it's different somehow. I know it's a disappointment to
you. I'm sorry. Thank you for all you've done for me.

Sheppey: All right. 'Ave it your own way. There'll always
be a 'ome for you 'ere when you want one.

Bessie: D'you mean to say you'd take me back?

Sheppey: Of course I would. I don't blame you. I only
want people to be 'appy.

Bessie: I think I know a thing or two about men, but I
don't mind saying you've got me beat. Well, so long.

Sheppey: You're not going now?

Bessie: Yes, I am. I can't stand it another minute. I'll just
get myself dressed and then I'll slip away without
saying anything to nobody.

Sheppey: All right. And don't forget when you feel like
coming you're welcome.

Bessie: It's a strange world and no mistake.

[*She goes out. In a moment* **Mrs Miller** *comes in.*]

Mrs Miller: I 'eard you come in. I couldn't leave my
kitchen. I was just making a nice calves-foot jelly for
Mrs Robinson.

Sheppey: That's right, my dear. She'll enjoy that.

Mrs Miller: I told you they was twins, didn't I?

Sheppey: Yes.

Mrs Miller: What did the doctor say about you?

Sheppey: Oh, we 'ad a rare set to. 'E 'ad a friend there,
another doctor, Ennismore 'is name was, a tip-top
swell, it appears, and Dr Jervis said as 'e was there we
might just as well profit by it and 'e examined me too.

Mrs Miller: I see.

Sheppey: A very nice gentleman, he was. Intelligent. He was very interested in my plan. He got me to tell him all about it. My word, he did ask me some funny questions. I couldn't 'ardly 'elp laughing. Asked me if I'd ever seen my dad 'ave 'is bath. Yes, I said, every Saturday night, 'e used to make me scrub 'is back for 'im.

Mrs Miller: You were gone a time.

Sheppey: I know I was. We must 'ave talked for nearly two hours. I left them at it. Dr Jervis said they'd 'ave a little chat and 'e'd come 'ere later.

[*There is a knock at the front door.*]

That might be 'im now.

Mrs Miller: Oh, I do hate doctors.

Sheppey: Why, you're not anxious, are you?

Mrs Miller: Yes.

Sheppey: That's silly. There's nothing the matter with me. I never felt better in my life.

[**Florrie** *opens the door.*]

Florrie: Mum, will you come a minute?

Sheppey: Is it the doctor? [*He goes to the door.*] Come in, doctor.

[**Dr Jervis** *comes in followed by* **Ernie**.]

Dr Jervis: Good afternoon, Mrs Miller.

Mrs Miller: Good afternoon, sir.

Dr Jervis: Your husband told you? By a piece of good luck a friend of mine, a West End specialist, happened to be there when Sheppey came.

Sheppey: I was just telling about 'im. 'E made quite an impression on me.

Dr Jervis: We've had a talk about you. Heart a bit weak, you know. We think a rest would do you good.

Sheppey: Me?

Dr Jervis: We want you to go into a home for a while where you'll be comfortable and looked after properly.

[**Mrs Miller, Florrie,** *and* **Ernie** *at once see what this means.* **Mrs Miller** *can hardly restrain a start of dismay.*]

Sheppey: I'm not going to no 'ome. Can't spare the time. I'm a busy man.

Mrs Miller: Couldn't we look after 'im 'ere?

Dr Jervis: It's not the same thing. My doctor friend is at the head of a very good hospital. You'll be under his direct care. I don't say you're seriously ill, but you're ill, and you want proper attention.

Sheppey: You know, doctors don't know everything.

Dr Jervis: They don't pretend to.

Florrie: It's silly to talk like that, Dad. If Dr Jervis says you're ill, you are ill.

Sheppey: I know more about me own 'ealth than 'e does.

Dr Jervis: Why do you say that? I'd never pretend to know as much as you do about the care of the hair.

Sheppey: Sit down, and just let me 'ave a look at your 'air.

Dr Jervis: Oh, my hair's all right.

Sheppey: That's what people say. There's many a man about London now with a bald 'ead who'd 'ave a good 'ead of 'air if he'd taken my advice in time.

Dr Jervis [*humouring him*]: All right, you have a look at it.

[*He sits down and* **Sheppey** *steps over to him. He takes a glass out of his pocket and inspects the doctor's hair.*]

Sheppey: Been falling out a bit lately?

Dr Jervis: A bit, you know. I'm getting on.

Sheppey: It's just as I thought. If you don't do something about it you'll be as bald as I am in six months.

Dr Jervis: Oh, I can't believe that.

Sheppey: It's true. And it's a pity. You've got beautiful 'air. I mean, it's not often one comes across a gentleman with 'air of this texture.

Dr Jervis: Funny you should say that. My wife always says I have nice hair.

Sheppey: She won't be able to say it much longer.

Dr Jervis: Well, I don't know what can be done about it.

Sheppey: I do. If you'll massage your 'ead for five minutes night and morning with our number three I guarantee that in six months you'll 'ave as fine a 'ead of 'air as you've ever 'ad in your life.

Dr Jervis: D'you expect me to believe that?

Sheppey: No.

Dr Jervis [*good-naturedly*]: Well, I'll tell you what I'll do: when I'm passing down Jermyn Street I'll drop in and buy myself a bottle.

Sheppey: You needn't do that. I always keep a small stock 'ere, in case any of my friends want any. I'll just pop along and put you up a little. Eight and six or thirteen and four?

Dr Jervis: Thirteen and four. I may as well be hanged for a sheep as a lamb.

Sheppey: You'll never regret it. It won't take me more than five minutes.

[*He goes out.*]

Dr Jervis: Of course I only did that to humour him, you know.

Mrs Miller: Oh, doctor, whatever do you mean?

Dr Jervis: My friend, Dr Ennismore, is one of the greatest authorities in England on diseases of the mind and he's made a thorough examination of your husband. He has no doubt at all that he's suffering from acute mania.

Mrs Miller: Oh, dear.

Dr Jervis: We want you to persuade him that it's for his own good to go into a home. I'll have another talk with him tomorrow myself. If he won't consent we're prepared to certify him.

Mrs Miller: Is that really necessary? I mean, I can't bear the thought of 'im being put away.

Dr Jervis: I must tell you that the prognosis in these cases is not favourable. It's much better that he should be put under restraint before he commits some act that may have unfortunate consequences to himself or to others.

Ernie: I don't want to say I told you so, but the fact remains, I said he was crazy from the beginning.

Dr Jervis: It's quite obvious that a sane man is not going to give all his money away to the poor. A sane man takes money from the poor. He runs chain stores, founds building societies, or engages in municipal work.

Mrs Miller: Sheppey always 'as liked people. I mean, you might almost say 'e loved 'is fellow-men.

Dr Jervis: That's not a healthy sign, you know. The normal man is selfish, grasping, destructive, vain and sensual. What is generally termed morality is forced upon him by the herd, and the obligation he is under to repress his natural instincts is undoubtedly the cause of many of the disorders of the mind. Dr Ennismore said to me just now that he had little doubt that philanthropy in general could always be ascribed to repressed homosexuality.

Ernie: Is it really? I call that very interesting.

Dr Jervis: He is of the opinion that, with rational education of the young, philanthropy could be entirely stamped out of this country.

Ernie: I should like to meet him. He sounds clever.

Dr Jervis: He asked Sheppey some very searching questions and it looks very much as if there was a distinct father complex at the bottom of his trouble.

Ernie: Oedipus and all that. I know.

Dr Jervis [*to* **Mrs Miller**]: He was asking me when you first noticed anything peculiar.

Mrs Miller: I never noticed anything peculiar, not till all of a sudden 'e said 'e wanted to live like Jesus.

Dr Jervis: Has he always been a religious man?

Mrs Miller: No, that's just it. I mean, 'e never went to church or anything like that. 'E liked to spend 'is Sunday mornings doing odd jobs about the 'ouse. If 'e'd been a bad man it would be different. It seems so funny for a good man to become religious.

Dr Jervis: Didn't you suspect something was wrong when you saw him reading the Bible?

Mrs Miller: I'll tell you exactly what 'appened. 'E always reads the *Morning Post*, on account of the society news, you know. 'E finds it useful with 'is customers to know who's engaged to be married and all that.

Dr Jervis: I see.

Mrs Miller: Well, when 'e was ill I went out and got it for 'im. And on the Monday morning when I took it in to 'im' 'e said, Mum, 'ave we got a Bible in the 'ouse? Yes, I said, and I give it 'im. I meant no 'arm. Naturally I thought 'e wanted it for a crossword puzzle.

Dr Jervis: That's the peculiar cunning of the insane. It's often very difficult indeed to get them to say what you want them to. Now I don't know if you remember, last week when I saw him I asked him if he saw things. He said he saw sin and wickedness beating with their wings. It struck me at the time. That beating with the wings – very suggestive. And then he talked of a great white light. Dr Ennismore is convinced he has visual hallucinations, but will he admit it? He's as obstinate as a mule.

Mrs Miller: 'E never 'as been. 'E was a man as would always listen to reason.

Dr Jervis: His general state is typical. The bright eyes and flushed cheeks. The restlessness and insomnia. Ennismore is a very careful man and he wouldn't say what wasn't a fact. He says he's never seen a prettier case of religious paranoia in all his practice.

Mrs Miller: I've never 'eard of there being any madness in 'is family. It's like a stigma on all of us.

Dr Jervis: Get that idea out of your head at once, Mrs Miller. Ennismore's opinion is that everybody's mad. He says we couldn't live in this world if we weren't.

[**Sheppey** *comes in with a bottle neatly made up into a paper parcel.*]

Sheppey: 'Ere you are, doctor. I've made it into a nice little package for you.

Dr Jervis: Would you like cash?

Sheppey: No, take it off my bill. I know our number

three. After you've once used it you'll never be able to do without it.

Dr Jervis: Well, I must be getting along.

Sheppey: I'll just show you out.

Dr Jervis: Good-bye, Mrs Miller. [*He nods to the others.*] Good evening.

Mrs Miller: Good evening, sir.

[**Dr Jervis** *goes out accompanied by* **Sheppey**.]

Ernie: I sympathize with you, Mrs Miller. I do indeed. But you must say it's the best that could have happened for all parties.

Florrie: It would have been a shame to throw all that good money away.

Ernie: What d'you say to going to the pictures, Florrie? Early show.

Florrie: Right ho. You don't want me, Mum, do you?

Mrs Miller [*a little doubtfully*]: No, dear.

Florrie: Why, what's the matter?

Mrs Miller: Well, I shouldn't 'ave thought you'd want to go to the pictures tonight, when your poor old dad . . .

Florrie: I can't do him any good by staying at home. And I want to go all I can these next few days, as I shan't be able to go all next month.

Ernie: Why not?

Florrie: I promised God I wouldn't, not if he made the doctors say poor Dad was potty.

Ernie: You're not going to pay any attention to that? That's only superstition.

Florrie: I don't care what it is. I've promised and I'm going to keep my promise. I may want something else one of these days, and then where should I be if I hadn't kept it?

Ernie: You don't suppose it had any effect really?

Florrie: No one can say that, Ernie. I promised I'd do something for God if he'd do something for me. Well, he has and I'm going to keep my word.

Ernie: Oh, well, darling, have it your own way.

Florrie: Besides, what with getting ready for the wedding

and poor Dad being in an asylum, we shan't have much
chance of going to the pictures next month anyway.

Ernie: You're a grand girl, Florrie. I don't know what I
should do without you.

Florrie: You wouldn't have liked breaking it off, would
you?

Ernie: Me? Why, the thought never entered my head.

Florrie: Oh, yes it did. And I don't blame you.

Ernie: Well, I don't mind telling you now that I was
having a bit of a struggle between my inclinations and
my duty to myself. And when I say my duty to myself,
of course I mean my duty to the community.

Mrs Miller [*with a sigh, tolerantly*]: Oh, go on with you.
After all one's only young once.

Florrie: Come on, Ernie. We don't want to get there when
it's half-over.

[*As they are going out* **Sheppey** *comes in.*]

Sheppey: 'Ulloa, where are you two off to?

Florrie: Going to the pictures. See you later.

[*They go out.*]

Mrs Miller: You look a bit tired, dear. Why don't you go
to our room and 'ave a lay down?

Sheppey: No, I don't fancy that. I'll just sit in my chair
and perhaps I'll 'ave forty winks. I don't feel very grand,
really. I've 'ad a busy day.

Mrs Miller: You won't be going out again, will you? Let
me take off your boots.

[*She goes down on her knees and begins to take them
off.*]

Sheppey: You've been a good wife to me, Ada.

Mrs Miller: Oh, don't be so silly. If you talk like that I
shall think you're ill and I shall put you right to bed
with a 'otwater bottle.

Sheppey: You 'ave, you know. I expect I've often been
aggravating and unreasonable like.

Mrs Miller: Oh, go on. If you want me to 'ave a good cry,
say so.

Sheppey: I expect this 'as been a disappointment to you, about the money, I mean. I know you wanted to finish paying for the 'ouse and a girl to do the rough work.

Mrs Miller: Don't let's talk about that, Sheppey.

Sheppey: We must, me dear. It'll be all right for Florrie. She's got Ernie. 'E's a bit conceited, but that's because 'e's young. 'E's a good boy really. Florrie'll lick 'im into shape all right. She'll turn 'im round 'er little finger, like you 'ave me, dear.

Mrs Miller: I like that.

Sheppey: But it's going to be different for you. I know that. That's why I want you to look at it like I do. It's the pain of the world that gets me.

Mrs Miller: Oh, Sheppey, don't you think that's just because you're run down?

Sheppey: I tell you I never felt better in me life. I feel so light in myself if it wasn't for me 'eavy boots I believe I'd float right away.

Mrs Miller: You would look funny, Sheppey, flying around like a butterfly.

Sheppey: I'm going to 'ave a grand time, Ada.

Mrs Miller: Are you, dear?

Sheppey: Don't think I'm not grateful for all you done for me, Ada. Don't think I'm not sorry to disappoint you. But I've got to do this.

Mrs Miller: I know you wouldn't do anything but what you thought was right, Sheppey.

Sheppey: You won't 'old it up against me, dear?

Mrs Miller: As if I'd ever 'old anything up against you, Sheppey. Aggravating as you may be.

Sheppey: It's many a day since you kissed me, Ada.

Mrs Miller: Go on with you. What would anyone want an old woman like me kissing them for?

Sheppey: First time I kissed you, you slapped my face good and proper.

Mrs Miller: I thought you was a bit too free and easy.

Sheppey: Come on, Ada. To show there's no ill feeling.
[*He leans forward and she puts up her face. They kiss one another gently on the lips.*]

Sheppey

Mrs Miller: It makes me feel quite foolish.

Sheppey: What 'ave you got for supper tonight?

Mrs Miller: Well, I've made a cottage pie.

Sheppey: D'you know what I'd fancy?

Mrs Miller: No.

Sheppey: I'd fancy a couple of kippers. You know I always 'ave liked kippers.

Mrs Miller: I know you 'ave. I'll tell you what I'll do. I'll run out in a little while and get them for you.

Sheppey: You're sure it's not too much trouble?

Mrs Miller: It's no trouble at all. Now you just sit down in your chair. See if you can 'ave forty winks.

Sheppey: All right.

Mrs Miller: I won't disturb you till supper's ready. We'll 'ave it the moment Florrie and Ernie come back.

Sheppey: I don't mind telling you that I shall enjoy a bit of a rest.

Mrs Miller: I'll draw the blind.

[*She goes to the window and does this. She goes out.* **Sheppey** *sits down in the winged grandfather's chair, so that he is hidden from sight. The stage is darkened to show the passage of a couple of hours.*

When the scene grows a little lighter, night has fallen. Through the blind is seen the light of an arc lamp in the street. The chair in which **Sheppey** *is sleeping is vaguely discernible. There is a knock at the door. No answer comes from* **Sheppey** *and the knock is repeated.*]

Sheppey: Come in.

[*The door is not opened.*]

Come in. [*He gets up.*] I thought I 'eard a knock.

[*The door is opened wide, silently; and as it opens it gives the impression that it has not been pushed but has swung open of its own accord.* **Bessie** *stands in the door. She wears a long black cloak, but no hat.*]

Sheppey: Oh, it's you, is it? I thought I 'eard a knock.

Bessie: I didn't knock.

94

Sheppey: Didn't you? I suppose I was dreaming. Come in, dear. [*She comes in and the door closes behind her.*]

Sheppey: Got somebody with you?

Bessie: No.

Sheppey: Who shut the door then? It's funny. I must be half asleep. [*He goes to the door, opens it and looks out.*] There's nobody there.

Bessie [*with the shadow of a smile*]: No.

Sheppey: You 'aven't been gone long.

Bessie: Have you been expecting me?

Sheppey: Thought better of it, I suppose. Well, I can't say I'm sorry. I'll put on some light.

[*He switches on a standard lamp. The room is now dimly lit.* **Bessie** *stands near the door, motionless.*]

What are you standing like that for? Come in.

Bessie: Thanks.

[*She enters into the room. There is something about her that seems strange to him. He cannot quite make it out. It makes him vaguely uneasy.*]

Sheppey: Did my old woman let you in?

Bessie: The house is empty.

Sheppey: I suppose she's popped out to get them kippers. We wasn't expecting you in to supper.

Bessie: I generally come before I'm wanted.

Sheppey: No, you don't, not 'ere. I said you was always welcome and I meant it.

Bessie: It's pleasant to hear that for once.

Sheppey: I say, why are you speaking so funny all of a sudden?

Bessie: Am I? I didn't know.

[*The cockney accent with which* **Bessie** *spoke has in fact disappeared, and this woman speaks now in ordinary English.*]

Sheppey: All posh. [*Imitating her*] The house is empty. It's pleasant to hear that for once. No good trying to be the perfect lady with me, you know.

Bessie: I'm afraid you must take me as I am.

Sheppey: Oh, go on, speak natural. 'Ave you been drinking?

[*She does not answer and he gives her a quick suspicious look.*]

What's the matter with you tonight? You are Bessie Legros, aren't you? You're just like her. [*He goes to her.*] And yet there's something different. [*Puzzled and astonished*] You're not Bessie Legros.

Woman: No.

Sheppey: Who are you?

Woman: Death.

Sheppey [*with his usual friendly good humour*]: Well, I'm glad you've told me. I shouldn't have known otherwise. Sit down, won't you?

Death: No, I won't do that.

Sheppey: In a hurry?

Death: I have no time to waste.

Sheppey: Are you on your way to Mrs Robinson's? My wife was making her some calves-foot jelly only this afternoon. If it's the twins I don't suppose they'll be sorry. They've got four already and Robinson's been out of work for eight months.

Death: Has he? No, I wasn't thinking of going there.

Sheppey: Well, you know your own business best.

Death: I have my whims and fancies.

Sheppey: Being a woman.

Death: You like your little joke, don't you?

Sheppey: I always 'ave. 'Aving a sense of 'umour 'as been an asset to me. I've often 'eard my customers say to the governor, No, I'll wait for Sheppey. 'E always gives me a good laugh.

Death: That's more than my customers can say of me.

Sheppey [*gently chaffing her*]: I suppose on the whole people would just as soon 'ave your room as your company.

Death: I'm not often welcome. And yet sometimes you'd think they'd be glad to see me.

Sheppey: Well, I don't know. It's not a very nice thing to say to a lady, but I think your looks are a bit against you.

Death: I felt there must be something.

Sheppey: Funny me taking you for Betty Legros. Now I come to talk to you you're not a bit like her. Of course she's what they call a common prostitute, but there's something you·· can't 'ardly 'elp liking about 'er. [*He pinches his arm.*]

Death: Why do you do that?

Sheppey: I was only pinching my arm. I wanted to see if I was awake. I'm dreaming, but I know I'm dreaming. That's funny, isn't it?

Death: What makes you think you're dreaming?

Sheppey: Well, I know I am. I'm sitting in my chair 'aving a nap really. I've been 'aving the most extraordinary dreams lately. I was telling the doctor about them only this afternoon. Our own doctor thought I was potty. [*With glee*] I got back on 'im all right. Sold 'im a bottle of our number three.

Death: That was clever of you.

Sheppey: I know it was. 'E tried to pretend 'e was only buying it to 'umour me. My eye and Betty Martin. He bought it because I 'ypnotized 'im. And 'e'll use it night and morning like I told 'im to. There's no one I couldn't sell our number three to. I could sell you a bottle if I wanted to.

Death: I don't think it would do me much good.

Sheppey: Now don't say that. When people say a thing like that it puts me on my mettle. Just let me 'ave a look at your 'air.

Death: I haven't got time just now.

Sheppey: I don't say you 'aven't got a good 'ead of 'air, but 'ow d'you know you're going to keep it? 'Ulloa, who's this?

[*The door opens and* **Cooper** *slinks in.*]

Cooper: It's me, governor.

Sheppey: You've come back then?

Cooper: Been waiting on the opposite side of the street till the coast was clear. They're all out.

Sheppey: Yes, I know they are.

Cooper: As I was going out I 'eard them talking. I was 'iding just outside the kitchen and I 'eard every word they said. They're going to shut you up, governor.

Sheppey: Me? What for?

Cooper: 'Cause you're barmy.

Sheppey: Don't be so silly.

Cooper: God's truth, governor. I swear it is. Florrie and that bloke of 'ers. They're going to shut you up so they can get 'old of your money. Your old woman's in it too.

Sheppey: You make me laugh. Why, my old woman wouldn't let them touch a 'air of my 'ead.

Cooper: They're going to try and make you go to the asylum peaceful, but if you won't they're going to sign you up.

Sheppey: Oh, is that what you think? And what are you going to do about it?

Cooper: Well, I've come to warn you.

Sheppey: That's very kind of you, I'm sure.

Cooper: When I thought you was in your right mind you give me the creeps. That's why I skipped. Now I know you're barmy – well, that's another story altogether. I'm used to people like that. My mother's uncle was barmy. Used to live with us. Thought 'e was a loaf of sugar. Wouldn't wash, because 'e thought 'e'd melt.

Sheppey: That's a funny idea.

Cooper: You've been a good sport to me. Saved me from a stretch. One good turn deserves another. You slip out of the 'ouse now with me when there's nobody about. I'll take care of you, see? Never mind about the money.

Sheppey [*to the woman*]: What do you think about that? I knew 'e was no worse than anybody else, really.

Cooper [*startled*]: Who are you talking to?

Sheppey: That lady there.

Cooper: Where? I don't see no lady.

Sheppey: Look again.

Cooper: There's no one there.

Sheppey: That's a good one. Looking straight at you and says there's no one there.

Death: I'm not surprised.

Sheppey [*to* **Cooper**]: Hear that?

Cooper: What?

Sheppey: She says she's not surprised.

Cooper: Nobody's spoke but you and me.

Sheppey: 'E don't seem to 'ear either.

Death: Why should he? I have nothing to say to him yet.

Sheppey: I was just going to sell her a bottle of our number three when you come in. Women think they're artful. They're just as easy as men really.

Cooper: Look 'ere, governor, if you want to get away you'd better look nippy. They'll be back in 'alf a mo'.

Sheppey: Not me. I ain't going to trust meself to a fellow that's as blind as a bat and as deaf as a post.

Cooper: Don't I tell you if you stay 'ere they'll shut you up?

Sheppey: Maybe you mean well and maybe you don't. Maybe you're the devil in disguise. I'm a respectable member of society and I'm not going on any 'arum-scarum adventures.

Cooper: Don't say the gipsy never warned you.

Sheppey: That's all right. I'm in the middle of an interesting conversation with this lady. I don't want to be disturbed.

Cooper: Oh, all right, 'ave it your own way.

[*He slips out of the room.* **Sheppey** *turns to* **Death** *with a smile.*]

Sheppey: Funny 'im not being able to see you.

Death: The hemp's not picked yet to make the rope that's waiting for him.

Sheppey: That's not a very nice thing to say about anybody.

Death: It all comes to the same thing in the end, you know.

Sheppey

Sheppey: But I say, if you ain't there really, 'ow is it I see you?

Death: Can't you guess?

Sheppey [*with a sudden movement of dismay*]: Look 'ere, you ain't come 'ere on my account?

Death: Yes.

Sheppey: You're joking. I thought you'd just come to 'ave a little chat. I'm sorry, my dear, there's nothing doing today. You must call again some other time.

Death: I'm too busy for that.

Sheppey: I don't think that's treating me right. Coming in all friendly and pleasant. If I'd known what you was after I'd 'ave nipped off with Cooper when 'e asked me.

Death: That wouldn't have helped you much.

Sheppey: I wish now I'd gone down to the Isle of Sheppey when the doctor advised it. You wouldn't 'ave thought of looking for me there.

Death: There was a merchant in Bagdad who sent his servant to market to buy provisions and in a little while the servant came back, white and trembling, and said, Master, just now when I was in the market-place I was jostled by a woman in the crowd and when I turned I saw it was death that jostled me. She looked at me and made a threatening gesture; now, lend me your horse, and I will ride away from this city and avoid my fate. I will go to Samarra and there death will not find me. The merchant lent him his horse, and the servant mounted it, and he dug his spurs in its flanks and as fast as the horse could gallop he went. Then the merchant went down to the market-place and he saw me standing in the crowd and he came to me and said, Why did you make a threatening gesture to my servant when you saw him this morning? That was not a threatening gesture, I said, it was only a start of surprise. I was astonished to see him in Bagdad, for I had an appointment with him tonight in Samarra.

Sheppey [*with a little shudder*]: D'you mean there's no escaping you?

Death: No.

Sheppey [*trying to wheedle her*]: I don't fancy the idea of leaving this world. I know my way about and I'm at 'ome 'ere. Seems silly at my age to go on a wild-goose chase like this.

Death: Are you afraid?

Sheppey: What of? The Judgement Day? [*With a little smile*] No, not really. You see, the way I look at it is this: I've 'ad dozens of apprentices under me, and often they was silly and inattentive and broke things, you know what boys are, fond of a lark; well, of course I told 'em off, but I never 'eld it up against them. I'm not going to believe in a God that's not got as much common sense and as much sense of 'umour as I 'ave.

Death: Are you ready then?

Sheppey: What for?

Death: To start.

Sheppey: Now? This minute? I never knew you meant that. Why, what's the 'urry? I must talk it over with my wife first. I never do a thing without consulting 'er.

Death: She can't help you now.

Sheppey: Besides, she's giving me kippers for my supper. She'd be terribly upset if I wasn't 'ere to eat them after she's taken all that trouble.

Death: Others will eat them in your place.

Sheppey: To tell you the truth, I'm feeling rather tired. I don't feel like making a journey tonight.

Death: It's an easy one.

Sheppey: And then there's another thing. I daresay you don't read the papers and 'aven't 'eard about it. I won over eight thousand pounds in the Irish Sweep and I've made up my mind to use it in a particular way. It would be ridiculous for me to pop off just when I'm going to do a bit of good in the world.

Death: It does happen like that sometimes. The world will get on quite well without you. You men, you find it hard to realize that.

[*There is the sound of the street door being closed.*]

Sheppey

Sheppey: There's my wife just come in. I'll call her, shall I?

Death: She wouldn't hear you if you did.

Sheppey: You know, we've never been separated since we married. I don't think she'll like me going off like this without 'er.

Death: She can't come with you on this journey.

Sheppey: She'll be quite lost in the 'ouse without 'aving me to look after. Of course I suppose in a way it'll be a rest for 'er. Cooking my dinner and washing me clothes. It won't 'urt 'er to take things a bit easy for the rest of 'er life. It'll seem strange to 'er just at first.

Death: People get used to it, you know.

Sheppey: Especially widows, I've noticed. Seems funny me talking of Ada as a widow. She'll take it terrible 'ard, you know.

Death: She'll get over it in time.

Sheppey: That's not much consolation to me. Look 'ere, I'll tell you what I'll do, I'll give you a thousand pounds of my Sweep money and you go out the way you came.

Death: Money's no use to me.

Sheppey: You know, I don't feel at all well. I think I ought to see the doctor.

Death: You'll feel better presently.

Sheppey: You seem to 'ave an answer to everything. Seems a pity, when you come to think of it, me not being able to do what I'd set me 'eart on. Of course, they kep' on telling me I'd do more 'arm than good. What was that other thing 'e said? Thy will be done. [*With a sigh*] Fact is, I'm so tired, I don't seem to mind any more.

Death: I know. It's often surprised me. People are so frightened beforehand, and the older they are the more frightened, but when it comes to the point they don't really mind.

Sheppey: There's just one thing I'd like to ask you before we go. What's on the other side really?

Death: I've often wondered.

Sheppey: Do you mean to say you don't know? [*She shakes her head.*] Are you going to tell me you go about taking people away, one after the other, young and old, whether they like it or not, and you don't know where it is they're going?

Death: It's no business of mine.

Sheppey: I don't think you're justified for a minute. I mean, you 'aven't got the right to take a responsibility like that.

Death: To tell you the truth, I've sometimes wondered if it isn't all a terrible misunderstanding.

Sheppey [*indignantly*]: All right, then. I'll just go and see for myself. Which way do we go?

Death: Out of the door.

Sheppey: That seems rather tame. I thought we'd fly out of the window or pop up the chimney. Something spectacular, you know.

Death: No.

Sheppey: Well, I'll just put on my boots. [*He looks round for them.*] There now. That artful old woman, she was afraid I'd go out and she's taken them away and 'id them.

Death: You'll have to come without.

Sheppey: I shall look funny walking about without my boots on.

Death: Nobody will notice.

Sheppey: I'll just put out the light. No good running up an electric light bill.

[*He switches off the electric light at the door. The door is opened and they pass out. In the empty room a rattle, the death rattle, is heard. It seems to come from the chair in which* **Sheppey** *was sleeping.*

The door is opened again and **Florrie** *and* **Ernie** *come in. He switches on the light.* **Ernie** *turns back and speaks to* **Mrs Miller** *in the passage.*]

Ernie: No, he's not here.

Florrie: Perhaps he's gone out.

Mrs Miller [*in the door*]: No, 'is 'at's in the 'all. I expect 'e's aving a lay down in our room. I'll let 'im be till supper's ready. You lay the table, Florrie.

Florrie: Right you are, Mum.

[**Mrs Miller** *disappears from sight.* **Florrie** *gets the tablecloth and the knives and forks from the sideboard.* **Ernie** *helps her to lay the cloth.*]

Ernie: No lodgers tonight, it appears.

Florrie: Thank goodness.

Ernie: What's happened to them?

Florrie: I don't know and I don't care. Though I don't mind Bessie really.

Ernie: Sorry I didn't have a talk to her. Oldest profession in the world, they say. It would have been interesting to clarify my views on the subject.

[**Mrs Miller** *comes in with the tray on which are glasses, a loaf of bread and a jug of water.*]

Mrs Miller: What was the picture like?

Florrie: Lovely.

Ernie: Bit sloppy for me. I hate all this sentiment.

Florrie: I saw you crying all right.

Ernie: What a lie.

Mrs Miller: It's nothing to be ashamed of. I like a good cry myself.

[*She goes out.*]

Ernie: Good-looking chap, the gangster. I'll admit that.

Florrie: He wasn't as good-looking as you.

Ernie: The rot you talk, Florrie.

Florrie: I mean it.

Ernie: Oh, do you?

[*They are standing together, close to the gramophone. He puts his arms round her and kisses her. Their lips linger.*]

Florrie: Love me, Ernie?

Ernie: I couldn't love anyone like I love you.

[*With his disengaged hand he switches on the gramophone. They begin to dance cheek to cheek.*]

Florrie: Mum's a bit low tonight.

Ernie: Worried about your dad, I suppose.

Florrie: Naturally she's anxious. The doctor told her the other day he might pop off any minute.

Ernie: Don't you believe it. They live for ever in asylums. He's good for another twenty years.

Florrie: Isn't it lovely to think of everything coming out all right?

Ernie: Must you talk?

[*He kisses her on the lips as they dance on.* **Mrs Miller** *comes in again with the tray. There is a cottage pie on it, and on a plate* **Sheppey's** *two kippers.*]

Mrs Miller: Really you're a disgrace, you two. Is that what you call laying the table?

[*They stop and Ernie turns off the music.*]

Ernie: The woman tempted me and I fell.

Florrie: That's right, blame me.

Ernie: I don't know what it is, but there's something about her I can't help liking.

Mrs Miller: Oh dear, don't be so silly. One of you's just as bad as the other. D'you think nobody's ever been in love before? Run up and tell your dad supper's ready, my girl.

[**Ernie's** *glance falls on the grandfather's chair.*]

Ernie: You needn't do that. Here he is ready and waiting.

[*He swings round the chair sideways so that an arm and a hand are seen to fall over the arm of the chair.*]

Florrie: Why, he's asleep.

[**Mrs Miller** *takes a step forward and stops suddenly.*]

Mrs Miller: That's not sleep. [*She looks at him for a moment.*]

He always said 'e was born lucky. He's died lucky too.

The Sacred Flame

A PLAY IN THREE ACTS

Characters

Maurice Tabret
Dr Harvester
Mrs Tabret
Nurse Wayland
Alice
Major Liconda
Stella Tabret
Colin Tabret

The action takes place at Gatley House, Mrs Tabret's residence, near London.

Act One

Scene: the drawing-room at Gatley House. It is a large easy room furnished comfortably in rather an old-fashioned way, with spacious chairs covered in faded chintz, great bowls of flowers, English china, Victorian water colours, and photographs in silver frames. It is the drawing-room of an elderly lady who had furnished it in the way she has since her childhood known a drawing-room furnished. An interior decorator has never been inside the door. No stranger entering it would cry, How lovely! but if he were sensitive to his surroundings he might think it a very good room to eat muffins in for tea and he would slip his hand behind the cushions on the sofa in the certainty that he would find fat little lavender bags in the corners.

It is now the height of June, the weather is very fine, and the french windows that lead into the garden are wide open. Through them you see the starry radiant night.

[*When the curtain rises, it discovers* **Maurice** *and* **Mrs Tabret, Nurse Wayland,** *and* **Dr Harvester. Mrs Tabret** *is working at her tapestry. She is a slim, small, grey-haired lady, with a gentle manner, but her face is determined; it has a ravaged look as though fate had borne her many a blow, but also a serenity that suggests that she has found in herself the character and courage to put up a good fight. She is dressed in semi-evening dress, in black.* **Nurse Wayland** *is reading a book. She is a girl of twenty-seven or so, handsome rather than pretty, with fine eyes, a little sullen, perhaps, and in her expression the hungry, somewhat pathetic look that some women have at her age. She is dressed not in uni-*

The Sacred Flame

form, but in a pretty, simple frock that sets off her fine figure.

Dr Harvester *and* **Maurice** *are playing chess.* **Dr Harvester** *is the family doctor; he is a youngish man, fresh-complexioned and of an open countenance, fair, clean and amiable. He wears a dinner jacket.* **Maurice** *is lying on an invalid bed in pyjamas and a bed-jacket. He is trim and neat, with his hair close-cropped and his face fresh-shaven; he has a handsome head and his manner is cheerful and even hearty; but he is very thin, his cheeks are pale and hollow, and his dark eyes look enormous. But they are constantly smiling. He gives no sign of being sorry for himself.*

There is a pause while the doctor considers the situation.]

Maurice [*with good-humoured sarcasm*]: Speed is the essence of this game, old boy!

Harvester: Don't let the brute bully me, Mrs Tabret.

Mrs Tabret [*smiling*]: I think you're quite capable of taking care of yourself, Doctor.

Maurice: If you moved your bishop you'd make things a bit awkward for me.

Harvester [*imperturbably, considering the game*]: When I want your advice, I'll ask for it.

Maurice: Mother, is that the way respectable general practitioners talked to their patients in the days of your far-distant youth?

Mrs Tabret: How on earth do you expect poor Nurse Wayland to read when you never for an instant hold your tongue? I can't even hear myself tatting.

Nurse [*looking up for an instant, with a pleasant smile*]: I don't mind, Mrs Tabret, don't bother about me.

Maurice: After listening to my sprightly conversation for nearly five years Nurse Wayland pays no more attention to me than if I were a deaf mute.

Mrs Tabret [*dryly*]: Who can blame her?

Maurice [*cheerily*]: Even when pain and anguish wring

my brow and I swear like fifty thousand troopers I never manage to bring the blush of shame to her maiden cheek.

Nurse [*smiling*]: I know it's exasperating.

Maurice: It's worse than that, Nurse. It's inconsiderate. It would relieve me to see you blench with horror and smother a sob of mortification in an adhesive bandage.... Watch the Doctor, he's about to move. Be very careful, old boy, the position is fraught with danger.

Harvester [*moving a piece*]: I'm going to move my knight.

Maurice: What would you say if I gave that pawn a little push and murmured check?

Harvester: I should say it was your right, but I should think it a trifle vulgar.

Maurice: Do you know what I'd do now in your place?

Harvester: No, I don't.

Maurice: I'd catch my foot in the leg of the table and kick it over accidentally. That's the only way you can save yourself from getting the worst hiding I've ever given you.

Harvester [*moving a piece*]: Go to the devil.

Maurice: Oh, you do that, do you? All right.

[**Alice**, *the maid, comes in.*]

Alice: If you please, ma'am, Major Liconda wants to know if it's too late for him to come in and have a drink.

Maurice: Of course not. Where is he?

Alice: He's at the door, sir.

Mrs Tabret: Ask him to come in.

Alice: Very good, ma'am.

[*She goes out.*]

Maurice: You know him, don't you, old boy?

Harvester: No, I've never met him. He's the fellow who's just taken that furnished house on the golf links, isn't he?

Mrs Tabret: Yes. I knew him years ago in India. That's why he came here.

Maurice: He was one of Mother's numerous admirers. I understand that she treated him very badly.

Harvester: I can well believe it. Does he still cherish a hopeless passion for you, Mrs Tabret?

Mrs Tabret [*taking the chaff in good part*]: I don't know at all, Dr Harvester. You'd better ask him.

Harvester: Is he a soldier?

Maurice: No, he was policeman. He's just retired. He's a very good chap, and I believe he's rather a good golfer. Colin has played with him two or three times.

Mrs Tabret: I'd asked him to dine tonight so that Maurice could get a game of bridge, but he couldn't come.

[**Alice** *comes in followed by* **Major Liconda**, *and, when she has announced him, goes out.*]

Alice: Major Liconda.

[*He is a tallish, middle-aged man, with grey hair and a sunburnt face, spare of build, active and alert. He wears a dinner jacket.*]

Mrs Tabret [*shaking hands with him*]: How d'you do? How very nice of you to look in.

Liconda: I was on my way home and saw that your lights were on, so I thought I'd just ask if anyone would like to give me a doch-an-dorris.

Mrs Tabret: Help yourself. [*With a gesture of the head*] The whisky's on the table.

Liconda [*going over to it and pouring himself out a drink*]: Thank you. How are you, Nurse?

Nurse: How do you do?

Liconda: And the patient?

Maurice [*lightly*]: Bearing up pretty well considering all he has to put up with.

Liconda [*smiling*]: You're in your usual high spirits.

Maurice: I have much to be thankful for, as the lady said when her husband was run over by a motor-bus just as he was stepping out of the office after insuring his life.

Harvester [*laughing*]: You fool, Maurice.

[*The two men shake hands.*]

Harvester: How d'you do?

Liconda: Mrs Tabret tells me you're a very good doctor.

Harvester: I take great pains to impress the fact on my patients.

Maurice: His only serious fault is that he thinks he can play chess.

Liconda: Don't let me disturb your game.

Maurice: It's finished.

Harvester: Not at all. I have three possible moves. [*Making one*] What do you say to that?

Maurice: Mate, you poor fish.

Harvester: Damn.

Mrs Tabret: Have you beaten him?

Maurice: Hollow.

Nurse: Shall I put the chess things away?

Maurice: If you wouldn't mind.

[*She takes the board and the chessmen and puts them away, while the conversation proceeds.*]

Liconda: I won't keep you up. I'll just swallow my drink and take myself off. I really only came to say I was sorry I couldn't come to dinner.

Maurice: There's no hurry, you know. I'm not going to bed for hours.

Mrs Tabret: We're really waiting up for Stella and Colin. They've gone to the opera.

Liconda: I'm a night owl. I never go to bed till I can help it.

Maurice: You're the man for my money.

Harvester: I've got a day's work before me. I'll just have a drop of Scotch to assuage the pangs of defeat and then I must run.

Maurice: Let's send the rest of them off to bed, Major, and have a good old gossip by ourselves.

Liconda: I'm willing.

Mrs Tabret: If you really want to stay up, Maurice, let Nurse Wayland get you ready and then you'll only just have to slip into bed, and Colin can help you.

Maurice: All right. What do you say to that, Nurse?

Nurse: Well, it's just as you like. I'm quite prepared to

The Sacred Flame

stay up until Mrs Maurice comes in. I'll put you to bed after you've said good night to her.

Maurice: No, come on. You're looking tired.

Mrs Tabret: You are looking a little peaked, Nurse. I think it's nearly time you had another holiday.

Nurse: Oh, I don't want a holiday for months.

Maurice: Put you shoulder to the wheel, Nurse, and gently trundle the wounded hero to his bedchamber.

Harvester: Shall I come and help?

Maurice: Not on your life. It's bad enough to be messed about by one person. I don't want a crowd, damn it.

Harvester: Sorry.

Maurice: I shall only be ten minutes.

[**Nurse Wayland** *wheels out the bed and closes the doors behind her.*]

Liconda: She seems a very nice woman, that nurse.

Mrs Tabret: Yes. She's extremely competent. And I must say she's very gentle and kind. Her patience is really wonderful.

Liconda: You've had her ever since poor Maurice crashed, haven't you?

Mrs Tabret: Oh, no. We had three or four before she came. All more or less odious.

Harvester: She's a rattling good nurse. I think you're lucky to have got her.

Mrs Tabret: I'm sure we are. The only fault I have to find with her is that she's so very reserved. There's nothing come-hither about her. Except for her month's holiday every August she's been with us all day and every day for nearly five years, and I only just know that her name's Beatrice. She calls the boys Mr Maurice and Mr Colin, and Stella she calls Mrs Maurice. She seems to be always a little on her guard. She certainly doesn't encourage familiarity.

Harvester: I can't imagine skylarking with her at a Sunday school treat, I must admit.

Mrs Tabret: And of course she's a little tactless. It never seems to occur to her that Maurice wants to be alone with his wife. Poor lamb, he has so little. He likes to say good night to Stella the last thing and he likes to say it without anyone looking on. That's why he's staying up now.

Liconda: Poor old boy.

Mrs Tabret: He can't bear the thought of going to sleep without kissing her. And Nurse Wayland always seems to find something to do just that last moment. He doesn't want to hurt her feelings by sending her out of the room, and he's terrified of being thought sentimental, so he uses every sort of trick and device to get her out of the way.

Harvester: But, good Lord, why don't you tell her? After all, there's no reason why a man shouldn't kiss his wife good night if he wants to.

Mrs Tabret: She's terribly sensitive. Haven't you noticed how often rather tactless people are? They'll stamp on your toes and then when you tuck them up out of harm's way they're so offended you feel quite miserable about it.

Liconda: I suppose Maurice is absolutely dependent upon her?

Mrs Tabret: Absolutely. All sorts of rather unpleasant things have to be done for him, poor dear, and he can't bear that anyone should know about them. Especially Stella.

Harvester: Yes, I've discovered that. He doesn't want Stella to have anything to do with his illness.

Liconda [to **Harvester**]: Is there really no chance of his getting better?

Harvester: I'm afraid not.

Mrs Tabret: It's a miracle that he's alive at all.

Harvester: He was terribly smashed up, you know. The lower part of his spine was broken and the plane caught fire and he was badly burnt.

Liconda: It was rotten bad luck.

Mrs Tabret: And when you think that he was flying all through the war and never even had a mishap. It seems so silly that this should happen just when he was trying a new machine. It was so unexpected.

Liconda: It seems such a pity he didn't stop flying when he married.

Mrs Tabret: It's easy to say that now.

Harvester: He was a born flyer. Fellows have told me that he seemed to have a sort of instinct for it.

Mrs Tabret: It was the one thing he was interested in. He wouldn't have given it up for anything in the world. And he was so good at it, it never occurred to me that he could have an accident, he always felt so safe.

Liconda: I've been told he was absolutely fearless.

Harvester: And you know, the strange thing is this, he's just as much interested in it all as he ever was. He follows all the important flights and the tests and so on. If anyone does a new stunt he's full of it.

Liconda: His courage amazes me. He never seems low or depressed.

Mrs Tabret: Never. His spirits are wonderful. It's one of the most anguishing things I know to see him, when he's in pain and there are beads of sweat on his brow, force a joke from his lips.

Harvester: I'm sorry to think Colin is going away so soon, Mrs Tabret. I think his being here has done Maurice a lot of good.

Mrs Tabret: When they were boys they were always great friends, and you know brothers aren't always.

Liconda: They're not, indeed.

Mrs Tabret: And Colin has been away so long. He went to Central America just before Maurice crashed, you know.

Liconda: Well, has he got to go back?

Mrs Tabret: He put all his share of his father's money in a coffee plantation and it's doing very well. He loves the life out there and it seems cruel to ask him to give it up to help us to look after his crippled brother.

Harvester: I think it would be very unfair. One has no

right to ask anyone to give up his own chance of making the best he can of life.

Mrs Tabret [*with a dry smile*]: At all events with the young one may ask, but the likelihood of their consenting is very slight.

Harvester: Not at all, Mrs Tabret. The country is full of desiccated females who've given up their lives to taking care of an invalid mother.

Liconda: When I was at Bath a little while ago I saw a good many couples like that, and to tell you the truth I sometimes wondered why the daughters didn't murder their mothers.

Harvester: They often do. Every doctor will tell you that he's had a case where he has a strong suspicion that some old woman who lived too long has been poisoned by her relatives. But he takes jolly good care not to say anything about it.

Liconda: Why?

Harvester: Oh, it's rotten for a man's practice. Nothing can do you so much damage as to be mixed up in a murder case.

Mrs Tabret: I've often pondered over the problem of the woman like myself who is no longer young and suffers from indifferent health. I'm not sure if the best way of dealing with us wouldn't be to do as some African tribes do. At a certain age take us to the river's brim and push us gently but firmly in.

Liconda [*with a smile*]: What happens if they swim?

Mrs Tabret: The family is prepared for that. They stand on the banks with brickbats and take pot shots at their struggling but aged grandmother. It discourages her efforts to get out.

[**Nurse Wayland** *opens the door and the* **Doctor**, *getting up, helps her to wheel back the bed on which* **Maurice** *is lying.*]

Maurice: Here we are again. I'm all fixed up and ready for any excitement. What about a tune on the gramophone?

The Sacred Flame

Harvester: I must go.

Mrs Tabret: And Nurse Wayland should go to bed.

Nurse: I'll just gather my things together and say good night. Are you sure Mrs Maurice and your brother won't go and have supper after the opera?

Maurice: I'm sure they will. I particularly told Stella she was to have a real bust. It's not often she goes on the loose, poor dear.

Nurse: Then they won't be home till four.

Maurice: Does that mean you disapprove of my staying up, you hard and brutal woman?

Nurse: Doesn't Dr Harvester?

Harvester: Very much. But I'm aware that Maurice has no intention of going to sleep till he knows his wife is safely home again, and my theory is that it only does people good now and then to do what they shouldn't.

Liconda: That is the kind of doctor for me.

Harvester: Hurry up and get a nice long lingering illness, will you, so that I can put down a hard court in my garden.

Liconda: I'll see what I can do about it.

Maurice [*pricking up his ears*]: What's that?

Mrs Tabret: What, Maurice?

Maurice: I thought I heard a car. Yes, by jove. It's Stella. I'd know the sound of that car in a thousand.

[*Now the sound of a car driving up is almost distinct.*]

Liconda: Do you mean to say you can hear from this distance?

Maurice: You bet your life I can. That's the family bus. Now just stay a minute and see Stella, Doctor. She's got her best bib and tucker on and she's a sight for sore eyes.

Liconda: What were they giving at the opera tonight?

Nurse: *Tristan.*

Maurice: That's why I insisted on Stella's going. It was after *Tristan* that we got engaged. D'you remember, Mother?

Mrs Tabret: Of course I do.

Maurice: We'd all been to hear it and then we went on to supper. I drove Stella round Regent's Park in a little two-seater I had then and I swore I'd go on driving round and round till she promised to marry me. *Tristan* had given her such an appetite that by the time we were half-way around the second time, she said, Oh, hell, if I must either marry you or die of starvation I'd sooner marry you.

Harvester: Is there a word of truth in this story, Mrs. Tabret?

Mrs Tabret: I don't know. They were both as mad as hatters in those days. All I know is that the rest of us had only just ordered our supper when they came in looking like a pair of cats who'd swallowed a canary and said they were engaged.

[*The door is opened and* **Stella** *comes in, followed by her brother-in-law,* **Colin Tabret**. **Stella** *is twenty-eight and beautiful. She is wearing an evening dress and an opera cloak.* **Colin**, *a tall, dark, handsome fellow in the early thirties, is in full evening dress, long coat, and white tie.*]

Maurice: Stella.

Stella: Darling. Have you missed me?

[*She goes over to him and lightly kisses him on the forehead.*]

Maurice: Why are you back already, you wretched girl? You promised me to go and have supper.

Stella: I was so thrilled and excited by the opera, I felt I simply couldn't eat a thing.

Maurice: Hang it all, you might have gone to Lucien's and had a dance or two and a bottle of bubbly! What's the good of my spending the eyes of my head on buying you a new dress when you won't let anyone see it. [*To* **Liconda**] She said it was too dressed up to go to the opera in, but I exercized my marital authority and made her.

Stella: Darling, I wanted to show it off in the intervals, but I hadn't the nerve and I kept my cloak on.

Maurice: Well, take it off now and show the gentlemen. The only way I managed to get them to stay was by promising to let them have a look at your new dress when you came home.

Stella: What nonsense. As if Major Liconda or Dr Harvester knew one frock from another.

Maurice: Don't be so damned contemptuous of the male sex, Stella. Take off your cloak and let's have a good look at you.

Stella: You brute, Maurice, you've made me feel shy now. [*She is sitting on the end of his bed and slips off her cloak.*]

Maurice: Stand up.

[*She hesitates a moment and then, still holding the cloak about her hips, stands up. She lets it fall to her feet.*]

Harvester: It's lovely.

[*She staggers a little and smothers a cry.*]

Maurice: Halloa, what's the matter?

[**Colin** catches her and helps her to a chair.]

Stella: It's nothing. I feel so frightfully faint.

Mrs Tabret: Oh, my dear.

Maurice: Stella.

[*The **Nurse** and the **Doctor** go up to her.*]

Harvester: It's all right, Maurice. Don't fuss. [*To **Stella***] Put your head down between your legs.

[*He puts his hand on her neck to force her head down. **Nurse Wayland** puts her hands to her side as though to support her. But **Stella** pushes her away.*]

Stella: No, don't. Don't come near me. I shall be all right again in a minute. It's silly of me.

Maurice: I'm sorry, darling. It was my fault.

Stella: It's nothing. I feel better already.

Mrs Tabret: My own belief is that she's just faint from lack of food. At what time did you dine?

Colin: We didn't dine. We just had some caviar and half a bottle of pop before the opera.

Mrs Tabret: You are a ridiculous pair.

Stella: I enjoy Wagner so much more on an empty stomach. I'm really quite all right now.

Mrs Tabret: Nurse, would you mind going to the kitchen and seeing if you can find anything for these silly young things to eat?

Nurse: Of course not. There ought to be some ham. I'll make them some sandwiches.

Mrs Tabret: Colin can get a bottle of champagne out of the cellar.

Colin: All right, Mother. Is there any ice in the house? I've got a thirst I wouldn't sell for twenty pounds.

[*He opens the door for* **Nurse Wayland** *and they both go out.*]

Liconda: Well, I'll say goodbye. [*To Stella*] I'm sorry you're feeling poorly.

Stella: I shall be all right when I've had something to eat. I think Mrs Tabret is quite right. What I want is a large ham sandwich with a lot of mustard on it.

Maurice: You're looking better, you know. Just for a moment you were as white as a sheet.

Liconda: Goodbye.

Mrs Tabret: Goodbye. It was so nice of you to look in. [*He goes out.*]

Harvester: I'll just stay a moment or two longer if you don't mind. I don't trust these young women who don't feed themselves properly.

[**Mrs Tabret** *gives* **Maurice** *and* **Stella** *a glance. She knows they want to have a moment to themselves.*]

Mrs Tabret [*to* **Dr Havester**]: Let's take a turn in the garden, shall we? It's so warm and lovely.

Harvester: Come on. And I hope Nurse Wayland has the sense to cut a sandwich for me, too.

[*The* **Doctor** *and* **Mrs Tabret** *go out. As soon as they are alone* **Stella** *goes over to her husband and gives* *him a long, loving kiss on the lips. He puts his arm round her neck.]*

Maurice: Darling.

[She releases herself and sitting down on the bed holds one of his thin, sick hands.]

Stella: I'm sorry I made such a fool of myself.

Maurice: You scared the life out of me, you little beast. Why didn't you go on to some place and have a bite before you came home?

Stella: I didn't want to. I wanted to get back.

Maurice: Will you give me your word of honour that you didn't go on to dance because you thought I should be waiting up for you?

Stella: Don't be an old silly. You know that I love to think you want me back so much. You don't imagine I care a hang about dancing.

Maurice: You little liar. How can anyone dance as well as you without being crazy about it? You're the best dancer I ever danced with.

Stella: Oh, but you know how one changes. All the dances are different now, and after all I'm not so young as I was either.

Maurice: You're twenty-eight. You're only a girl. You ought to be having the time of your life. Oh, my dear, it is rotten for you.

Stella: Oh, darling, don't. You mustn't think that. Don't imagine for a moment that I've given up a thing that meant anything to me.

Maurice: You must allow me to have my own opinion. Anyhow it's been a snip having old Colin here. It's damned well forced you to go out.

Stella: Darling, you talk as though I was shut up like a nun. I'm always going out. I see all the plays.

Maurice: Yes, at matinées with my mother. She's a dear old thing, but she's not precisely exhilarating. After all, when one's young one wants to be with young people. One wants to say and do all sorts of things that seem merely silly to the elderly. They smile indulgently because they have the tolerance of wise old people. Damn it all, one doesn't want their indulgence. One wants to play the fool because one's young. And it's wise for the young to be rather foolish.

Stella: My dear, you mustn't be epigrammatic. They tell me it's so out of date.

Maurice: I was hoping you'd dance till your feet were dropping off and then go for a spin in the moonlight. Do you remember, we did that once one night and we had breakfast at a pub on the river in our evening things. What a lark!

Stella: We were a pair of lunatics in those days. I was much too tired to do anything like that. I only wanted to get home.

Maurice: The honest fact is that you've lost the habit of going on a binge.

Stella: I don't want to go on a binge if you can't come with me.

Maurice: That is perfectly idiotic of you, my poor child. I wish that silly ass Colin weren't going away so soon.

Stella: He only came home for six months and he's stayed nearly a year.

Maurice: You promised you'd try to persuade him to stay on for a bit.

Stella: He must get back to his work.

Maurice: Why can't he sell his old plantation and settle down here?

Stella: He'd be a fish out of water in England. When a man's got used to the sort of life he's lived out there it's frightfully difficult for him to settle down in an office or something like that.

Maurice: I suppose it is really. I should have hated it, too. I wasn't really thinking of myself, and Mother must be used to having a pair of useless sons by now. I was thinking of you.

Stella: I'm quite capable of thinking of myself, darling. I'm a very selfish woman.

Maurice: My poor child, you mustn't think because I've got a broken back I'm a drivelling imbecile.

Stella: How can I think anything else when I see you fussing like an old hen with an only chick because you imagine I may be having a rather thin time? I'm not having a thin time. You never try to prevent me from doing anything I want to. No one could be more considerate than you are. I'm busy all day long and the days just fly past. I don't know what it is to be bored. Why, I haven't time for half the things I want to do.

Maurice: Yes, you're wonderful . . . You've always been wonderful. You've made the best of a bad job, all right. I've had to. But why should you? Resignation. I've had to set my teeth and learn it. But what has a girl like you to do with resignation?

Stella: Oh, darling, don't talk like that. You mustn't think such things. I married you because I loved you. What a foul brute I should be if I stopped loving you now that you want my love more than ever.

Maurice: Oh, my dear, we can't love because we ought to. Love comes and goes and we can none of us help ourselves.

Stella [*with a sharp look at him*]: Maurice, what do you mean? [*She looks away.*] Has there been anything in my behaviour to lead you to think that I wasn't the same as I'd always been?

Maurice [*with deep affection*]: No, darling. You've been angelic always, always. [*Taken aback*] Why, what's the matter? You suddenly went quite white. You're not feeling faint again?

Stella: No. I didn't know I went white.

Maurice: You know, if I've seemed often to take for granted all you've done for me you mustn't think I'm not conscious all the time how much I owe you.

Stella: That's very silly of you, my pet. I don't know that I've done anything for you at all except be moderately civil. You've never let me.

Maurice: I've never let you nurse me. Not on your life. I couldn't have borne that you should have anything to do with the disgusting side of illness. [*With a grin*] My precious, I don't want you to smell of antiseptics. I want you to smell of the dawn. I'm so grateful to you, Stella.

Stella: God knows, you've got no cause to be.

Maurice [*casually*]: You know that I'm never going to get well, Stella, don't you?

Stella: I don't indeed. It's a long business, we know that, but I'm absolutely convinced you'll get at all events very much better.

Maurice: They tell me that one of these days they'll try operating again to see if they can't possibly put me right. But I know they're lying. They pretend they can do something in order to give me hope, and I pretend to believe them because it's the easiest thing to do. I know I'm here for life, Stella.

[*There is a moment's pause. This is the first time that* **Stella** *has realized that* **Maurice** *knows his case is hopeless.*]

Stella [*very earnestly*]: Then let's take what comfort we can in the great joy we've had in one another in the days when you were well and strong. I shall always be grateful for the happiness you gave me and for your love, your great love.

Maurice: Do you think that's changed? No. I love you as deeply, as devotedly as I ever did. I'm not often silly and sentimental, am I, Stella?

Stella [*with a little smile*]: Is it so silly to be sentimental? No, you're not often.

Maurice: You're everything in the world to me, Stella. People have been most awfully kind to me, and it's not till you're crocked up as I am that you find out how kind people are. They've been simply topping. But there's not one of them that I wouldn't see in hell if it would save you from unhappiness or trouble.

Stella [*in a lighter tone, going back to her chaffing way*

The Sacred Flame

with him]: Well, I wouldn't tell them if I were you. I don't believe they'd awfully like it.

Maurice [*with a smile*]: I ought to be frightened because I'm so dependent on you, but I'm not because I know, not just with my mind or my heart, but with every nerve in me, with every little feeling and every pain, how good you are.

Stella [*trying to take his speech lightly*]: Now, darling, you really are exaggerating. If you go on like this I shall send you to bed.

Maurice: My precious. You can laugh at me, but I see the tears in your lovely eyes.

Stella [*with sudden emotion*]: Maurice, I'm a very weak, a very imperfect, and a very sinful woman.

Maurice [*suddenly changing, but still with the greatest affection*]: Come down to earth, you silly little ass.

Stella [*unable not to feel a trifle anxious*]: Why are you saying all this to me just tonight?

Maurice [*smiling*]: One can't always jump through a hoop to make people laugh. It's hardly becoming in a gentleman approaching middle age who's chained to an invalid bed. You must forgive me if my flow of jokes sometimes runs dry.

Stella: You're sure you're not worrying about anything?

Maurice: You know, when you're shut up as I am you find out all sorts of interesting things. Being an invalid fortunately has its compensations. Of course, people are very sympathetic, but you mustn't abuse their sympathy. They ask you how you are, but they don't really care a damn. Why should they? Life is for the living and I'm dead.

Stella [*strangely harassed*]: Maurice, oh, my darling.

Maurice: You soon cotton on to it and you say you're as fit as a fiddle. You must take care not to bore the people who come to see you and you soon discover that it bores them if you talk about yourself. Let them talk about themselves. That always interests them and they say, What an intelligent fellow he is. Make jokes. Make all the jokes you can – good, bad, and indifferent; when you've made them laugh, they feel they needn't be sorry for you, and that's a relief to them. And when they go away they feel so kindly disposed towards you.

Stella: Oh, my precious, you break my heart. It's so cruel to think that you should have had to learn such bitter truths.

Maurice: My dear, they're not so bitter as all that. That's only human nature and I get a lot of fun out of observing it. I'm not so terribly to be pitied. I've learnt to take pleasure in all sorts of things, other people's affairs and books and so on, that I never cared a tinker's damn for before. I should never have mentioned it, only I wanted to tell you that it's you who've given me the courage to carry on. I'm not unhappy. I don't know how many years I shall hang on, but if you'll help me, darling, I think I can make a pretty good job of it. I owe everything to you. Nothing matters to me very much when I know I shall see you tomorrow and the next day and the day after that and always. And when I've had a bit of pain I think to myself when you come in next you'll kiss me, and I feel the tenderness of your lips on my beating heart.

Stella [*shattered by emotion*]: Maurice, I'm unworthy of such love. I'm so ashamed. I'm so selfish. I'm so thoughtless.

Maurice: Never.

Stella: Why did you make me go out tonight? Did you think it was any pleasure to me?

Maurice: I didn't care. I was thinking of my pleasure. I wanted you to hear again the music we'd heard together that night we got engaged. I was crazy about you. Do you remember how you cried in the second act when Tristan and Isolde sing that duet of theirs and I held your hand in the dark? Why did you cry?

Stella: I cried beeause I loved you and I was happy.

Maurice: Did you cry tonight?

Stella: I don't know.

Maurice: You know, that music is stunning, isn't it?

Stella [*smiling through her tears*]: People seem to think it's above the average.

Maurice: You seemed to carry it still in your eyes when you came in. They were bright and shining. They were like great deep pools of light. You've never looked so beautiful as you looked tonight. You made the Venus of Milo look like a lump of cheese.

Stella [*recovered now and chaffing him again*]: Go on, darling, I can bear much more in the same strain.

Maurice: I could go on for weeks.

Stella: No, then I'd be afraid you were prejudiced. Go on till the sandwiches come in.

Maurice: Give me your hands.

Stella: No, I won't. Let's be sensible and talk about what's going to win the Grand National.

Maurice: Of course the honest-to-God truth is that you're ever so much lovelier than when I married you. What is there that gives you this sudden new radiance? You look like a goddess who's just created a world and is about to step upon it for the first time.

Stella: I don't know why I should look any different from usual.

Maurice: I watch your face. I know every change in it from day to day. A year ago you had a strained, almost a hunted, look, but now lately you've had an aïr that is strangely peaceful. You've gained a sort of beautiful serenity.

Stella: My poor lamb. I'm afraid that can only be due to advancing years. Soon you'll discover the first wrinkle on my forehead and then the first white hair.

Maurice: No, no. You must never grow old. I couldn't bear it. Oh, how cruel that all that beauty, all that superb and shining youth of yours . . .

Stella [*interrupting him quickly*]: No, don't, Maurice, I beseech you.

Maurice: It would have been better for both of us if I'd been killed when I crashed. I'm no use to you, I'm no use to anybody.

Stella: Oh, Maurice, how can you say that? Don't you know how desperately afraid I was when they told me you were hurt and how relieved, how infinitely thankful, when they told me at last, after days and days of anguish, that you would live?

Maurice: They should never have let me. Why didn't they put me out of my misery when I was all smashed up? It only wanted an injection a little stronger than usual. That was the cruelty – to bring me back to life. Cruel to me and ten times more cruel to you.

Stella: I won't let you say it. It's not true. It's not true.

Maurice: I think I could have borne it if we'd had a child. Oh, Stella, if we'd only had a little kid and I could think to myself that it was you and me. And you would have something to console you. After all, it's a woman's destiny to have children. You wouldn't have felt that you had entirely wasted your life.

Stella: But, Maurice, my dear, I don't feel I've wasted my life. You're not yourself tonight. You're ill and tired. Oh, what has come over you?

Maurice: I love you, Stella. I want to take you in my arms as I used to. I want to press my lips to yours and see your eyes close and your head fall back and feel your dear soft body grow tense with desire. Stella, Stella. I can't bear it. [*He bursts into tears, clinging to her.*]

Stella: Maurice, darling. Don't. Don't cry.

[*He sobs hysterically while she rocks him to and fro like a mother with her child. Then he gets hold of himself.*]

Maurice [*with a complete change of tone, in a matter-of-fact voice*]: Oh, my God, what a damned fool I am. Give me a handkerchief.

[*She gives him one from under the pillow and he blows his nose.*]

Stella: My dear, you did frighten me.

Maurice: It's what they call a nerve storm. It's lucky it

was only you there. It would have been a pretty kettle of fish if Nurse Wayland had seen me like that.

Stella [*trying to laugh with him*]: It would have been a much prettier kettle of fish if I'd seen you clinging to her capacious bosom.

Maurice: Now you mention it I must admit it is rather capacious.

Stella: They're not worn now.

Maurice: I say, you haven't got a glass, have you?

Stella: My angel, how do you imagine I apply lipstick to my ruby lips? [*She takes a little glass out of her bag and hands it to him.*]

Maurice [*laughing at himself*]: For an intrepid aviator I look rather tear-stained, if I may say so. [*He wipes his eyes with the handkerchief.*]

Stella: Let me powder your nose. You can't think what a comfort it is after you've been upset.

Maurice: Go on with you. You can give me a whisky and soda if you like.

Stella: All right. But I'll powder mine.

Maurice: I feel like a house on fire now.

Stella: I wish someone would explain how it is that a dab of powder can in the twinkling of an eye reduce a woman's nose from an unwieldy lump to a dear little thing that no one can deny is her best feature.

Maurice: These are the miracles of science that we read about.

Stella: Now I'll get you your whisky and soda.

Maurice: Here's Colin. I'll have a glass of bubbly instead.
  [**Colin** *comes in with a tray on which are glasses, ice, and a bottle of champagne.*]

Colin: I'm afraid I've been a devil of a time.

Maurice: I knew you couldn't be trusted in the cellar by yourself. We were just going to send a search party after you.

Colin: Well, first I couldn't find anything to break the ice with and then I couldn't find the nippers to cut the wire. And then I thought I might as well put the car away. I didn't want to leave it outside all night.

Maurice: Meanwhile Stella is famishing.

Colin: Nurse Wayland is just coming. She's making some sandwiches with bacon and they smell a fair treat.

[*The* **Nurse** *comes in with a covered entrée dish.*]

Stella: Here she is. That is kind of you, Nurse. If there's anything I adore it's bacon sandwiches.

Nurse: I haven't brought any knives and forks. I thought you could eat with your fingers.

Stella: Heavenly.

Colin: I'll just bolt up and change my coat. I might just as well be comfortable and I shan't be a minute.

Stella: Well, I'm not going to wait for you.

Colin: All right. Go right ahead. But leave me my fair share or else all is over between us.

[*He goes out.* **Stella** *goes to the window.*]

Stella: Dr Harvester, come and eat a sandwich before it gets cold.

Maurice: I don't think I'll wait to see you people make pigs of yourselves. I think I'll turn in.

Stella: Aren't you going to have a drink with us?

Maurice: I don't think I will if you don't mind. I'm rather tired.

Stella: Oh, I am sorry, Maurice. But there's nothing to stay up for if you're tired.

Maurice: You might look in on your way up to bed, Stella.

Stella: Yes, rather. But I shan't disturb you if you're asleep.

Maurice: I shan't be asleep. I've got a bit of a head. I'll just lie still in the dark and it'll go away.

[*As* **Nurse Wayland** *starts to wheel him out,* **Mrs Tabret** *and* **Dr Harvester** *come in.*]

Harvester: Did I hear you calling me?

Stella: You did. Maurice is going to bed.

Mrs Tabret: Oh, I'm glad. It's fearfully late. Good night, old boy. Sleep well. [*She leans over and kisses him on the forehead.*]

Maurice: Good night, Mother. Bless you.

Harvester: Let me give you a hand, Nurse.

Nurse: I can manage perfectly. I'm so used to wheeling the invalid bed and he weighs nothing.

Maurice: I never weighed more than ten stone eight when I was well.

Harvester: Never mind. Let me push him in. I'd like to.

Maurice: Let the man do something for his money, Nurse. [*Putting on a cockney accent*] You bring me drops and me powder puff, dearie.

[*The **Nurse** opens the door and **Dr Harvester** pushes the bed out.*]

Stella: Don't be long, Doctor, or the sandwiches will be stone cold.

[*The door is closed. **Stella** and **Mrs Tabret** are left alone.*]

Stella: Maurice is rather nervous tonight.

Mrs Tabret: Yes, I noticed it.

Stella: I'm sorry I went to the opera.

Mrs Tabret: My dear, you go out so little.

Stella: I haven't the inclination, really.

Mrs Tabret: I'm afraid you're awfully tired.

Stella [*with a smile*]: Dead.

Mrs Tabret: Why don't you eat something?

Stella: No, I'll wait till the others come.

Mrs Tabret: Whatever happens, darling, I want you to know that I'm deeply grateful for all you've done for Maurice.

Stella [*startled*]: Why do you say that? You don't think he's any worse?

Mrs Tabret: No, I think he's just about the same as usual.

Stella: He does get a little nervous and high-strung sometimes.

Mrs Tabret: Yes, I know.

Stella: You startled me. I don't know why you should suddenly say a thing like that.

Mrs Tabret [*smiling*]: Is there any reason I shouldn't?

Stella: It sounded strangely ominous.

Mrs Tabret: I feel I'd like you to know that I realize what a great sacrifice you've made for him for so many years. You musn't think that I've taken it as a matter of course.

Stella: Oh, my dear, don't. It would be inhuman if I didn't feel unspeakably sorry for Maurice. It's awful for him, poor darling. Naturally if there was anything I could do to make things a little easier for him I was anxious to do it.

Mrs Tabret: After all, you didn't marry him to be the helpmate of a hopeless cripple.

Stella: One takes the rough with the smooth.

Mrs Tabret: I know it's very irksome to have an old woman like me always living with you. It's difficult to be a mother-in- law and welcome.

Stella [*charmingly*]: My dear, you've been kindness itself to me. What should I have done without you?

Mrs Tabret: I will admit that I've tried not to be a pest. You'd have been within your rights if you'd refused to have me to live here. I must thank you for all you've done for me, too.

Stella: Oh, my dear, you make me feel quite shy.

Mrs Tabret: You're a very young and a very beautiful woman. You have the right to live your life just as everyone else has. For six years now you've given up everything to be the sole comfort of a man who was your husband only because a legal ceremony had joined you together.

Stella: No, no. Because love had joined us together.

Mrs Tabret: My poor child, I'm so desperately sorry for you. Whatever the future may have in store I shall never forget your courage, your self-sacrifice, and your patience.

Stella [*puzzled and a little frightened*]: I don't understand what you mean.

Mrs Tabret [*with a tolerant and ironic smile*]: Don't you? Well, let us suppose that this is the anniversary of my wedding day and my thoughts have been much occupied with the ups and downs, the fortunes and misfortunes of married life.

[**Colin** *comes in. He has taken off his long evening coat and wears a very shabby old golf coat.*]

Colin: Hulloa, where are the others?

Stella: Maurice has gone to bed. Dr Harvester is just coming.

Mrs Tabret: Now, come on, children. Sit down and have something to eat.

Colin: I'll pour out some wine, shall I?

[*He pours out three glasses of champagne while* **Stella** *helps herself to a sandwich.*]

Stella: Hm. Scrumptious.

Mrs Tabret: Nurse Wayland makes them well, doesn't she?

Stella: Marvellously.

[**Dr Harvester** *comes in.*]

Stella: If you don't hurry up you'll be too late. They're simply divine.

Harvester: I'll just have one and swallow a glass of bubbly and bolt. It's any old time and I've got to be up bright and early in the morning.

Colin: Is Maurice all right?

Harvester: Oh, fairly. He's a bit down tonight for some reason. I don't know why. He was in great spirits earlier in the evening.

Mrs Tabret: I expect he's just tired. He *would* sit up.

Harvester: Nurse Wayland says that something has happened to upset him. Is that true?

Mrs Tabret: Not that I know of.

Harvester: He says he's got a headache. I've left him a sleeping draught that he can take if he can't get off or wakes in the night and feels restless.

Stella: I'll go in and see him before I go to bed. If he can only get a good rest I'm sure he'll be his usual self tomorrow.

Mrs Tabret: Sit with him a little, Stella.

Stella: Of course I will.

Harvester: Well, I must be off. Good night, Mrs Tabret. I've had a jolly evening.

Mrs Tabret: I'll come and see you to the door and then I shall go up to bed. Good night, children.

Stella: Good night.

[*They kiss one another and then* **Mrs Tabret** *kisses* **Colin**.]

Mrs Tabret: Good night, Colin dear. Don't stay up too late, either of you.

Colin: And put out the lights and see that the windows are properly closed and the safety catch is in place. I will, Mother.

Mrs Tabret [*pleased with his chaff, to* **Dr Harvester**]: You see how these boys treat me. They have no respect for their aged mother.

Colin: A certain amount of restrained affection, however.

Mrs Tabret: Bless you, my dear, now and always.

Harvester: Good night.

Stella: Good night. We shall see you in a day or two, I suppose.

Harvester: I expect so.

Colin: Good night, old boy.

[**Dr Harvester** *and* **Mrs Tabret** *go out.* **Colin** *goes over to the windows and shuts them and draws the curtains. The moment the door closes on* **Mrs Tabret**, **Stella** *puts down the sandwich she has been making a pretence of eating. She stands looking out into space. When* **Colin** *has finished shutting up, he turns off most of the lights so that the room is shrouded in darkness and there is only light on* **Stella**. *He turns to her.*]

Colin: Stella . . . Stella.

[*She gives a stifled sob and looks at him, misery in her eyes.*]

Stella: Oh, Colin. The anguish.

Colin [*going towards her*]: My poor child.

Stella: Don't touch me. Oh, what shall I do? Colin, what have we done?

Colin: Darling.

Stella: Maurice was so strange tonight. I couldn't make him out. I was almost afraid he suspected.

Colin: Impossible.

Stella: He must never know. Never! I'd do anything in the world to prevent it.

Colin: I'm so terribly sorry.

Stella: We're in a hopeless pass. Hopeless. Why did you ever love me? Why did I ever love you?

Colin: Stella.

[*He stretches out his arms, but she turns away.*]

Stella: Oh, I'm so ashamed. [*She hides her face with her hands.*]

Act Two

The scene is the same as in the preceding act.
Next morning, and about midday.

[**Colin** *is seated at a writing-table writing letters.* **Major Liconda** *is shown in by the* **Maid**. *He is in golfing things.*]

Alice: Major Liconda.

Colin [*getting up*]: Oh, how do you do?

[*The Maid goes out.*]

Liconda: My dear boy, what an awful thing. I'm absolutely horrified. I've only just this minute heard.

Colin: It's nice of you to have come. As you can imagine we're all very much upset.

Liconda: I've been playing golf. I went out early. I had a match at nine. Someone told me at the club-house when I got in. I could hardly believe it.

Colin: I'm afraid it's true all the same.

Liconda: But Maurice seemed comparatively well last night.

Colin: Anyhow no worse than usual.

Liconda: I thought him in such good spirits. He was full of fun. He was cracking jokes.

Colin: Yes, I know.

Liconda: Of course, I know nothing. You know Blake at the club? I don't know if you've ever played with him.

Colin: No. But I've met him.

Liconda: Well, he came up when I was standing at the bar having a drink and said to me: I say, have you heard that poor Maurice Tabret died last night? By George, it gave me a shock. You know, when one isn't as young as one was, it always gives one a turn to hear of the death of someone you knew.

Colin: I suppose it does.

Liconda: Blake hadn't heard any of the details. Was he taken suddenly worse in the night?

Colin: No, he said he was rather tired. Stella and I were going to have a snack before going to bed. He said he wouldn't wait. It was very natural, it was getting a bit late, you know. Harvester was here and he went along with him and Nurse Wayland and helped to put him to bed. He seemed all right then.

Liconda: Did he just die in his sleep?

Colin: I suppose so.

Liconda: What a mercy. That's the best way, isn't it? We'd all give something to know for certain that when our time came we'd pass out like that.

Colin: He can't have felt ill, or he'd have rung. He had a bell-push under his pillow and it rings in Nurse Wayland's room. She'd have been down like a flash if there'd been a sound.

Liconda: She heard nothing?

Colin: Nothing.

Liconda: When did you find out then?

Colin: Well, you see, sometimes, if he'd had a poorish night, you know, he slept rather late in the morning. And he was always allowed to sleep on. You know what nurses are. However rotten a night you've had they come bustling in at the crack of dawn and they don't care a damn if you're sleeping or not. You must be washed and have your hair brushed and your pillows shaken.

Liconda: Don't I know it? I never know which I dread most, an attack of malaria or a really efficient nurse.

Colin: Well, Stella stopped all that. She insisted that no one should go in to Maurice till he rang.

Liconda: Poor devil, at all events when he was asleep he was happy.

Colin: I believe it was the only matter on which there'd been any friction between Stella and Nurse Wayland. You know, Nurse Wayland is really a very good sort. She was never any trouble in the house and she was always good-tempered and that sort of thing.

Liconda: Oh, I know. It struck me that she was a thoroughly nice girl.

Colin: When she first came she wanted to get Maurice ready for the day as she called it, at eight o'clock every morning. Routine, you know. And she said if he was tired he could go to sleep again afterwards. But Stella put her foot down. She said she didn't want to interfere with anything else, but on that point she insisted. And Nurse Wayland could either knuckle under or go.

Liconda: Quite right.

Colin: We were just finishing breakfast, about half past nine, I think, Stella and I and Mother, when Nurse Wayland came in. She never has breakfast. She just makes herself a cup of cocoa when she gets up at seven.

Liconda: My God, these women, what a genius they have for doing the uncomfortable thing.

Colin: I noticed she was very white. She said she'd just been in to Maurice. I never heard him ring, said Stella. You know what these jerry-built houses are. You hear every bell in the house.

Liconda: Yes, mine's like that.

Colin: He didn't ring, said Nurse Wayland. It was so late I thought I'd just peep in and see if he was all right. Then Stella got right up on her hind legs. I won't have

it, she said. I've forbidden you to go in till he rings.
How dare you disobey me. I've never seen Stella in such
a passion. I saw that Nurse Wayland was trembling. She
looked all funny. Scared, you know. But not of Stella.
I had a sort of suspicion something was wrong. Hold
hard, Stella, I said. I got up. Is anything the matter,
Nurse? I asked. She gave a sort of cry and clenched her
hands. I'm afraid he's dead, she said.

Liconda: Good God! How awful.

Colin: Stella gave a sort of gasp and then she went into
a dead faint.

Liconda: Your poor mother.

Colin: Mother was wonderful. You know when half a
dozen things happen at a time, you seem to see them
all separately and yet together. I sprang forward to help
Stella. She'd fallen on the floor with a thump. I don't
know, for a moment I was afraid the shock had killed
her. And I saw Mother sitting at the table with a piece
of toast in her hand. And she just looked at Nurse
Wayland, I don't know, as though she couldn't understand. She was awfully white and then she began to
tremble. She never made a sound. She shrank back into
her chair and seemed all of a sudden to become an old,
old woman.

Liconda: Why didn't the fool break it to you more gently?

Colin: Then Mother stood up. She got hold of herself
quicker than any of us. I never knew she had such
nerve.

Liconda: She's a woman in a thousand. I knew that.

Colin: You'd better go for Dr Harvester, she said to me.
[*With a sudden falter*] By God, I shall never get the
sound of her voice out of my ears.

Liconda: Hold on, old man. It's no good you going to
pieces. Don't tell me any more if it upsets you.

Colin [*pulling himself together*]: No, I'm all right. There's
nothing more to tell. Mother said, Nurse and I'll see to
Stella. Don't you bother. That seemed to pull Nurse
Wayland up. She came forward and she and Mother

began to try to get Stella round. I went into Maurice's room. I felt his pulse and I put my hand on his heart. He looked as if he was asleep. I knew he was dead. I got the car and went to Dr Harvester's. He'd started on his rounds, but they knew where he'd gone more or less and I bolted after him. Luckily I caught him and I brought him back with me. He said he thought poor Maurice had been dead for a good two hours.

Liconda: Did he say what had happened?

Colin: He thinks it may have been an embolism. Or perhaps heart failure, you know.

Liconda: How about Stella?

Colin: She's all right, thank God. She came to after a bit. My God, she did give me a fright.

Liconda: I don't wonder.

Colin: Harvester wanted her to go to bed, but she wouldn't. She's in Maurice's room now.

Liconda: What about your mother?

Colin: Harvester's with her. He had to go and see some patients, but he said he'd come back, and he turned up just before you did. Here he is.

[*As he says these words,* **Dr Harvester** *comes in. He and* **Major Liconda** *shake hands.*]

Harvester: Hulloa, Major.

Liconda: This is a very sad errand that has brought you here, Doctor.

Harvester: It's naturally been a dreadful shock to Mrs Tabret and Stella.

Liconda: How is Mrs Tabret?

Harvester: She's bearing up wonderfully. She's very much upset, but she's trying not to show it. She has a great deal of self-control.

Liconda: I wonder if she'd like to see me.

Harvester: I'm sure she would.

Colin: Shall I run up and see?

Liconda: It would be very kind of you, Colin. Say that if she doesn't want to be bothered with me she has only to say so. I shall quite understand. I don't want to be a nuisance, but if it'll be any comfort to her to see me I shall be only too glad.

Colin: All right.

[*He goes out.*]

Liconda: You know, I've known Mrs Tabret for over thirty years. Her husband was in the Indian Civil.

Harvester: Yes, she told me.

Liconda: They were almost the first people I got to know at all well when I went out to India. She's one of the best, you know. She always was. Everybody liked her.

Harvester: Of course, I've seen a good deal of her during the last five years. She's really been wonderful. So has Stella, for the matter of that.

Liconda: One can't help being rather thankful it's all over.

Harvester: He never had a chance of getting better, poor devil.

Liconda: Yes, you said that last night.

Harvester: Of course, he might have gone on for years like that. But what was the good? It was rotten for him and rotten for everyone connected with him.

Liconda: You can't say that any of them grudged the sacrifices they had to make for his sake.

Harvester: No. Rather not. They were awfully good to him.

Liconda: I could wish the end hadn't come quite so suddenly.

Harvester: Oh, why? It's much better that he should have passed out like that rather than get inflammation of the lungs or something of that sort that he just hadn't the strength to fight against.

Liconda: So far as he was concerned, yes. I was thinking of his mother and Stella.

[**Nurse Wayland** *comes in. She wears her nurse's uniform.*]

Harvester: Hulloa, Nurse. I thought you were having a rest.

Liconda: Good morning.

The Sacred Flame

Nurse: Good morning, Major. I'm glad you came round. Mrs Tabret will be glad to see you.

Harvester: I told you to go and lie down, Nurse.

Nurse: I couldn't. I was too restless.

Harvester: Then why don't you go for a walk? You can do no good by sitting about and moping.

Liconda: I'm afraid it's been as great a shock to Nurse Wayland as to the rest of us. After all, she'd been looking after Maurice for a long time.

Nurse: Yes, it's been a great shock to me. He was a dear. One couldn't help admiring him. He bore his terrible misfortune with so much courage.

Harvester: He was topping. There's no doubt about that.

Nurse: I naturally grew attached to him. He was always so gay and so grateful for what one did for him.

Liconda: I suppose you'll try to get a good long holiday before you take another job.

Nurse: I haven't made any plans yet.

Harvester: What about those friends of yours who live on the South Coast? Why don't you spend a few weeks with them? To tell you the truth, you're looking all in.

Nurse [*listlessly*]: Am I?

Harvester: You must try not to take it too hard.

Nurse: A nurse naturally doesn't like to lose a patient. Especially so unexpectedly.

Harvester: It was always on the cards that he'd go out suddenly.

Nurse: Like a candle that you blow out when you don't want it any more. Where does the flame go then?

[**Dr Harvester** *looks at her for a moment reflectively.*]

Harvester [*kindly*]: My dear, I'm afraid you're taking poor Maurice's death a good deal more to heart than is quite wise.

Nurse [*with bitterness*]: Did you think he was only a case to me? Even a nurse is human. Strange as it may seem, she has a heart like other people.

Harvester: Of course she has a heart. But it doesn't do

her or her patients any good if she allows her emotions to get the better of her common sense.

Nurse: Does that mean you think I've been inefficient?

Harvester: No, of course not. Heaven knows, you never spared yourself. Perhaps you've been trying to do a little too much for your strength. You take my advice, my dear, and go for a holiday. What you want is a real rest.

Nurse: What is it, in your opinion, that Maurice Tabret actually died of?

Harvester: Heart failure.

Nurse: Everybody dies of heart failure.

Harvester: Of course. But that's as good a thing as any to put on the death certificate.

Nurse: Are you going to have a post-mortem?

Harvester: No, why should I? It's quite unnecessary.

Nurse [*looking him full in the face*]: I don't agree with you.

Harvester [*without a trace of asperity*]: I'm sorry. But it's my affair. If I'm prepared to sign the death certificate I don't know that anyone else has any right to say anything about it.

Nurse: You've told me half a dozen times that Maurice Tabret might have lived for years.

Harvester: So he might. I can tell you now that it's a blessing for everybody concerned with him that he didn't.

Nurse [*very deliberately*]: Dr Harvester, Maurice Tabret was murdered.

Harvester: What are you talking about?

Nurse: Do you want me to repeat it? Maurice Tabret was murdered.

Harvester: Rubbish.

Liconda: I daresay you're not quite yourself this morning, Nurse. It's very natural. But you must try to be reasonable. You oughtn't to say things that you can't possibly mean.

Nurse: I'm in complete possession of my senses, Major Liconda, and I know perfectly well what I'm saying.

Liconda: Do you mean to say that you intended that statement to be taken literally?

Nurse: Quite.

Liconda [*gravely*]: It's a very serious one, you know.

Nurse: I'm aware of that.

Harvester: It's grotesque.

Nurse: You've known me for five years, Dr Harvester. Have I ever given you to imagine that I'm a neurotic or hysterical woman, given to talking in a wild and exaggerated way?

Liconda: Let us listen to what Nurse Wayland has to say. Do you mean by any chance that you are dissatisfied with the way your patient was treated by Dr Harvester?

Harvester: By George, that never occurred to me. Is that it, Nurse? Don't hesitate to say anything you want to. I shan't be in the least offended. I don't want to put on any frills, and if there's anything that's making you miserable it's much better that you should say it. I'll try to explain.

Nurse: So far as I could judge you did everything for Maurice Tabret that medical skill could do.

Liconda: Besides, he was surely seen by several specialists.

Harvester: Half a dozen at the least.

Liconda: Well, Nurse Wayland?

Nurse: I am a trained nurse, Major Liconda; you can't imagine that if Maurice Tabret had died as the result of an error in treatment on Dr Harvester's part I should be so heartless as to distress the relatives by mentioning it.

Harvester: 1 don't want to seem flippant on such an occasion, but I am forced to say that your magnanimity overwhelms me, Nurse Wayland.

Nurse: You can be flippant or condescending or sarcastic, Dr Harvester. It means nothing to me.

Liconda [*with a thin smile*]: I'm sure it will do no harm if we're all civil to one another, at least for a little while longer.

Nurse: I've made a definite charge and I stick to it.

Harvester: The charge being that some person or persons unknown murdered Maurice Tabret?

Nurse: Yes.

Harvester: But, my dear, why should anyone want to murder poor Maurice?

Nurse: That at present is no business of mine.

Harvester: Now, look here, Nurse, you know just as well as I do that everyone connected with him was devoted to Maurice. No one was ever more surrounded with love and affection than he was. It's incredible that anyone should even have *wished* him harm.

Nurse: Whatever I may think or may not think I am at liberty to keep to myself. I am not in the witness-box.

Harvester: The witness-box? [*Mockingly*] Do you already see yourself giving sensational evidence at the Old Bailey?

Nurse: I can honestly say that I can imagine nothing more hateful than the notoriety that would be forced upon me if I were obliged to appear in court.

Harvester: There'd be notoriety all right. This is the sort of thing that would be jam for the papers. Come, now, be a sport, Nurse Wayland; you know just as well as I do that Maurice died of natural causes. What on earth is the use of making a fuss and getting everyone upset?

Nurse: If he died of natural causes a post-mortem will prove it and then I shall have nothing more to say.

Harvester [*irritably*]: I'm not going to have a post-mortem. You know how the relatives hate it.

Nurse: Are you afraid of what it will show?

Harvester [*with decision*]: Not on your life.

Nurse [*defiantly*]: I warn you that if you sign the death certificate I shall go straight to the coroner and make a protest.

Harvester: I should have thought the Tabrets had had enough to put up with, without being obliged to go through the ordeal you want to force upon them.

Nurse: Major Liconda, you were in the Indian Police,

weren't you? You ought to know about such things. Will you tell me what is the duty of a nurse who has reason to believe that her patient has come to his death by foul play?

Liconda: That is a question I'd sooner you hadn't asked me. I suppose her duty is quite clear. But I think she should be very sure that her reasons are valid before she exposes to distress and publicity a family that has treated her with unvarying kindness.

Harvester: What are your reasons, anyway? You've made a charge, but to the best of my recollection you haven't given us an inkling of what it's based on.

Nurse: If you'd been willing to have a post-mortem nothing need have been said till we knew the results of it. But you've put me with my back to the wall. Major Liconda is right. Everyone in this house has treated me with the greatest consideration. I do at least owe it to them to make no charges that may directly or indirectly concern them behind their backs.

Harvester: Does that mean you want them sent for?

Nurse: Please.

Liconda: I think it's best. You've been so definite, Nurse Wayland, that neither Dr Harvester nor I can keep the matter to ourselves. However distressing it may be I think Maurice's family should know what you have to say.

Nurse: I'm quite prepared to tell them. In point of fact, I think Mrs Tabret is just coming.

Liconda: Where is Stella?

Harvester: Do you want her, too?

Liconda: I think it's better.

Harvester: I'll see if I can find her.

Liconda: I believe she's in Maurice's room.

[**Harvester** *goes out.*]

Nurse: Don't judge me till you've heard all I have to say, Major Liconda.

Liconda [*with a certain severity*]: Miss Wayland, I happen to be a very old friend of the Tabrets and deeply attached to Mrs Tabret. I regret that you should think it your duty at this moment of all others to add to their great sorrow. I can only hope that you will be shown not to have been justified.

Nurse: In that case you will have good reason to throw me out of the house, bag and baggage.

Liconda: It is not my house, Miss Wayland, and I doubt whether Colin Tabret would be willing to depute to me that pleasant task.

Nurse: I'm just as glad to know who are my friends and who are my enemies.

[**Mrs Tabret** *comes in with* **Colin**. *She goes up to* **Major Liconda** *with a little smile. She is calm and composed.*]

Mrs Tabret: My dear old friend.

Liconda: I felt that I must come and see you for a moment, my dear. I'm sure you know how deeply I sympathize with you, but I wanted to tell you that if in any way I can be of service to you . . .

Mrs Tabret [*interrupting him with a little smile*]: It was very kind of you to come, and just like you.

Liconda: I'm relieved to see that you're bearing so bravely what must have been a bitter blow.

Mrs Tabret: I am trying to put my own feelings away out of sight and mind. I want only to think that my son has ended his long martyrdom. He had a brave, a carefree, and a happy nature. He was not meant to live on a bed of sickness.

Liconda: I remember when he was a boy how amazing his vitality was.

Mrs Tabret: I will not weep because he is dead. I will rejoice because he is free.

[**Stella** *comes in from the garden, followed by* **Dr Harvester**. *She is all in white.*]

Stella: Dr Harvester told me you were here and wanted to see me.

Liconda: I wanted first of all to tell you how much I feel for you in your sad loss.

Stella: You know, Maurice and I often talked of death. He was never afraid of it. He'd faced it often enough during the war. He didn't attach very much importance to it. He couldn't bear any of the trappings of woe. He told me that he didn't wish me to wear mourning for him. He said that if he died I was to carry on as usual. He wanted me to go about and do things exactly as if he were alive.

Mrs Tabret: He loved you so much, Stella. He put your happiness above everything.

Stella: I know.

Colin: Those lines of Stevenson's keep ringing in my ears: 'Home is the sailor, home from the sea.'

Liconda: 'And the hunter home from the hill.' They're very moving to us who've spent our lives in distant places.

Stella: You know, Maurice never quite believed that with this life everything ended for him. He didn't believe in a great many things that many people still more or less believe in ...

Mrs Tabret [*interrupting*]: I could never bring myself to teach my children what I couldn't myself believe. When they were little and I used to sit in the evenings in our house and look at the multitudinous stars sweeping across the blue sky of India and thought of what we are, so transitory and so insignificant, and yet with such a capacity for suffering, such a passion for beauty, I was overwhelmed by the mystery and the immensity of the universe. I could not conceive what was the cause of all those worlds I saw above me, nor what was the power that guided them, but my heart was filled with amazement and awe. What I vaguely divined was too stupendous to fit into the limits of any creed of men.

Stella: You know how Maurice was always laughing and joking. Even when he was speaking seriously he kept a little twinkle in his eye, so that you weren't quite sure he wasn't making fun of himself. I think he'd never quite grown out of some of those beliefs that I suppose he'd acquired unconsciously in his childhood from nurses and servants.

Mrs Tabret: We always had native ayahs. Heaven knows what they taught the children.

Stella: He didn't believe with his reason, but in some strange way with his nerves or his heart, that perhaps there was something in the Eastern notion of the transmigration of souls.

Liconda: I wonder if one ever entirely ceases to believe in what one has been taught as a child.

Stella: I think deep down in him was the faith that when his soul left his poor wounded body it would find another tenement. I think he had so much vitality that he felt it impossible that he should not live again on this earth.

Mrs Tabret: Ah, I've so often wished I had that comforting faith. Oh, to have a second chance and a third, to pass from life to life, purging yourself of imperfection and atoning for your sins, till at last you lose yourself in the infinite peace of the infinite soul of God.

Stella [*turning to* **Nurse Wayland**]: I had something to say to you, Nurse. You'll be leaving us very soon now, I suppose?

Nurse: I suppose so.

Stella: I want to thank you for everything you did for Maurice, and I want you to know how deeply grateful I am to you.

Nurse: I did no more than my duty.

Stella [*with a charming smile*]: Oh, no, you did much more than that. If it had been only your duty you could never have been so immensely thoughtful. You could never have anticipated Maurice's wants. You've been so awfully kind.

Nurse [*a trifle sullenly*]: Your husband was a very easy patient. He was always anxious not to give trouble.

Stella: I've got a little plan that I want to tell you about. I've talked it over with Mrs Tabret and she very much approves of it. You've had a long and hard time here. And your month's holiday a year has been very little rest. You've often talked to me about your sister in Japan and I know how much you've wanted to travel. If you'll allow me I should like to make it possible for you to go out to the East and have a good time.

Nurse [*stonily on the defensive*]: I don't think I understand what you mean.

Stella [*a little shyly, but in a manner that is disarming*]: Well, my dear, a nurse's salary is never very large. I know that Maurice has left me everything he had and we've been living so economically, I shall be quite well off in a modest way. It would be dear of you if you'd let me make you a present of a few hundred pounds, a thousand, say, to make it a round sum, so that you could go for a nice long journey and need not think of earning your living for a while.

Nurse [*hoarsely, trembling in her effort to control herself*]: Do you think I would take money from you? Is that what you take me for?

Stella [*surprised, but not taking her very seriously*]: But what on earth is the harm of it? Come, Nurse, don't be unreasonable. You know I don't want to offend you.

Nurse: What I've done I've been paid for. If I wasn't satisfied with the payment I received I only had to go.

Stella [*taken aback, as though she had been suddenly slapped in the face*]: Nurse, what is the matter? What have I said? Why do you speak to me like that?

Harvester: You mustn't take what Nurse Wayland says too literally. She really isn't herself today.

Liconda: No, Harvester, it's no good taking up that attitude. The position is much too serious. Stella, I've got something very unpleasant to tell you. I would sooner not have added to your present trouble, but I'm afraid it can't be avoided.

Stella: What is it?

Liconda: Nurse Wayland is not satisfied that Maurice died from heart failure.

Stella: But if Dr Harvester says so? Surely he knows best.

Harvester: I am prepared to sign the death certificate. I have no doubt in my mind of the cause of death.

Liconda: Nurse Wayland thinks there ought to be a post-mortem.

Stella [*with the utmost determination*]: Never. Never. Poor Maurice's body has suffered enough. I won't have him cut about to satisfy an idle curiosity. I absolutely refuse.

Liconda: I understand that an autopsy cannot be held except with the consent of the next of kin.

Nurse: Or on the order of the coroner.

Stella: What does she mean by that?

Liconda: I'm afraid she means that if you persist in your refusal she will go to the proper authority and make the statement she has already made to Dr Harvester and me.

Stella: What is the statement?

Liconda: Do you wish to repeat it, Nurse Wayland?

Nurse [*very coolly, almost with insolence*]: Not particularly. I have no objection to your doing so.

Harvester: Do you really insist on going through with this, Nurse? What you said to the Major and me was more or less confidential, wasn't it? Don't you think you'd better reflect a little more? If anything further is said the matter must necessarily go out of our control. I think you should consider the consequences of your attitude and the harm that may arise.

Nurse: I can't keep silent. I should never forgive myself.

Liconda: Nurse Wayland states that Maurice's death was not due to his illness, but to some other cause.

Stella: I'm dreadfully sorry, but I don't understand. What other cause could have brought about his death?

Liconda: She says he was murdered.

[**Colin** *and* **Stella** *start*. **Mrs Tabret** *smothers a cry*.]

Stella: Murdered? You must be mad, Nurse.

Liconda: Harvester and I have pointed out to her that he was regarded by everyone connected with him with the greatest affection.

Colin: It's preposterous.

Stella: After the first shock I'm almost inclined to laugh. Really, Nurse, you must be very nervous and overwrought to have got such an idea in your head. Is that why you were so funny when I asked you to accept enough money to take a year's holiday?

Nurse: I had no wish that the matter should go so far now. If Dr Harvester had agreed to my suggestion of having a post-mortem nothing need have been said till it was discovered if my suspicions were justified or not.

Harvester: Willing to wound and yet afraid to strike, Nurse Wayland.

Nurse [*turning on him*]: You have forced me into this position, Dr Harvester. I only did my duty in telling you my very grave suspicions, and the moment I did, you took up a definitely hostile attitude towards me.

Harvester: Well, if you want to know, I thought you silly, nervous, and hysterical. Good heavens, I've been in practice long enough to know how wildly people talk. I should be kept pretty busy if I paid any attention, for instance, to what one woman says about another.

Nurse: Or is it that you're frightened to death of a scandal? You know that notoriety does a doctor no good, and you think it would hurt your practice if anything came of this that got into the papers. You don't want to have a post-mortem because if there is anything you don't want to know it. Deny it if you can.

Harvester: I admit I shouldn't welcome publicity. I put all the money I had into buying my practice and I don't suppose it would do it any good if I were mixed up in an unpleasant case.

Mrs Tabret: People want their doctor to be like their central heating: efficient, but not obtrusive.

Harvester: But I can honestly say that if it were my duty I wouldn't let my own interests stop me from doing it. In this case I don't think it is my duty. I am quite satisfied that there is no reason why I shouldn't sign the necessary documents.

Colin: All that is neither here nor there. Nurse Wayland has presumably some grounds for her statement. Perhaps she'd better give them.

Liconda: Yes, she has. I thought it better she should speak before all concerned.

Nurse: It was my wish to do so. I don't want to do anything underhand.

Stella: Go on, Nurse Wayland.

Nurse [*to* **Liconda**]: I daresay you know that Mr Maurice often had bouts of sleeplessness. Dr Harvester had prescribed various sedatives. But he found that chloralin was the one he supported best. [To **Harvester**] Is that true?

Harvester: Quite. Chloralin is a new preparation in tabloid form. It's more convenient than the liquid chloral we've been in the habit of using. I explained to Maurice the danger of his growing dependent on drugs and begged him not to take a dose without my permission or Nurse Wayland's.

Nurse: I'm quite sure that he never did.

Harvester: So am I. He was very sensible and he understood my point. He certainly wasn't lacking in self-control.

Nurse: Will you tell Major Liconda what instructions you gave me last night?

Harvester: He was excited and wrought up. I asked Nurse Wayland to give him a tabloid and told him that if he woke in the night he could take it. I thought he'd probably drop off for half an hour or so and then wake up and not be able to get to sleep again.

Nurse: I dissolved a tabloid in half a glass of water and put it by his side. I noticed that there were only five tabloids left in the bottle and I made up my mind to order some more. This morning the bottle was empty.

Stella [*puzzled*]: That's very strange.

Nurse: Very!

Harvester: How did you happen to notice?

Nurse: I was tidying up. I thought it better to put away all the medicines and dressings and so on.

Stella [*to* **Harvester**]: Would five tabloids have a fatal effect?

Nurse: Six. I left one dissolved in water by the side of his bed.

Harvester: Yes, there's little doubt that the effect would be fatal.

Stella: It's all incredible. It's surely much more likely that someone took them for his own use.

Colin: Are you absolutely sure that last night the bottle contained five tabloids?

Nurse: Absolutely. If anyone took them for his own use it must have been after I went to bed.

Stella: But no one went into Maurice's room last night after that but me. I went in to say good night to him.

Liconda: How do you know that no one else went into his room?

Stella: Who could have? There was only Colin and Mother.

Liconda [*to* **Mrs Tabret**]: You went upstairs as I was letting myself out, Millie.

Mrs Tabret: I was very tired. [*With the shadow of a smile*] I didn't see any reason to wait while Colin and Stella and the Doctor ate a bacon sandwich.

Liconda: You didn't go into Maurice's room last night, Colin?

Colin: No, why should I? I don't want a sleeping-draught to make me sleep.

Stella: You're not under the impression that I took the tabloids, I suppose, Nurse Wayland?

Harvester: If you had you could presumably produce at least four of them. Believe me, if you'd taken twenty-five grains of chloralin at midnight you wouldn't be standing there now.

Nurse: The fact remains that five tabloids disappeared last night. Where are they?

Harvester: There's always the possibility that they were taken maliciously by someone who wanted to make trouble.

Nurse: Do you mean me, Dr Harvester? What do you think I can get out of making trouble? Really I don't know how such a stupid idea can have crossed your mind. Why should I have asked you to have a post-mortem if I knew for certain – as I must if I'd taken the tabloids out of sheer malice – that it would discover nothing?

Colin: Isn't it possible that they could have been taken by somebody this morning?

Liconda: Who?

Colin: The housemaid, for instance.

Liconda: Chloralin is not a very common drug. I shouldn't have thought a housemaid would ever have heard of it. It's not as though it were aspirin or veronal.

Harvester: I don't know about that. There have been cases in the papers. It's not safe to take it for granted that a house maid wouldn't have got into the habit of taking something when she couldn't sleep.

Stella: Well, it's very easy to make sure. It's Alice who did Maurice's room. Let us send for her.

Nurse: That is unnecessary. She was frightened at the idea of going in. I told her she need not and said I would clean up the room and put everything to rights myself. I'm quite sure she has not been in this morning.

Stella: What are we to do, Mother?

Mrs Tabret: You must do exactly what you think fit.

Liconda [*to the* **Doctor**]: Is it possible that Maurice can have died from chloral poisoning?

Harvester: I have told you that I am satisfied that death was due to natural causes.

Liconda: I wasn't asking that.

Harvester: Yes, of course it's possible. But I don't for an instant believe it.

Nurse: I know that this must add awfully to your grief, Mrs Tabret. I can't tell you how sorry I am. It seems dreadful that I should have to repay all your kindness to me by increasing your troubles.

Mrs Tabret: My dear, I'm quite ready to believe that you will do nothing and say nothing but what you think is right.

Stella: I'm all confused. It's come as such a dreadful shock. [*To the* **Nurse**] Do you *really* think that Maurice died of an overdose of his sleeping-draught?

Nurse [*very deliberately, looking her straight in the eyes*]: I do.

Stella: It's awful.

Nurse [*still looking at* **Stella**]: I think I should tell you that when I found the tabloids were missing I looked in the glass in which I'd dissolved the one I'd prepared for him. There was still about a dessertspoonful of liquid in the bottom of it. I have put it aside and I suggest that it should be analysed.

Mrs Tabret [*with faint mockery*]: You are wasted on your profession, Nurse Wayland. You have all the makings of a detective.

Liconda: But wouldn't a draught in which half a dozen tabloids had been dissolved be very unpalatable?

Harvester: It would be rather bitter. I suppose if one swallowed it down at a gulp one would hardly notice till one had already drunk it.

Stella: It all sounds very circumstantial. I'm afraid there's a dreadful probability in Nurse Wayland's story.

Colin: But, my dear, it's absurd. Who on earth would have thought of murdering Maurice? It's out of the question.

Stella: Oh, that, yes. I wasn't thinking of that. Nurse Wayland can't seriously think that anyone deliberately gave Maurice an overdose of his sleeping-draught. But I'm beginning to be desperately afraid that perhaps he took it himself.

Harvester: Suicide?

Stella [*with distress*]: He wasn't himself last night. He was very strange. I'd never seen him so nervous.

Liconda: Was there any reason for that?

Stella [*after a moment's hesitation*]: I'm afraid so. You see I'd been to *Tristan*. And we'd seen it together the night we got engaged. It upset him to think of the past.

Liconda: Did he speak of suicide?

Stella: No.

Liconda: Had he ever done so?

Stella: Never. I don't believe it had entered his head.

Liconda: What made you think he was upset last night?

Stella [*much moved*]: He did a thing he'd never done before. It was dreadfully painful. He cried. He cried in my arms.

Nurse: Why, exactly?

Stella [*desperately*]: Really, Miss Wayland, there are some things I can't tell you. What passed between my husband and myself was between ourselves. It concerned nobody but us.

Nurse: I beg your pardon. I should have thought it better for your own sake to be frank.

Stella: What do you mean? Are you accusing me of holding anything back?

Nurse: I'm not accusing anybody.

Liconda: My dear, I won't ask you anything that is painful for you to answer. But there's just this. If there's anything in what Miss Wayland says I suppose there'll have to be an inquest. The coroner will certainly ask you if your husband said anything at all that might indicate that suicide was in his mind.

Stella [*with a deep sigh*]: He said it would have been better if the accident had killed him outright. But he wasn't thinking of himself, he was thinking of me.

Liconda: That's very important.

Stella: Oh, Nurse, don't be hard on us. Don't be vindictive because I've been rather sharp with you. My nerves are all on edge today. After all, it's rather natural, isn't it? If poor Maurice did take an overdose of something, can't you square it with your conscience to say nothing about it? He had so little to live for. Can't you spare us the distress and horror of a post-mortem and an inquest?

Liconda: The question is if Dr Harvester is still willing to sign the death certificate.

Harvester: I think Nurse Wayland may very well have been mistaken about the tabloids. I can see no reason why I shouldn't.

Nurse [*deliberately*]: But you see, I am quite convinced that Maurice Tabret did not commit suicide.

Liconda: For what reason?

Nurse: Well, here's one of them. There was a little liquid still in the glass from which he drank. About a dessert-spoonful. You remember I mentioned that, and I put the glass away so that the liquid could be examined.

Liconda: Yes.

Nurse: Surely if a man were going to commit suicide he would drink the entire contents of the glass either in one gulp or two. He wouldn't risk making a bad job of what he was about by leaving something at the bottom. Least of all a man like Maurice Tabret.

Colin: That seems very far-fetched to me.

Liconda: I must say it seems rather a small point.

Colin: Besides, the stuff hasn't been analysed yet.

Liconda: Is your conviction based on nothing more than that, Nurse Wayland?

Nurse: No, it is not. Although Maurice Tabret was very good and I didn't believe he would ever take a tabloid without leave, one knows that it's very easy to get into the habit of drug-taking and then you can't be certain about anyone. Isn't that so, Dr Harvester?

Harvester: Yes, I suppose it is.

Nurse: Sometimes he was terribly depressed. I didn't think it wise to let him have within reach the power of putting an end to himself.

Stella: I never saw him depressed.

Nurse [*bitterly*]: I know you didn't. You never saw anything.

Stella: Nurse Wayland, what have I done to you? Why do

you talk to me like that? Your face is all twisted with hate of me. I don't understand.

Nurse: Don't you?

[*The two women stare at one another for a moment, then* **Stella** *gives a little shudder and turns her head away.*]

Stella: I'm beginning to be frightened of you. What sort of a woman are you that we've had in this house for five years?

Mrs Tabret [*in a soothing tone*]: There's nothing to be frightened of, darling. Don't give way to your nerves.

Nurse [*to Stella*]: Because he joked and laughed when you were there, did it never occur to you that there were moments when he was overwhelmed with black misery?

Stella [*with deep sympathy*]: Poor lamb, why did he insist on hiding it from me?

Nurse [*with a sort of restrained violence*]: His one aim was to make his suffering easy for you to bear. Whatever pain he had, he hid from you so that you shouldn't have the distress of being sorry for him.

Stella: It's dreadful that you should say such things. You make me feel that I was so cruel to him.

Nurse [*with increasing bitterness*]: Everything had to be hidden from you. When you were coming the medicine bottles and the dressings had to be put away, so that there should be nothing to remind you that there was anything the matter with him.

Stella: I would willingly have done everything for him that you did. It was his most earnest wish that I shouldn't concern myself with the horrid part of his illness.

Mrs Tabret: That is true, Nurse. I'm sorry you don't think that Stella did all she could for Maurice. As his mother I'm perhaps no less competent to judge than you. I have only admiration for her unselfishness and consideration.

Stella: Oh, Mother.

Mrs Tabret: I always think we do best by people when we help them in the way they want to be helped rather than in the way we may think they should be helped. I would sooner someone gave me a vanity bag that I hankered after than a shawl to wrap round my old bones that I didn't happen to want.

Liconda: There's something in that, Nurse Wayland.

Mrs Tabret: I'm sure that Stella did Maurice most good by answering him back in the same strain when he chaffed her and when he laughed, laughing with him.

Nurse: I was nothing. I was only his paid nurse. He didn't try to hide from me the despair that filled his heart. He didn't have to pretend to me. He didn't have to be good-tempered or amusing with me. He could be morose and he knew I wouldn't mind. He could quarrel with me and then say he was sorry if he'd hurt me and know he couldn't hurt me. To make you laugh he plastered his face with flour and painted his nose red and jumped through a hoop. You only saw the white mask of the clown; I saw his naked, tortured, triumphant soul.

Stella [*the truth dawning on her, the truth that the nurse had loved him*]: What are you telling us, Nurse Wayland?

Nurse: I'm telling the truth at last.

Stella: I wonder if you know what a strange truth it is.

Liconda: But, Nurse, what you've been saying suggests that he did have at least moments of despair when he must have thought of suicide. We know that he was overwrought last night. If his death was not due to natural causes, surely it's extremely likely that he brought it about himself.

Nurse: It was just one of those moments that I was on my guard against. The chloralin was kept in the bathroom on an upper shelf that he could not possibly have got at. I had to stand on a chair myself to reach it.

Liconda: If a man is determined to do a thing he can often surmount difficulties that others would have thought insuperable.

Nurse: Ask Dr Harvester if it would have been possible for Maurice Tabret to cross the room and go into the bathroom and stand up on a chair.

Harvester: He had absolutely no power in the lower part of his body. His back was broken by the accident and the spinal cord terribly injured.

Liconda: Couldn't he have crawled into the bathroom?

Harvester: With a great deal of difficulty. Yes, I think he might have done that.

Nurse: Could he have stood up on a chair?

Harvester: No, I'm bound to admit that is absolutely out of the question.

Liconda: If he'd got into the bathroom, couldn't he have fished down the bottle with a stick or something?

Harvester: Perhaps.

Nurse: Why do you say that, Dr Harvester? You know that he couldn't sit upright without help.

Harvester: I'm not so anxious to put the worst construction on everything as you seem to be, Nurse Wayland.

Nurse: And if he'd got the bottle down, how could he have put it up in its place again?

Harvester [*irritably*]: After all, we don't know yet that Maurice died of an overdose of chloralin.

Liconda: The matter can't be left like this, Harvester. I'm afraid there'll have to be an inquest.

Harvester: Yes, obviously, I can't sign the death certificate now. I shall have to communicate with the coroner.

Nurse: I'm sorry, Dr Harvester.

Harvester: I bet you are. I suppose you think it's very self-seeking of me not to want to be mixed up in a scandal. I suppose I ought to laugh through a horse collar at the prospect of smashing up a practice that I paid good money for and have spent seven years in building up.

Liconda: Oh, come now, it's not going to be as bad as that. However distressing an inquiry may be to Maurice's family, I don't see how it can affect his doctor. For a hopeless invalid to take an overdose of his sleeping draught is not so uncommon as to excite much comment.

Harvester: That, no.

Liconda: Many of us can only admire a man who has a fatal illness and prefers to end his life painlessly rather than endure useless suffering. He is more merciful to himself and to those he loves.

Nurse: Dr Harvester knows as well as I do that if Maurice Tabret died of an overdose of chloralin he couldn't have taken it himself. There's only one word for it and you all know it. It was murder.

Harvester: That's why I'm absolutely convinced that he died of natural causes. I can't offer an explanation for the disappearance of those damned tabloids, but there must be an explanation.

Colin: The most likely one is that Nurse Wayland was mistaken. Surely it's only reasonable to suppose that if anyone had taken out half a dozen tabloids he would have put others in their place, aspirin or chlorate of potash or something, so that they wouldn't be missed.

Nurse: People don't think of everything. It's only because a murderer makes some mistake that he's caught.

Harvester: But, damn it all, no one commits a murder without a motive. No one had the smallest reason to wish Maurice dead.

Nurse: How do you know?

Harvester: Good God, how do I know that two and two are four? I know that everybody was devoted to him. And with reason, damn it. He was the best fellow in the world.

Nurse: Did you know that his wife was going to have a baby?

Stella [*with a gasp*]: You fiend!

Colin [*aghast*]: Stella!

Nurse: I suspected it last night when she nearly fainted. This morning I knew for certain.

Stella: What do you mean? Are you accusing me of having murdered my husband?

Liconda [*very gravely*]: Is it true what she says, Stella?
[*There is a pause.* **Stella** *does not speak. There is anguish in her eyes.* **Alice**, *the parlourmaid, comes briskly in, breaking the tension with the affairs of every day.*]

Alice: Shall I keep lunch back, madam?

Mrs Tabret: Is it one o'clock? No, you can serve up.

Colin: We can't have lunch now, Mother.

Mrs Tabret: Why not? Lay for two extra. Major Liconda and Dr Harvester will be lunching.

Alice: Very good, madam.
[*She goes out.*]

Colin: Mother, it's impossible. How can we all sit down together as though nothing had happened?

Mrs Tabret: I think it's just as well. We have a great deal more to say to one another. It will do none of us any harm to talk of other things for half an hour.

Stella: I couldn't, I couldn't. Let me stay here.

Mrs Tabret [*firmly*]: I insist on your coming, my dear.

Harvester: I must bolt round to my house, Mrs Tabret. I'll have a bite there and come back immediately afterwards.

Mrs Tabret: Very well.

Liconda: My dear, I couldn't think of imposing myself on you.

Mrs Tabret [*with a grim smile*]: You must eat. Will you come, Nurse Wayland?

Nurse: No.

Mrs Tabret: I'll have something sent up to your room.

Nurse: I want nothing.

Mrs Tabret: You may when it comes.
[*Alice comes in again.*]

Alice: Lunch is served, madam.

Mrs Tabret [*giving Stella her hand*]: Come, Stella.

Act Three

The scene is the same as in the preceding acts.
Half an hour has passed.
  [**Stella** *is standing at one of the windows looking into*
  the garden. **Colin** *comes in from the hall and she*
  turns round.]
Colin: Stella.
Stella: Have you finished already?
Colin: More or less. I told Mother I wanted to see if you
  were all right.
Stella: Yes, I'm all right.
Colin: It was awful sitting there as though nothing had
  happened. I don't know what induced Mother to make
  us go through that farce.
Stella [*with a shrug*]: I dare say it was very sensible. With
  the servants there it was obvious that we had to hold
  our tongues. It gave us all a chance to collect ourselves.
Colin: I'm afraid you didn't eat a thing.
Stella [*smiling*]: You ate enough for both of us.
Colin: Did you think it was rotten of me?
Stella: No, I think it comforted me. To see you wolf
  down great mouthfuls of lamb and green peas made me
  realize that this nightmare isn't the whole of things.
  The world is going on all around us. Whatever we may
  be suffering the buses are going down Piccadilly and
  the trains are running in and out of Paddington Station.
Colin: Stella, is it true?
Stella: Is what true?
Colin: What that woman said.
Stella: About the baby? I suppose so. Yes, it's true.
Colin: Oh, Stella.
Stella: I wasn't sure. I was afraid. I thought it might be a
  false alarm. It's only quite lately that I've been certain.

Colin: Why didn't you tell me?

Stella: I didn't want to.

Colin: Not at all? Were you going to let me go away without knowing?

Stella: It was only a month before you were going back to Guatemala. I didn't want to spoil those last weeks for you. Because I worried there didn't seem to be any reason why you should be worried, too.

Colin: But what were you going to do?

Stella: I don't know. I was looking for some way out. I thought it would be easier when you were gone. Whatever happened, I thought I'd like to keep you out of it.

Colin: Why?

Stella: I don't know, unless because I love you.

Colin: Aren't I there to share your troubles with you?

Stella: I suppose women are very silly, when they tell a man that they're going to have a child by him, it seems rather an important moment to them. I suppose they feel happy and a little frightened and awed. They want to be made a fuss of. I couldn't expect you to feel joy or pride, but only consternation.

Colin: Oh, my sweetness, don't you know how devotedly I love you?

Stella: No, don't. Don't say anything that's going to upset me. I don't want to get emotional. If we've got to talk it over we'd better try to talk it over as calmly as we can.

Colin: What is that dreadful woman going to say now?

Stella: I don't know. I don't care . . . I don't know why I say that. I'm frightened to death.

Colin: You must keep a stiff upper lip.

Stella: Oh, Colin, whatever happens you'll stand by me, won't you?

Colin: Yes, I swear it.

[**Dr Harvester** *comes in from the garden.*]

Harvester: Oh, have you finished your luncheon already?

Stella [*forcing a smile to her lips*]: I'm afraid I couldn't make much of a pretence at eating. I wanted to be alone for a minute and came in here.

Colin: I think Mother and Major Liconda will be here directly. They were just starting coffee when I left them.

Harvester: Where's Nurse Wayland? I came back rather soon because 1 thought I'd like to have a chat with her alone.

Stella: Colin will go and fetch her. I suppose she lunched in her room.

Colin: Right-ho.

[*He goes out.*]

Harvester: I say, my dear, I hope this is going to come out all right.

Stella: It doesn't look much like it, does it?

Harvester: My word, you're cool.

Stella: When the earth is opening under your feet and the heavens are falling it doesn't seem much use to run about like a frightened hen.

Harvester: Do you mind my giving you a bit of advice?

Stella [*with a shade of irony*] : I'd welcome it, but I think it's very unlikely I shall take it.

Harvester: Well, it's just this, if I were you I'd take very great care not to say anything to put up Nurse Wayland's back.

Stella: She can't very well make things much more disagreeable than she has already.

Harvester: I'm not so sure of that. That's why I wanted to see her alone. You know she's not a bad sort, really. Now that she's had half an hour to calm down, I don't see why she shouldn't be more reasonable.

Stella: I wouldn't count on it in your place.

Harvester: I don't myself see what Nurse Wayland has to get out of making a fuss.

Stella: She's a very conscientious woman and she mistakes her hatred of me for the call of duty.

Harvester: The good are difficult to get on with, aren't they?

Stella [*smiling*]: Fortunately they're so few, it's not often they seriously inconvenience the rest of us.

Harvester: Nurse Wayland has got her knife into you all right.

Stella: Dr Harvester, will you tell me something?

Harvester: If I can.

Stella: Do you think it possible that Maurice could have guessed – my condition?

Harvester: I shouldn't think so.

Stella: I'm so thankful. I couldn't have borne the thought that he died rather than expose me to shame and disgrace. He was capable of it, you know.

Harvester: I'm afraid that if Maurice died of an overdose of chloral he can't have taken it himself.

Stella: But who could have given it him?

Harvester: That is the question, isn't it?

Stella: Wild and fantastic notions pass through my mind and one is more incredible than the other.

Harvester: I know.

Stella: Why couldn't that wretched woman leave me for a moment alone with my sorrow? My heart is burning with grief. I reproach myself so bitterly. I'm so ashamed of myself. You never knew Maurice in the old days. He was such a gallant figure. When I was in his room just now before all this horror burst upon us, I wept for myself as well as him. I wept for all the love I'd borne him in years gone by. Oh, how cruel death is.

Harvester: I know. However often your trade brings you in contact with it, you are overcome with the same dismay. It's so desperately final.

Stella: I can't believe that it's final. It would be too unfair. Why shouldn't it be true what Maurice believed – that we are born again? Will you think me silly and childish if I tell you something? I have a strange, mystical feeling that that brave spirit has entered into the child that I shall bear, and that in him Maurice, forgiving me the wrong I did him, will live out the life that was his due.

Harvester: There are some who think that if you only

The Sacred Flame

believe enough that a thing is true, it becomes true. Who am I to decide such matters?

[*The door is opened and* **Colin** *comes in immediately followed by the* **Nurse**.]

Colin: Here is Nurse Wayland.

Stella: Oh, Nurse, Dr Harvester wishes to speak to you by himself. Colin and I will go into the garden.

Nurse: It's very kind of you. But I have nothing private to say to Dr Harvester and I do not wish to listen to anything Dr Harvester has to say that anyone else may not hear. I want to do nothing underhand.

Harvester: I'm not going to ask you to do anything underhand.

Nurse: I know exactly what you want to say to me. You're going to point out that everyone here has been very kind to me and very generous. And they're prepared to be still kinder and still more generous. And if I make a scandal I shall be exposed to every sort of unpleasantness and very likely have great difficulty in getting another job. On the other hand, if I hold my tongue I can go to Japan and have a good time. Well, I won't.

Stella [*coolly*]: That seems very definite.

Harvester: All the same, I don't see how it can hurt you to listen to me for five minutes.

Stella: Now I put my foot down. I'm not prepared to allow an appeal on my behalf to be made to Nurse Wayland.

Colin: I think I hear my mother and the Major.

Harvester: Then it's too late.

[**Colin** *goes over to the door and opens it for them.* **Mrs Tabret** *and* **Major Liconda** *enter.*]

Mrs Tabret: Have we kept you waiting? I hope you had everything you wanted in your room, Nurse.

Nurse: Everything, thank you, Mrs Tabret.

Mrs Tabret: Won't you sit down? There's no use in your tiring yourself.

Nurse [*sitting down*]: Thank you.

Mrs Tabret: Have you been talking things over?

Harvester: I've only just come, Mrs Tabret.

Mrs Tabret: I suppose we are in Nurse Wayland's hands. What have you decided to do, Nurse Wayland?

Nurse: I must do what I think is my duty, Mrs Tabret.

Mrs Tabret: Of course. We should all do our duty, and how difficult it would be if at the same time we did not often make ourselves a trifle disagreeable to others.

Nurse: Mrs Tabret, Major Liconda asked your daughter-in-law a question just before luncheon. She didn't answer it.

Liconda [*to Stella*]: I am afraid you must have thought me very impertinent. Nurse Wayland said that you were going to have a baby, and I asked you if it was true.

Stella: It's quite true.

Liconda [*struggling with his embarrassment*]: I'm in a very false position. I am conscious that I am interfering in matters that are no affair of mine.

Stella: My dear Major, I know that you are kindness itself. You've known Mrs Tabret for ages and Maurice and Colin when they were small boys.

Liconda: All the same you must see how difficult it is for me to ask the question that inevitably rises in one's mind.

Stella: I'll answer without your asking. Of course it's quite impossible that Maurice should have been the father of the child I'm going to have. Since his accident he has been my husband only in name.

Colin [*going up to her and putting his hand round her shoulders*]: I am the father, Major Liconda.

Nurse [*astounded*]: You?

Mrs Tabret [*ironically*]: Do you mean to say that it escaped your sharp eyes, Nurse, that Colin and Stella were in love with one another?

Stella [*with a little frightened gasp*]: Did you know?

Mrs Tabret: I think nowadays the young are apt to think their elders even more stupid than advancing years generally make them.

Stella: Oh, Mother, what must you think of me?

Mrs Tabret [*dryly*]: Do you very much care?

Stella: I suppose I ought to be terribly ashamed of myself. I must be sincere. I don't want to make a pretence of remorse that I don't feel. I can no more help loving Colin than I can help the rain falling or the trees bursting into leaf. I'm proud of the child he's given me.

Nurse: You're shameless.

Stella [*to Mrs Tabret*]: But *you* have every right to think that I treated Maurice abominably. He's beyond the reach of pain, but I bitterly regret the pain I've caused you. I have no excuses to make for myself.

Mrs Tabret: My dear, don't you remember what I said to you last night? I thanked you for all you had done for Maurice. Did you think I was talking at random? I knew then that you were going to have a baby and that Colin was its father.

Colin: Mother, I blame myself so awfully.

Stella: You mustn't do that, darling. [*To* **Mrs Tabret**] If a woman doesn't want a man to make love to her she can very easily prevent it. Living side by side, in the same house for so many months, there's no reason why he should ever have looked upon me as anything but his sister. I was shameless. I didn't prevent him from making love to me because I wanted him to make love to me. I made him love me.

Colin: Oh, Stella, how could I help loving you? I don't blame myself for that. I blame myself because when I knew I loved you I didn't bolt.

Mrs Tabret: Am I right in thinking that then it was too late?

Colin: Do you remember, when we were kids in India they used to tell us of children who could recollect their past lives. They'd know who was who in the village and recognize the things that had belonged to them before and go straight to places that otherwise they couldn't have found. That's how I felt when I fell in love with Stella. I felt that I'd loved her always and that her love was home to me.

Stella: Whatever you may think of me, Mother, and however badly you think I've behaved, I ask you to believe
that I didn't give myself to Colin to gratify any passing
whim. I loved him with all my heart.

Mrs Tabret: My dear, I know. You say you made him love
you. Why do you say that except that you love him so
much? You can't persuade yourself that this miracle
should have happened that he loves you, too, unless
you had done it. Love is always diffident. One can never
be certain of love, one can only be certain of affection.

Stella: You mustn't think I didn't struggle against the
madness that possessed me. I said to myself that the
only return I could make Maurice for all the devotion
he gave me was by remaining faithful to him and loyal.

Mrs Tabret: I'm sure you did.

Stella: I told myself that Maurice was a cripple, bedridden,
sick, the victim of an unforeseen misfortune, and that
it would be foul of me to betray him. I tried to drive
Colin away. I was beastly to him, rude and sarcastic,
and then the dumb misery in his eyes broke my heart.
I did everything except ask him to go. I couldn't do
that. I couldn't. I pretended to myself that it was on
your account and on Maurice's. You hadn't seen him
for so long. Maurice was so pleased to have him here.

Mrs Tabret: It's quite true that I hadn't seen Colin for a
long time, and Maurice was tremendously pleased to
have him here.

Nurse [*with exasperation*]: I don't understand you, Mrs
Tabret. You seem to be going out of your way to find
excuses for your daughter-in-law. If you knew what
was going on, why didn't you stop it?

Mrs Tabret: I'm afraid I shall shock you, Miss Wayland;
I want to put it as delicately as I can, but it's a matter
that we English have made indelicate by prudishness
and hypocrisy. Stella is young, healthy, and normal.
Why should I imagine she has not got the instincts that
I had at her age? The sexual instinct is as normal as

hunger and as pressing as the desire to sleep. Why should she be deprived of its satisfaction?

Nurse [*with a little shiver of disgust*]: It seems to me that the modern world is obsessed by sex. Is there nothing else in it? After all, the answer is that you can't go without food and you can't go without sleep. But you can go without the satisfaction of your sexual appetites.

Harvester: But at what price of nervous disorders, crabbedness, and unhealthy emotions.

Mrs Tabret: When Maurice's accident made it impossible for him and Stella ever to live again as man and wife I asked myself if she would be able to support so false a relationship. They had loved one another as two healthy young things love. Their love was deep and passionate, but it was rooted in sex. It might have come about with time that it would have acquired a more spiritual character, it might have been that the inevitable trials of life endured together would have given birth to an affection and a confidence in one another that might have given a new glow to the fading fires of passion. They did not have the time.

Nurse [*to* **Stella**, *with irony*]: May I ask how long you'd been married?

Stella: I was married to Maurice about a year before he crashed.

Nurse: A year. A whole year.

Mrs Tabret: Out of his suffering a new love did spring up in Maurice's heart, a hungry, clinging, dependent love. I didn't know how long Stella would be content with that.

Nurse [*bitterly*]: No one could say that you had much trust in human nature.

Mrs Tabret: I have a great deal. As much, in fact, as experience has taught me is justified. I knew that Stella's pity was infinite.

Stella: Oh, infinite. Poor lamb.

Mrs Tabret: I knew it was so great that she mistook it for love, and I prayed that she would never find out her mistake. She meant everything in the world to Maurice. Everything. At first it was easier when we were struggling for his life, but when he settled down to being a chronic invalid and we knew that he would never be anything else I was seized with a great fear. I feared that the time would come when she felt she couldn't stand any longer the miserable life that was all he had to offer her. If she wanted to go I felt we hadn't the right to prevent her, and I knew that if she went Maurice would die.

Stella: I would never have left him. It never entered my head that it was possible.

Mrs Tabret: I saw the strain that it began to be on her nerves. She was as kind as ever, and as gentle, but it was an effort, and what is the good you do worth unless you do it naturally as the flowers give their scent?

Nurse: I have never been given to understand that good is only good if it's easy to do.

Mrs Tabret: I don't suppose it is, but if it's difficult then I think it benefits the person who does it rather than the person it's done to. That is why it is more blessed to give than to receive.

Nurse: I don't understand you. I think what you say is odious and cynical.

Mrs Tabret: Then I'm afraid you'll think what I'm going to say now even more cynical and odious. I found myself half wishing that Stella should take a lover.

Nurse [*with horror*]: Mrs Tabret!

Mrs Tabret: I was willing to shut my eyes to anything so long as she stayed with Maurice. I wanted her to be kind and thoughtful and affectionate to him, and I didn't care for the rest.

Nurse [*brokenly*]: I had such a deep respect for you, Mrs Tabret. I admired you so much. I used to think that when I was your age I'd like to be a woman like you.

Mrs Tabret: When Colin came back and after a while I realized that he and Stella were in love with one another, I did nothing to prevent the almost inevitable consequences. I didn't deliberately say it to myself in so many words, that would have shocked me, but in my heart was a feeling that this would make it all right for Maurice. She wouldn't go now. She was bound to this house by a stronger tie than pity or kindness.

Liconda: Didn't it strike you what great dangers you were exposing them to?

Mrs Tabret: I didn't care. I only thought of Maurice. When they were children I think I loved them equally. But since his accident I haven't had room in my heart for anyone but Maurice. He was everything to me. For him I was prepared to sacrifice Colin and Stella. [*With a little gesture of appeal to* **Stella**] I hope they'll forgive me.

Stella: Oh, my dear, as though there was anything for me to forgive.

Nurse: You'll only laugh at me if I say I'm shocked. I can't help it. I'm shocked to the very depths of my soul.

Mrs Tabret: I was afraid you would be.

Nurse: I would have gone to the stake for my belief that no unclean thought had ever entered your head. Didn't it revolt you to think that your son's wife was having an affair with a man under your own roof?

Mrs Tabret: I suppose I'm not very easily revolted. I've lived too long abroad to think that my own standard of right and wrong is the only one possible. We all know nowadays that morality isn't one and the same in all countries and at all times. There are many things, for instance, that we think right here and they think wrong in India . . .

Liconda: And contrariwise.

Mrs Tabret: But I wonder why people don't see that morality isn't the same for everyone at the same time in the same country. I'm not sure that I'd go as far as to say that there's a morality for the rich and a morality for the poor, though I'm doubtful, but I do think there's a morality for the young and a morality for the old. Perhaps we should all look upon these matters very differently if our moral rules hadn't been made by persons who had forgotten the passion and the high spirits of youth. Do you think it so very wicked if two young things surrender to the instincts that nature has planted in them?

Nurse: Did the probable result never occur to you?

Mrs Tabret: A baby? It persuades me of Stella's essential innocence. If she'd been a loose or abandoned woman she would have known how to avoid such an accident.

Nurse [*sardonically*]: You must admit at all events that Maurice's death has come in the very nick of time to get her out of a very awkward predicament.

Stella: Nurse, what a cruel – what a heartless thing to say.

Liconda [*sternly*]: You must be very careful, Nurse. That sounds extremely like an accusation.

Nurse: I wanted to accuse nobody. Do me the justice to admit that I started by saying that I was not satisfied with the circumstances and thought there should be a post-mortem. That was my right and my duty. Isn't that so, Dr Harvester?

Harvester: I suppose it is.

Nurse: You've forced me to this. You asked me who could have a motive for murdering Maurice Tabret. In self-defence I was obliged to tell you that his wife was going to have a child of which he couldn't be the father.

Stella: You talk of your duty, Miss Wayland. Are you sure that your motive for all this is anything more than your bitter hatred of me?

Nurse [*scornfully*]: Why should I hate you? Believe me, I only despise you.

Stella: You hate me because you were in love with Maurice.

Nurse [*violently*]: I? What do you mean? You're insulting me. How dare you say that?

Stella [*coolly*]: You gave it away. It had often seemed to me that you were fonder of Maurice than a nurse generally is of her patient and I used to chaff him about it.

It never struck me that it was serious till this morning.
Then you betrayed yourself in every word you said.
You were madly in love with Maurice.

Nurse [*defiantly*]: And if I was, what of it?

Stella: Nothing, except that it's my turn to be shocked. I
think it was rather horrible and disgusting.

Nurse [*with increasing emotion*]: Yes, I loved him. My
love grew as I saw yours fade. I loved him because he
was so helpless and so dependent on me. I loved him
because he was like a child in my arms. I never showed
him my love, I would sooner have died, and I was
ashamed because sometimes I thought, notwithstanding everything, he saw it. But if he saw it he understood
and was sorry for me. He knew how bitter it is to long
for the love of someone who has no love to give you.
My love meant nothing to him, he had no room in his
heart for any love but the love of you, and you had no
use for it. He asked for bread and you gave him a stone.
You think you were so kind and considerate. If you'd
loved him as I loved him you'd have seen how less than
nothing was all you did for him. I could think of a
hundred ways to give him happiness, they would have
meant nothing to him, and you hadn't the love to think
of them.

Stella: Miss Wayland, I'm sorry for what I said just now.
It was stupid of me and rather horrid. I suppose there
is something beautiful in love, of whatever kind it is.
Will you let me thank you for the love you gave my
husband?

Nurse [*violently*]: No, it's an impertinence to offer me
your thanks.

Stella: I'm sorry you should think that . . . It's quite true
that I didn't love Maurice, at least not with the love of
a woman for a man. I'm deeply conscious of the fact,
and often I reproached myself because I couldn't feel —
when at one moment I hadn't been able to help feeling.
It seemed so ungrateful and so unkind. He was no more

to me than a very dear friend for whom I was desperately sorry.

Nurse: Do you think he wanted your pity?

Stella: I know he didn't. But pity was all I had to give
him. Who was it that said that pity was akin to love?
There's all the world between them.

Nurse [*with angry vehemence*]: Yes, all the hideousness
of sex.

Stella; And do you believe there was nothing of sex in
your love for Maurice? It was because I felt that there
was in it an abnormal aborted sexuality that at the first
moment it gave me a little shiver of repulsion.

Nurse [*with a passionate emotion*]: No. No. My love for
that poor boy was as pure and as spiritual as my love
for God. There was never a shadow of self in it. My
love was compassion and Christian charity. I never
asked anything but to be allowed to serve and tend
him. It was a sufficient reward for me to be able to
wash and dry his poor wasted limbs and to hold the
mirror in front of him while he shaved. I never touched
his lips till they were cold in death. And now I've lost
everything that made life lovely to me. What was he
to you? What was he to his mother? To me he was my
child, my friend, my lover, my god. And you killed
him.

Stella: That's a lie!

Liconda: Come, Nurse Wayland, you have no right to say
that.

Nurse [*beside herself*]: It's true and you know it!

Liconda [*impatiently*]: I know nothing of the kind. I only
know that you've worked yourself into a state in which
you are saying all sorts of things for which you have
no justification.

Stella [*with a tolerant shrug of the shoulders*]: My dear,
I could no more have killed Maurice than I could walk
a tightrope. Doesn't it occur to you that there was
nothing to prevent my leaving him? Who could have
blamed me?

The Sacred Flame

Nurse: How would you have lived? You haven't a penny of your own. I've heard you tell Maurice a hundred times that you had to mind your p's and q's because he was your only means of livelihood.

Stella: I certainly shouldn't have repeated a feeble little joke so often. I suppose I could have worked.

Nurse [*scornfully*]: You!

Stella: I've noticed that the average woman who works for a living looks upon it as a little miracle and can never believe that any other can be clever enough to do the same thing. I needn't have become a nurse, you know. I might have made hats or invented a face-cream.

Nurse: Do you think this is the time to make cheap jokes?

Stella: I shouldn't have thought so. But you surely began when you accused me of poisoning my husband.

Nurse: Do you know what it means to work for one's living? Do you think one doesn't often feel tired and ill but goes on because it's one's job? Do you think one doesn't want to go and have fun like other girls? All your life you've been petted and spoiled and pampered. And you were going to have a child. How could you have worked?

Colin: You're really going too far, Miss Wayland. We can't stand here and let you insult Stella. The situation is preposterous.

Stella: There was Colin, you know, Miss Wayland. I don't think he would have left me in the lurch.

Colin: He certainly wouldn't.

Nurse: And what would you have had to go through before he could marry you? Not only exposure to your husband. But the divorce court. It wouldn't have been a very pretty case.

Stella: It would have been horrible.

Nurse [*with a gesture towards* **Colin**]: Do you think his love would have stood that test? Are you sure he wouldn't have hated you for the disgrace you had thrust upon him? Men are sensitive, you know, more sensitive than women, and they're afraid of scandal.

Stella: I may not be typical of my sex. I don't think I should like it either.

Nurse [*with all the scorn of which she is capable*]: You don't have to tell me that. Why are you letting me stand here and talk as I'm talking, but that you think you can persuade me or bribe me into holding my tongue? Why haven't these men, who are your friends and who hate me, thrown me out? Because they're afraid of me. They're afraid of scandal. They're afraid of publicity. Is that true?

Stella: Very probably.

Nurse: And you're not only afraid of scandal, you're afraid of your neck.

Stella: No, that's not true.

Nurse: You were in a hopeless situation. There was only one way out of your difficulties. You know as well as I do that your treachery, your monstrous cruelty would have broken your husband's heart. You couldn't face that. You preferred to kill him.

Stella: You've known me for five years, Nurse Wayland. I don't know how you can think me capable of such wickedness.

Nurse: Your husband trusted and loved you. He was bed-ridden. He was defenceless. I know that if you'd had a spark of decent feeling you couldn't have treated him as you did. If you were capable of being unfaithful to him you were capable of killing him.

Mrs Tabret [*with her thin smile*]: Are you not falling into a rather vulgar error, my dear? I know that when people talk of a good woman they mean a chaste one, but isn't that a very narrow view of goodness? Chastity is a very excellent thing, but it isn't the whole of virtue. There's kindness and courage and consideration for others. I'm not sure if there isn't also humour and common sense.

Nurse: Are you defending her for having been untrue to your son?

Mrs Tabret: I'm excusing her, Nurse Wayland. I know she gave Maurice all she could. The rest was not in her power.

Nurse: Oh, I know how you look upon these things. Nothing matters very much. There's no guilt in sin and no merit in virtue.

Mrs Tabret: May I tell you a little story about myself? When I was still a young woman, with a husband and two children, I fell madly in love with a young officer who had charge of the police in my husband's district and he fell madly in love with me.

Liconda: Millie!

Mrs Tabret: I'm an old woman now and he's an elderly retired major. But in those days we were all the world to one another. I didn't yield to my love on account of my boys. It nearly broke my heart. Now, you know, I'm very glad I didn't. One recovers from the pain of love. When I look at that funny old-fashioned major now I wonder why he ever excited in me such turbulent emotions. I could have told Colin and Stella that in thirty years it wouldn't matter much if they'd resisted their love. But people don't learn from the experience of others.

Nurse: You resisted, you can always say that you clung to the right.

Mrs Tabret: I think it was easier then, you know, for in that far-distant time we attached more importance to chastity than we do now. Yes, I resisted, but because I know the anguish it was, I feel I have the right to forgive those who were less virtuous, or perhaps only more courageous, than I.

Nurse: It is only by overcoming temptation that we strengthen our souls.

Mrs Tabret: Perhaps. But I've sometimes noticed that our most spectacular victories are over temptations that don't really tempt us very much. When I consider human nature and temptation I can't help thinking of a river and its banks. So long as too much water doesn't flow down between them the banks do their work very well, but let a flood come and they're useless. The river overflows and havoc follows.

Stella: Oh, my dear, you're so kind and so wise.

Mrs Tabret: No, darling, I'm only so old.

Liconda [kindly, but quite firmly]: Stella, Miss Wayland's accusation is very definite and must be met.

Stella: Her accusation is absurd.

Liconda: If Maurice died of an overdose of chloral, it was administered by somebody.

Stella: I suppose so.

Liconda: Can you suggest anyone who had the slightest motive for wishing he was dead?

Stella: No.

Liconda: I'm sure you want to help us to get at the truth. You must forgive me if I ask you some embarrassing questions.

Stella: Of course.

Liconda: What did you propose to do when you discovered you were going to have a baby?

Stella: I was frightened. At first I couldn't believe it. I didn't know what to do.

Liconda: You were aware that it couldn't be concealed very long?

Stella: Naturally. I thought something would happen. I was distracted.

Liconda: Did you tell anyone?

Stella: No, I was trying to screw up courage to ask Dr Harvester what I had better do. I didn't mind for myself. It was Maurice I was thinking of.

Liconda: You must have had some plan.

Stella: Oh, a hundred. I thought of nothing else day and night. I tried to find out if there wasn't some place I could go to. I thought if the worst came to the worst I could get Dr Harvester to say I was ill and run down and wanted a change and I could go away till the baby was born.

The Sacred Flame

Liconda: I suppose you never thought of making a clean breast of it to Maurice?

Stella: No, never. It would have broken his heart. He would have forgiven me. He loved me so much. But I couldn't bear that he should lose that immense belief he had in me. It meant everything to him.

Liconda: You appear to have been the last person who saw him alive?

Stella: Yes, I went in to say good night to him just before I went up to bed.

Liconda: What did you say to him then?

Stella: Nothing particular.

Liconda: Didn't you say that he'd been very much upset? He'd cried.

Stella: Yes. Earlier in the evening, before he went to bed.

Liconda: Why was he upset?

Stella: Need I tell you? It was so very private.

Liconda: No, of course not. I have no right to ask you anything. Only there is something very strange about the whole thing and for your own sake I think it would be better if you told us everything.

Stella: He broke down because he couldn't love me as he wanted to love me. He would have so liked to have a baby.

Liconda: And when you said good night to him did he make no further reference to that?

Stella: No, none. He'd quite recovered. He was in perfectly good spirits again.

Liconda: What did he say?

Stella: He just asked me if we'd enjoyed our snack and then he said, You'd better get off to bed. I said, I'm simply dropping, and I kissed him and said, Good night, old thing.

Liconda: How long were you in his room?

Stella: Five minutes.

Liconda: Did he say that he felt sleepy?

Stella: No.

Liconda: I suppose you knew where the chloralin was kept.

Stella: Vaguely. I knew that all his bottles and things were in the bathroom. He hated his bedroom to be littered about.

Liconda: Did he ask you for anything before you went?

Stella: No, there was nothing he wanted. Nurse Wayland had fixed him up quite comfortably.

Nurse [*to* **Stella** *freezingly*]: You don't understand. Major Liconda is giving you an opportunity of saying that your husband asked you for the chloralin and you, thinking no harm, gave it to him. You saw him take out five or six tabloids and then you replaced the bottle on the shelf.

Stella [*with irony*]: I never thought of that. That would have been quite a good way out if I'd poisoned my husband. No, Major, Maurice never asked me for the chloralin and I never gave it to him.

Nurse: May I ask a question now?

Stella: Certainly.

Nurse: Why were you so upset when I came in this morning and told you I'd been into your husband's room?

Stella: Do you mean when you said he was dead? Did you expect me to go on eating an egg as though you'd said it was a fine day?

Nurse: No, you didn't know he was dead then. You couldn't have known unless you'd had second sight.

Stella: Oh, I see what you mean now. I was angry with you for going into his room before he called. Sleep is such a precious and lovely thing. I think one should never wake anyone without reason.

Nurse: Are you sure you weren't afraid I'd gone into his room too soon? Supposing he'd been still alive and it had been possible to save him?

Stella: You've quite made up your mind that I murdered Maurice, haven't you?

Nurse: I'm not the only one.

Stella: What makes you think that?

Nurse: Why do you suppose the Major gave you that loop hole by suggesting that your husband asked you to give him the tabloids?

Liconda [*with some acerbity*]: You have done what you thought your duty, Miss Wayland. Well and good. If now you have other things to do, I don't think we need take up any more of your time.

Nurse: I'll go. There's nothing more for me to do here. I know you all hate me and you think I've done what I've done from unworthy motives. I started packing my things while you were having lunch. I shall be ready in ten minutes.

Mrs Tabret: You must take your time, Nurse.

Nurse: Believe me, I'm just as anxious to leave this house as you are to get rid of me. I shall be grateful if I can have a taxi rung up.

Mrs Tabret: Colin will get on to the rank. Perhaps you'd better get on at once, darling.

Colin: All right, Mother.

[*He opens the door for the Nurse and follows her out. The others watch her go in silence. The door is closed.*]

Mrs Tabret: Poor Miss Wayland. She has right on her side, you know, and she feels like a criminal. One can't help feeling sorry for a girl who has so much virtue and so little charm.

Liconda: Might I speak to Stella alone for a minute?

Mrs Tabret: If you wish to. Come with me, Dr Harvester.

Harvester: With pleasure.

Mrs Tabret: It's too bad that you should have to waste so much time on what is no business of yours.

Harvester: Believe me, I'd give a farm to be quite certain of that.

[*They go out.*]

Liconda: Stella, what are you going to do?

Stella: I don't know. What can I do? I feel like a rat in a trap.

Liconda: It's obvious that the matter can't rest here. It can't be hushed up now.

Stella: What is going to happen, then?

Liconda: I suppose Dr Harvester must communicate with the coroner. There'll be a post-mortem. If, as I'm afraid seems almost certain, Maurice is found to have died of an overdose of chloral there'll be an inquest and we shall have to await the verdict of the jury.

Stella: And then?

Liconda: If they find that poison was administered by a person unknown I imagine that the police will step in. I am afraid you must be prepared for a very terrible ordeal.

Stella: Do you mean that I should be tried for murder?

Liconda: It might be that the Director of Public Prosecutions would think that there was insufficient evidence to justify him in instituting proceedings.

Stella: Whatever else I've done you must know that it's incredible that I can be guilty of such a monstrous crime.

Liconda: Let us get the facts quite straight. I'm afraid it's no good blinking them. You were going to have a child of which Maurice was not the father. You were desperately anxious that he shouldn't know of your condition.

Stella: Desperately.

Liconda: Something had happened between you that had greatly distressed him. You were the last person that saw him. He was allowed to sleep on in the morning as long as he could. You were very angry when you found the nurse had gone into his room. He was dead. Five tabloids of chloralin are missing from the bottle and he couldn't possibly have got them himself. Who gave them to him?

Stella: How can I tell?

Liconda: My dear, you know that I desire to help you. I am your friend. It's no good beating about the bush. You're in a frightful situation.

Stella: Do *you* think I'm guilty?

The Sacred Flame

Liconda: Do you want the truth?

Stella: Yes.

Liconda: I don't know.

Stella [*as though she were thinking it over*]: I see.

Liconda: Of course, it's only circumstantial, but it all hangs together pretty well. You can hardly be surprised if suspicion falls on you.

Stella [*with a touch of humour*]: It hangs together beautifully. If I didn't know I hadn't poisoned Maurice I should say I must be guilty. There's only one thing I can say on the other side. I should have thought anyone who knew me at all would know I couldn't have poisoned Maurice.

Liconda: In the course of my career I've had to do with a lot of crime. To me one of the shattering things about it has been to notice that the most law-abiding and decent person may be driven to commit one. There are very few of us who can say that we shall certainly never do so. Sometimes crime seems to come to a man as accidentally as a chimney pot may fall on his head when he's walking down the street.

Stella [*with a shudder*]: It's rather terrible.

Liconda: It's not my business to judge you. I can only feel the deepest sympathy for the dreadful position you are in. You know what we English are and how uncharitably we regard sexual delinquencies. A jury would be greatly prejudiced against you when they were told that you had committed adultery with your brother-in-law.

Stella: Poor Colin. He'll have to put up with a good deal, won't he?

Liconda: Do you love him very much?

Stella: I love him as I never loved Maurice. My love for Maurice was open and sunny. It seemed as natural as the air I breathe. I thought it would last for ever. But in my love for Colin there is all my pain and my remorse and the bitterness of knowing that it's possible for love to die.

Liconda: Yes, that is bitter, isn't it? It makes life look such a sell.

Stella: Wouldn't it be possible in any way to keep Colin out of it?

Liconda: Oh, I'm afraid not. Anyhow that is a question we can discuss with the lawyers. We must find out who are the best people to go to. There's one thing I should like to impress upon you at once. Don't try to hide anything from your lawyers. The only chance an accused person has is to tell his advisers the absolute truth.

Stella: I have told the truth from the beginning.

Liconda: I hope to God you have.

[**Colin** *comes in. She sweeps up to him in a sudden storm of agitation.*]

Stella: Oh, Colin, you believe in me, don't you? You know I couldn't have done what they accuse me of.

Colin [*taking her in his arms*]: Darling. Darling.

Stella: Oh, Colin, I'm so frightened.

Colin: There's nothing to be frightened of. You're innocent. They can't touch you.

Stella: Whatever happens it means that we're finished. All our love is going to be told to everyone and they'll make us appear beastly and vicious. They'll say horrible things about me. They'll never know how hard I tried to resist. People blame you because you fall, they give you no credit for the effort you made to save yourself. The past counts for nothing.

Colin: It's so cruel that I who'd give my life for you should have brought all this misery on you.

Stella: How can I expect you to stay loving me when we've gone through what we've got to go through? Oh, the shame of it. Where should we go to hide our heads?

Colin: 1 shall love you always. You're all the world to me. You're all the world I want.

Stella: Men used to try to flirt with me. It meant so little, I only laughed at them. Until you came the thought never entered my head that I could be unfaithful to

Maurice. I wasn't troubled. I just put all that side of life on one side and never thought of it. I never knew I loved you till it was too late.

Colin: The only thing I ask you is never to regret that you loved me, whatever happens.

Stella: No, I shall never do that. I can't.

Colin [*with all his tenderness*]: Oh, my love. My sweetness.

Stella: But what a rotten trick fate has played on me. I look as though I were a bad, beastly woman, and when I look into my heart I can't see any wickedness. What a punishment because I couldn't resist the love that swept me up, as a gust of wind in March sweeps up last year's dead leaf.

Colin: Whatever the punishment is we can bear it together. Let's take our medicine, Stella; whatever happens, they can't take us away from one another.

Stella [*desperately*]: Major Liconda, what are we to do? Can't you say something to help us?

Liconda [*very gravely, in a low voice*]: How can I advise you? I can only tell you what I should do in your place.

Stella: What is that?

Liconda: If I were innocent I should stick it out. I should say to myself I may have sinned, I don't know, the world says so and the world is my judge. Whatever I did, I did because I couldn't help it and I'm willing to put up with what is coming to me. But if I were guilty, if in a moment of terror or madness I had committed an act for which the punishment of the law is death, I wouldn't wait to let justice take its course. I would take the surest, quickest way to put myself beyond the reach of the law.

Stella: I am innocent.

Liconda: If you hadn't been I should have told you that in the drawer of my writing-desk is a loaded revolver and that no one would prevent your going the few steps to my house and letting yourself in through the study window.

[**Stella** *looks at him in horror, fear making her heart beat furiously, he drops his eyes and turns his head away. There is a terrible silence. Then* **Nurse Wayland** *comes in. She wears now a coat and skirt and carries a hat in her hand. Stella pulls herself together. She addresses the Nurse with relief. She is cool and urbane.*]

Stella: You've been very quick, Nurse.

Nurse: I found I had practically nothing left to pack. I've asked Alice to have my trunk taken downstairs.

Stella: The gardener's here today. He can give her a hand.

Nurse: Might I say good-bye to Mrs Tabret before I go?

Stella: I'm sure she'd like you to. She's in the garden.

Nurse: I'll go to her.

Stella: Oh, don't bother. Colin will call her. She only went out because Major Liconda had something he wished to say to me in private.

[**Colin** *goes to the window and calls.*]

Colin: Mother.

Mrs Tabret [*from the garden*]: Are you calling me, Colin?

Colin: Nurse Wayland is just going. She would like to say good-bye to you.

Mrs Tabret: I'll come.

[*The four persons in the room stand in silence. To all of them the moment is fateful.* **Mrs Tabret** *comes in, followed by* **Dr Harvester**.]

Mrs Tabret [*with a little smile as though nothing very serious had happened*]: Is your taxi here, dear?

Nurse: Yes, I saw it drive up from my window. Mrs Tabret, I couldn't go without thanking you for all your kindness to me during the five years I've lived here.

Mrs Tabret: My dear, you were never any trouble. It was never difficult to be kind to you.

Nurse: I'm dreadfully sorry to have to repay all you've done for me by bringing this confusion and unhappiness upon you. I know you must hate me. It seems frightful, but I do ask you to believe that I can't help myself.

Mrs Tabret: Before we part, my dear, I should like if I

could to release your spirit from the bitterness that is making you so unhappy. We're none of us all of a piece, you know. We haven't one self but half a dozen. That's why you're wrong to have been jealous of Stella. You gave Maurice everything that one self of him craved and that self of his was — yours. It may be that we can be all things to all men, but can any of us be all things to one man, can any man be all things to any one of us? I knew a self of Maurice that none of you knew, I gave him something that no one else could give. I did not interfere with anyone. How ungenerous it would have been of me to resent the passion that bound him to Stella and the tender, comradely habit that bound him to you. God bless you for the kindness you showed my poor Maurice and for the unselfish love you bore him.

[*She takes* **Nurse Wayland's** *hands and kisses her on both cheeks.*]

Nurse [*with a sob*]: I'm so desperately unhappy.

Mrs Tabret: Oh, my dear, you mustn't lose your admirable self-control. No one can make an omelette without breaking eggs. And, such is the depravity of human nature, I suppose even the most respectable citizen feels a slight twinge of discomfort when he delivers the criminal to justice.

Liconda: I suppose you will leave an address, Miss Wayland. Dr Harvester will communicate with the proper authorities and I have no doubt they will want to get in touch with you.

Harvester: I shall go and see the coroner and put the facts before him. Would you like to come with me, Nurse?

Nurse: No.

Harvester: If Mrs Tabret doesn't mind I'll ring up his place from here and find out if he's in.

Mrs Tabret: Of course, I don't mind, but before you do that may I say a few words?

Harvester: As many as you like.

Mrs Tabret: I'll try to be brief. Nurse Wayland is mistaken in thinking that Stella was the last person who saw Maurice alive. I saw him and spoke to him later.

Nurse [*with utter amazement*]: You!

Harvester: But was he wide awake? If he'd taken thirty grains of chloralin he'd have been certainly very drowsy, if not comatose.

Mrs Tabret: Wait a minute, Dr Harvester. Let me tell you my story in my own way.

Harvester: I beg your pardon.

Mrs Tabret: You know that Maurice's room was just under mine. His windows were always wide open and when he couldn't sleep, and put on his light, I could see the reflection from my room. Then I used to slip down and sit by him and we'd put out the light and talk. Sometimes we talked about his childhood in India and I used to tell him of my own youth. But sometimes we'd talk about things that few men care to speak of in the broad light of day. He'd tell me of his great love for Stella and how anxious he was for her welfare and happiness. We'd talk of the mystery that surrounds the life of man. And often he would fall asleep and I stole softly away. We never mentioned these long conversations we had. [*With a little ironical smile*] The position of a woman living in the same house with her son and her daughter-in-law is a trifle delicate and I didn't want Stella to think that I was in any way taking her place.

Stella: My dear, I wouldn't have grudged you anything.

Mrs Tabret: There was no need to. But one shouldn't put human nature to too great a strain. The self that Maurice gave me during those long watches of the night was a self that only I, his mother, could respond to ... I couldn't sleep last night. There was no light in Maurice's room, but I felt strangely that he was lying awake, too. I went downstairs and into the garden and looked in at his window. He saw my shadow and said, Is that you, Mother? I thought you might come in.

Harvester: What time was that?

Mrs Tabret: I don't know. Perhaps an hour after you'd left. He told me that he'd taken his sleeping-draught but it didn't seem to be having any effect. He said he felt awfully wide awake. And then he said, Mother, be a sport and give me another, it can't hurt just for once, and I do want to have a decent sleep.

Harvester: Somehow or other he was very nervous last night. I suppose his usual dose wasn't any good.

Mrs Tabret [*very quietly*]: Very early after his accident I had promised Maurice that if life became intolerable to him I would give him the means of putting an end to it.

Stella: Oh, God!

Mrs Tabret: I said that if his sufferings were so great that he couldn't bear them any more and he solemnly asked me to help him, I wouldn't shirk the responsibility of giving him whatever drug was necessary to put to a painless end an existence he was no longer willing to endure. And sometimes he'd say to me, Does the promise still hold? And I answered, Yes, dear, it holds.

Stella [*with the greatest agitation*]: Did he ask you last night?

Mrs Tabret: No.

Liconda: What happened then?

Mrs Tabret: I knew that Stella's love meant everything to Maurice and I knew that she had none to give him because she had given all her love to Colin. What do we any of us live for but our illusions and what can we ask of others but that they should allow us to keep them? It was an illusion that sustained poor Maurice in his sufferings, and if he lost it he lost everything. Stella had done as much for him as even I, his mother, could ask of her. I was not so selfish as to demand from her the sacrifice of all that makes a woman's life worth while.

Stella: Why didn't you give me the chance?

Mrs Tabret: Years ago, when for my sons' sake I put aside the great love I bore to that funny old major standing there, I thought that no greater sacrifice could ever be asked of me. I know now it was nothing. For I loved Maurice. I adored him. I am so lonely now he is dead. It was a lovely dream that he dreamed, and I loved him too much to let him ever awake from it. I gave him life and I took life away from him.

Nurse [*horror-struck*]: Mrs Tabret! It's impossible! How dreadful!

Liconda: Millie! Millie! What are you going to tell us?

Mrs Tabret: I went into the bathroom and climbed on the chair and got the bottle of chloralin. I took five tabloids, as you know, Nurse Wayland, and I dissolved them in a glass of water. I took it in to Maurice and he drank it at a gulp. But it was bitter; he mentioned it, and I suppose that's why he left a little at the bottom of the glass. I sat by the side of his bed holding his hand till he fell asleep, and when I withdrew my hand I knew it was a sleep from which he would never awake. He dreamed his dream to the end.

Stella [*taking her in her arms*]: Oh, Mother, Mother. What have you done? And what will be the end of this? Oh, I'm so terrified.

Mrs Tabret [*gently releasing herself*]: My dear, don't bother about me. What I did I did deliberately and I am quite ready to put up with the consequences. I do not seek to shirk them.

Stella: It's my fault. It's my weakness. How can I ever forgive myself? What have I done?

Mrs Tabret: You mustn't be silly and sentimental. You love Colin and Colin loves you. You mustn't think about me nor distress yourselves at what happens to me. You must go away and in America you can marry and have your child and you must forget the past and the dead. For you are young and the young have a right to life and the future belongs to them.

Colin: Mother, darling. Oh, Mother, you make me so ashamed.

Mrs Tabret: My son, I love you, too. I have your happiness very much at heart.

Liconda: Millie. My dear, dear Millie.

Mrs Tabret [*with a slightly grim smile*]: Well, Nurse Wayland, you see you were quite right. Of course, I ought to have replaced the tabloids by others, aspirin or chlorate of potash, but as you said just now murderers often make mistakes and I'm not an habitual criminal.

[*There is a moment's pause.*]

Nurse: Dr Harvester, are you still willing to sign the death certificate?

Harvester: Yes.

Nurse: Then sign it. If there were ever any question I am prepared to swear that I left the tabloids on Maurice's table by his bed.

Stella: Nurse Wayland!

Mrs Tabret [*to* **Harvester**]; Isn't it a dreadful risk you're taking?

Harvester: Damn it, I don't care.

Liconda: Oh, Nurse, we're so grateful to you, so infinitely grateful.

[**Nurse Wayland** *throws herself down on her knees and clasps* **Mrs Tabret** *in her arms.*]

Nurse: Oh, Mrs Tabret, I've been so horrible. I've been petty and revengeful. I never knew how mean I was.

Mrs Tabret: Come, come, my dear, don't let any of us get emotional. We are both of us lonely women now. Let us cleave to one another. So long as you and I can keep our love for Maurice alive in our hearts he is not entirely dead.

The Circle

A PLAY IN THREE ACTS

Characters

Arnold Champion-Cheney, M.P.
A Footman
Mrs Shenstone
Elizabeth
Edward Luton
Clive Champion-Cheney
Butler
Lady Catherine Champion-Cheney
Lord Porteous

The action takes place at Aston-Adey, Arnold Champion-Cheney's house in Dorset.

Act One

The scene is a stately drawing-room at Aston-Adey, with fine pictures on the walls and Georgian furniture. Aston-Adey has been described with many illustrations, in Country Life. It is not a house, but a place. Its owner takes a great pride in it, and there is nothing in the room which is not of the period. Through the french windows at the back can be seen the beautiful gardens which are one of the features.

It is a fine summer morning.

[**Arnold** *comes in. He is a man of about thirty-five, tall and good-looking, fair, with a clean-cut, sensitive face. He has a look that is intellectual, but somewhat bloodless. He is very well dressed.*]

Arnold [*calling*]: Elizabeth! [*He goes to the window and calls again*] Elizabeth! [*He rings the bell. While he is waiting he gives a look round the room. He slightly alters the position of one of the chairs. He takes an ornament from the chimney-piece and blows the dust from it.*]

[*A* **Footman** *comes in.*]

Oh, George! See if you can find Mrs Cheney, and ask her if she'd be good enough to come here.

Footman: Very good, sir.

[*The* **Footman** *turns to go.*]

Arnold: Who is supposed to look after this room?

Footman: I don't know, sir.

Arnold: I wish when they dust they'd take care to replace the things exactly as they were before.

Footman: Yes, sir.

Arnold [*dismissing him*]: All right.

[*The* **Footman** *goes out. He goes again to the window and calls.*]

The Circle

Arnold: Elizabeth! [*He sees* **Mrs Shenstone**.] Oh, Anna, do you know where Elizabeth is?

[**Mrs Shenstone** *comes in from the garden. She is a woman of forty, pleasant and of elegant appearance.*]

Anna: Isn't she playing tennis?

Arnold: No, I've been down to the tennis court. Something very tiresome has happened.

Anna: Oh?

Arnold: I wonder where the deuce she is.

Anna: When do you expect Lord Porteous and Lady Kitty?

Arnold: They're motoring down in time for luncheon.

Anna: Are you sure you want me to be here? It's not too late yet, you know. I can have my things packed and catch a train for somewhere or other.

Arnold: No, of course we want you. It'll make it so much easier if there are people here. It was exceedingly kind of you to come.

Anna: Oh, nonsense!

Arnold: And I think it was a good thing to have Teddie Luton down.

Anna: He is so breezy, isn't he?

Arnold: Yes, that's his great asset. I don't know that he's very intelligent, but, you know, there are occasions when you want a bull in a china shop. I sent one of the servants to find Elizabeth.

Anna: I dare say she's putting on her shoes. She and Teddie were going to have a single.

Arnold: It can't take all this time to change one's shoes.

Anna [*with a smile*]: One can't change one's shoes without powdering one's nose, you know.

[**Elizabeth** *comes in. She is a very pretty creature in the early twenties. She wears a light summer frock.*]

Arnold: My dear, I've been hunting for you everywhere. What *have* you been doing?

Elizabeth: Nothing! I've been standing on my head.

Arnold: My father's here.

Elizabeth [*startled*]: Where?

Arnold: At the cottage. He arrived last night.

Elizabeth: Damn!

Arnold [*good-humouredly*]: I wish you wouldn't say that, Elizabeth.

Elizabeth: If you're not going to say Damn when a thing's damnable, when are you going to say Damn?

Arnold: I should have thought you could say, Oh, bother or something like that.

Elizabeth: But that wouldn't express my sentiments. Besides, at that speech day when you were giving away the prizes you said there were no synonyms in the English language.

Anna [*smiling*]: Oh, Elizabeth! It's very unfair to expect a politician to live in private up to the statements he makes in public.

Arnold: I'm always willing to stand by anything I've said. There are no synonyms in the English language.

Elizabeth: In that case I shall be regretfully forced to continue to say Damn whenever I feel like it.

[**Edward Luton** *shows himself at the window. He is an attractive youth in flannels.*]

Teddie: I say, what about this tennis?

Elizabeth: Come in. We're having a scene.

Teddie [*entering*]: How splendid! What about?

Elizabeth: The English language.

Teddie: Don't tell me you've been splitting your infinitives.

Arnold [*with the shadow of a frown*]: I wish you'd be serious, Elizabeth. The situation is none too pleasant.

Anna: I think Teddie and I had better make ourselves scarce.

Elizabeth: Nonsense! You're both in it. If there's going to be any unpleasantness we want your moral support. That's why we asked you to come.

Teddie: And I thought I'd been asked for my blue eyes.

Elizabeth: Vain beast! And they happen to be brown.

Teddie: Is anything up?

Elizabeth: Arnold's father arrived last night.

Teddie: Did he, by Jove! I thought he was in Paris.

The Circle

Arnold: So did we all. He told me he'd be there for the next month.

Anna: Have you seen him?

Arnold: No! He rang me up. It's a mercy he had a telephone put in the cottage. It would have been a pretty kettle of fish if he'd just walked in.

Elizabeth: Did you tell him Lady Catherine was coming?

Arnold: Of course not. I was flabbergasted to know he was here. And then I thought we'd better talk it over first.

Elizabeth: Is he coming along here?

Arnold: Yes. He suggested it, and I couldn't think of any excuse to prevent him.

Teddie: Couldn't you put the other people off?

Arnold: They're coming by car. They may be here any minute. It's too late to do that.

Elizabeth: Besides, it would be beastly.

Arnold: I knew it was silly to have them here. Elizabeth insisted.

Elizabeth: After all, she is your mother, Arnold.

Arnold: That meant precious little to her when she – went away. You can't imagine it means very much to me now.

Elizabeth: It's thirty years ago. It seems so absurd to bear malice after all that time.

Arnold: I don't bear malice, but the fact remains that she did me the most irreparable harm. I can find no excuse for her.

Elizabeth: Have you ever tried to?

Arnold: My dear Elizabeth, it's no good going over all that again. The facts are lamentably simple. She had a husband who adored her, a wonderful position, all the money she could want, and a child of five. And she ran away with a married man.

Elizabeth: Lady Porteous is not a very attractive woman, Arnold. [*To* **Anna**] Do you know her?

Anna [*smiling*]: Forbidding is the word, I think.

Arnold: If you're going to make little jokes about it, I have nothing more to say.

Anna: I'm sorry, Arnold.

Elizabeth: Perhaps your mother couldn't help herself – if she was in love?

Arnold: And had no sense of honour, duty, or decency? Oh, yes, under those circumstances you can explain a great deal.

Elizabeth: That's not a very pretty way to speak of your mother.

Arnold: I can't look on her as my mother.

Elizabeth: What you can't get over is that she didn't think of you. Some of us are more mother and some of us more woman. It gives me a little thrill when I think that she loved that man so much. She sacrificed her name, her position, and her child to him.

Arnold: You really can't expect the said child to have any great affection for the mother who treated him like that.

Elizabeth: No, I don't think I do. But I think it's a pity after all these years that you shouldn't be friends.

Arnold: I wonder if you realize what it was to grow up under the shadow of that horrible scandal. Everywhere, at school, and at Oxford, and afterwards in London, I was always the son of Lady Kitty Cheney. Oh, it was cruel, cruel!

Elizabeth: Yes, I know, Arnold. It was beastly for you.

Arnold: It would have been bad enough if it had been an ordinary case, but the position of the people made it ten times worse. My father was in the House then, and Porteous – he hadn't succeeded to the title – was in the House too; he was Under-Secretary for Foreign Affairs, and he was very much in the public eye.

Anna: My father always used to say he was the ablest man in the party. Everyone was expecting him to be Prime Minister.

Arnold: You can imagine what a boon it was to the British public. They hadn't had such a treat for a generation.

The most popular song of the day was about my
mother. Did you ever hear it? 'Naughty Lady Kitty.
Thought it such a pity . . . '

Elizabeth [*interrupting*]: Oh, Arnold, don't!

Arnold: And then they never let people forget them. If
they'd lived quietly in Florence and not made a fuss
the scandal would have died down. But those constant
actions between Lord and Lady Porteous kept on
reminding everyone.

Teddie: What were they having actions about?

Arnold: Of course my father divorced his wife, but Lady
Porteous refused to divorce Porteous. He tried to force
her by refusing to support her and turning her out of her
house, and heaven knows what. They were constantly
wrangling in the law courts.

Anna: I think it was monstrous of Lady Porteous.

Arnold: She knew he wanted to marry my mother, and
she hated my mother. You can't blame her.

Anna: It must have been very difficult for them.

Arnold: That's why they've lived in Florence. Porteous
has money. They found people there who were willing
to accept the situation.

Elizabeth: This is the first time they've ever come to
England.

Arnold: My father will have to be told, Elizabeth.

Elizabeth: Yes.

Anna [*to* **Elizabeth**]: Has he ever spoken to you about
Lady Kitty?

Elizabeth: Never.

Arnold: I don't think her name has passed his lips since
she ran away from this house thirty years ago.

Teddie: Oh, they lived here?

Arnold: Naturally. There was a house-party, and one evening neither Porteous nor my mother came down to
dinner. The rest of them waited. They couldn't make
it out. My father sent up to my mother's room, and a
note was found on the pincushion.

Elizabeth [*with a faint smile*]: That's what they did in the Dark Ages.

Arnold: I think he took a dislike to this house from that horrible night. He never lived here again, and when I married he handed the place over to me. He just has a cottage now on the estate that he comes to when he feels inclined.

Elizabeth: It's been very nice for us.

Arnold: I owe everything to my father. I don't think he'll ever forgive me for asking these people to come here.

Elizabeth: I'm going to take all the blame on myself, Arnold.

Arnold [*irritably*]: The situation was embarrassing enough anyhow. I don't know how I ought to treat them.

Elizabeth: Don't you think that'll settle itself when you see them?

Arnold: After all, they're my guests. I shall try and behave like a gentleman.

Elizabeth: I wouldn't. We haven't got central heating.

Arnold [*taking no notice*]: Will she expect me to kiss her?

Elizabeth [*with a smile*]: Surely.

Arnold: It always makes me uncomfortable when people are effusive.

Anna: But I can't understand why you never saw her before.

Arnold: I believe she tried to see me when I was little, but my father thought it better she shouldn't.

Anna: Yes, but when you were grown up?

Arnold: She was always in Italy. I never went to Italy.

Elizabeth: It seems to me so pathetic that if you saw one another in the street you wouldn't recognize each other.

Arnold: Is it my fault?

Elizabeth: You've promised to be very gentle with her and very kind.

Arnold: The mistake was asking Porteous to come too.

It looks as though we condoned the whole thing. And how am I to treat him? Am I to shake him by the hand and slap him on the back? He absolutely ruined my father's life.

Elizabeth [*smiling*]: How much would you give for a nice motor accident that prevented them from coming?

Arnold: I let you persuade me against my better judgement, and I've regretted it ever since.

Elizabeth [*good-humouredly*]: I think it's very lucky that Anna and Teddie are here. I don't foresee a very successful party.

Arnold: I'm going to do my best. I gave you my promise and I shall keep it. But I can't answer for my father.

Anna: Here is your father.

[**Mr Champion-Cheney** *shows himself at one of the french windows.*]

C.-C.: May I come in through the window, or shall I have myself announced by a supercilious flunkey?

Elizabeth: Come in. We've been expecting you.

C.-C.: Impatiently, I hope, my dear child.

[**Mr Champion-Cheney** *is a tall man in the early sixties, spare, with a fine head of grey hair and an intelligent, somewhat ascetic face. He is very carefully dressed. He is a man who makes the most of himself. He bears his years jauntily. He kisses* **Elizabeth** *and then holds out his hand to* **Arnold**.]

Elizabeth: We thought you'd be in Paris for another month.

C.-C.: How are you, Arnold? I always reserve to myself the privilege of changing my mind. It's the only one elderly gentlemen share with pretty women.

Elizabeth: You know Anna.

C.-C.: [*shaking hands with her*]: Of course I do. How very nice to see you here. Are you staying long?

Anna: As long as I'm welcome.

Elizabeth: And this is Mr Luton.

C.-C.: How do you do? Do you play bridge?

Luton: I do.

C.-C.: Capital. Do you declare without top honours?

Luton: Never.

C.-C.: Of such is the kingdom of heaven. I see that you are a good young man.

Luton: But, like the good in general, I am poor.

C.-C.: Never mind; if your principles are right, you can play ten shillings a hundred without danger. I never play less, and I never play more.

Arnold: And you – are you going to stay long, Father?

C.-C.: To luncheon, if you'll have me.

[**Arnold** *gives* **Elizabeth** *a harassed look.*]

Elizabeth: That'll be jolly.

Arnold: I didn't mean that. Of course you're going to stay for luncheon. I meant, how long are you going to stay down here?

C.-C.: A week.

[*There is a moment's pause. Everyone but* **Champion-Cheney** *is slightly embarrassed.*]

Teddie: I think we'd better chuck our tennis.

Elizabeth: Yes. I want my father-in-law to tell me what they're wearing in Paris this week.

Teddie: I'll go and put the rackets away.

[**Teddie** *goes out.*]

Arnold: It's nearly one o'clock, Elizabeth.

Elizabeth: I didn't know it was so late.

Anna [*to* **Arnold**]: I wonder if I can persuade you to take a turn in the garden before luncheon.

Arnold [*jumping at the idea*]: I'd love it.

[**Anna** *goes out of the window, and as he follows her he stops irresolutely.*]

I want you to look at this chair I've just got. I think it's rather good.

C.-C.: Charming.

Arnold: About 1750, I should say. Good design, isn't it? It hasn't been restored or anything.

C.-C.: Very pretty.

Arnold: I think it was a good buy, don't you?

C.-C.: Oh, my dear boy, you know I'm entirely ignorant about these things.

Arnold: It's exactly my period ... I shall see you at luncheon, then.

[*He follows* **Anna** *through the window.*]

C.-C.: Who is that young man?

Elizabeth: Mr Luton. He's only just been demobilized. He's the manager of a rubber estate in the F.M.S.

C.-C.: And what are the F.M.S. when they're at home?

Elizabeth: The Federated Malay States. He joined up at the beginning of the war. He's just going back there.

C.-C.: And why have we been left alone in this very marked manner?

Elizabeth: Have we? I didn't notice it.

C.-C.: I suppose it's difficult for the young to realize that one may be old without being a fool.

Elizabeth: I never thought you that. Everyone knows you're very intelligent.

C.-C.: They certainly ought to by now. I've told them often enough. Are you a little nervous?

Elizabeth: Let me feel my pulse. [*She puts her finger on her wrist.*] It's perfectly regular.

C.-C.: When I suggested staying to luncheon Arnold looked exactly like a dose of castor oil.

Elizabeth: I wish you'd sit down.

C.-C.: Will it make it easier for you? [*He takes a chair.*] You have evidently something very disagreeable to say to me.

Elizabeth: You won't be cross with me?

C.-C.: How old are you?

Elizabeth: Twenty-five.

C.-C.: I'm never cross with a woman under thirty.

Elizabeth: Oh, then, I've got ten years.

C.-C.: Mathematics?

Elizabeth: No, paint.

C.-C.: Well?

Elizabeth [*reflectively*]: I think it would be easier if I sat on your knees.

C.-C.: That is a pleasing taste of yours, but you must take care not to put on weight.

[*She sits down on his knees.*]

Elizabeth: Am I bony?

C.-C.: On the contrary . . . I'm listening.

Elizabeth: Lady Catherine's coming here.

C.-C.: Who's Lady Catherine?

Elizabeth: Your – Arnold's mother.

C.-C.: Is she?

[*He withdraws himself a little and* **Elizabeth** *gets up.*]

Elizabeth: You mustn't blame Arnold. It's my fault. I insisted. He was against it. I nagged him till he gave way. And then I wrote and asked her to come.

C.-C.: I didn't know you knew her.

Elizabeth: I don't. But I heard she was in London. She's staying at Claridge's. It seemed so heartless not to take the smallest notice of her.

C.-C.: When is she coming?

Elizabeth: We're expecting her in time for luncheon.

C.-C.: As soon as that? I understand the embarrassment.

Elizabeth: You see we never expected you to be here. You said you'd be in Paris for another month.

C.-C.: My dear child, this is your house. There's no reason why you shouldn't ask whom you please to stay with you.

Elizabeth: After all, whatever her faults, she's Arnold's mother. It seemed so unnatural that they should never see one another. My heart ached for that poor lonely woman.

C.-C.: I never heard that she was lonely, and she certainly isn't poor.

Elizabeth: And there's something else. I couldn't ask her by herself. It would have been so – so insulting. I asked Lord Porteous, too.

C.-C.: I see.

Elizabeth: I dare say you'd rather not meet them.

C.-C.: I dare say they'd rather not meet me. I shall get a capital luncheon at the cottage. I've noticed you always get the best food if you come in unexpectedly and have the same as they're having in the servants' hall.

Elizabeth: No one's ever talked to me about Lady Kitty. It's always been a subject that everyone has avoided. I've never even seen a photograph of her.

C.-C.: The house was full of them when she left. I think I told the butler to throw them in the dust-bin. She was very much photographed.

Elizabeth: Won't you tell me what she was like?

C.-C.: She was very like you, Elizabeth, only she had dark hair instead of red.

Elizabeth: Poor dear! It must be quite white now.

C.-C.: I dare say. She was a pretty little thing.

Elizabeth: But she was one of the great beauties of her day. They say she was lovely.

C.-C.: She had the most adorable little nose, like yours . . .

Elizabeth: D'you like my nose?

C.-C.: And she was very dainty, with a beautiful little figure; very light on her feet. She was like a marquise in an old French comedy. Yes, she was lovely.

Elizabeth: And I'm sure she's lovely still.

C.-C.: She's no chicken, you know.

Elizabeth: You can't expect me to look at it as you and Arnold do. When you're loved as she's loved you may grow old, but you grow old beautifully.

C.-C.: You're very romantic.

Elizabeth: If everyone hadn't made such a mystery of it I dare say I shouldn't feel as I do. I know she did a great wrong to you and a great wrong to Arnold. I'm willing to acknowledge that.

C.-C.: I'm sure it's very kind of you.

Elizabeth: But she loved and she dared. Romance is such an illusive thing. You read of it in books, but it's seldom you see it face to face. I can't help it if it thrills me.

C.-C.: I am painfully aware that the husband in these cases is not a romantic object.

Elizabeth: She had the world at her feet. You were rich.

She was a figure in society. And she gave up everything for love.

C.-C. [*dryly*]: I'm beginning to suspect it wasn't only for her sake and for Arnold's that you asked her to come here.

Elizabeth: I seem to know her already. I think her face is a little sad, for a love like that doesn't leave you gay, it leaves you grave, but I think her pale face is unlined. It's like a child's.

C.-C.: My dear, how you let your imagination run away with you!

Elizabeth: I imagine her slight and frail.

C.-C.: Frail, certainly.

Elizabeth: With beautiful thin hands and white hair. I've pictured her so often in that Renaissance palace that they live in, with old masters on the walls and lovely carved things all round, sitting in a black silk dress with old lace round her neck and old-fashioned diamonds. You see, I never knew my mother; she died when I was a baby. You can't confide in aunts with huge families of their own. I want Arnold's mother to be a mother to me. I've got so much to say to her.

C.-C.: Are you happy with Arnold?

Elizabeth: Why shouldn't I be?

C.-C.: Why haven't you got any babies?

Elizabeth: Give us a little time. We've only been married three years.

C.-C.: I wonder what Hughie is like now?

Elizabeth: Lord Porteous?

C.-C.: He wore his clothes better than any man in London. You know he'd have been Prime Minister if he'd remained in politics.

Elizabeth: What was he like then?

C.-C.: He was a nice-looking fellow. Fine horseman. I suppose there was something very fascinating about him. Yellow hair and blue eyes, you know. He had a very good figure. I like him. I was his parliamentary secretary. He was Arnold's godfather.

Elizabeth: I know.

C.-C.: I wonder if he ever regrets.

Elizabeth: I wouldn't.

C.-C.: Well, I must be strolling back to my cottage.

Elizabeth: You're not angry with me?

C.-C.: Not a bit.

[*She puts up her face for him to kiss. He kisses her on both cheeks and then goes out. In a moment* **Teddie's** *seen at the window.*]

Teddie: I saw the old blighter go.

Elizabeth: Come in.

Teddie: Everything all right?

Elizabeth: Oh, quite, as far as he's concerned. He's going to keep out of the way.

Teddie: Was it beastly?

Elizabeth: No, he made it very easy for me. He's a nice old thing.

Teddie: You were rather scared.

Elizabeth: A little. I am still. I don't know why.

Teddie: I guessed you were. I thought I'd come and give you a little moral support. It's ripping here, isn't it?

Elizabeth: It is rather nice.

Teddie: It'll be jolly to think of it when I'm back in the F.M.S.

Elizabeth: Aren't you homesick sometimes?

Teddie: Oh, everyone is now and then, you know.

Elizabeth: You could have got a job in England if you'd wanted to, couldn't you?

Teddie: Oh, but I love it out there. England's ripping to come back to, but I couldn't live here now. It's like a woman you're desperately in love with as long as you don't see her, but when you're with her she maddens you so that you can't bear her.

Elizabeth [*smiling*]: What's wrong with England?

Teddie: I don't think anything's wrong with England. I expect something's wrong with me. I've been away too long. England seems to me full of people doing things they don't want to because other people expect it of them.

Elizabeth: Isn't that what you call a high degree of civilization?

Teddie: People seem to me so insincere. When you go to parties in London they're all babbling about art, and you feel that in their hearts they don't care twopence about it. They read the books that everybody is talking about because they don't want to be out of it. In the F.M.S. we don't get very many books, and we read those we have over and over again. They mean so much to us. I don't think the people over there are half so clever as the people at home, but one gets to know them better. You see, there are so few of us that we have to make the best of one another.

Elizabeth: I imagine that frills are not much worn in the F.M.S. It must be a comfort.

Teddie: It's not much good being pretentious where everyone knows exactly who you are and what your income is.

Elizabeth: I don't think you want too much sincerity in society. It would be like an iron girder in a house of cards.

Teddie: And then, you know, the place is ripping. You get used to a blue sky and you miss it in England.

Elizabeth: What do you do with yourself all the time?

Teddie: Oh, one works like blazes. You have to be a pretty hefty fellow to be a planter. And then there's ripping bathing. You know, it's lovely, with palm trees all along the beach. And there's shooting. And now and then we have a little dance to a gramophone.

Elizabeth [*pretending to tease him*]: I think you've got a young woman out there, Teddie.

Teddie [*vehemently*]: Oh, no!

[*She is a little taken aback by the earnestness of his disclaimer. There is a moment's silence, then she recovers herself.*]

Elizabeth: But you'll have to marry and settle down one of these days, you know.

Teddie: I want to, but it's not a thing you can do lightly.

Elizabeth: I don't know why there more than elsewhere.

Teddie: In England if people don't get on they go their own ways and jog along after a fashion. In a place like that you're thrown a great deal on your own resources.

Elizabeth: Of course.

Teddie: Lots of girls come out because they think they're going to have a good time. But if they're empty-headed, then they're just faced with their own emptiness and they're done. If their husbands can afford it they go home and settle down as grass-widows.

Elizabeth: I've met them. They seem to find it a very pleasant occupation.

Teddie: It's rotten for their husbands, though.

Elizabeth: And if the husbands can't afford it?

Teddie: Oh, then they tipple.

Elizabeth: It's not a very alluring prospect.

Teddie: But if the woman's the right sort she wouldn't exchange it for any life in the world. When all's said and done, it's we who've made the Empire.

Elizabeth: What sort is the right sort?

Teddie: A woman of courage and endurance and sincerity. Of course, it's hopeless unless she's in love with her husband.

[*He is looking at her earnestly and she, raising her eyes, gives him a long look. There is silence between them.*]

Teddie: My house stands on the side of a hill, and the coconut trees wind down to the shore. Azaleas grow in my garden, and camellias, and all sorts of ripping flowers. And in front of me is the winding coast-line, and then the blue sea.

[*A pause.*]

Do you know that I'm awfully in love with you?

Elizabeth [*gravely*]: I wasn't quite sure. I wondered.

Teddie: And you?

[*She nods slowly.*]

I've never kissed you.

Elizabeth: I don't want you to.

[*They look at one another steadily. They are both grave.* **Arnold** *comes in hurriedly.*]

Arnold: They're coming, Elizabeth.

Elizabeth [*as though returning from a distant world*]: Who?

Arnold [*impatiently*]: My dear! My mother, of course. The car is just coming up the drive.

Teddie: Would you like me to clear out?

Arnold: No, no! For goodness' sake stay.

Elizabeth: We'd better go and meet them, Arnold.

Arnold: No, no; I think they'd much better be shown in. I feel simply sick with nervousness.

[*Anna comes in from the garden.*]

Anna: Your guests have arrived.

Elizabeth: Yes, I know.

Arnold: I've given orders that luncheon should be served at once.

Elizabeth: Why? It's not half past one already, is it?

Arnold: I thought it would help. When you don't know exactly what to say you can always eat.

[*The* **Butler** *comes in and announces.*]

Butler: Lady Catherine Champion-Cheney. Lord Porteous.

[**Lady Kitty** *comes in followed by* **Porteous**, *and the* **Butler** *goes out.* **Lady Kitty** *is a gay little lady, with dyed red hair and painted cheeks. She is somewhat outrageously dressed. She never forgets that she has been a pretty woman and she still behaves as if she were twenty-five.* **Lord Porteous** *is a very bald, elderly gentleman in loose, rather eccentric clothes. He is snappy and gruff. This is not at all the couple that* **Elizabeth** *expected and for a moment she stares at them with round startled eyes.* **Lady Kitty** *goes up to her with outstretched hands.*]

Lady Kitty: Elizabeth! Elizabeth! [*She kisses her*

effusively.] What an adorable creature! [*Turning to* **Porteous**] Hughie, isn't she adorable?

Porteous [*with a grunt*]: Ugh!

[**Elizabeth**, *smiling now, turns to him and gives him her hand.*]

Elizabeth: How d'you do?

Porteous: Damnable road you've got down here. How d'you do, my dear? Why d'you have such damnable roads in England?

[**Lady Kitty's** *eyes fall on* **Teddie** *and she goes up to him with her arms thrown back, prepared to throw them round him.*]

Lady Kitty: My boy, my boy! I should have known you anywhere!

Elizabeth [*hastily*]: That's Arnold.

Lady Kitty [*without a moment's hesitation*]: The image of his father! I should have known him anywhere! [*She throws her arms round his neck.*] My boy, my boy!

Porteous [*with a grunt*]: Ugh!

Lady Kitty: Tell me, would you have known me again? Have I changed?

Arnold: I was only five, you know, when – when you . . .

Lady Kitty [*emotionally*]: I remember as if it was yesterday. I went up into your room. [*With a sudden change of manner*] By the way, I always thought that nurse drank. Did you ever find out if she really did?

Porteous: How the devil can you expect him to know that, Kitty?

Lady Kitty: You've never had a child, Hughie; how can you tell what they know and what they don't?

Elizabeth [*coming to the rescue*]: This is Arnold, Lord Porteous.

Porteous [*shaking hands with him*]: How d'you do? I knew your father.

Arnold: Yes.

Porteous: Alive still?

Arnold: Yes.

Porteous: He must be getting on. Is he well?

Arnold: Very.

Porteous: Ugh! Takes care of himself I suppose. I'm not at all well. This damned climate doesn't agree with me.

Elizabeth [*to* **Lady Kitty**]: This is Mrs Shenstone. And this is Mr Luton. I hope you don't mind a very small party.

Lady Kitty [*shaking hands with* **Anna** *and* **Teddie**]: Oh, no, I shall enjoy it. I used to give enormous parties here. Political, you know. How nice you've made this room!

Elizabeth: Oh, that's Arnold.

Arnold [*nervously*]: D'you like this chair? I've just bought it. It's exactly my period.

Porteous [*bluntly*]: It's a fake.

Arnold [*indignantly*]: I don't think it is for a minute.

Porteous: The legs are not right.

Arnold: I don't know how you can say that. If there is anything right about it, it's the legs.

Lady Kitty: I'm sure they're right.

Porteous: You know nothing whatever about it, Kitty.

Lady Kitty: That's what you think. *I* think it's a beautiful chair. Hepplewhite?

Arnold: No, Sheraton.

Lady Kitty: Oh, I know. *The School for Scandal.*

Porteous: Sheraton, my dear. Sheraton.

Lady Kitty: Yes, that's what I say. I acted the screen scene at some amateur theatricals in Florence, and Ermete Novelli, the great Italian tragedian, told me he'd never seen a Lady Teazle like me.

Porteous: Ugh!

Lady Kitty [*to* **Elizabeth**]: Do you act?

Elizabeth: Oh, I couldn't. I should be too nervous.

Lady Kitty: I'm never nervous. I'm a born actress. Of course, if I had my time over again I'd go on the stage. You know, it's extraordinary how they keep young. Actresses, I mean. I think it's because they're always playing different parts. Hughie, do you think Arnold takes after me or after his father? Of course I think he's the very image of me. Arnold, I think I ought to tell

The Circle

you that I was received into the Catholic Church last winter. I'd been thinking about it for years, and last time we were at Monte Carlo I met such a nice monsignore. I told him what my difficulties were and he was too wonderful. I knew Hughie wouldn't approve, so I kept it a secret. [*To* **Elizabeth**] Are you interested in religion? I think it's too wonderful. We must have a long talk about it one of these days. [*Pointing to her frock*] Callot?

Elizabeth: No, Worth.

Lady Kitty: I knew it was either Worth or Callot. Of course, it's line that's the important thing. I go to Worth myself and I always say to him, Line, my dear Worth, line. What is the matter, Hughie?

Porteous: These new teeth of mine are so damned uncomfortable.

Lady Kitty: Men are extraordinary. They can't stand the smallest discomfort. Why, a woman's life is uncomfortable from the moment she gets up in the morning till the moment she goes to bed at night. And d'you think it's comfortable to sleep with a mask on your face?

Porteous: They don't seem to hold up properly.

Lady Kitty: Well, that's not the fault of your teeth. That's the fault of your gums.

Porteous: Damned rotten dentist. That's what's the matter.

Lady Kitty: I thought he was a very nice dentist. He told me my teeth would last till I was fifty. He has a Chinese room. It's so interesting; while he scrapes your teeth he tells you all about the dear Empress Dowager. Are you interested in China? I think it's too wonderful. You know they've cut off their pigtails. I think it's such a pity. They were so picturesque.

[*The* **Butler** *comes in.*]

Butler: Luncheon is served, sir.

Elizabeth: Would you like to see your rooms?

Porteous: We can see our rooms after luncheon.

Lady Kitty: I must powder my nose, Hughie.

Porteous: Powder it down here.

Lady Kitty: I never saw anyone so inconsiderate.

Porteous: You'll keep us all waiting half an hour. I know you.

Lady Kitty [*fumbling in her bag*]: Oh, well, peace at any price, as Lord Beaconsfield said.

Porteous: He said a lot of damned silly things, Kitty, but he never said that.

[**Lady Kitty's** *face changes. Perplexity is followed by dismay and consternation.*]

Lady Kitty: Oh!

Elizabeth: What is the matter?

Lady Kitty [*with anguish*]: My lipstick.

Elizabeth: Can't you find it?

Lady Kitty: I had it in the car. Hughie, you remember that I had it in the car.

Porteous: I don't remember anything about it.

Lady Kitty: Don't be so stupid, Hughie. Why, when we came through the gates I said: My home, my home! and I took it out and put some on my lips.

Elizabeth: Perhaps you dropped it in the car.

Lady Kitty: For heaven's sake send someone to look for it.

Arnold: I'll ring.

Lady Kitty: I'm absolutely lost without my lipstick. Lend me yours, darling, will you?

Elizabeth: I'm awfully sorry. I'm afraid I haven't got one.

Lady Kitty: Do you mean to say you don't use a lipstick?

Elizabeth: Never.

Porteous: Look at her lips. What the devil d'you think she wants muck like that for?

Lady Kitty: Oh, my dear, what a mistake you make! You must use a lipstick. It's so good for the lips. Men like it, you know. I couldn't live without a lipstick.

[**Champion-Cheney** *appears at the window holding in his upstretched hand a little gold case.*]

C.-C. [*as he comes in*]: Has any one here lost a diminutive utensil containing, unless I am mistaken, a favourite preparation for the toilet?

[**Arnold** *and* **Elizabeth** *are thunderstruck at his appearance and even* **Teddie** *and* **Anna** *are taken aback. But* **Lady Kitty** *is overjoyed.*]

Lady Kitty: My lipstick!

C.-C.: I found it in the drive and I ventured to bring it in.

Lady Kitty: It's Saint Antony. I said a little prayer to him when I was hunting in my bag.

Porteous: Saint Antony be blowed! It's Clive, by God!

Lady Kitty [*startled, her attention suddenly turning from the lipstick*]: Clive!

C.-C.: You didn't recognize me. It's many years since we met.

Lady Kitty: My poor Clive, your hair has gone quite white!

C.-C. [*holding out his hand*]: I hope you had a pleasant journey down from London.

Lady Kitty [*offering him her cheek*]: You may kiss me, Clive.

C.-C. [*kissing her*]: You don't mind, Hughie?

Porteous [*with a grunt*]: Ugh!

C.-C. [*going up to him cordially*]: And how are you, my dear Hughie?

Porteous: Damned rheumatic if you want to know. Filthy climate you have in this country.

C.-C.: Aren't you going to shake hands with me, Hughie?

Porteous: I have no objection to shaking hands with you.

C.-C.: You've aged, my poor Hughie.

Porteous: Someone was asking me how old you were the other day.

C.-C.: Were they surprised when you told them?

Porteous: Surprised! They wondered you weren't dead.

[*The* **Butler** *comes in.*]

Butler: Did you ring, sir?

Arnold: No. Oh, yes, I did. It doesn't matter now.

C.-C. [*as the* **Butler** *is going*]: One moment. My dear Elizabeth, I've come to throw myself on your mercy.

My servants are busy with their own affairs. There's not a thing for me to eat in my cottage.

Elizabeth: Oh, but we shall be delighted if you'll lunch with us.

C.-C.: It either means that or my immediate death. from starvation. You don't mind, Arnold?

Arnold: My dear father!

Elizabeth [*to the* **Butler**]: Mr Cheney will lunch here.

Butler: Very good, ma'am.

C.-C. [*to* **Lady Kitty**]: And what do you think of Arnold?

Lady Kitty: I adore him.

C.-C.: He's grown, hasn't he? But then you'd expect him to do that in thirty years.

Arnold: For God's sake let's go in to lunch, Elizabeth!

Act Two

The scene is the same as in the preceding act.

[*When the curtain rises* **Porteous** *and* **Lady Kitty**, **Anna** *and* **Teddie** *are playing bridge.* **Elizabeth** *and* **Champion-Cheney** *are watching.* **Porteous** *and* **Lady Kitty** *are partners.*]

C.-C.: When will Arnold be back, Elizabeth?

Elizabeth: Soon, I think.

C.-C.: Is he addressing a meeting?

Elizabeth: No, it's only a conference with his agent and one or two constituents.

Porteous [*irritably*]: How any one can be expected to play bridge when people are shouting at the top of their voices all round them, I for one cannot understand.

Elizabeth [*smiling*]: I'm so sorry.

Anna: I can see your hand, Lord Porteous.

Porteous: It may help you.

Lady Kitty: I've told you over and over again to hold your cards up. It ruins one's game when one can't help seeing one's opponent's hand.

Porteous: One isn't obliged to look.

Lady Kitty: What was Arnold's majority at the last election?

Elizabeth: Seven hundred and something.

C.-C.: He'll have to fight for it if he wants to keep his seat next time.

Porteous: Are we playing bridge, or talking politics?

Lady Kitty: I never find that conversation interferes with my game.

Porteous: You certainly play no worse when you talk than when you hold your tongue.

Lady Kitty: I think that's a very offensive thing to say, Hughie. Just because I don't play the same game as you do, you think I can't play.

Porteous: I'm glad you acknowledge it's not the same game as I play. But why in God's name do you call it bridge?

C.-C.: I agree with Kitty. I hate people who play bridge as though they were at a funeral and knew their feet were getting wet.

Porteous: Of course you take Kitty's part.

Lady Kitty: That's the least he can do.

C.-C.: I have a naturally cheerful disposition.

Porteous: You've never had anything to sour it.

Lady Kitty: I don't know what you mean by that, Hughie.

Porteous [*trying to contain himself*]: Must you trump my ace?

Lady Kitty [*innocently*]: Oh, was that your ace, darling?

Porteous [*furiously*]: Yes, it was my ace.

Lady Kitty: Oh, well, it was the only trump I had. I shouldn't have made it anyway.

Porteous: You needn't have told them that. Now she knows exactly what I've got.

Lady Kitty: She knew before.

Porteous: How could she know?

Lady Kitty: She said she'd seen your hand.

Anna: Oh, I didn't. I said I could see it.

Lady Kitty: Well, I naturally supposed that if she could see it she did.

Porteous: Really, Kitty, you have the most extraordinary ideas.

C.-C.: Not at all. If any one is such a fool as to show me his hand, of course I look at it.

Porteous [*fuming*]: If you study the etiquette of bridge, you'll discover that onlookers are expected not to interfere with the game.

C.-C.: My dear Hughie, this is a matter of ethics, not of bridge.

Anna: Anyhow, I get the game. And rubber.

Teddie: I claim a revoke.

Porteous: Who revoked?

Teddie: You did.

Porteous: Nonsense. I've never revoked in my life.

Teddie: I'll show you. [*He turns over the tricks to show the faces of the cards.*] You threw away a club on the third heart trick and you have another heart.

Porteous: I never had more than two hearts.

Teddie: Oh, yes, you had. Look here. That's the card you played on the last trick but one.

Lady Kitty [*delighted to catch him out*]: There's no doubt about it, Hughie. You revoked.

Porteous: I tell you I did not revoke. I never revoke.

C.-C.: You did, Hughie, I wondered what on earth you were doing.

Porteous: I don't know how anyone can be expected not to revoke when there's this confounded chatter going on all the time.

Teddie: Well, that's another hundred to us.

Porteous [*to* **Champion-Cheney**]: I wish you wouldn't breathe down my neck. I never can play bridge when there's somebody breathing down my neck.

[*The party have risen from the bridge-table, and they scatter about the room.*]

The Circle

Anna: Well, I'm going to take a book and lie down in the hammock till it's time to dress.

Teddie [*who has been adding up*]: I'll put it down in the book, shall I?

Porteous [*who has not moved, setting out the cards for a patience*]: Yes, yes, put it down. I never revoke.

    [**Anna** *goes out.*]

Lady Kitty: Would you like to come for a little stroll, Hughie?

Porteous: What for?

Lady Kitty: Exercise.

Porteous: I hate exercise.

C.-C.: [*looking at the patience*]: The seven goes on the eight.

    [**Porteous** *takes no notice.*]

Lady Kitty: The seven goes on the eight, Hughie.

Porteous: I don't choose to put the seven on the eight.

C.-C.: That knave goes on the queen.

Porteous: I'm not blind, thank you.

Lady Kitty: The three goes on the four.

C.-C.: All these go over.

Porteous [*furiously*]: Am I playing this patience, or are you playing it?

Lady Kitty: But you're missing everything.

Porteous: That's my business.

C.-C.: It's no good losing your temper over it, Hughie.

Porteous: Go away, both of you. You irritate me.

Lady Kitty: We were only trying to help you, Hughie.

Porteous: I don't want to be helped. I want to do it by myself.

Lady Kitty: I think your manners are perfectly deplorable, Hughie.

Porteous: It's simply maddening when you're playing patience and people won't leave you alone.

C.-C.: We won't say another word.

Porteous: That three goes. I believe it's coming out. If I'd been such a fool as to put that seven up I shouldn't have been able to bring these down.

[*He puts down several cards while they watch him silently.*]

Lady Kitty and C.-C. [*together*]: The four goes on the five.

Porteous [*throwing down the cards violently*]: Damn you! Why don't you leave me alone? It's intolerable.

C.-C.: It was coming out, my dear fellow.

Porteous: I know it was coming out. Confound you!

Lady Kitty: How petty you are, Hughie!

Porteous: Petty, be damned! I've told you over and over again that I will not be interfered with when I'm playing patience.

Lady Kitty: Don't talk to me like that, Hughie.

Porteous: I shall talk to you as I please.

Lady Kitty [*beginning to cry*]: Oh, you brute! You brute! [*She flings out of the room.*]

Porteous: Oh, damn! Now she's going to cry.

[*He shambles out into the garden.* **Champion-Cheney, Elizabeth,** *and* **Teddie** *are left alone. There is a moment's pause.* **Champion-Cheney** *looks from* **Teddie** *to* **Elizabeth,** *with an ironical smile.*]

C.-C.: Upon my soul, they might be married. They frip so much.

Elizabeth [*frigidly*]: It's been nice of you to come here so often since they arrived. It's helped to make things easy.

C.-C.: Irony? It's a rhetorical form not much favoured in this blessed plot, this earth, this realm, this England.

Elizabeth: What exactly are you getting at?

C.-C.: How slangy the young women of the present day are! I suppose the fact that Arnold is a purist leads you to the contrary extravagance.

Elizabeth: Anyhow you know what I mean.

C.-C. [*with a smile*]: I have a dim, groping suspicion.

Elizabeth: You promised to keep away. Why did you come back the moment they arrived?

C.-C.: Curiosity, my dear child. A surely pardonable curiosity.

Elizabeth: And since then you've been here all the time.

You don't generally favour us with so much of your company when you're down at your cottage.

C.-C.: I've been excessively amused.

Elizabeth: It has struck me that whenever they started fripping you took a malicious pleasure in goading them on.

C.-C.: I don't think there's much love lost between them now, do you?

[**Teddie** *is making as though to leave the room.*]

Elizabeth: Don't go, Teddie.

C.-C.: No, please don't. I'm only staying a minute. We were talking about Lady Kitty just before she arrived. [*To* **Elizabeth**] Do you remember? The pale, frail lady in black satin and old lace.

Elizabeth [*with a chuckle*]: You are a devil, you know.

C.-C.: Ah, well, he's always had the reputation of being a humorist and a gentleman.

Elizabeth: Did you expect her to be like that, poor dear?

C.-C.: My dear child, I hadn't the vaguest idea. You were asking me the other day what she was like when she ran away. I didn't tell you half. She was so gay and so natural. Who would have thought that animation would turn into such frivolity, and that charming impulsiveness lead to such a ridiculous affectation?

Elizabeth: It rather sets my nerves on edge to hear the way you talk of her.

C.-C.: It's the truth that sets your nerves on edge, not I.

Elizabeth: You loved her once. Have you no feeling for her at all?

C.-C.: None. Why should I?

Elizabeth: She's the mother of your son.

C.-C.: My dear child, you have a charming nature, as simple, frank, and artless as hers was. Don't let pure humbug obscure your common sense.

Elizabeth: We have no right to judge. She's only been here two days. We know nothing about her.

C.-C.: My dear, her soul is as thickly rouged as her face. She hasn't an emotion that's sincere. She's tinsel. You

think I'm a cruel, cynical old man. Why, when I think
of what she was, if I didn't laugh at what she has
become I should cry.

Elizabeth: How do you know she wouldn't be just the
same now if she'd remained your wife? Do you think
your influence would have had such a salutary effect
on her?

C.-C. [*good-humouredly*]: I like you when you're bitter
and rather insolent.

Elizabeth: D'you like me enough to answer my question?

C.-C.: She was only twenty-seven when she went away.
She might have become anything. She might have
become the woman you expected her to be. There are
very few of us who are strong enough to make
circumstances serve us. We are the creatures of our
environment. She's a silly worthless woman because
she's led a silly worthless life.

Elizabeth [*disturbed*]: You're horrible today.

C.-C.: I don't say it's I who could have prevented her from
becoming this ridiculous caricature of a pretty woman
grown old. But life could. Here she would have had the
friends fit to her station, and a decent activity, and
worthy interests. Ask her what her life has been all
these years among divorced women and kept women
and the men who consort with them. There is no more
lamentable pursuit than a life of pleasure.

Elizabeth: At all events she loved and she loved greatly.
I have only pity and affection for her.

C.-C.: And if she loved what d'you think she felt when
she saw that she had ruined Hughie? Look at him. He
was tight last night after dinner and tight the night
before.

Elizabeth: I know.

C.-C.: And she took it as a matter of course. How long
do you suppose he's been getting tight every night? Do
you think he was like that thirty years ago? Can you
imagine that that was a brilliant young man, whom

everyone expected to be Prime Minister? Look at him now. A grumpy sodden old fellow with false teeth.

Elizabeth: You have false teeth, too.

C.-C.: Yes, but damn it all, they fit. She's ruined him and she knows she's ruined him.

Elizabeth [*looking at him suspiciously*]: Why are you saying all this to me?

C.-C.: Am I hurting your feelings.

Elizabeth: I think I've had enough for the present.

C.-C.: I'll go and have a look at the gold-fish. I want to see Arnold when he comes in. [*Politely*] I'm afraid we've been boring Mr Luton.

Teddie: Not at all.

C.-C.: When are you going back to the F.M.S.?

Teddie: In about a month.

C.-C.: I see.

[*He goes out.*]

Elizabeth: I wonder what he has at the back of his head.

Teddie: D'you think he was talking *at* you?

Elizabeth: He's as clever as a bagful of monkeys.

[*There is a moment's pause. **Teddie** hesitates a little, and when he speaks it is in a different tone. He is grave and somewhat nervous.*]

Teddie: It seems very difficult to get a few minutes alone with you. I wonder if you've been making it difficult?

Elizabeth: I wanted to think.

Teddie: I've made up my mind to go away tomorrow.

Elizabeth: Why?

Teddie: I want you altogether or not at all.

Elizabeth: You're so arbitrary.

Teddie: You said you – you said you cared for me.

Elizabeth: I do.

Teddie: Do you mind if we talk it over now?

Elizabeth: No.

Teddie [*frowning*]: It makes me feel rather shy and awkward. I've repeated to myself over and over again exactly what I want to say to you, and now all I'd prepared seems rather footling.

Elizabeth: I'm so afraid I'm going to cry.

Teddie: I feel it's all so tremendously serious and I think we ought to keep emotion out of it. You're rather emotional, aren't you?

Elizabeth [*half smiling and half in tears*]: So are you for the matter of that.

Teddie: That's why I wanted to have everything I meant to say to you cut and dried. I think it would be awfully unfair if I made love to you and all that sort of thing, and you were carried away. I wrote it all down and thought I'd send it you as a letter.

Elizabeth: Why didn't you?

Teddie: I got the wind up. A letter seems so – so cold. You see, I love you so awfully.

Elizabeth: For goodness' sake don't say that.

Teddie: You mustn't cry. Please don't, or I shall go all to pieces.

Elizabeth [*trying to smile*]: I'm sorry. It doesn't mean any thing really. It's only tears running out of my eyes.

Teddie: Our only chance is to be awfully matter-of-fact.
[*He stops for a moment. He finds it quite difficult to control himself. He clears his throat. He frowns with annoyance at himself.*]

Elizabeth: What's the matter?

Teddie: I've got a sort of lump in my throat. It is idiotic. I think I'll have a cigarette.
[*She watches him in silence while he lights a cigarette.*]
You see, I've never been in love with anyone before, not really. It's knocked me endways. I don't know how I can live without you now . . . Does that old fool know I'm in love with you?

Elizabeth: I think so.

Teddie: When he was talking about Lady Kitty smashing up Lord Porteous's career I thought there was something at the back of it.

Elizabeth: I think he was trying to persuade me not to smash up yours.

The Circle

Teddie: I'm sure that's very considerate of him, but I don't happen to have one to smash. I wish I had. It's the only time in my life I've wished I were a hell of a swell so that I could chuck it all and show you how much more you are to me than anything else in the world.

Elizabeth [*affectionately*]: You're a dear old thing, Teddie.

Teddie: You know, I don't really know how to make love, but if I did I couldn't do it now because I just want to be absolutely practical.

Elizabeth [*chaffing him*]: I'm glad you don't know how to make love. It would be almost more than I could bear.

Teddie: You see, I'm not at all romantic and that sort of thing. I'm just a common or garden businessman. All this is so dreadfully serious and I think we ought to be sensible.

Elizabeth [*with a break in her voice*]: You owl!

Teddie: No, Elizabeth, don't say things like that to me. I want you to consider all the pros and cons, and my heart's thumping against my chest, and you know I love you, I love you, I love you.

Elizabeth [*in a sigh of passion*]: Oh, my precious.

Teddie [*impatiently, but with himself rather than with Elizabeth*]: Don't be idiotic, Elizabeth. I'm not going to tell you that I can't live without you and a lot of muck like that. You know that you mean everything in the world to me. [*Almost giving it up as a bad job*] Oh, my God!

Elizabeth [*her voice faltering*]: D'you think there's anything you can say to me that I don't know already?

Teddie [*desperately*]: But I haven't said a single thing I wanted to. I'm a businessman and I want to put it all in a business way, if you understand what I mean.

Elizabeth [*smiling*]: I don't believe you're a very good businessman.

Teddie [*sharply*]: You don't know what you're talking about. I'm a first-rate businessman, but somehow this

228

is different. [*Hopelessly*] I don't know why it won't go right.

Elizabeth: What are we going to do about it?

Teddie: You see, it's not just because you're awfully pretty that I love you. I'd love you just as much if you were old and ugly. It's you I love, not what you look like. And it's not only love; love be blowed. It's that I *like* you so tremendously. I think you're such a ripping good sort. I just want to be with you. I feel so jolly and happy just to think you're there. I'm so awfully *fond* of you.

Elizabeth [*laughing through her tears*]: I don't know if this is your idea of introducing a business proposition.

Teddie: Damn you, you won't let me.

Elizabeth: You said, Damn you.

Teddie: I meant it.

Elizabeth: Your voice sounded as if you meant, you perfect duck.

Teddie: Really, Elizabeth, you're intolerable.

Elizabeth: I'm doing nothing.

Teddie: Yes, you are, you're putting me off my blow. What I want to say is perfectly simple. I'm a very ordinary businessman.

Elizabeth: You've said that before.

Teddie [*angrily*]: Shut up. I haven't got a bob besides what I earn. I've got no position. I'm nothing. You're rich and you're a big pot and you've got everything that anyone can want. It's awful cheek my saying anything to you at all. But after all there's only one thing that really matters in the world, and that's love. I love you. Chuck all this, Elizabeth, and come to me.

Elizabeth: Are you cross with me?

Teddie: Furious.

Elizabeth: Darling!

Teddie: If you don't want me tell me so at once and let me get out quickly.

Elizabeth: Teddie, nothing in the world matters anything to me but you. I'll go wherever you take me. I love you.

Teddie [*all to pieces*] Oh, my God!

Elizabeth: Does it mean as much to you as that? Oh, Teddie!

Teddie [*trying to control himself*]: Don't be a fool, Elizabeth.

Elizabeth: It's you're the fool. You're making me cry.

Teddie: You're so damned emotional.

Elizabeth: Damned emotional yourself. I'm sure you're a rotten businessman.

Teddie: I don't care what you think. You've made me so awfully happy. I say, what a lark life's going to be.

Elizabeth: Teddie, you are an angel.

Teddie: Let's get out quick. It's no good wasting time, Elizabeth.

Elizabeth: What?

Teddie: Nothing. I just like to say Elizabeth.

Elizabeth: You fool.

Teddie: I say, can you shoot?

Elizabeth: No.

Teddie: I'll teach you. You don't know how ripping it is to start out from your camp at dawn and travel through the jungle. And you're so tired at night and the sky's all starry. It's a fair treat. Of course I didn't want to say anything about that till you'd decided. I'd made up my mind to be absolutely practical.

Elizabeth [*chaffing him*] The only practical thing you said was that love is the only thing that really matters.

Teddie [*happily*]: Pull the other leg next time, will you? I should hate to have one longer than the other.

Elizabeth: Isn't it fun being in love with someone who's in love with you?

Teddie: I say, I think I'd better clear out at once, don't you? It seems rather rotten to stay on in – in this house.

Elizabeth: You can't go tonight. There's no train.

Teddie: I'll go tomorrow. I'll wait in London till you're ready to join me.

Elizabeth: I'm not going to leave a note on the pincushion like Lady Kitty, you know. I'm going to tell Arnold.

Teddie: Are you? Don't you think there'll be an awful bother?

Elizabeth: I must face it. I should hate to be sly and deceitful.

Teddie: Well, then, let's face it together.

Elizabeth: No, I'll talk to Arnold by myself.

Teddie: You won't let anyone influence you?

Elizabeth: No.

[*He holds out his hand and she takes it. They look into one another's eyes with grave, almost solemn affection. There is the sound outside of a car driving up.*]

Elizabeth: There's the car. Arnold's come back. I must go and bathe my eyes. I don't want them to see I've been crying.

Teddie: All right. [*As she is going*] Elizabeth.

Elizabeth [*stopping*]: What?

Teddie: Bless you.

Elizabeth [*affectionately*]: Idiot!

[*She goes out of the door and **Teddie** through the french window into the garden. For an instant the room is empty. **Arnold** comes in. He sits down and takes some papers out of his dispatch-case. Lady Kitty enters. He gets up.*]

Lady Kitty: I saw you come in. Oh, my dear, don't get up. There's no reason why you should be so dreadfully polite to me.

Arnold: I've just rung for a cup of tea.

Lady Kitty: Perhaps we shall have the chance of a little talk. We don't seem to have had five minutes by ourselves. I want to make your acquaintance, you know.

Arnold: I should like you to know that it's not by my wish that my father is here.

Lady Kitty: But I'm so interested to see him.

Arnold: I was afraid that you and Lord Porteous must find it embarrassing.

Lady Kitty: Oh, no. Hughie was his greatest friend. They were at Eton and Oxford together. I think your father

has improved so much since I saw him last. He wasn't
good-looking as a young man, but now he's quite handsome.

[*The* **Footman** *brings in a tray on which are tea-
things.*]

Lady Kitty: Shall I pour it out for you?

Arnold: Thank you very much.

Lady Kitty: Do you take sugar?

Arnold: No. I gave it up during the war.

Lady Kitty: So wise of you. It's so bad for the figure.
Besides being patriotic, of course. Isn't it absurd that I
should ask my son if he takes sugar or not? Life is
really very quaint. Sad, of course, but oh, so quaint!
Often I lie in bed at night and have a good laugh to
myself as I think how quaint life is.

Arnold: I'm afraid I'm a very serious person.

Lady Kitty: How old are you now, Arnold?

Arnold: Thirty-five.

Lady Kitty: Are you really? Of course, I was a child when
I married your father.

Arnold: Really. He always told me you were twenty-two.

Lady Kitty: Oh, what nonsense! Why, I was married out
of the nursery. I put my hair up for the first time on
my wedding-day.

Arnold: Where is Lord Porteous?

Lady Kitty: My dear, it sounds too absurd to hear you call
him Lord Porteous. Why don't you call him – Uncle
Hughie?

Arnold: He doesn't happen to be my uncle.

Lady Kitty: No, but he's your godfather. You know, I'm
sure you'll like him when you know him better. I'm
so hoping that you and Elizabeth will come and stay
with us in Florence. I simply adore Elizabeth. She's too
beautiful.

Arnold: Her hair is very pretty.

Lady Kitty: It's not touched up, is it?

Arnold: Oh, no.

Lady Kitty: I just wondered. It's rather a coincidence that

her hair should be the same colour as mine. I suppose
it shows that your father and you are attracted by just
the same thing. So interesting, heredity, isn't it?

Arnold: Very.

Lady Kitty: Of course, since I joined the Catholic Church
I don't believe in it any more. Darwin and all that sort
of thing. Too dreadful. Wicked, you know. Besides, it's
not very good form, is it?

[**Champion-Cheney** *comes in from the garden.*]

C.-C.: Do I intrude?

Lady Kitty: Come in, Clive. Arnold and I have been
having such a wonderful heart-to-heart talk.

C.-C.: Very nice.

Arnold: Father, I stepped in for a moment at the Harveys'
on my way back. It's simply criminal what they're
doing with that house.

C.-C.: What are they doing?

Arnold: It's an almost perfect Georgian house and they've
got a lot of dreadful Victorian furniture. I gave them
my ideas on the subject, but it's quite hopeless. They
said they were attached to their furniture.

C.-C.: Arnold should have been an interior decorator.

Lady Kitty: He has wonderful taste. He gets that from
me.

Arnold: I suppose I have a certain flair. I have a passion
for decorating houses.

Lady Kitty: You've made this one charming.

C.-C.: D'you remember, we just had chintzes and comfortable chairs when we lived here, Kitty?

Lady Kitty: Perfectly hideous, wasn't it?

C.-C.: In those days gentlemen and ladies were not
expected to have taste.

Arnold: You know, I've been looking at this chair again.
Since Lord Porteous said the legs weren't right I've been
very uneasy.

Lady Kitty: He only said that because he was in a bad
temper.

C.-C.: His temper seems to me very short these days, Kitty.

Lady Kitty: Oh, it is.

Arnold: You feel he knows what he's talking about. I gave seventy-five pounds for that chair. I'm very seldom taken in. I always think if a thing's right you feel it.

C.-C.: Well, don't let it disturb your night's rest.

Arnold: But, my dear father, that's just what it does. I had a most horrible dream about it last night.

Lady Kitty: Here is Hughie.

Arnold: I'm going to fetch a book I have on Old English furniture. There's an illustration of a chair which is almost identical with this one.

[*Porteous comes in.*]

Porteous: Quite a family gathering, by George!

C.-C.: I was thinking just now we'd make a very pleasing picture of a typical English home.

Arnold: I'll be back in five minutes. There's something I want to show you, Lord Porteous.

[*He goes out.*]

C.-C.: Would you like to play piquet with me, Hughie?

Porteous: Not particularly.

C.-C.: You were never much of a piquet player, were you?

Porteous: My dear Clive, you people don't know what piquet is in England.

C.-C.: Let's have a game then. You may make money.

Porteous: I don't want to play with you.

Lady Kitty: I don't know why not, Hughie.

Porteous: Let me tell you that I don't like your manner.

C.-C.: I'm sorry for that. I'm afraid I can't offer to change it at my age.

Porteous: I don't know what you want to be hanging around here for.

C.-C.: A natural attachment to my home.

Porteous: If you'd had any tact you'd have kept out of the way while we were here.

C.-C.: My dear Hughie, I don't understand your attitude

at all. If I'm willing to let bygones be bygones why should you object?

Porteous: Damn it all, they're not bygones.

C.-C.: After all, I am the injured party.

Porteous: How the devil are you the injured party?

C.-C.: Well, you did run away with my wife, didn't you?

Lady Kitty: Now, don't let's go into ancient history. I can't see why we shouldn't all be friends.

Porteous: I beg you not to interfere, Kitty.

Lady Kitty: I'm very fond of Clive.

Porteous: You never cared two straws for Clive. You only say that to irritate me.

Lady Kitty: Not at all. I don't see why he shouldn't come and stay with us.

C.-C.: I'd love to. I think Florence in spring-time is delightful. Have you central heating?

Porteous: I never liked you, I don't like you now, and I never shall like you.

C.-C.: How very unfortunate! Because I liked you, I like you now, and I shall continue to like you.

Lady Kitty: There's something very nice about you, Clive.

Porteous: If you think that, why the devil did you leave him?

Lady Kitty: Are you going to reproach me because I loved you? How utterly, utterly, utterly detestable you are!

C.-C.: Now, now, don't quarrel with one another.

Lady Kitty: It's all his fault. I'm the easiest person in the world to live with. But really he'd try the patience of a saint.

C.-C.: Come, come, don't get upset, Kitty. When two people live together there must be a certain amount of give and take.

Porteous: I don't know what the devil you're talking about.

C.-C.: It hasn't escaped my observation that you are a little inclined to frip. Many couples are. I think it's a pity.

Porteous: Would you have the very great kindness to mind your own business?

Lady Kitty: It is his business. He naturally wants me to be happy.

C.-C.: I have the very greatest affection for Kitty.

Porteous: Then why the devil didn't you look after her properly?

C.-C.: My dear Hughie, you were my greatest friend. I trusted you. It may have been rash.

Porteous: It was inexcusable.

Lady Kitty: I don't know what you mean by that, Hughie.

Porteous: Don't, don't, don't try and bully me, Kitty.

Lady Kitty: Oh, I know what you mean.

Porteous: Then why the devil did you say you didn't?

Lady Kitty: When I think that I sacrificed everything for that man! And for thirty years I've had to live in a filthy marble palace with no sanitary conveniences.

C.-C.: D'you mean to say you haven't got a bathroom?

Lady Kitty: I've had to wash in a tub.

C.-C.: My poor Kitty, how you've suffered!

Porteous: Really, Kitty, I'm sick of hearing of the sacrifices you made. I suppose you think I sacrificed nothing. I should have been Prime Minister by now if it hadn't been for you.

Lady Kitty: Nonsense!

Porteous: What do you mean by that? Everyone said I should be Prime Minister. Shouldn't I have been Prime Minister, Clive?

C.-C.: It was certainly the general expectation.

Porteous: I was the most promising young man of my day. I was bound to get a seat in the Cabinet at the next election.

Lady Kitty: They'd have found you out just as I've found you out. I'm sick of hearing that I ruined your career. You never had a career to ruin. Prime Minister! You haven't the brain. You haven't the character.

C.-C.: Cheek, push, and a gift of the gab will serve very well instead, you know.

Lady Kitty: Besides, in politics it's not the men that matter. It's the women at the back of them. I could have made Clive a Cabinet Minister if I'd wanted to.

Porteous: Clive?

Lady Kitty: With my beauty, my charm, my force of character, my wit, I could have done anything.

Porteous: Clive was nothing but my political secretary. When I was Prime Minister I might have made him Governor of some Colony or other. Western Australia, say. Out of pure kindliness.

Lady Kitty [*with flashing eyes*]: D'you think I would have buried myself in Western Australia? With my beauty? My charm?

Porteous: Or Barbados, perhaps.

Lady Kitty [*furiously*]: Barbados! Barbados can go to – Barbados.

Porteous: That's all you'd have got.

Lady Kitty: Nonsense! I'd have India.

Porteous: I would never have given you India.

Lady Kitty: You would have given me India.

Porteous: I tell you I wouldn't.

Lady Kitty: The King would have given me India. The nation would have insisted on my having India. I would have been a vice-reine or nothing.

Porteous: I tell you that as long as the interests of the British Empire – Damn it all, my teeth are coming out! [*He hurries from the room.*]

Lady Kitty: It's too much. I can't bear it any more. I've put up with him for thirty years and now I'm at the end of my tether.

C.-C.: Calm yourself, my dear Kitty.

Lady Kitty: I won't listen to a word. I've quite made up my mind. It's finished, finished, finished. [*With a change of tone*] I was so touched when I heard that you never lived in this house again after I left it.

C.-C.: The cuckoos have always been very plentiful. Their note has a personal application which, I must say, I have found extremely offensive.

The Circle

Lady Kitty: When I saw that you didn't marry again I couldn't help thinking that you still loved me.

C.-C.: I am one of the few men I know who is able to profit by experience.

Lady Kitty: In the eyes of the Church I am still your wife. The Church is so wise. It knows that in the end a woman always comes back to her first love. Clive, I am willing to return to you.

C.-C.: My dear Kitty, I couldn't take advantage of your momentary vexation with Hughie to let you take a step which I know you would bitterly regret.

Lady Kitty: You've waited for me a long time. For Arnold's sake.

C.-C.: Do you think we really need bother about Arnold? In the last thirty years he's had time to grow used to the situation.

Lady Kitty [*with a little smile*]: I think I've sown my wild oats, Clive.

C.-C.: I haven't. I was a good young man, Kitty.

Lady Kitty: I know.

C.-C.: And I'm very glad, because it has enabled me to be a wicked old one.

Lady Kitty: I beg your pardon.

[**Arnold** *comes in with a large book in his hand.*]

Arnold: I say, I've found the book I was hunting for. Oh, isn't Lord Porteous here?

Lady Kitty: One moment, Arnold. Your father and I are busy.

Arnold: I'm so sorry.

[*He goes out into the garden.*]

Lady Kitty: Explain yourself, Clive.

C.-C.: When you ran away from me, Kitty, I was sore and angry and miserable. But above all I felt a fool.

Lady Kitty: Men are so vain.

C.-C.: But I was a student of history, and presently I reflected that I shared my misfortune with very nearly all the greatest men.

Lady Kitty: I'm a great reader myself. It has always struck me as peculiar.

C.-C.: The explanation is very simple. Women dislike intelligence, and when they find it in their husbands they revenge themselves on them in the only way they can, by making them – well, what you made me.

Lady Kitty: It's ingenious. It may be true.

C.-C.: I felt I had done my duty by society and I determined to devote the rest of my life to my own entertainment. The House of Commons had always bored me excessively and the scandal of our divorce gave me an opportunity to resign my seat. I have been relieved to find that the country got on perfectly well without me.

Lady Kitty: But has love never entered your life?

C.-C.: Tell me frankly, Kitty, don't you think people make a lot of unnecessary fuss about love?

Lady Kitty: It's the most wonderful thing in the world.

C.-C.: You're incorrigible. Do you really think it was worth sacrificing so much for?

Lady Kitty: My dear Clive, I don't mind telling you that if I had my time over again I should be unfaithful to you, but I should not leave you.

C.-C.: For some years I was notoriously the prey of a secret sorrow. But I found so many charming creatures who were anxious to console that in the end it grew rather fatiguing. Out of regard to my health I ceased to frequent the drawing-rooms of Mayfair.

Lady Kitty: And since then?

C.-C.: Since then I have allowed myself the luxury of assisting financially a succession of dear little things, in a somewhat humble sphere, between the ages of twenty and twenty-five.

Lady Kitty: I cannot understand the infatuation of men for young girls. I think they're so dull.

C.-C.: It's a matter of taste. I love old wine, old friends, and old books, but I like young women. On their twenty-fifth birthday I give them a diamond ring and tell them they must no longer waste their youth and

The Circle

beauty on an old fogey like me. We have a most affecting scene, my technique on these occasions is perfect, and then I start all over again.

Lady Kitty: You're a wicked old man, Clive.

C.-C.: That's what I told you. But, by George! I'm a happy one.

Lady Kitty: There's only one course open to me now.

C.-C.: What is that!

Lady Kitty [*with a flashing smile*]: To go and dress for dinner.

C.-C.: Capital. I will follow your example.

[*As* **Lady Kitty** *goes out* **Elizabeth** *comes in.*]

Elizabeth: Where is Arnold?

C.-C.: He's on the terrace. I'll call him.

Elizabeth: Don't bother.

C.-C.: I was just strolling along to my cottage to put on a dinner jacket. [*As he goes out*] Arnold.

[*Exit* **Champion-Cheney.**]

Arnold: Hulloa! [*He comes in*] Oh, Elizabeth, I've found an illustration here of a chair which is almost identical with mine. It's dated 1750. Look!

Elizabeth: That's very interesting.

Arnold: I want to show it to Porteous. [*Moving a chair which has been misplaced*] You know, it does exasperate me the way people will not leave things alone. I no sooner put a thing in its place than somebody moves it.

Elizabeth: It must be maddening for you.

Arnold: It is. You are the worst offender. I can't think why you don't take the pride that I do in the house. After all, it's one of the show-places in the county.

Elizabeth: I'm afraid you find me very unsatisfactory.

Arnold [*good-humouredly*]: I don't know about that. But my two subjects are politics and decoration. I should be a perfect fool if I didn't see that you don't care two straws about either.

Elizabeth: We haven't very much in common, Arnold, have we?

Arnold: I don't think you can blame me for that.

Elizabeth: I don't. I blame you for nothing. I have no fault to find with you.

Arnold [*surprised at her significant tone*]: Good gracious me, what's the meaning of all this?

Elizabeth: Well, I don't think there's any object in beating about the bush. I want you to let me go.

Arnold: Go where?

Elizabeth: Away. For always.

Arnold: My dear child, what are you talking about?

Elizabeth: I want to be free.

Arnold [*amused rather than disconcerted*]: Don't be ridiculous, darling. I daresay you're run down and want a change. I'll take you over to Paris for a fortnight if you like.

Elizabeth: I shouldn't have spoken to you if I hadn't quite made up my mind. We've been married for three years and I don't think it's been a great success. I'm frankly bored by the life you want me to lead.

Arnold: Well, if you'll allow me to say so, the fault is yours. We lead a very distinguished, useful life. We know a lot of extremely nice people.

Elizabeth: I'm quite willing to allow that the fault is mine. But how does that make it any better? I'm only twenty-five. If I've made a mistake I have time to correct it.

Arnold: I can't bring myself to take you very seriously.

Elizabeth: You see, I don't love you.

Arnold: Well, I'm awfully sorry. But you weren't obliged to marry me. You've made your bed and I'm afraid you must lie on it.

Elizabeth: That's one of the falsest proverbs in the English language. Why should you lie on the bed you've made if you don't want to? There's always the floor.

Arnold: For goodness' sake don't be funny, Elizabeth.

Elizabeth: I've quite made up my mind to leave you, Arnold.

The Circle

Arnold: Come, come, Elizabeth, you must be sensible. You haven't any reason to leave me.

Elizabeth: Why should you wish to keep a woman tied to you who wants to be free?

Arnold: I happen to be in love with you.

Elizabeth: You might have said that before.

Arnold: I thought you'd take it for granted. You can't expect a man to go on making love to his wife after three years. I'm very busy. I'm awfully keen on politics and I've worked like a dog to make this house a thing of beauty. After all, a man marries to have a home, but also because he doesn't want to be bothered with sex and all that sort of thing. I fell in love with you the first time I saw you and I've been in love ever since.

Elizabeth: I'm sorry, but if you're not in love with a man his love doesn't mean very much to you.

Arnold: It's so ungrateful. I've done everything in the world for you.

Elizabeth: You've been very kind to me. But you've asked me to lead a life I don't like and that I'm not suited for. I'm awfully sorry to cause you pain, but now you must let me go.

Arnold: Nonsense! I'm a good deal older than you are and I think I have a little more sense. In your interest as well as in mine I'm not going to do anything of the sort.

Elizabeth [*with a smile*]: How can you prevent me? You can't keep me under lock and key.

Arnold: Please don't talk to me as if I were a foolish child. You're my wife and you're going to remain my wife.

Elizabeth: What sort of a life do you think we should lead? Do you think there'd be any more happiness for you than for me?

Arnold: But what is it precisely that you suggest?

Elizabeth: Well, I want you to let me divorce you.

Arnold [*astounded*]: Me? Thank you very much. Are you under the impression I'm going to sacrifice my career for a whim of yours?

Elizabeth: How will it do that?

Arnold: My seat's wobbly enough as it is. Do you think I'd be able to hold it if I were in a divorce case? Even if it were a put up job, as most divorces are nowadays, it would damn me.

Elizabeth: It's rather hard on a woman to be divorced.

Arnold [*with sudden suspicion*]: What do you mean by that? Are you in love with someone?

Elizabeth: Yes.

Arnold: Who?

Elizabeth: Teddie Luton.

[*He is astonished for a moment, then bursts into a laugh.*]

Arnold: My poor child, how can you be so ridiculous? Why, he hasn't a bob. He's a perfectly commonplace young man. It's so absurd I can't even be angry with you.

Elizabeth: I've fallen desperately in love with him, Arnold.

Arnold: Well, you'd better fall desperately out.

Elizabeth: He wants to marry me.

Arnold: I daresay he does. He can go to hell.

Elizabeth: It's no good talking like that.

Arnold: Is he your lover?

Elizabeth: No, certainly not.

Arnold: It shows that he's a mean skunk to take advantage of my hospitality to make love to you.

Elizabeth: He's never even kissed me.

Arnold: I'd try telling that to the horse marines if I were you.

Elizabeth: It's because I wanted to do nothing shabby that I told you straight out how things were.

Arnold: How long have you been thinking of this?

Elizabeth: I've been in love with Teddie ever since I knew him.

Arnold: And you never thought of me at all, I suppose.

Elizabeth: Oh, yes, I did. I was miserable. But I can't help myself. I wish I loved you, but I don't.

243

Arnold: I recommend you to think very carefully before you do anything foolish.

Elizabeth: I have thought very carefully.

Arnold: By God, I don't know why I don't give you a sound hiding. I'm not sure if that wouldn't be the best thing to bring you to your senses.

Elizabeth: Oh, Arnold, don't take it like that.

Arnold: How do you expect me to take it? You come to me quite calmly and say: 'I've had enough of you. We've been married three years and I think I'd like to marry somebody else now. Shall I break up your home? What a bore for you! Do you mind my divorcing you? It'll smash up your career, will it? What a pity!' Oh, no, my girl, I may be a fool, but I'm not a damned fool.

Elizabeth: Teddie is leaving here by the first train tomorrow. I warn you that I mean to join him as soon as he can make the necessary arrangements.

Arnold: Where is he?

Elizabeth: I don't know. I suppose he's in his room.

[**Arnold** *goes to the door and calls.*]

Arnold: George!

[*For a moment he walks up and down the room impatiently.* **Elizabeth** *watches him. The* **Footman** *comes in.*]

Footman: Yes, sir.

Arnold: Tell Mr Luton to come here at once.

Elizabeth: Ask Mr Luton if he wouldn't mind coming here for a moment.

Footman: Very good, madam.

[*Exit* **Footman**.]

Elizabeth: What are you going to say to him?

Arnold: That's my business.

Elizabeth: I wouldn't make a scene if I were you.

Arnold: I'm not going to make a scene.

[*They wait in silence.*]

Why did you insist on my mother coming here?

Elizabeth: It seemed to me rather absurd to take up the attitude that I should be contaminated by her when . . .

Arnold [*interrupting*]: When you were proposing to do exactly the same thing. Well, now you've seen her what do you think of her? Do you think it's been a success? Is that the sort of woman a man would like his mother to be?

Elizabeth: I've been ashamed. I've been so sorry. It all seemed dreadful and horrible. This morning I happened to notice a rose in the garden. It was all overblown and bedraggled. It looked like a painted old woman. And I remembered that I'd looked at it a day or two ago. It was lovely then, fresh and blooming and fragrant. It may be hideous now, but that doesn't take away from the beauty it had once. That was real.

Arnold: Poetry, by God! As if this were the moment for poetry!

[**Teddie** *comes in. He has changed into a dinner jacket.*]

Teddie [*to* **Elizabeth**]: Did you want me?

Arnold: I sent for you.

[**Teddie** *looks from* **Arnold** *to* **Elizabeth**. *He sees that something has happened.*]

When would it be convenient for you to leave this house?

Teddie: I was proposing to go tomorrow morning. But I can very well go at once if you like.

Arnold: I do like.

Teddie: Very well. Is there anything else you wish to say to me?

Arnold: Do you think it was a very honourable thing to come down here and make love to my wife?

Teddie: No, I don't. I haven't been very happy about it. That's why I wanted to go away.

Arnold: Upon my word you're cool.

Teddie: I'm afraid it's no good saying I'm sorry and that sort of thing. You know what the situation is.

Arnold: Is it true that you want to marry Elizabeth?

Teddie: Yes. I should like to marry her as soon as ever I can.

Arnold: Have you thought of me at all? Has it struck you that you're destroying my home and breaking up my happiness?

Teddie: I don't see how there could be much happiness for you if Elizabeth doesn't care for you.

Arnold: Let me tell you that I refuse to have my home broken up by a twopenny-halfpenny adventurer who takes advantage of a foolish woman. I refuse to allow myself to be divorced. I can't prevent my wife from going off with you if she's determined to make a damned fool of herself but this I tell you: nothing will induce me to divorce her.

Elizabeth: Arnold, that would be monstrous.

Teddie: We could force you.

Arnold: How?

Teddie: If we went away together openly you'd have to bring an action.

Arnold: Twenty-four hours after you leave this house I shall go down to Brighton with a chorus-girl. And neither you nor I will be able to get a divorce. We've had enough divorces in our family. And now get out, get out, get out!

[**Teddie** *looks uncertainly at* **Elizabeth**.]

Elizabeth [*with a little smile*]: Don't bother about me. I shall be all right.

Arnold: Get out! Get out!

Act Three

The scene is still the same.

It is the night of the same day as that on which takes place the action of the second act.

[**Champion-Cheney** and **Arnold**, *both in dinner jackets, are discovered.* **Champion-Cheney** *is seated.* **Arnold** *walks restlessly up and down the room.*]

C.-C.: I think, if you'll follow my advice to the letter, you'll probably work the trick.

Arnold: I don't like it, you know. It's against all my principles.

C.-C.: My dear Arnold, we all hope that you have before you a distinguished political career. You can't learn too soon that the most useful thing about a principle is that it can always be sacrificed to expediency.

Arnold: But supposing it doesn't come off? Women are incalculable.

C.-C.: Nonsense! Men are romantic. A woman will always sacrifice herself if you give her the opportunity. It is her favourite form of self-indulgence.

Arnold: I never know whether you're a humorist or a cynic, Father.

C.-C.: I'm neither, my dear boy; I'm merely a very truthful man. But people are so unused to the truth that they're apt to mistake it for a joke or a sneer.

Arnold [*irritably*]: It seems so unfair that this should happen to me.

C.-C.: Keep your head, my boy, and do what I tell you.
   [**Lady Kitty** *and* **Elizabeth** *come in.* **Lady Kitty** *is in a gorgeous evening gown.*]

Elizabeth: Where is Lord Porteous?

C.-C.: He's on the terrace. He's smoking a cigar. [*Going to window*] Hughie!
   [**Porteous** *comes in.*]

Porteous [*with a grunt*]: Yes? Where's Mrs Shenstone?

Elizabeth: Oh, she had a headache. She's gone to bed.
   [*When* **Porteous** *comes in* **Lady Kitty** *with a very haughty air purses her lips and takes up an illustrated paper.* **Porteous** *gives her an irritated look, takes another illustrated paper, and sits himself down at the other end of the room. They are not on speaking terms.*]

C.-C.: Arnold and I have just been down to my cottage.

Elizabeth: I wondered where you'd gone.

C.-C.: I came across an old photograph album this

afternoon. I meant to bring it along before dinner, but I forgot, so we went and fetched it.

Elizabeth: Oh, do let me see it. I love old photographs.

[*He gives her the album, and she, sitting down, puts it on her knees and begins to turn over the pages. He stands over her.* **Lady Kitty** *and* **Porteous** *take surreptitious glances at one another.*]

C.-C.: I thought it might amuse you to see what pretty women looked like five-and-thirty years ago. That was the day of beautiful women.

Elizabeth: Do you think they were more beautiful then than they are now?

C.-C.: Oh, much. Now you see lots of pretty little things, but very few beautiful women.

Elizabeth: Aren't their clothes funny?

C.-C. [*pointing to a photograph*]: That's Mrs Langtry.

Elizabeth: She has a lovely nose.

C.-C.: She was the most wonderful thing you ever saw. Dowagers used to jump on chairs in order to get a good look at her when she came into a drawing-room. I was riding with her once, and we had to have the gates of the livery stable closed when she was getting on her horse because the crowd was so great.

Elizabeth: And who's that?

C.-C.: Lady Lonsdale. That's Lady Dudley.

Elizabeth: This is an actress, isn't it?

C.-C.: It is, indeed. Ellen Terry. By George, how I loved that woman!

Elizabeth [*with a smile*]: Dear Ellen Terry!

C.-C.: That's Bwabs. I never saw a smarter man in my life. And Oliver Montagu. Henry Manners with his eyeglass.

Elizabeth: Nice-looking, isn't he? And this?

C.-C.: That's Mary Anderson. I wish you could have seen her in *A Winter's Tale*. Her beauty just took your breath away. And look! There's Lady Randolph. Bernal Osborne – the wittiest man I ever knew.

Elizabeth: I think it's too sweet. I love their absurd bustles and those tight sleeves.

C.-C.: What figures they had! In those days a woman wasn't supposed to be as thin as a rail and as flat as a pancake.

Elizabeth: Oh, but aren't they laced in? How could they bear it?

C.-C.: They didn't play golf then, and nonsense like that, you know. They hunted, in a tall hat and a long black habit, and they were very gracious and charitable to the poor in the village.

Elizabeth: Did the poor like it?

C.-C.: They had a very thin time if they didn't. When they were in London they drove in the Park every afternoon, and they went to ten-course dinners, where they never met anybody they didn't know. And they had their box at the opera when Patti was singing or Madame Albani.

Elizabeth: Oh, what a lovely little thing! Who on earth is that?

C.-C.: That?

Elizabeth: She looks so fragile, like a piece of exquisite china, with all those furs on and her face up against her muff and the snow falling.

C.-C.: Yes, there was quite a rage at that time for being taken in an artificial snowstorm.

Elizabeth: What a sweet smile, so roguish and frank, and debonair! Oh, I wish I looked like that. Do tell me who it is.

C.-C.: Don't you know?

Elizabeth: No.

C.-C.: Why – it's Kitty.

Elizabeth: Lady Kitty! [*To* **Lady Kitty**] Oh, my dear, do look. It's too ravishing. [*She takes the album over to her impulsively.*] Why didn't you tell me you looked like that? Everybody must have been in love with you.

[**Lady Kitty** *takes the album and looks at it. Then*

she lets it slip from her hands and covers her face with her hands. She is crying.]

[*In consternation*] My dear, what's the matter? Oh, what have I done? I'm so sorry.

Lady Kitty: Don't, don't talk to me. Leave me alone. It's stupid of me.

[**Elizabeth** *looks at her for a moment perplexed then, turning round, slips her arm in* **Champion-Cheney's** *and leads him out on to the terrace.*]

Elizabeth [*as they are going, in a whisper*]: Did you do that on purpose?

[**Porteous** *gets up and goes to* **Lady Kitty**. *He puts his hand on her shoulder. They remain thus for a little while.*]

Porteous: I'm afraid I was very rude to you before dinner, Kitty.

Lady Kitty [*taking his hand which is on her shoulder*]: It doesn't matter. I'm sure I was very exasperating.

Porteous: I didn't mean what I said, you know.

Lady Kitty: Neither did I.

Porteous: Of course I know that I'd never have been Prime Minister.

Lady Kitty: How can you talk such nonsense, Hughie? No one would have had a chance if you'd remained in politics.

Porteous: I haven't the character.

Lady Kitty: You have more character than anyone I've ever met.

Porteous: Besides, I don't know that I much wanted to be Prime Minister.

Lady Kitty: Oh, but I should have been so proud of you. Of course you'd have been Prime Minister.

Porteous: I'd have given you India, you know. I think it would have been a very popular appointment.

Lady Kitty: I don't care twopence about India. I'd have been quite content with Western Australia.

Porteous: My dear, you don't think I'd have let you bury yourself in Western Australia?

Lady Kitty: Or Barbados.

Porteous: Never. It sounds like a cure for flat feet. I'd have kept you in London.

[*He picks up the album and is about to look at the photograph of Lady Kitty. She puts her hand over it.*]

Lady Kitty: No, don't look.

[*He takes her hand away.*]

Porteous: Don't be so silly.

Lady Kitty: Isn't it hateful to grow old?

Porteous: You know, you haven't changed much.

Lady Kitty [*enchanted*]: Oh, Hughie, how can you talk such nonsense?

Porteous: Of course you're a little more mature, but that's all. A woman's all the better for being rather mature.

Lady Kitty: Do you really think that?

Porteous: Upon my soul I do.

Lady Kitty: You're not saying it just to please me?

Porteous: No, no.

Lady Kitty: Let me look at the photograph again.

[*She takes the album and looks at the photograph complacently.*]

The fact is, if your bones are good, age doesn't really matter. You'll always be beautiful.

Porteous [*with a little smile, almost as if he were talking to a child*]: It was silly of you to cry.

Lady Kitty: It hasn't made my eyelashes run, has it?

Porteous: Not a bit.

Lady Kitty: It's very good stuff I use now. They don't stick together either.

Porteous: Look here, Kitty, how much longer do you want to stay here?

Lady Kitty: Oh, I'm quite ready to go whenever you like.

Porteous: Clive gets on my nerves. I don't like the way he keeps hanging about you.

Lady Kitty [*surprised, rather amused, and delighted*]: Hughie, you don't mean to say you're jealous of poor Clive?

Porteous: Of course I'm not jealous of him, but he does

look at you in a way that I can't help thinking rather objectionable.

Lady Kitty: Hughie, you may throw me downstairs like Amy Robsart; you may drag me about the floor by the hair of my head; I don't care, you're jealous. I shall never grow old.

Porteous: Damn it all, the man was your husband.

Lady Kitty: My dear Hughie, he never had your style. Why, the moment you come into a room everyone looks and says, Who the devil is that?

Porteous: What? You think that, do you? Well, I daresay there's something in what you say. These damned Radicals can say what they like, but, by God, Kitty, when a man's a gentleman – well, damn it all, you know what I mean.

Lady Kitty: I think Clive has degenerated dreadfully since we left him.

Porteous: What do you say to making a bee-line for Italy and going to San Michele?

Lady Kitty: Oh, Hughie! It's years since we were there.

Porteous: Wouldn't you like to see it again – just once more?

Lady Kitty: Do you remember the first time we went? It was the most heavenly place I'd ever seen. We'd only left England a month, and I said I'd like to spend all my life there.

Porteous: Of course, I remember. And in a fortnight it was yours, lock, stock, and barrel.

Lady Kitty: We were very happy there, Hughie.

Porteous: Let's go back once more.

Lady Kitty: I daren't. It must be all peopled with the ghosts of our past. One should never go again to a place where one has been happy. It would break my heart.

Porteous: Do you remember how we used to sit on the terrace of the old castle and look at the Adriatic? We might have been the only people in the world, you and I, Kitty.

Lady Kitty [*tragically*]: And we thought our love would last forever.

[*Enter* **Champion-Cheney**.]

Porteous: Is there any chance of bridge this evening?

C.-C.: I don't think we can make up a four.

Porteous: What a nuisance that boy went away like that! He wasn't a bad player.

C.-C.: Teddie Luton?

Lady Kitty: I think it was very funny his going without saying good-bye to anyone.

C.C.: The young men of the present day are very casual.

Porteous: I thought there was no train in the evening.

C.-C.: There isn't. The last train leaves at 5-45.

Porteous: How did he go then?

C.-C.: He went.

Porteous: Damned selfish I call it.

Lady Kitty [*intrigued*]: Why did he go, Clive?

[**Champion-Cheney** *looks at her for a moment reflectively*.]

C.-C.: I have something very grave to say to you. Elizabeth wants to leave Arnold.

Lady Kitty: Clive! What on earth for?

C.C.: She's in love with Teddie Luton. That's why he went. The men of my family are really very unfortunate.

Porteous: Does she want to run away with him?

Lady Kitty [*with consternation*]: My dear, what's to be done?

C.-C.: I think you can do a great deal.

Lady Kitty: I? What?

C.-C.: Tell her, tell her what it means.

[*He looks at her fixedly. She stares at him*.]

Lady Kitty: Oh, no, no!

C.C.: She's a child. Not for Arnold's sake. For her sake. You must.

Lady Kitty: You don't know what you're asking.

C.-C.: Yes, I do.

Lady Kitty: Hughie, what shall I do?

Porteous: Do what you like. I shall never blame you for anything.

[*The* **Footman** *comes in with a letter on a salver. He hesitates on seeing that* **Elizabeth** *is not in the room.*]

C.-C.: What is it?

Footman: I was looking for Mrs Champion-Cheney, sir.

C.-C.: She's not here. Is that a letter?

Footman: Yes, sir. It's just been sent up from the Champion Arms.

C.-C.: Leave it. I'll give it to Mrs Cheney.

Footman: Very good, sir.

[*He brings the tray to* **Clive**, *who takes the letter. The* **Footman** *goes out.*]

Porteous: Is the Champion Arms the local pub?

C.-C. [*looking at the letter*]: It's by way of being a hotel, but I never heard of anyone staying there.

Lady Kitty: If there was no train I suppose he had to go there.

C.-C.: Great minds. I wonder what he has to write about.

[*He goes to the door leading on to the garden.*] Elizabeth.

Elizabeth [*outside*]: Yes.

C.-C.: Here's a note for you.

[*There is silence. They wait for* **Elizabeth** *to come. She enters.*]

Elizabeth: It's lovely in the garden tonight.

C.-C.: They've just sent this up from the Champion Arms.

Elizabeth: Thank you.

[*Without embarrassment she opens the letter. They watch her while she reads it. It covers three pages. She puts it away in her bag.*]

Lady Kitty: Hughie, I wish you'd fetch me a cloak. I'd like to take a little stroll in the garden, but after thirty years in Italy I find these English summers rather chilly.

[*Without a word* **Porteous** *goes out.* **Elizabeth** *is lost in thought.*]

I want to talk to Elizabeth, Clive.

C.-C.: I'll leave you.

[*He goes out.*]

Lady Kitty: What does he say?

Elizabeth: Who?

Lady Kitty: Mr Luton.

Elizabeth [*giving a little start, then looking at* **Lady Kitty**]: They've told you?

Lady Kitty: Yes. And now they have I think I knew it all along.

Elizabeth: I don't expect you to have much sympathy for me. Arnold is your son.

Lady Kitty: So pitifully little.

Elizabeth: I'm not suited for this sort of existence. Arnold wants me to take what he calls my place in Society. Oh, I get so bored with those parties in London. All those middle-aged painted women, in beautiful clothes, lolloping round ball-rooms with rather old young men. And the endless luncheons where they gossip about so-and-so's love affairs.

Lady Kitty: Are you very much in love with Mr Luton?

Elizabeth: I love him with all my heart.

Lady Kitty: And he?

Elizabeth: He's never cared for anyone but me. He never will.

Lady Kitty: Will Arnold let you divorce him?

Elizabeth: No, he won't hear of it. He refuses even to divorce me.

Lady Kitty: Why?

Elizabeth: He thinks a scandal will revive all the old gossip.

Lady Kitty: Oh, my poor child.

Elizabeth: It can't be helped. I'm quite willing to accept the consequences.

Lady Kitty: You don't know what it is to have a man tied to you only by his honour. When married people don't get on they can separate, but if they're not married it's impossible. It's a tie that only death can sever.

The Circle

Elizabeth: If Teddie stopped caring for me I shouldn't want him to stay with me for five minutes.

Lady Kitty: One says that when one's sure of a man's love, but when one isn't any more – oh, it's so different. In those circumstances one's got to keep a man's love. It's the only thing one has.

Elizabeth: I'm a human being. I can stand on my own feet.

Lady Kitty: Have you any money of your own?

Elizabeth: None.

Lady Kitty: Then how can you stand on your own feet? You think I'm a silly, frivolous woman, but I've learnt something in a bitter school. They can make what laws they like, they can give us the suffrage, but when you come down to bedrock it's the man who pays the piper who calls the tune. Woman will only be the equal of man when she earns her living in the same way that he does.

Elizabeth [*smiling*]: It sounds rather funny to hear you talk like that.

Lady Kitty: A cook who marries a butler can snap her fingers in his face because she can earn just as much as he can. But a woman in your position and a woman in mine will always be dependent on the men who keep them.

Elizabeth: I don't want luxury. You don't know how sick I am of all this beautiful furniture. These over-decorated houses are like a prison in which I can't breathe. When I drive about in a Callot frock and a Rolls-Royce I envy the shop-girl in a coat and skirt whom I see jumping on the tailboard of a bus.

Lady Kitty: You mean that if need be you could earn your own living?

Elizabeth: Yes.

Lady Kitty: What could you be? A nurse or a typist? It's nonsense. Luxury saps a woman's nerve. And when she's known it once it becomes a necessity.

Elizabeth: That depends on the woman.

Lady Kitty: When we're young we think we're different from everyone else, but when we grow a little older we discover we're all very much of a muchness.

Elizabeth: You're very kind to take so much trouble about me.

Lady Kitty: It breaks my heart to think that you're going to make the same pitiful mistake that I made.

Elizabeth: Oh, don't say it was that, don't, don't.

Lady Kitty: Look at me, Elizabeth, and look at Hughie. Do you think it's been a success? If I had my time over again do you think I'd do it again? Do you think he would?

Elizabeth: You see, you don't know how much I love Teddie.

Lady Kitty: And do you think I didn't love Hughie? Do you think he didn't love me?

Elizabeth: I'm sure he did.

Lady Kitty: Oh, of course in the beginning it was heavenly. We felt so brave and adventurous and we were so much in love. The first two years were wonderful. People cut me, you know, but I didn't mind. I thought love was everything. It is a little uncomfortable when you come upon an old friend and go towards her eagerly, so glad to see her, and are met with an icy stare.

Elizabeth: Do you think friends like that are worth having?

Lady Kitty: Perhaps they're not very sure of themselves. Perhaps they're honestly shocked. It's a test one had better not put one's friends to if one can help it. It's rather bitter to find how few one has.

Elizabeth: But one has some.

Lady Kitty: Yes, they ask you to come and see them when they're quite certain no one will be there who might object to meeting you. Or else they say to you, My dear, you know I'm devoted to you, and I wouldn't mind at all, but my girl's growing up – I'm sure you understand, you won't think it unkind of me if I don't ask you to the house?

The Circle

Elizabeth [*smiling*]: That doesn't seem to me very serious.

Lady Kitty: At first I thought it rather a relief, because it threw Hughie and me together more. But, you know, men are funny. Even when they are in love they're not in love all day long. They want change and recreation.

Elizabeth: I'm not inclined to blame them for that, poor dears.

Lady Kitty: Then we settled in Florence. And because we couldn't get the society we'd been used to, we became used to the society we could get. Loose women and vicious men. Snobs who liked to patronize people with a handle to their names. Vague Italian princes who were glad to borrow a few francs from Hughie and seedy countesses who liked to drive with me in the Cascine. And then Hughie began to hanker after his old life. He wanted to go big-game shooting, but I dared not let him go. I was afraid he'd never come back.

Elizabeth: But you knew he loved you.

Lady Kitty: Oh, my dear, what a blessed institution marriage is – for women, and what fools they are to meddle with it! The Church is so wise to take its stand on the indi – indi –

Elizabeth: Solu –

Lady Kitty: Bility of marriage. Believe me, it's no joke when you have to rely only on yourself to keep a man. I could never afford to grow old. My dear, I'll tell you a secret that I've never told a living soul.

Elizabeth: What is that?

Lady Kitty: My hair is not naturally this colour.

Elizabeth: Really?

Lady Kitty: I touch it up. You would never have guessed, would you?

Elizabeth: Never.

Lady Kitty: Nobody does. My dear, it's white, prematurely of course, but white. I always think it's a symbol of my life. Are you interested in symbolism? I think it's too wonderful.

Elizabeth: I don't think I know very much about it.

Lady Kitty: However tired I've been I've had to be brilliant and gay. I've never let Hughie see the aching heart behind my smiling eyes.

Elizabeth [*amused and touched*]: You poor dear.

Lady Kitty: And when I saw he was attracted by someone else the fear and the jealousy that seized me! You see, I didn't dare make a scene as I should have done if I'd been married. I had to pretend not to notice.

Elizabeth [*taken aback*]: But do you mean to say he fell in love with anyone else?

Lady Kitty: Of course he did eventually.

Elizabeth [*hardly knowing what to say*]: You must have been very unhappy.

Lady Kitty: Oh, I was, dreadfully. Night after night I sobbed my heart out when Hughie told me he was going to play cards at the club and I knew he was with that odious woman. Of course, it wasn't as if there weren't plenty of men who were only too anxious to console me. Men have always been attracted by me, you know.

Elizabeth: Oh, of course, I can quite understand it.

Lady Kitty: But I had my self-respect to think of. I felt that whatever Hughie did I would do nothing that I should regret.

Elizabeth: You must be very glad now.

Lady Kitty: Oh, yes. Notwithstanding all my temptations I've been absolutely faithful to Hughie in spirit.

Elizabeth: I don't think I quite understand what you mean.

Lady Kitty: Well, there was a poor Italian boy, young Count Castel Giovanni, who was so desperately in love with me that his mother begged me not to be too cruel. She was afraid he'd go into a consumption. What could I do? And then, oh, years later, there was Antonio Melita. He said he'd shoot himself unless I – well, you understand I couldn't let the poor boy shoot himself.

Elizabeth: D'you think he really would have shot himself?

The Circle

Lady Kitty: Oh, one never knows, you know. Those Italians are so passionate. He was really rather a lamb. He had such beautiful eyes.

[**Elizabeth** *looks at her for a long time and a certain horror seizes her of this dissolute, painted old woman.*]

Elizabeth [*hoarsely*]: Oh, but I think that's – dreadful.

Lady Kitty: Are you shocked? One sacrifices one's life for love and then one finds that love doesn't last. The tragedy of love isn't death or separation. One gets over them. The tragedy of love is indifference.

[**Arnold** *comes in.*]

Arnold: Can I have a little talk with you, Elizabeth?

Elizabeth: Of course.

Arnold: Shall we go for a stroll in the garden?

Elizabeth: If you like.

Lady Kitty: No, stay here. I'm going out anyway.

[*Exit* **Lady Kitty**.]

Arnold: I want you to listen to me for a few minutes, Elizabeth. I was so taken aback by what you told me just now that I lost my head. I was rather absurd and I beg your pardon. I said things I regret.

Elizabeth: Oh, don't blame yourself. I'm sorry that I should have given you occasion to say them.

Arnold: I want to ask you if you've quite made up your mind to go.

Elizabeth: Quite.

Arnold: Just now I seem to have said all that I didn't want to say and nothing that I did. I'm stupid and tongue-tied. I never told you how deeply I loved you.

Elizabeth: Oh, Arnold.

Arnold: Please let me speak now. It's so very difficult. If I seemed absorbed in politics and the house, and so on, to the exclusion of my interest in you, I'm dreadfully sorry. I suppose it was absurd of me to think you would take my great love for granted.

Elizabeth: But, Arnold, I'm not reproaching you.

Arnold: I'm reproaching myself. I've been tactless and

neglectful. But I do ask you to believe that it hasn't
been because I didn't love you. Can you forgive me?

Elizabeth: I don't think that there's anything to forgive.

Arnold: It wasn't till today when you talked of leaving
me that I realized how desperately in love with you I
was.

Elizabeth: After three years?

Arnold: I'm so proud of you. I admire you so much. When
I see you at a party, so fresh and lovely, and everybody
wondering at you, I have a sort of little thrill because
you're mine, and afterwards I shall take you home.

Elizabeth: Oh, Arnold, you're exaggerating.

Arnold: I can't imagine this house without you. Life
seems all of a sudden all empty and meaningless. Oh,
Elizabeth, don't you love me at all?

Elizabeth: It's much better to be honest. No.

Arnold: Doesn't my love mean anything to you?

Elizabeth: I'm very grateful to you. I'm sorry to cause you
pain. What would be the good of my staying with you
when I should be wretched all the time?

Arnold: Do you love that man as much as all that? Does
my unhappiness mean nothing to you?

Elizabeth: Of course it does. It breaks my heart. You see,
I never knew I meant so much to you. I'm so touched.
And I'm so sorry, Arnold, really sorry. But I can't help
myself.

Arnold: Poor child, it's cruel of me to torture you.

Elizabeth: Oh, Arnold, believe me, I have tried to make
the best of it. I've tried to love you, but I can't. After
all, one either loves or one doesn't. Trying is no help.
And now I'm at the end of my tether. I can't help the
consequences – I must do what my whole self yearns
for.

Arnold: My poor child, I'm so afraid you'll be unhappy.
I'm so afraid you'll regret.

Elizabeth: You must leave me to my fate. I hope you'll
forget me and all the unhappiness I've caused you.

261

[*There is a pause. Arnold walks up and down the room reflectively. He stops and faces her.*]

Arnold: If you love this man and want to go to him I'll do nothing to prevent you. My only wish is to do what is best for you.

Elizabeth: Arnold, that's awfully kind of you. If I'm treating you badly at least I want you to know that I'm grateful for all your kindness to me.

Arnold: But there's one favour I should like you to do me. Will you?

Elizabeth: Oh, Arnold, of course I'll do anything I can.

Arnold: Teddie hasn't very much money. You've been used to a certain amount of luxury, and I can't bear to think that you should do without anything you've had. It would kill me to think that you were suffering any hardship or privation.

Elizabeth: Oh, but Teddie can earn enough for our needs. After all, we don't want much money.

Arnold: I'm afraid my mother's life hasn't been very easy, but it's obvious that the only thing that's made it possible is that Porteous was rich. I want you to let me make you an allowance of two thousand a year.

Elizabeth: Oh, no, I couldn't think of it. It's absurd.

Arnold: I beg you to accept it. You don't know what a difference it will make.

Elizabeth: It's awfully kind of you, Arnold. It humiliates me to speak about it. Nothing would induce me to take a penny from you.

Arnold: Well, you can't prevent me from opening an account at my bank in your name. The money shall be paid in every quarter whether you touch it or not, and, if you happen to want it, it will be there waiting for you.

Elizabeth: You overwhelm me, Arnold. There's only one thing I want you to do for me. I should be very grateful if you would divorce me as soon as you possibly can.

Arnold: No, I won't do that. But I'll give you cause to divorce me.

Elizabeth: You!

Arnold: Yes. But of course you'll have to be very careful for a bit. I'll put it through as quickly as possible, but I'm afraid you can't hope to be free for over six months.

Elizabeth: But, Arnold, your seat and your political career!

Arnold: Oh, well, my father gave up his seat under similar circumstances. He's got along very comfortably without politics.

Elizabeth: But they're your whole life.

Arnold: After all one can't have it both ways. You can't serve God and Mammon. If you want to do the decent thing you have to be prepared to suffer for it.

Elizabeth: But I don't want you to suffer for it.

Arnold: At first I rather hesitated at the scandal. But I daresay that was only weakness on my part. In the circumstances I should have liked to keep out of the Divorce Court if I could.

Elizabeth: Arnold, you're making me absolutely miserable.

Arnold: What you said before dinner was quite right. It's nothing for a man, but it makes so much difference to a woman. Naturally I must think of you first.

Elizabeth: That's absurd. It's out of the question. Whatever there's to pay I must pay it.

Arnold: It's not very much I'm asking for, Elizabeth.

Elizabeth: I'm taking everything from you.

Arnold: It's the only condition I make. My mind is absolutely made up. I will never divorce you, but I will enable you to divorce me.

Elizabeth: Oh, Arnold, it's cruel to be so generous.

Arnold: It's not generous at all. It's the only way I have of showing you how deep and passionate and sincere my love is for you.

[*There is a silence. He holds out his hand.*]
Good night. I have a great deal of work to do before I go to bed.

Elizabeth: Good night.

Arnold: Do you mind if I kiss you?

The Circle

Elizabeth [*with agony*]: Oh, Arnold!

[*He gravely kisses her on the forehead and then goes out.* **Elizabeth** *stands lost in thought. She is shattered.* **Lady Kitty** *and* **Porteous** *come in.* **Lady Kitty** *wears a cloak.*]

Lady Kitty: You're alone, Elizabeth?

Elizabeth: That note you asked me about, Lady Kitty, from Teddie . . .

Lady Kitty: Yes?

Elizabeth: He wanted to have a talk with me before he went away. He's waiting for me in the summer house by the tennis court. Would Lord Porteous mind going down and asking him to come here?

Porteous: Certainly. Certainly.

Elizabeth: Forgive me for troubling you. But it's very important.

Porteous: No trouble at all.

[*He goes out.*]

Lady Kitty: Hughie and I will leave you alone.

Elizabeth: But I don't want to be left alone. I want you to stay.

Lady Kitty: What are you going to say to him?

Elizabeth [*desperately*]: Please don't ask me questions. I'm so frightfully unhappy.

Lady Kitty: My poor child.

Elizabeth: Oh, isn't life rotten? Why can't one be happy without making other people unhappy?

Lady Kitty: I wish I knew how to help you. I'm simply devoted to you. [*She hunts about in her mind for something to do or say.*] Would you like my lip-stick?

Elizabeth [*smiling through her tears*]: Thanks. I never use one.

Lady Kitty: Oh, but just try. It's such a comfort when you're in trouble.

[*Enter* **Porteous** *and* **Teddie**.]

Porteous: I brought him. He said he'd be damned if he'd come.

Lady Kitty: When a lady sent for him? Are these the manners of the young men of today?

Teddie: When you've been solemnly kicked out of a house once I think it seems rather pushing to come back again as though nothing had happened.

Elizabeth: Teddie, I want you to be serious.

Teddie: Darling, I had such a rotten dinner at that pub. If you ask me to be serious on the top of that I shall cry.

Elizabeth: Don't be idiotic, Teddie. [*Her voice faltering*] I'm so utterly wretched.

[*He looks at her for a moment gravely.*]

Teddie: What is it?

Elizabeth: I can't come away with you, Teddie.

Teddie: Why not?

Elizabeth [*looking away in embarrassment*]: I don't love you enough.

Teddie: Fiddle!

Elizabeth [*with a flash of anger*] : Don't say Fiddle to me.

Teddie: I shall say exactly what I like to you.

Elizabeth: I won't be bullied.

Teddie: Now look here, Elizabeth, you know perfectly well that I'm in love with you, and I know perfectly well that you're in love with me. So what are you talking nonsense for?

Elizabeth [*her voice breaking*]: I can't say it if you're cross with me.

Teddie [*smiling very tenderly*]: I'm not cross with you, silly.

Elizabeth: It's harder still when you're being rather an owl.

Teddie [*with a chuckle*]: Am I mistaken in thinking you're not very easy to please?

Elizabeth: Oh, it's monstrous. I was all wrought up and ready to do anything, and now you've thoroughly put me out. I feel like a great big fat balloon that someone has put a long pin into. [*With a sudden look at him*] Have you done it on purpose?

Teddie: Upon my soul I don't know what you're talking about.

Elizabeth: I wonder if you're really much cleverer than I think you are.

Teddie [*taking her hands and making her sit down*]: Now tell me exactly what you want to say. By the way, do you want Lady Kitty and Lord Porteous to be here?

Elizabeth: Yes.

Lady Kitty: Elizabeth asked us to stay.

Teddie: Oh, I don't mind, bless you. I only thought you might feel rather in the way.

Lady Kitty [*frigidly*]: A gentlewoman never feels in the way, Mr Luton.

Teddie: Won't you call me Teddie? Everybody does, you know. [**Lady Kitty** *tries to give him a withering look, but she finds it very difficult to prevent herself from smiling.* **Teddie** *strokes* **Elizabeth's** *hands. She draws them away.*]

Elizabeth: No, don't do that. Teddie, it wasn't true when I said I didn't love you. Of course I love you. But Arnold loves me, too. I didn't know how much.

Teddie: What has he been saying to you?

Elizabeth: He's been very good to me, and so kind. I didn't know he could be so kind. He offered to let me divorce him.

Teddie: That's very decent of him.

Elizabeth: But don't you see, it ties my hands. How can I accept such a sacrifice? I should never forgive myself if I profited by his generosity.

Teddie: If another man and I were devilish hungry and there was only one mutton chop between us, and he said, You eat it, I wouldn't waste a lot of time arguing. I'd wolf it before he changed his mind.

Elizabeth: Don't talk like that. It maddens me. I'm trying to do the right thing.

Teddie: You're not in love with Arnold, you're in love with me. It's idiotic to sacrifice your life for a slushy sentiment.

Elizabeth: After all, I did marry him.

Teddie: Well, you made a mistake. A marriage without love is no marriage at all.

Elizabeth: I made the mistake. Why should he suffer for it? If anyone has to suffer it's only right that I should.

Teddie: What sort of a life do you think it would be with him? When two people are married it's very difficult for one of them to be unhappy without making the other unhappy too.

Elizabeth: I can't take advantage of his generosity.

Teddie: I daresay he'll get a lot of satisfaction out of it.

Elizabeth: You're being beastly, Teddie. He was simply wonderful. I never knew he had it in him. He was really noble.

Teddie: You are talking rot, Elizabeth.

Elizabeth: I wonder if you'd be capable of acting like that.

Teddie: Acting like what?

Elizabeth: What would you do if I were married to you and came and told you I loved somebody else and wanted to leave you?

Teddie: You have very pretty blue eyes, Elizabeth. I'd black first one and then the other. And after that we'd see.

Elizabeth: You damned brute!

Teddie: I've often thought I wasn't quite a gentleman. Had it never struck you?

[*They look at one another for a while.*]

Elizabeth: You know, you are taking an unfair advantage of me. I feel as if I came to you quite unsuspectingly and when I wasn't looking you kicked me on the shins.

Teddie: Don't you think we'd get on rather well together?

Porteous: Elizabeth's a fool if she don't stick to her husband. It's bad enough for the man, but for the woman – it's damnable. I hold no brief for Arnold. He plays bridge like a fool. Saving your presence, Kitty, I think he's a prig.

Lady Kitty: Poor dear, his father was at his age. I daresay he'll grow out of it.

The Circle

Porteous: But you stick to him, Elizabeth, stick to him. Man is a gregarious animal. We're members of a herd. If we break the herd's laws we suffer for it. And we suffer damnably.

Lady Kitty: Oh, Elizabeth, my dear child, don't go. It's not worth it. It's not worth it. I tell you that, and I've sacrificed everything to love.

[A pause.]

Elizabeth: I'm afraid.

Teddie [*in a whisper*]: Elizabeth.

Elizabeth: I can't face it. It's asking too much of me. Let's say good-bye to one another, Teddie. It's the only thing to do. And have pity on me. I'm giving up all my hope of happiness.

[He goes up to her and looks into her eyes.]

Teddie: But I wasn't offering you happiness. I don't think my sort of love tends to happiness. I'm jealous. I'm not a very easy man to get on with. I'm often out of temper and irritable. I should be fed to the teeth with you sometimes, and so would you be with me. I daresay we'd fight like cat and dog, and some times we'd hate each other. Often you'd be wretched and bored stiff and lonely, and often you'd be frightfully homesick, and then you'd regret all you'd lost. Stupid women would be rude to you because we'd run away together. And some of them would cut you. I don't offer you peace and quietness. I offer you unrest and anxiety. I don't offer you happiness. I offer you love.

Elizabeth [*stretching out her arms*]: You hateful creature, I absolutely adore you.

[He throws his arms round her and kisses her passionately on the lips.]

Lady Kitty: Of course the moment he said he'd give her a black eye I knew it was finished.

Porteous [*good-humouredly*]: You are a fool, Kitty.

Lady Kitty: I know I am, but I can't help it.

Teddie: Let's make a bolt for it now.

Elizabeth: Shall we?

Teddie: This minute.

Porteous: You're damned fools, both of you, damned fools. If you like you can have my car.

Teddie: That's awfully kind of you. As a matter of fact, I got it out of the garage. It's just along the drive.

Porteous [*indignantly*]: How do you mean, you got it out of the garage?

Teddie: Well, I thought there'd be a lot of bother, and it seemed to me the best thing would be for Elizabeth and me not to stand upon the order of our going, you know. Do it now. An excellent motto for a businessman.

Porteous: Do you mean to say you were going to steal my car?

Teddie: Not exactly. I was only going to bolshevize it, so to speak.

Porteous: I'm speechless. I'm absolutely speechless.

Teddie: Hang it all, I couldn't carry Elizabeth all the way to London. She's so damned plump.

Elizabeth: You dirty dog!

Porteous [*spluttering*]: Well, well, well! . . . [*Helplessly*] I like him, Kitty, it's no good pretending I don't. I like him.

Teddie: The moon's shining, Elizabeth. We'll drive all through the night.

Porteous: They'd better go to San Michele. I'll wire to have it got ready for them.

Lady Kitty: That's where we went when Hughie and I. . . . [*Faltering*] Oh, you dear things, how I envy you.

Porteous [*mopping his eyes*]: Now don't cry, Kitty. Confound you, don't cry.

Teddie: Come, darling.

Elizabeth: But I can't go like this.

Teddie: Nonsense! Lady Kitty will lend you her cloak. Won't you?

Lady Kitty [*taking it off*]: You're capable of tearing it off my back if I don't.

Teddie [*putting the cloak on* **Elizabeth**]: And we'll buy you a tooth-brush in London in the morning.

Lady Kitty: She must write a note for Arnold. I'll put it on her pincushion.

Teddie: Pincushion be blowed. Come, darling. We'll drive through the dawn and through the sunrise.

Elizabeth [*kissing* **Lady Kitty** *and* **Porteous**]: Good-bye. Good-bye.

[**Teddie** *stretches out his hand and she takes it. Hand in hand they go out into the night.*]

Lady Kitty: Oh, Hughie, how it all comes back to me. Will they suffer all we suffered? And have we suffered all in vain?

Porteous: My dear, I don't know that in life it matters so much what you do as what you are. No one can learn by the experience of another because no circumstances are quite the same. If we made rather a hash of things perhaps it was because we were rather trivial people. You can do anything in this world if you're prepared to take the consequences, and consequences depend on character.

[*Enter* **Champion-Cheney**, *rubbing his hands. He is as pleased as Punch.*]

C.-C.: Well, I think I've settled the hash of that young man.

Lady Kitty: Oh?

C.-C.: You have to get up very early in the morning to get the better of your humble servant.

[*There is the sound of a car starting.*]

Lady Kitty: What is that?

C.-C.: It sounds like a car. I expect it's your chauffeur taking one of the maids for a joy-ride.

Porteous: Whose hash are you talking about?

C.-C.: Mr Edward Luton's, my dear Hughie. I told Arnold exactly what to do and he's done it. What makes a prison? Why, bars and bolts. Remove them and a prisoner won't want to escape. Clever, I flatter myself.

Porteous: You were always that, Clive, but at the moment you're obscure.

C.-C.: I told Arnold to go to Elizabeth and tell her she could have her freedom. I told him to sacrifice himself all along the line. I know what women are. The moment every obstacle was removed to her marriage with Teddie Luton, half the allurement was gone.

Lady Kitty: Arnold did that?

C.-C.: He followed my instructions to the letter. I've just seen him. She's shaken. I'm willing to bet five hundred pounds to a penny that she won't bolt. A downy old bird, eh? Downy's the word. Downy.

[*He begins to laugh. They laugh too. Presently they are all three in fits of laughter.*]

The Constant Wife

A COMEDY IN THREE ACTS

Characters

Mrs Culver
Bentley, *the butler*
Martha Culver
Barbara Fawcett
Constance Middleton
Marie-Louise
John Middleton, F.R.C.S.
Bernard Kersal
Mortimer Durham

*The action of the play takes place in John's house
in Harley Street.*

Act One

Scene: Constance's drawing-room. It is a room furnished with singularly good taste. Constance has a gift for decoration and has made this room of hers both beautiful and comfortable.

It is afternoon.

> [**Mrs Culver** *is seated alone. She is an elderly lady with a pleasant face and she is dressed in walking costume. The door is opened and* **Bentley** *the butler introduces* **Martha Culver.** *This is her daughter and a fine young woman.*]

Bentley: Miss Culver.

> [*He goes out.*]

Martha [*with astonishment*]: Mother.

Mrs Culver [*very calmly*]: Yes, darling.

Martha: You're the last person I expected to find here. You never told me you were coming to see Constance.

Mrs Culver [*good-humouredly*]: I didn't intend to till I saw in your beady eye that you meant to. I thought I'd just as soon be here first.

Martha: Bentley says she's out.

Mrs Culver: Yes . . . Are you going to wait?

Martha: Certainly.

Mrs Culver: Then I will, too.

Martha: That'll be very nice.

Mrs Culver: Your words are cordial, but your tone is slightly frigid, my dear.

Martha: I don't know what you mean by that, Mother.

Mrs Culver: My dear, we've known one another a great many years, haven't we? More than we always find it convenient to mention.

Martha: Not at all. I'm thirty-two. I'm not in the least ashamed of my age. Constance is thirty-six.

Mrs Culver: And yet we still think it worth while to be a trifle disingenuous with one another. Our sex takes a natural pleasure in dissimulation.

Martha: I don't think anyone can accuse me of not being frank.

Mrs Culver: Frankness of course is the pose of the moment. It is often a very effective screen for one's thoughts.

Martha: I think you're being faintly disagreeable to me, Mother.

Mrs Culver: I, on the other hand, think you're inclined to be decidedly foolish.

Martha: Because I want to tell Constance something she ought to know?

Mrs Culver: Ah, I *was* right then. And it's to tell her that you've broken an engagement, and left three wretched people to play cut-throat.

Martha: It is.

Mrs Culver: And may I ask why you think Constance ought to know?

Martha: Why? Why? Why? That's one of those questions that really don't need answering.

Mrs Culver: I've always noticed that the questions that really don't need answering are the most difficult to answer.

Martha: It isn't at all difficult to answer. She ought to know the truth because it's the truth.

Mrs Culver: Of course truth is an excellent thing, but before one tells it one should be quite sure that one does so for the advantage of the person who hears it rather than for one's own self-satisfaction.

Martha: Mother, Constance is a very unhappy person.

Mrs Culver: Nonsense. She eats well, sleeps well, dresses well, and she's losing weight. No woman can be unhappy in those circumstances.

Martha: Of course if you won't understand it's no use my trying to make you. You're a darling, but you're the most unnatural mother. Your attitude simply amazes me.

[*The door opens and* **Bentley** *ushers in* **Mrs Fawcett.**
Mrs Fawcett *is a trim, business-like woman of forty.*]

Bentley: Mrs Fawcett.

Mrs Culver: Oh, Barbara, how very nice to see you.

Barbara [*going up to her and kissing her*]: Bentley told me you were here and Constance was out. What are you doing?

Mrs Culver: Bickering.

Barbara: What about?

Mrs Culver: Constance.

Martha: I'm glad you've come, Barbara . . . Did you know that John was having an affair with Marie-Louise?

Barbara: I hate giving a straight answer to a straight question.

Martha: I suppose everyone knows but us. How long have you known? They say it's been going on for months. I can't think how it is we've only just heard it.

Mrs Culver [*ironically*]: It speaks very well for human nature that with the masses of dear friends we have it's only today that one of them broke the news to us.

Barbara: Perhaps the dear friend only heard it this morning.

Martha: At first I refused to believe it.

Mrs Culver: Only quite, quite at first, darling. You surrendered to the evidence with an outraged alacrity that took my breath away.

Martha: Of course I put two and two together. After the first shock I understood everything. I'm only astonished that it never occurred to me before.

Barbara: Are you very much upset, Mrs Culver?

Mrs Culver: Not a bit. I was brought up by a very strict mother to believe that men were naturally wicked. I am seldom surprised at what they do and never upset.

Martha: Mother has been simply maddening. She treats it as though it didn't matter a row of pins.

Mrs Culver: Constance and John have been married for

fifteen years. John is a very agreeable man. I've sometimes wondered whether he was any more faithful to
his wife than most husbands, but as it was really no
concern of mine I didn't let my mind dwell on it.

Martha: Is Constance your daughter or is she not your
daughter?

Mrs Culver: You certainly have a passion for straight
questions, my dear. The answer is yes.

Martha: And are you prepared to sit there quietly and let
her husband grossly deceive her with her most intimate
friend?

Mrs Culver: So long as she doesn't know I can't see that
she's any the worse. Marie-Louise is a nice little thing,
silly of course, but that's what men like, and if John is
going to deceive Constance it's much better that it
should be with someone we all know.

Martha [*to Barbara*]: Did you ever hear a respectable
woman – and Mother is respectable . . .

Mrs Culver [*interrupting*]: Oh, quite.

Martha: Talk like that?

Barbara: You think that something ought to be done
about it?

Martha: I am determined that something shall be done
about it.

Mrs Culver: Well, my dear, I'm determined that there's
at least one thing you shan't do and that is to tell
Constance.

Barbara [*a trifle startled*]: Is that what you want to do?

Martha: Somebody ought to tell her. If Mother won't I
must.

Barbara: I'm extremely fond of Constance. Of course I've
known what was going on for a long time and I've been
dreadfully worried.

Martha: John has put her into an odious position. No man
has the right to humiliate his wife as he has humiliated
Constance. He's made her perfectly ridiculous.

Mrs Culver: If women were ridiculous because their
husbands are unfaithful to them, there would surely be

a great deal more merriment in the world than there
is.

Barbara [*delighted to have a good gossip*]: You know they
were lunching together today?

Martha: We hadn't heard that. But they were dining
together the night before last.

Mrs Culver [*brightly*]: We know what they had to eat for
dinner. Do you know what they had to eat for
luncheon?

Martha: Mother.

Mrs Culver: Well, I thought she seemed rather uppish
about the lunch.

Martha: You have no sense of decency, Mother.

Mrs Culver: Oh, my dear, don't talk to me about decency.
Decency died with dear Queen Victoria.

Barbara [*to* **Mrs Culver**]: But you can't approve of John
having an open and flagrant intrigue with Constance's
greatest friend.

Mrs Culver: It may be that with advancing years my
arteries have hardened. I am unable to attach any great
importance to the philanderings of men. I think it's
their nature. John is a very hard-working surgeon. If he
likes to lunch and dine with a pretty woman now and
then I don't think he's much to blame. It must be
very tiresome to have three meals a day with the same
woman for seven days a week. I'm a little bored at
seeing Martha opposite me at the dinner-table. And
men can't stand boredom as well as women.

Martha: I'm sure I'm very much obliged to you, Mother.

Barbara [*significantly*]: But they're not only lunching and
dining together.

Mrs Culver: You fear the worst, my dear?

Barbara [*with solemnity*]: I know the worst.

Mrs Culver: I always think that's such a comfort. With
closed doors and no one listening to us, so long as a
man is kind and civil to his wife do you blame him
very much if he strays occasionally from the narrow
path of virtue?

The Constant Wife

Martha: Do you mean to say that you attach no importance to husbands and wives keeping their marriage vows?

Mrs Culver: I think wives should.

Barbara: But that's grossly unfair. Why should *they* any more than men?

Mrs Culver: Because on the whole they like it. We ascribe a great deal of merit to ourselves because we're faithful to our husbands. I don't believe we deserve it for a minute. We're naturally faithful creatures and we're faithful because we have no particular inclination to be anything else.

Barbara: I wonder.

Mrs Culver: My dear, you are a widow and perfectly free. Have you really had any great desire to do anything that the world might say you shouldn't?

Barbara: I have my business. When you work hard eight hours a day you don't much want to be bothered with love. In the evening the tired business woman wants to go to a musical comedy or play cards. She doesn't want to be worried with adoring males.

Martha: By the way, how is your business?

Barbara: Growing by leaps and bounds. As a matter of fact I came here today to ask Constance if she would like to come in with me.

Mrs Culver: Why should she? John earns plenty of money.

Barbara: Well, I thought if things came to a crisis she might like to know that her independence was assured.

Mrs Culver: Oh, you want them to come to a crisis, too?

Barbara: No, of course I don't. But, you know, they can't go on like this. It's a miracle that Constance hasn't heard yet. She's bound to find out soon.

Mrs Culver: I suppose it's inevitable.

Martha: I hope she'll find out as quickly as possible. I still think it's Mother's duty to tell her.

Mrs Culver: Which I have no intention of doing.

Martha: And if Mother won't I think I ought.

Mrs Culver: Which I have no intention of permitting.

Martha: He's humiliated her beyond endurance. Her position is intolerable. I have no words to express my opinion of Marie-Louise, and the first time I see her I shall tell her exactly what I think of her. She's a horrid, ungrateful, mean, and contemptible little cat.

Barbara: Anyhow, I think it would be a comfort to Constance to know that if anything happened she has me to turn to.

Mrs Culver: But John would make her a handsome allowance. He's a very generous man.

Martha [*indignantly*]: Do you think Constance would accept it?

Barbara: Martha's quite right, Mrs Culver. No woman in those circumstances would take a penny of his money.

Mrs Culver: That's what she'd say. But she'd take care that her lawyer made the best arrangement he could. Few men know with what ingenuity we women can combine the disinterested gesture with a practical eye for the main chance.

Barbara: Aren't you rather cynical, Mrs Culver?

Mrs Culver: I hope not. But when women are alone together I don't see why they shouldn't tell the truth now and then. It's a rest from the weary round of pretending to be something that we quite well know we're not.

Martha [*stiffly*]: I'm not aware that I've ever pretended to be anything I wasn't.

Mrs Culver: I dare say not, my dear. But I've always thought you were a little stupid. You take after your poor father. Constance and I have the brains of the family.

[**Constance** *comes into the room. She is a handsome woman of six and thirty. She has been out and wears a hat.*]

Barbara [*eagerly*]: Constance.

Constance: I'm so sorry I wasn't in. How nice of you all to wait. How are you, Mother darling?

[*She kisses them one after another.*]

The Constant Wife

Martha: What have you been doing all day, Constance?

Constance: Oh, I've been shopping with Marie-Louise. She's just coming up.

Barbara [*with dismay*]: Is she here?

Constance: Yes. She's telephoning.

Martha [*ironically*]: You and Marie-Louise are quite inseparable.

Constance: I like her. She amuses me.

Martha: Were you lunching together?

Constance: No, she was lunching with a beau.

Martha [*with a glance at* **Mrs Culver**]: Oh, really. [*Breezily*] John always comes home to luncheon, doesn't he?

Constance [*with great frankness*]: When he doesn't have to be at the hospital too early.

Martha: Was he lunching with you today?

Constance: No. He was engaged.

Martha: Where?

Constance: Good heavens, I don't know. When you've been married as long as I have you never ask your husband where he's going.

Martha: I don't know why not.

Constance [*smiling*]: Because he might take it into his head to ask *you*.

Mrs Culver: And also because if you're a wise woman you have confidence in your husband.

Constance: John has never given me a moment's uneasiness yet.

Martha: You're lucky.

Constance [*with her tongue in her cheek*]: Or wise.

[**Marie-Louise** *appears. She is a very pretty little thing, beautifully dressed, of the clinging, large-eyed type.*]

Marie-Louise: Oh, I didn't know there was a party.

Mrs Culver: Martha and I are just going.

Constance: You know my mother, Marie-Louise.

Marie-Louise: Of course I do.

Constance: She's a very nice mother.

Mrs Culver: With her head screwed on the right way and very active for her years.

[**Marie-Louise** *kisses* **Barbara** *and* **Martha.**]

Marie-Louise: How do you do.

Martha [*looking at her dress*]: That's new, isn't it, Marie-Louise?

Marie-Louise: Yes, I've never had it on before.

Martha: Oh, did you put it on because you were lunching with a beau?

Marie-Louise: What makes you think I was lunching with a beau?

Martha: Constance told me so.

Constance: It was only a guess on my part. [*To* **Marie-Louise**] When we met I noticed that your eyes were shining and you had that pleased, young look a woman always gets when someone has been telling her she's the most adorable thing in the world.

Martha: Tell us who it was, Marie-Louise.

Constance: Do nothing of the kind, Marie-Louise. Keep it a secret and give us something to gossip about.

Barbara: How is your husband, dear?

Marie-Louise: Oh, he's very well. I've just been telephoning to him.

Barbara: I never saw anyone adore his wife so obviously as he adores you.

Marie-Louise: Yes, he's sweet, isn't he?

Barbara: But doesn't it make you a little nervous sometimes? It must be nerve-racking to be obliged to live up to such profound devotion. It would be a dreadful shock if he ever found out that you were not everything he thought you.

Constance [*charmingly*]: But Marie-Louise is everything he thinks her.

Marie-Louise: And even if I weren't I think it would require more than the evidence of his eyes to persuade him.

Constance: Listen. There's John. [*She goes to the door and calls*] John! John!

The Constant Wife

John [*downstairs*]: Hulloa.

Constance: Are you coming up? Marie-Louise is here.

John: Yes, I'm just coming.

Constance: He's been operating all the afternoon. I expect he's tired out.

Martha [*with a look at* **Marie-Louise**]: I dare say he only had a sandwich for luncheon.

[**John** *comes in. He is a tall, spare man of about forty.*]

John: Good Lord, I never saw such a lot of people. How is my mother-in-law?

Mrs Culver: Mother-in-lawish.

John [*kissing* **Mrs Culver**, *then speaking to* **Barbara**]: You know, I only married Constance because her mother wouldn't have me.

Mrs Culver: I was too young at the time to marry a boy twenty years younger than myself.

Constance: It hasn't prevented you from flirting outrageously with the creature ever since. It's lucky I'm not a jealous woman.

John: What have you been doing all day, darling?

Constance: I've been shopping with Marie-Louise.

John [*shaking hands with Marie-Louise*]: Oh, how do you do? Did you lunch together?

Martha: No, she lunched with a beau.

John: I wish it had been me. [*To* **Marie-Louise**] What have you been doing with yourself lately? We haven't seen you for ages.

Marie-Louise: You're never about. Constance and I almost live in one another's pockets.

John: How's that rich husband of yours?

Marie-Louise: I've just been speaking to him. Isn't it a bore, he's got to go down to Birmingham for the night.

Constance: You'd better come and dine with us.

Marie-Louise: Oh, it's awfully nice of you. But I'm tired out. I shall just go to bed and have an egg.

John: I was just going to tell you, Constance. I shan't be in this evening. I've got an acute appendix to do.

Constance: Oh, what a nuisance.

Martha: You've got a wonderful profession, John. If you ever want to do anything or go anywhere you've only got to say you've got an operation and no one can prove it's a lie.

Constance: Oh, my dear, you mustn't put suspicions into my innocent head. It would never occur to John to be so deceitful. [*To* **John**] Would it?

John: I think I'd have to go an awful long way before I managed to deceive you, darling.

Constance [*with a little smile*]: Sometimes I think you're right.

Marie-Louise: I do like to see a husband and wife so devoted to one another as you and John. You've been married fifteen years, haven't you?

John: Yes. And it doesn't seem a day too much.

Marie-Louise: Well, I must be running along. I'm late already. Good-bye, darling. Good-bye, Mrs Culver.

Constance: Good-bye, darling. We've had such a nice afternoon.

Marie-Louise [*giving her hand to* **John**]: Good-bye.

John: Oh, I'll come downstairs with you.

Martha: I was just going, Marie-Louise. I'll come with you.

Marie-Louise [*with presence of mind*]: John, I wonder if you'd mind looking at my knee for a minute. It's been rather painful for the last day or two.

John: Of course not. Come into my consulting-room. These knee-caps are troublesome things when you once get them out of order.

Martha [*firmly*]: I'll wait for you. You won't be long, will you? We might share a taxi.

Marie-Louise: I've got my car.

Martha: Oh, how nice! You can give me a lift then.

Marie-Louise: Of course. I shall be delighted.

[**John** *opens the door for* **Marie-Louise**. *She goes out and he follows her.* **Constance** *has watched this little scene coolly, but with an alert mind.*]

The Constant Wife

Martha: What is the matter with her knee?

Constance: It slips.

Martha: What happens then?

Constance: She slips too.

Martha: Are you never jealous of these women who come and see John in his consulting-room?

Constance: He always has a nurse within call in case they should attempt to take liberties with him.

Martha [*amiably*]: Is the nurse there now?

Constance: And anyway I can't help thinking that the sort of woman who wants to be made love to in a consulting-room with a lively odour of antiseptics is the sort of woman who wears horrid undies. I could never bring myself to be jealous of her.

Martha: Marie-Louise gave me two of her chemises to copy only the other day.

Constance: Oh, did she give you the cerise one with the Irish lace insertions? I thought that sweet. I've copied that.

Barbara: It's true that Marie-Louise is very pretty.

Constance: Marie-Louise is a darling. But she and John have known each other far too long. John likes her of course, but he says she has no brain.

Martha: Men don't always say what they think.

Constance: Fortunately, or we shouldn't always know what they feel.

Martha: Don't you think John has any secrets from you?

Constance: I'm sure of it. But of course a good wife always pretends not to know the little things her husband wishes to keep hidden from her. That is an elementary rule in matrimonial etiquette.

Martha: Don't forget that men were deceivers ever.

Constance: My dear, you talk like a confirmed spinster. What woman was ever deceived that didn't want to be? Do you really think that men are mysterious? They're children. Why, my dear, John at forty isn't nearly so grown up as Helen at fourteen.

Barbara: How is your girl, Constance?

Constance: Oh, she's very well. She loves boarding-school, you know. They're like little boys, men. Sometimes of course they're rather naughty and you have to pretend to be angry with them. They attach so much importance to such entirely unimportant things that it's really touching. And they're so helpless. Have you never nursed a man when he's ill? It wrings your heart. It's just like a dog or a horse. They haven't got the sense to come in out of the rain, poor darlings. They have all the charming qualities that accompany general incompetence. They're sweet and good and silly and tiresome and selfish. You can't help liking them, they're so ingenuous and so simple. They have no complexity or finesse. I think they're sweet, but it's absurd to take them seriously. You're a wise woman, Mother. What do you think?

Mrs Culver: I think you're not in love with your husband.

Constance: What nonsense.

[**John** *comes in.*]

John: Marie-Louise is waiting for you, Martha. I've just put a little bandage round her knee.

Constance: I hope you weren't rough.

Martha [*to* **Constance**]: Good-bye, dear. Are you coming, Mother?

Mrs Culver: Not just yet.

Martha: Good-bye, Barbara.

[**Martha** *and* **John** *go out.*]

Barbara: Constance, I've got a suggestion to make to you. You know that my business has been growing by leaps and bounds and I simply cannot get along alone any more. I was wondering if you'd like to come in with me.

Constance: Oh, my dear, I'm not a business woman.

Barbara: You've got marvellous taste and you have ideas. You could do all the decorating and I'd confine myself to buying and selling furniture.

Constance: But I've got no capital.

Barbara: I've got all the capital I want. I must have help and I know no one more suitable than you. We'd go fifty-fifty and I think I can promise that you'd make a thousand to fifteen hundred a year.

Constance: I've been an idle woman so long. I think I'd find it dreadfully hard to work eight hours a day.

Barbara: Won't you think it over? It's very interesting, you know. You're naturally energetic. Don't you get bored with doing nothing all the time?

Constance: I don't think John would like it. After all, it would look as though he couldn't afford to support me.

Barbara: Oh, not nowadays, surely. There's no reason why a woman shouldn't have a career just as much as a man.

Constance: I think my career is looking after John – running a house for him, entertaining his friends, and making him happy and comfortable.

Barbara: Don't you think it rather a mistake to put all your eggs in one basket? Supposing that career failed you?

Constance: Why should it?

Barbara: Of course I hope it won't. But men, you know, are fluctuating and various. Independence is a very good thing, and a woman who stands on her own feet financially can look upon the future with a good deal of confidence.

Constance: It's sweet of you, but so long as John and I are happy together I think I should be a fool to do anything that would vex him.

Barbara: Of course I'm in no immediate hurry. One never knows what the future will bring forth. I want you to know that if you change your mind the job is open to you. I don't think I shall ever find anyone so competent as you. You have only to say the word.

Constance: Oh, Barbara, you are kind to me. It's a splendid offer and I'm ever so grateful to you. Don't think me horrid if I say I hope I shall never need to accept it.

Barbara: Of course not. Good-bye, darling.

Constance: Good-bye, dear.

[*They kiss, and* **Barbara** *goes out.* **Constance** *rings the bell.*]

Mrs Culver: Are you quite happy, dear?

Constance: Oh, quite. Don't I look it?

Mrs Culver: I'm bound to say you do. So far as I can judge by the look of you I should say you haven't a trouble in the world.

Constance: You'd be wrong. My cook has given notice and she makes the best meringues I've ever eaten.

Mrs Culver: I like John.

Constance: So do I. He has all the solid qualities that make a man a good husband, an agreeable temper, a sense of humour, and an entire indifference to petty extravagance.

Mrs Culver: How right you are, darling, to realize that those are the solid qualities.

Constance: It's not the seven deadly virtues that make a man a good husband, but the three hundred pleasing amiabilities.

Mrs Culver: Of course one has to compromise in life. One has to make the best of things. One mustn't expect too much from people. If one wants to be happy in one's own way one must let others be happy in theirs. If one can't get this, that, and the other the wise thing is to make up one's mind to do without it. The great thing is not to let vanity warp one's reasonable point of view.

Constance: Mother, mother, pull yourself together.

Mrs Culver: Everybody's so clever nowadays. They see everything but the obvious. I've discovered that I only have to say it quite simply in order to be thought a most original and amusing old lady.

Constance: Spare me, darling.

Mrs Culver [*affectionately*]: If at any time anything went wrong with you, you would tell your mother, wouldn't you?

Constance: Of course.

Mrs Culver: I hate the thought that you might be unhappy and let a foolish pride prevent you from letting me console and advise you.

Constance [*with feeling*]: It wouldn't, Mother dear.

Mrs Culver: I had rather an odd experience the other day. A little friend of mine came to see me and told me that her husband was neglecting her. I asked her why she told me and not her own mother. She said that her mother had never wanted her to marry and it would mortify her now to have to say that she had made a mistake.

Constance: Oh, well, John never neglects me, Mother.

Mrs Culver: Of course I gave her a good talking to. She didn't get much sympathy from me.

Constance [*with a smile*]: That was very unkind, wasn't it?

Mrs Culver: I have my own ideas about marriage. If a man neglects his wife it's her own fault, and if he's systematically unfaithful to her in nine cases out of ten she only has herself to blame.

Constance [*ringing the bell*]: Systematically is a grim word.

Mrs Culver: No sensible woman attaches importance to an occasional slip. Time and chance are responsible for that.

Constance: And, shall we say, masculine vanity?

Mrs Culver: I told my little friend that if her husband was unfaithful to her it was because he found other women more attractive. Why should she be angry with him for that? Her business was to be more attractive than they.

Constance: You are not what they call a feminist, Mother, are you?

Mrs Culver: After all, what is fidelity?

Constance: Mother, do you mind if I open the window?

Mrs Culver: It is open.

Constance: In that case do you mind if I shut it? I feel that when a woman of your age asks such a question I should make some sort of symbolic gesture.

Mrs Culver: Don't be ridiculous. Of course I believe in fidelity for women. I suppose no one has ever questioned the desirability of that. But men are different. Women should remember that they have their homes and their name and position and their family, and they should learn to close their eyes when it's possible they may see something they are not meant to.

[**Bentley** *comes in.*]

Bentley: Did you ring, madam?

Constance: Yes. I am expecting Mr Bernard Kersal. I'm not at home to anybody else.

Bentley: Very good, madam.

Constance: Is Mr Middleton in?

Bentley: Yes, madam. He's in the consulting-room.

Constance: Very well.

[**Bentley** *goes out.*]

Mrs Culver: Is that a polite way of telling me that I had better take myself off?

Constance: Of course not. On the contrary I particularly want you to stay.

Mrs Culver: Who is this mysterious gentleman?

Constance: Mother. Bernard.

Mrs Culver: That says nothing to me at all. Not Saint Bernard, darling?

Constance: Pull yourself together, my pet. You must remember Bernard Kersal. He proposed to me.

Mrs Culver: Oh, my dear, you cannot expect me to remember the names of all the young men who proposed to you.

Constance: Yes, but he proposed more than any of the others.

Mrs Culver: Why?

Constance: I suppose because I refused him. I can't think of any other reason.

Mrs Culver: He made no impression on me.

Constance: I don't suppose he tried to.

Mrs Culver: What did he look like?

Constance: He was tall.

The Constant Wife

Mrs Culver: They were all tall.

Constance: He had brown hair and brown eyes.

Mrs Culver: They all had brown hair and brown eyes.

Constance: He danced divinely.

Mrs Culver: They all danced divinely.

Constance: I very nearly married him, you know.

Mrs Culver: Why didn't you?

Constance: I think he was a trifle too much inclined to lie down on the floor and let me walk over him.

Mrs Culver: In short he had no sense of humour.

Constance: I was quite certain that he loved me, and I was never absolutely sure that John did.

Mrs Culver: Well, you're sure now, dear, aren't you?

Constance: Oh, yes. John adores me.

Mrs Culver: And what's this young man coming for today?

Constance: He's not such a very young man any more. He was twenty-nine then and so he must be nearly forty-five now.

Mrs Culver: He isn't still in love with you?

Constance: I shouldn't think so. Do you think it possible after fifteen years? It's surely very unlikely. Don't look at me like that, Mother. I don't like it.

Mrs Culver: Don't talk stuff and nonsense to me, child. Of course you know if he's in love with you or not.

Constance: But I haven't seen him since I married John. You see he lives in Japan. He's a merchant or something in Kôbe. He was here during the war on leave. But that was when I was so dreadfully ill and I didn't see him.

Mrs Culver: Oh! Why's he here now then? Have you been corresponding with him?

Constance: No. One can't write letters to anyone one never sees for fifteen years. He always sends me flowers on my birthday.

Mrs Culver: That's rather sweet of him.

Constance: And the other day I had a letter from him saying he was in England and would like to see me. So I asked him to come today.

Mrs Culver: I wondered why you were so smart.

Constance: Of course he may be terribly changed. Men go off so dreadfully, don't they? He may be bald and fat now.

Mrs Culver: He may be married.

Constance: Oh, if he were I don't think he'd want to come and see me, would he?

Mrs Culver: I see you're under the impression that he's still in love with you.

Constance: Oh, I'm not.

Mrs Culver: Then why are you so nervous?

Constance: It's only natural that I shouldn't want him to think me old and haggard. He adored me, Mother. I suppose he still thinks of me as I was then. It wouldn't be very nice if his face fell about a yard and a half when he came into the room.

Mrs Culver: I think I'd much better leave you to face the ordeal alone.

Constance: Oh, no, Mother, you must stay. I particularly want you. You see, he may be awful and I may wish I'd never seen him again. It'll be so much easier if you're here. I may not want to be alone with him at all.

Mrs Culver: Oh.

Constance [*with a twinkle in her eye*]: On the other hand I may.

Mrs Culver: It seems to me you're putting me in a slightly embarrassing situation.

Constance: Now listen. If I think he's awful we'll just talk about the weather and the crops for a few minutes and then we'll have an ominous pause and stare at him. That always makes a man feel a perfect fool and the moment a man feels a fool he gets up and goes.

Mrs Culver: Sometimes they don't know how to, poor dears, and the earth will never open and swallow them up.

Constance: On the other hand if I think he looks rather

nice I shall just take out my handkerchief and carelessly place it on the piano.

Mrs Culver: Why?

Constance: Darling, in order that you may rise to your aged feet and say, well, you really must be running along.

Mrs Culver: Yes, I know that, but why should you carelessly place your handkerchief on the piano?

Constance: Because I am a creature of impulse. I shall have an impulse to place my handkerchief on the piano.

Mrs Culver: Oh, very well. But I always mistrust impulses. [**Bentley** *enters and announces* **Bernard Kersal.** *He is a tall good-looking man, sunburned and of healthy appearance. He is evidently very fit and he carries his forty-five years well.*]

Bentley: Mr Kersal.

Constance: How do you do? Do you remember my mother?

Bernard [*shaking hands with her*]: I'm sure she doesn't remember me.

[**Constance** *takes a small handkerchief out of her bag.*]

Mrs Culver: That is the soft answer that turneth away wrath.

Constance: It's rather late for tea, isn't it? Would you like a drink?

[*As she says this she goes towards the bell and places her handkerchief on the piano.*]

Bernard: No, thanks. I've just this moment had one.

Constance: To brace you for seeing me?

Bernard: I was nervous.

Constance: Have I changed as much as you expected?

Bernard: Oh, that's not what I was nervous about.

Mrs Culver: Is it really fifteen years since you saw Constance?

Bernard: Yes. I didn't see her when I was last in England. When I got demobbed I had to go out to Japan again and get my business together. I haven't had a chance to come home before.

[**Constance** *has been giving her mother significant looks, but her mother does not notice then.* **Constance** *takes a second handkerchief out of her bag and when the opportunity arises places it neatly on the piano beside the first one.*]

Mrs Culver: And are you home for long?

Bernard: A year.

Mrs Culver: Have you brought your wife with you?

Bernard: I'm not married.

Mrs Culver: Oh, Constance said you were married to a Japanese lady.

Constance: Nonsense, Mother. I never said anything of the sort.

Mrs Culver: Oh, perhaps I was thinking of Julia Linton. She married an Egyptian pasha. I believe she's very happy. At all events he hasn't killed her yet.

Bernard: How is your husband?

Constance: He's very well. I dare say he'll be in presently.

Bernard: Haven't you got a little sister? I suppose she's out now?

Mrs Culver: He means Martha. She's come out and gone in again.

Constance: She was not so very much younger than me, you know. She's thirty-two now.

[**Mrs Culver** *has taken no notice of the handkerchiefs and in desperation* **Constance** *takes a third from her bag and places it beside the other two.*]

Mrs Culver: Do you like the East, Mr Kersal?

Bernard: One has a pretty good time there, you know.

[*Now* **Mrs Culver** *catches sight of the three handkerchiefs and starts.*]

Mrs Culver: I wonder what the time is.

Constance: It's late, Mother. Are you dining out tonight? I suppose you want to have a lie-down before you dress for dinner.

Mrs Culver: I hope I shall see you again, Mr Kersal.

The Constant Wife

Bernard: Thank you very much.

[**Constance** *accompanies her to the door.*]

Mrs Culver: Good-bye, darling. [*In a whisper*] I couldn't remember if the handkerchiefs meant go or stay.

Constance: You had only to use your eyes. You can see at a glance that he is the kind of man one would naturally want to have a heart-to-heart talk with after fifteen years.

Mrs Culver: You only confused me by putting more and more handkerchiefs on the piano.

Constance: For goodness' sake go, Mother. [*Aloud*] Goodbye, my sweet. I'm sorry you've got to run away so soon.

Mrs Culver: Good-bye.

[*She goes out and* **Constance** *comes back into the room.*]

Constance: Did you think it very rude of us to whisper? Mother has a passion for secrets.

Bernard: Of course not.

Constance: Now let's sit down and make ourselves comfortable. Let me look at you. You haven't changed much. You're a little thinner and perhaps a little more lined. Men are so lucky, if they have any character they grow better-looking as they grow older. Do you know I'm thirty-six now?

Bernard: What does that matter?

Constance: Shall I tell you something? When you wrote and suggested coming here I was delighted at the thought of seeing you again and wrote at once making a date. And then I was panic-stricken. I would have given almost anything not to have sent that letter. And all today I've had such a horrible feeling at the pit of my stomach. Didn't you see my knees wobble when you came into the room?

Bernard: In God's name, why?

Constance: Oh, my dear, I think you must be a little stupid. I should be a perfect fool if I didn't know that when I was a girl I was very pretty. It's rather a pang when you are forced to the conclusion that you're not quite so pretty as you were. People don't tell one. One tries to hide it from oneself. Anyhow I thought I'd rather know the worst. That's one of the reasons I asked you to come.

Bernard: Whatever I thought you can hardly imagine that I should be deliberately rude.

Constance: Of course not. But I watched your face. I was afraid I'd see there: By God, how she's gone off.

Bernard: And did you?

Constance: You were rather shy when you came in. You weren't thinking of me.

Bernard: It's quite true, fifteen years ago you were a pretty girl. Now you're lovely. You're ten times more beautiful than you were then.

Constance: It's nice of you to say so.

Bernard: Don't you believe it?

Constance: I think you do. And I confess that's sufficiently gratifying. Now tell me, why aren't you married? It's time you did, you know, or it'll be too late. You'll have a very lonely old age if you don't.

Bernard: I never wanted to marry anyone but you.

Constance: Oh, come, you're not going to tell me that you've never been in love since you were in love with me?

Bernard: No, I've been in love half a dozen times, but when it came to the point I found I still loved you best.

Constance: I like you for saying that. I shouldn't have believed it if you'd said you'd never loved anybody else and I should have been vexed with you for thinking me such a fool as to believe it.

Bernard: You see, it was you I loved in the others. One because she had hair like yours and another because her smile reminded me of your smile.

Constance: I hate to think that I've made you unhappy.

Bernard: But you haven't. I've had a very good time; I've enjoyed my work; I've made a bit of money; and I've had a lot of fun. I don't blame you for having married John instead of me.

Constance: Do you remember John?

Bernard: Of course I do. He was a very nice fellow. I dare say he's made you a better husband than I should have. I've had my ups and downs. I'm very irritable sometimes. John's been able to give you everything you wanted. You were much safer with him. By the way, I suppose I can still call you Constance.

Constance: Of course. Why not? Do you know, I think you have a very nice nature, Bernard.

Bernard: Are you happy with John?

Constance: Oh, very. I don't say that he has never given me a moment's uneasiness. He did once, but I took hold of myself and saw that I mustn't be silly. I'm very glad I did. I think I can quite honestly say that ours has been a very happy and successful marriage.

Bernard: I'm awfully glad to hear that. Do you think it's cheek to ask if John loves you?

Constance: I'm sure he loves me.

Bernard: And do you love him?

Constance: Very much.

Bernard: May I make you a short speech?

Constance: If I may interrupt at suitable moments.

Bernard: I hope you're going to let me see a great deal of you during this year I've got at home.

Constance: I want to see a great deal of you.

Bernard: There's just one thing I want to get off my chest and then I needn't refer to it again. I am just as madly in love with you as I was when I asked you to marry me fifteen years ago. I think I shall remain in love with you all my life. I'm too old a dog to learn new tricks. But I want you to know that you needn't have the smallest fear that I shall make a nuisance of myself. I should think it an awfully caddish thing to try to come between you and John. I suppose we all want to be happy, but I don't believe the best way of being that is to try to upset other people's happiness.

Constance: That's not such a very long speech after all. At a public dinner they would hardly even call it a few remarks.

Bernard: All I ask for is your friendship and if in return I care to give you my love I don't see that it's anyone's business but my own.

Constance: I don't think it is. I think I can be a very good friend, Bernard.

[*The door opens and* **John** *comes in.*]

John: Oh, I'm sorry. I didn't know you were engaged.

Constance: I'm not. Come in. This is Bernard Kersal.

John: How do you do?

Bernard: I'm afraid you don't remember me.

John: If you ask me point-blank I think it's safer to confess I don't.

Constance: Don't be so silly, John. He used to come to Mother's.

John: Before we were married, d'you mean?

Constance: Yes. You spent several week-ends with us together.

John: My dear, that was fifteen years ago. I'm awfully sorry not to remember you, but I'm delighted to see you now.

Constance: He's just come back from Japan.

John: Oh, well, I hope we shall see you again. I'm just going along to the club to have a rubber before dinner, darling. [*To* **Bernard**] Why don't you dine here with Constance? I've got an acute appendix and she'll be all alone, poor darling.

Bernard: Oh, that's awfully kind of you.

Constance: It would be a friendly act. Are you free?

Bernard: Always to do a friendly act.

Constance: Very well. I shall expect you at eight-fifteen.

The Constant Wife

Act Two

The scene is the same. A fortnight has passed.
   [**Martha** *in walking costume and a hat is looking at
   an illustrated paper.* **Bentley** *comes in.*]
Bentley: Mr Kersal is here, miss.
Martha: Oh! Ask him if he won't come up.
Bentley: Very good, miss. [*He goes out and in a moment
   comes in again to announce* **Bernard**.] Mr Kersal.
   [*Exit* **Bentley**.]
Martha: Constance is dressing. She won't be very long.
Bernard: Oh, I see. Well, there's no violent hurry.
Martha: You're taking her to Ranelagh, aren't you?
Bernard: That was the idea. I know some of the fellows
   who are playing today.
Martha: Are you having a good time in London?
Bernard: Marvellous. When a man's lived in the East as
   long as I have, he's apt to feel rather out of it when he
   comes home. But Constance and John have been rip-
   ping to me.
Martha: Do you like John?
Bernard: Yes. He's been awfully kind.
Martha: Do you know, I remember you quite well.
Bernard: Oh, you can't. You were a kid when I used to
   come down and stay with your mother.
Martha: I was sixteen. Do you imagine I wasn't thrilled
   to the marrow by Constance's young men?
Bernard: There were a good many of them. I should have
   thought your marrow got callous.
Martha: But you were one of the serious ones. I always
   thought you terribly romantic.
Bernard: I was terribly romantic. I think it's becoming in
   the young.

Martha: I don't think it's unbecoming in the not quite as young.

Bernard: Don't think I'm romantic now. I make a considerable income and I'm putting on weight. The price of silk has ousted love's young dream in my manly bosom.

Martha: You're an unconscionable liar.

Bernard: To which I can only retort that you're excessively rude.

Martha: You were madly in love with Constance in those days, weren't you?

Bernard: You know, it's so long ago I forget.

Martha: I advised her to marry you rather than John.

Bernard: Why?

Martha: Well, for one thing you lived in Japan. I would have married anyone who would take me there.

Bernard: I live there still.

Martha: Oh, I don't want to marry you.

Bernard: I couldn't help suspecting that.

Martha: I could never really quite understand what she saw in John.

Bernard: I suppose she loved him.

Martha: I wonder if she ever regrets that she married John rather than you.

Bernard: Well, don't. She's perfectly satisfied with John and wouldn't change him for anything in the world.

Martha: It's exasperating, isn't it?

Bernard: I don't think so. It must make it much more comfortable for a husband and wife to be content with one another.

Martha: You're in love with her still, aren't you?

Bernard: Not a bit.

Martha: Upon my soul, you've got a nerve. Why, you donkey, you're giving it away all the time. Do you know what you look like when she's in the room? Have you any idea how your eyes change when they rest on her? When you speak her name it sounds as though you were kissing it.

Bernard: I thought you were an odious child when you

were sixteen, Martha, and now that you're thirty-two I think you're a horrible woman.

Martha: I'm not really. But I'm very fond of Constance and I'm inclined to be rather fond of you.

Bernard: Don't you think you could show your attachment by minding your own business?

Martha: Why does it make you angry because I've told you that no one can see you with Constance for five minutes without knowing that you adore her?

Bernard: My dear, I'm here for one year. I want to be happy. I don't want to give trouble or cause trouble. I value my friendship with Constance and I hate the idea that anything should interfere with it.

Martha: Hasn't it occurred to you that she may want more than your friendship?

Bernard: No, it has not.

Martha: You need not jump down my throat.

Bernard: Constance is perfectly happy with her husband. You must think me a damned swine if you think I'm going to butt in and try to smash up a perfectly wonderful union.

Martha: But, you poor fool, don't you know that John has been notoriously unfaithful to Constance for ages?

Bernard: I don't believe it.

Martha: Ask anyone you like. Mother knows it. Barbara Fawcett knows it. Everyone knows it but Constance.

Bernard: That certainly isn't true. Mrs Durham told me when I met her at dinner two or three days ago that John and Constance were the most devoted couple she'd ever known.

Martha: Did Marie-Louise tell you that?

Bernard: She did.

[**Martha** *begins to laugh. She can hardly restrain herself.*]

Martha: The nerve. Marie-Louise. Oh, my poor Bernard. Marie-Louise is John's mistress.

Bernard: Marie-Louise is Constance's greatest friend.

Martha: Yes.

Bernard: If this is a pack of lies I swear I'll damned well wring your neck.

Martha: All right.

Bernard: That was a silly thing to say. I'm sorry.

Martha: Oh, I don't mind. I like a man to be violent. I think you're just the sort of man Constance needs.

Bernard: What the devil do you mean by that?

Martha: It can't go on. Constance is being made perfectly ridiculous. Her position is monstrous. I thought she ought to be told and as everyone else seemed to shirk the job I was prepared to do it myself. My mother was so disagreeable about it, I've had to promise not to say a word.

Bernard: You're not under the delusion that I'm going to tell her?

Martha: No, I don't really think it would come very well from you. But things can't go on. She's bound to find out. All I want you to do is to . . . well, stand by.

Bernard: But Marie-Louise has got a husband. What about him?

Martha: His only ambition in life is to make a million. He's the sort of fool who thinks a woman loves him just because he loves her. Marie-Louise can turn him round her little finger.

Bernard: Has Constance never suspected?

Martha: Never. You've only got to look at her. Really, her self-confidence sometimes is positively maddening.

Bernard: I wonder if it wouldn't be better that she never did find out. She's so happy. She's entirely carefree. You've only got to look at that open brow and those frank, trustful eyes.

Martha: I thought you loved her.

Bernard: Enough to want her happiness above all things.

Martha: You *are* forty-five, aren't you? I forgot that for a moment.

Bernard: Dear Martha. You have such an attractive way of putting things.

The Constant Wife

[**Constance's** *voice on the stairs is heard calling:* Bentley, Bentley.]

Martha: Oh, there's Constance. I can't imagine where Mother is. I think I'll go into the brown room and write a letter.

[**Bernard** *takes no notice of what she says nor does he make any movement when she goes out. A moment later* **Constance** *comes in.*]

Constance: Have I kept you waiting?

Bernard: It doesn't matter.

Constance: Hulloa! What's up?

Bernard: With me? Nothing. Why?

Constance: You look all funny. Why are your eyes suddenly opaque?

Bernard: I didn't know they were.

Constance: Are you trying to hide something from me?

Bernard: Of course not.

Constance: Have you had bad news from Japan?

Bernard: No. Far from it. Silk is booming.

Constance: Then you're going to tell me that you've just got engaged to a village maiden.

Bernard: No, I'm not.

Constance: I hate people who keep secrets from me.

Bernard: I have no secrets from you.

Constance: Do you think I don't know your face by now?

Bernard: You'll make me vain. I would never have ventured to think that you took the trouble to look twice at my ugly face.

Constance [*with sudden suspicion*]: Wasn't Martha here when you came? She hasn't gone, has she?

Bernard: She's waiting for her mother. She's gone into another room to write letters.

Constance: Did you see her?

Bernard [*trying to be very casual*]: Yes. We had a little chat about the weather.

Constance [*immediately grasping what has happened*]: Oh – don't you think we ought to be starting?

Bernard: There's plenty of time. It's no good getting there too early.

Constance: Then I'll take off my hat.

Bernard: And it's jolly here, isn't it? I love your room.

Constance: Do you think it's a success? I did it myself. Barbara Fawcett wants me to go into the decorating business. She's in it, you know, and she's making quite a lot of money.

Bernard [*smiling to hide his anxiety in asking the question*]: Aren't you happy at home?

Constance [*breezily*]: I don't think it necessarily means one's unhappy at home because one wants an occupation. One may very easily grow tired of going to parties all the time. But as a matter of fact I refused Barbara's offer.

Bernard [*insisting*]: You are happy, aren't you?

Constance: Very.

Bernard: You've made *me* very happy during this last fortnight. I feel as though I'd never been away. You've been awfully kind to me.

Constance: I'm very glad you think so. I don't know that I've done anything very much for you.

Bernard: Yes, you have. You've let me see you.

Constance: I let the policeman at the corner do that, you know.

Bernard: You mustn't think that because I take care only to talk to you of quite casual things I don't still love you with all my heart.

Constance [*quite coolly*]: We agreed when first you came back that your feelings were entirely your business.

Bernard: Do you mind my loving you?

Constance: Oughtn't we all to love one another?

Bernard: Don't tease me.

Constance: My dear, I can't help being pleased and flattered and rather touched. It is rather wonderful that anyone should care for me . . .

Bernard [*interrupting*]: So much?

Constance: After so many years.

The Constant Wife

Bernard: If anyone had asked me fifteen years ago if I could love you more than I loved you then I should have said it was impossible. I love you ten times more than I ever loved you before.

Constance [*going on with her own speech*]: But I don't in the least want you to make love to me now.

Bernard: I know. I'm not going to. I know you far too well.

Constance [*amused and a trifle taken aback*]: I don't quite know what you've been doing for the last five minutes.

Bernard: I was merely stating a few plain facts.

Constance: Oh, I beg your pardon. I thought it was something quite different. I'm afraid you might mistake my meaning if I said I'm quite curious to see how you *do* make love.

Bernard [*good-humouredly*]: I have a notion that you're laughing at me.

Constance: In the hope of teaching you to laugh at yourself.

Bernard: I've been very good during the last fortnight, haven't I?

Constance: Yes, I kept on saying to myself: I wonder if a pat of butter really would melt in his mouth.

Bernard: Well, for just a minute I'm going to let myself go.

Constance: I wouldn't if I were you.

Bernard: Yes, but you're not. I want to tell you just once that I worship the ground you tread on. There's never been anyone in the world for me but you.

Constance: Oh, nonsense. There have been half a dozen. We are seven.

Bernard: They were all you. I love you with all my heart. I admire you more than any woman I've ever met. I respect you. I'm an awful fool when it comes to the point. I don't know how to say all I've got in my heart without feeling like a perfect ass. I love you. I want you to know that if ever you're in trouble I should look upon it as the greatest possible happiness to be allowed to help you.

Constance: That's very kind of you. I don't see why I should be in any trouble.

Bernard: Always and in all circumstances you can count on me absolutely. I will do anything in the world for you. If ever you want me you have only to give me a sign. I should be proud and happy to give my life for you.

Constance: It's sweet of you to say so.

Bernard: Don't you believe it?

Constance [*with a charming smile*]: Yes.

Bernard: I should like to think that it meant – oh, not very much, but just a little to you.

Constance [*almost shaken*]: It means a great deal. I thank you.

Bernard: Now we won't say anything more about it.

Constance [*recovering her accustomed coolness*]: But why did you think it necessary to say all this just now?

Bernard: I wanted to get it off my chest.

Constance: Oh, really.

Bernard: You're not angry with me?

Constance: Oh, Bernard, I'm not that kind of a fool at all – It's a pity that Martha doesn't marry.

Bernard: Don't think that I'm going to marry her.

Constance: I don't. I merely thought that a husband would be a pleasant and useful occupation for her. She's quite a nice girl, you know. A liar, of course, but otherwise all right.

Bernard: Oh?

Constance: Yes, a terrible liar, even for a woman . . . Shall we start now? It's no good getting there when the polo is over.

Bernard: All right. Let's start.

Constance: I'll put my hat on again. By the way, you haven't had a taxi waiting all this time, have you?

Bernard: No, I've got a car. I thought I'd like to drive you down myself.

The Constant Wife

Constance: Open or shut?

Bernard: Open.

Constance: Oh, my dear, then I must get another hat. A broad brim like this is such a bore in an open car.

Bernard: Oh, I am sorry.

Constance: It doesn't matter a bit. I shall only be a minute. And why on earth shouldn't one be comfortable if one can?

[*She goes out. In a moment* **Bentley** *shows in* **Marie-Louise**.]

Marie-Louise: Oh, how do you do. [*To* **Bentley**] Will you tell Mr Middleton at once?

Bentley: Yes, madam.

[*Exit* **Bentley**.]

Marie-Louise [*rather flustered*]: I particularly wanted to see John for a minute and there are patients waiting to see him, so I asked Bentley if he couldn't come here.

Bernard: I'll take myself off.

Marie-Louise: I'm awfully sorry, but it's rather urgent. John hates to be disturbed like this.

Bernard: I'll go into the next room.

Marie-Louise: Are you waiting for Constance?

Bernard: Yes, I'm taking her to Ranelagh. She's changing her hat.

Marie-Louise: I see. Bentley told me she was upstairs. Good-bye. I shall only be a minute.

[**Bernard** *goes into the adjoining room just as* **John** *comes in.*]

Oh, John, I'm sorry to drag you away from your patients.

John: There's nothing urgent. They can wait for a few minutes.

[**Bernard** *has closed the door behind him, and* **John's** *tone changes. They speak now in a low voice and quickly.*]

Is anything the matter?

Marie-Louise: Mortimer.

John: What about Mortimer?

Marie-Louise: I'm convinced he suspects.

John: Why?

Marie-Louise: He was so funny last night. He came into my room to say good night to me. He sat on my bed. He was chatting nicely and he was asking what I'd been doing with myself all the evening . . .

John: Presumably you didn't tell him.

Marie-Louise: No, I said I'd been dining here. And suddenly he got up and just said good night and went out. His voice was so strange that I couldn't help looking at him. He was as red as a turkey cock.

John: Is that all?

Marie-Louise: He never came in to say good morning to me before he went to the City.

John: He may have been in a hurry.

Marie-Louise: He's never in too much of a hurry for that.

John: I think you're making a mountain out of a mole heap.

Marie-Louise: Don't be stupid, John. Can't you see I'm as nervous as a cat?

John: I can. But I'm trying to persuade you there's nothing to be nervous about.

Marie-Louise: What fools men are. They never will see that it's the small things that matter. I tell you I'm frightened out of my wits.

John: You know there's a devil of a distance between suspicion and proof.

Marie-Louise: Oh, I don't think he could prove anything. But he can make himself awfully unpleasant. Supposing he put ideas in Constance's head?

John: She'd never believe him.

Marie-Louise: If the worst came to worst I could manage Mortimer. He's awfully in love with me. That always gives one such an advantage over a man.

John: Of course you can twist Mortimer round your little finger.

Marie-Louise: I should die of shame if Constance knew.

The Constant Wife

After all, she's my greatest friend and I'm absolutely devoted to her.

John: Constance is a peach. Of course I don't believe there's anything in this at all, but, if there were, I'd be in favour of making a clean breast of it to Constance.

Marie-Louise: Never!

John: I expect she'd kick up a row. Any woman would. But she'd do anything in the world to help us out.

Marie-Louise: A lot you know about women. She'd help you out, I dare say. But she'd stamp on me with both feet. That's only human nature.

John: Not Constance's.

Marie-Louise: Upon my word, it's lucky I'm fairly sure of you, John, or the way you talk of Constance would really make me jealous.

John: Thank God you can smile. You're getting your nerve back.

Marie-Louise: It's been a comfort to talk it over. It doesn't seem so bad now.

John: I'm sure you've got nothing to be frightened about.

Marie-Louise: I dare say it was only my fancy. It was a stupid risk to take all the same.

John: Perhaps. Why did you look so devilish pretty?

Marie-Louise: Oughtn't you to be getting back to your wretched patients?

John: I suppose so. Will you stop and see Constance?

Marie-Louise: I may as well. It would look rather odd if I went away without saying how d'you do to her.

John [*going*]: I'll leave you then. And don't worry.

Marie-Louise: I won't. I dare say it was only a guilty conscience. I'll go and have my hair washed.

[*As* **John** *is about to go,* **Martha** *comes in followed by* **Bernard**.]

Martha [*with an almost exaggerated cordiality*]: I had no idea you were here, Marie-Louise.

Marie-Louise: It's not very important.

Martha: I was just writing letters, waiting for Mother, and Bernard's only just told me.

Marie-Louise: I wanted to see John about something.

Martha: I hope you haven't got anything the matter with you, darling.

Marie-Louise: No. Mortimer's been looking rather run down lately and I want John to persuade him to take a holiday.

Martha: Oh, I should have thought he'd be more likely to take a physician's advice than a surgeon's in a thing like that.

Marie-Louise: He's got a tremendous belief in John, you know.

Martha: In which I'm sure he's justified. John is so very reliable.

John: What can I do for you, Martha? If you'd like me to cut out an appendix or a few tonsils I shall be happy to oblige you.

Martha: My dear John, you've only left me the barest necessities of existence as it is. I don't think I could manage with anything less than I have.

John: My dear, as long as a woman has a leg to stand on she need not despair of exciting her surgeon's sympathy and interest.

[**Constance** *comes in with* **Mrs Culver**.]

Marie-Louise [*kissing her*]: Darling.

Constance: How is your knee, still slipping?

Marie-Louise: It always gives me more or less trouble, you know.

Constance: Yes, of course. I think you're very patient. In your place I should be furious with John. Of course I would never dream of consulting him if I had anything the matter with me.

Mrs Culver: I'm sorry I've been so long, Martha. Have you been very impatient?

Martha: No, I've been passing the time very pleasantly.

Mrs Culver: For others, darling, or only for yourself?

Constance: I met Mother on the stairs and she came up with me while I changed my hat. Bernard is taking me down to Ranelagh.

The Constant Wife

John: Oh, that'll be jolly.

Bernard: We shall be dreadfully late.

Constance: Does it matter?

Bernard: No.

> [**Bentley** *comes in with a card on a small salver and takes it to* **Constance**. *She looks at the card and hesitates.*]

Constance: How very odd.

John: What's the matter, Constance?

Constance: Nothing. [*For an instant she reflects.*] Is he downstairs?

Bentley: Yes, madam.

Constance: I don't know why he should send up a card. Show him up.

Bentley: Very good, madam.

> [*Exit* **Bentley**.]

John: Who is it, Constance?

Constance: Come and sit down, Marie-Louise.

Marie-Louise: I must go and so must you.

Constance: There's plenty of time. Do you like this hat?

Marie-Louise: Yes. I think it's sweet.

Constance: What are *you* doing here, John? Haven't you got any patients today?

John: Yes, there are two or three waiting. I'm just going down. As a matter of fact I thought I deserved a cigarette. [*He puts his hand to his hip pocket.*] Hang, I've mislaid my cigarette-case. You haven't seen it about, Constance?

Constance: No, I haven't.

John: I looked for it everywhere this morning. I can't think where I left it. I must ring up the nursing-home and ask if I left it there.

Constance: I hope you haven't lost it.

John: Oh, no. I'm sure I haven't. I've just put it somewhere.

> [*The door opens and* **Bentley** *announces the visitor.*]

Bentley: Mr Mortimer Durham.

Marie-Louise [*startled out of her wits*]: Oh!

Constance [*quickly, seizing her wrist*]: Sit still, you fool.
  [**Mortimer Durham** *comes in. He is a stoutish biggish
  man of about forty, with a red face and an irascible
  manner. At the moment he is a prey to violent
  emotion.* **Bentley** *goes out.*]
  Hulloa, Mortimer. What are you doing in these parts at
  this hour? Why on earth did you send up a card?
  [*He stops and looks round.*]
Marie-Louise: What is the matter, Mortimer?
Mortimer [*to* **Constance**, *with difficulty restraining his
  fury*]: I thought you might like to know that your hus-
  band is my wife's lover.
Marie-Louise: Morty!
Constance [*keeping a firm hand on* **Marie-Louise** *and
  very coolly to* **Mortimer**]: Oh? What makes you think
  that?
Mortimer [*taking a gold cigarette-case out of his pocket*]:
  Do you recognize this? I found it under my wife's pillow
  last night.
Constance: Oh, I am relieved. I couldn't make out where
  I'd left it. [*Taking it from him*] Thank you so much.
Mortimer [*angrily*]: It's not yours.
Constance: Indeed it is. I was sitting on Marie-Louise's
  bed and I must have slipped it under the pillow without
  thinking.
Mortimer: It has John's initials on it.
Constance: I know. It was presented to him by a grateful
  patient and I thought it much too nice for him, so I
  just took it.
Mortimer: What sort of fool do you take me for,
  Constance?
Constance: My dear Morty, why should I say it was my
  cigarette-case if it wasn't?
Mortimer: They had dinner together.
Constance: My poor Morty, I know that. You were going
  to a City banquet or something, and Marie-Louise rang
  up and asked if she might come and take pot-luck with
  us.

Mortimer: Do you mean to say she dined here?

Constance: Isn't that what she told you?

Mortimer: Yes.

Constance: It's quite easy to prove. If you won't take my word for it we can ring for the butler, and you can ask him yourself . . . Ring the bell, John, will you?

Mortimer [*uneasily*]: No, don't do that. If you give me your word, of course I must take it.

Constance: That's very kind of you. I'm grateful to you for not exposing me to the humiliation of making my butler corroborate my statement.

Mortimer: If Marie-Louise was dining here why were you sitting on her bed?

Constance: John had to go out and do an operation, and Marie-Louise wanted to show me the things she'd got from Paris, so I walked round to your house. It was a lovely night. You remember that, don't you?

Mortimer: Damn it, I've got more important things to do than look at the night.

Constance: We tried them all on and then we were rather tired, so Marie-Louise got into bed and I sat down and we talked.

Mortimer: If you were tired why didn't you go home and go to bed?

Constance: John had promised to come round and fetch me.

Mortimer: And did he? At what time did he come?

John: I couldn't manage it. The operation took much longer than I expected. It was one of those cases where when you once start cutting you really don't know where to stop. You know the sort of thing, don't you, Mortimer?

Mortimer: No, I don't. How the devil should I?

Constance: All that is neither here nor there. This is a terrible accusation you've made against John and Marie-Louise and I'm very much upset. But I will remain perfectly calm till I've heard everything. Now let me have your proofs.

Mortimer: My proofs? What d'you mean? The cigarette-case. When I found the cigarette-case I naturally put two and two together.

Constance [*with her eyes flashing*]: I quite understand, but why did you make them five?

Mortimer [*emphatically, in order not to show that he is wavering*]: It isn't possible that I should have made a mistake.

Constance: Even the richest of us may err. I remember when Mr Pierpont Morgan died, he was found to own seven million dollars of worthless securities.

Mortimer [*uneasily*]: You don't know what a shock it was, Constance. I had the most implicit confidence in Marie-Louise. I was knocked endways. I've been brooding over it ever since till I was afraid I should go mad.

Constance: And do you mean to say that you've come here and made a fearful scene just because you found my cigarette case in Marie-Louise's room? I can't believe it. You're a man of the world and a business-man. You're extremely intelligent. Surely you have something to go upon. You must be holding something back. Don't be afraid of hurting my feelings. You've said so much now that I must insist on your saying everything. I want the truth and the whole truth.

[*There is a pause.* **Mortimer** *looks from* **Marie-Louise**, *who is quietly weeping, to Constance with the utmost bewilderment.*]

Mortimer: I'm afraid I've made a damned fool of myself.

Constance: I'm afraid you have.

Mortimer: I'm awfully sorry, Constance. I beg your pardon.

Constance: Oh, don't bother about me. You've exposed me to the most bitter humiliation. You've sown seeds of distrust between me and John which can never be . . . [*She looks for a word.*]

Mrs Culver [*supplying it*]: Fertilized.

Constance [*ignoring it*]: Uprooted. But I don't matter. It's Marie-Louise's pardon you must beg.

The Constant Wife

Mortimer [*humbly*]: Marie-Louise.

Marie-Louise: Don't touch me. Don't come near me.

Mortimer [*to* **Constance**, *miserably*]: You know what jealousy is.

Constance: Certainly not. I think it's a most ugly and despicable vice.

Mortimer [*to* **Marie-Louise**]: Marie-Louise, I'm sorry. Won't you forgive me?

Marie-Louise: You've insulted me before all my friends. You know how devotedly I love Constance. You might have accused me of having an affair with anyone else – but not John.

Constance: Not her greatest friend's husband. The milkman or the dustman if you like, but not her greatest friend's husband.

Mortimer: I've been a perfect swine. I don't know what came over me. I really wasn't responsible for my actions.

Marie-Louise: I've loved you all these years. No one has ever loved you as I've loved you. Oh, it's cruel, cruel.

Mortimer: Come away, darling. I can't say here what I want to say.

Marie-Louise: No, no, no.

Constance [*putting her hand on his arm, gently*]: I think you'd better leave her here for a little while, Morty. I'll talk to her when you've gone. She's naturally upset. A sensitive little thing like that.

Mortimer: We're dining with the Vancouvers at 8.15.

Constance: For eighty-thirty. I promise I'll send her home in good time to dress.

Mortimer: She'll give me another chance?

Constance: Yes, yes.

Mortimer: I'd do anything in the world for her.

[**Constance** *puts her fingers to her lips and then points significantly to the pearl chain she is wearing. For a second* **Mortimer** *does not understand, but as soon as her notion dawns on him he gives a pleased nod.*]

You're the cleverest woman in the world. [*As he goes out he stops and holds out his hand to* John.] Will you shake hands with me, old man? I made a mistake and I'm man enough to acknowledge it.

John [*very cordially*]: Not at all, old boy. I quite agree that it did look fishy, the cigarette-case. If I'd dreamt that Constance was going to leave an expensive thing like that lying about all over the place, I'm hanged if I'd have let her pinch it.

Mortimer: You don't know what a weight it is off my mind. I felt a hundred when I came here, and now I feel like a two-year-old.

[*He goes out. The moment the door is closed behind him there is a general change in every attitude. The tension disappears and there is a feeling of relief.*]

John: Constance, you're a brick. I shall never forget this. Never, so long as I live. And by George, what presence of mind you showed. I went hot and cold all over, and you never batted an eyelash.

Constance: By the way, here is your cigarette-case. You'd better have a ring made and hang it on your key-chain.

John: No, no. Keep it. I'm too old to take these risks.

Constance: By the way, did anyone see you go into Morty's house last night?

John: No, we let ourselves in with Marie-Louise's latch key.

Constance: That's all right then. If Mortimer asks the servants they can tell him nothing. I had to take that chance.

Marie-Louise [*with a little gesture of ashamed dismay*]: Oh, Constance, what must you think of me?

Constance: I? Exactly the same as I thought before. I think you're sweet, Marie-Louise.

Marie-Louise: You have every right to be angry with me.

Constance: Perhaps, but not the inclination.

Marie-Louise: Oh, it's not true. I've treated you shamefully. You've made me feel such a pig. And you had

your chance to get back on me and you didn't take it.
I'm so ashamed.

Constance [*amused*]: Because you've been having an affair
with John, or because you've been found out?

Marie-Louise: Oh, Constance, don't be heartless. Say anything you like, curse me, stamp on me, but don't smile
at me. I'm in a terrible position.

Constance: And you want me to make a scene. I know
and I sympathize. [*Very calmly*] But the fact is that
Mortimer told me nothing I didn't know before.

Marie-Louise [*aghast*]: Do you mean to say that you've
known all along?

Constance: All along, darling. I've been spending the last
six months in a desperate effort to prevent my friends
and relations from telling me your ghastly secret. It's
been very difficult sometimes. Often Mother's profound understanding of life, Martha's passion for truth
at any price, and Barbara's silent sympathy, have
almost worn me down. But until today the t's were not
definitely crossed nor the i's distinctly dotted, and I
was able to ignore the facts that were staring at me –
rather rudely, I must say – in the face.

Marie-Louise: But why, why? It's not human. Why didn't
you do anything?

Constance: That, darling, is my affair.

Marie-Louise [*thinking she understands*] Oh, I see.

Constance [*rather tartly*]: No, you don't. I have always
been absolutely faithful to John. I have not winked at
your intrigue in order to cover my own.

Marie-Louise [*beginning to be a little put out*]: I almost
think you've been laughing at me up your sleeve all
the time.

Constance [*good-humouredly*]: Oh, my dear, you mustn't
be offended just because I've taken away from you the
satisfaction of thinking that you have been deceiving
me all these months. I should hate you to think me
capable of an intentional meanness.

Marie-Louise: My head's going round and round.

Constance: Such a pretty head, too. Why don't you go and lie down? You want to look your best if you're dining with the Vancouvers.

Marie-Louise: I wonder where Mortimer is?

Constance: You know that pearl necklace you showed me the other day and you said that Mortimer thought it cost a lot of money — well, he's gone to Cartier's to buy it for you.

Marie-Louise [*excitedly*]: Oh, Constance, do you think he has?

Constance: I think all men are born with the knowledge that when they have wounded a woman's soul — and our souls are easily wounded — the only cure is a trifling, but expensive jewel.

Marie-Louise: Do you think he'll have the sense to bring it home with him so that I can wear it tonight?

Constance: Oh, my dear, don't be such a fool as to accept it with alacrity. Remember that Mortimer has grievously insulted you, he's made the most shocking accusation that a man can make against his wife, he's trampled on your love, and now he's destroyed your trust in him.

Marie-Louise: Oh, how right you are, Constance.

Constance: Surely I need not tell you what to do. Refuse to speak to him, but never let him get a word of defence in edgeways. Cry enough to make him feel what a brute he is, but not enough to make your eyes swell. Say you'll leave him and run sobbing to the door, but take care to let him stop you before you open it. Repeat yourself. Say the same thing over and over again — it wears them down — and if he answers you take no notice, but just say it again. And at last when you've reduced him to desperation, when his head is aching as though it would split, when he's sweating at every pore, when he's harassed and miserable and haggard and broken — then consent as an unmerited favour, as a sign of your forgiving temper and the sweetness of your nature, to accept, no, don't consent, deign to accept the pearl necklace for which the wretch has just paid ten thousand pounds.

Marie-Louise [*with peculiar satisfaction*]: Twelve, darling.

Constance: And don't thank him. That wouldn't be playing the game. Let him thank you for the favour you do him in allowing him to make you a paltry gift. Have you got your car here?

Marie-Louise: No, I was in such a state when I came I took a taxi.

Constance: John, do take Marie-Louise down and put her in a taxi.

John: All right.

Marie-Louise: No, not John. I couldn't. After all, I have some delicacy.

Constance: Oh, have you? Well, let Bernard go.

Bernard: I shall be pleased.

Constance [*to* **Bernard**]: But come back, won't you?

Bernard: Certainly.

Marie-Louise [*kissing* **Constance**]: This has been a lesson to me, darling. I'm not a fool, Constance. I can learn.

Constance: At least prudence, I hope.

[**Marie-Louise** *goes out followed by* **Bernard Kersal**.]

John: How did you guess that Marie-Louise had said she was dining here?

Constance: She's too crafty a woman to invent a new lie when an old one will serve.

John: It would have been awkward if Mortimer had insisted on asking Bentley if it was true.

Constance: I knew he wouldn't dare. It's only if a man's a gentleman that he won't hesitate to do an ungentlemanly thing. Mortimer is on the boundary line and it makes him careful.

Martha [*significantly*]: Don't you imagine your patients are growing a trifle restless, John?

John: I like to keep them waiting. They grow more and more nervous as the minutes pass and when I recommend an operation that will cost them two hundred and fifty pounds they are too shaken to protest.

Martha [*pursing her lips*]: I can't imagine you'll very much like to hear what I'm determined to say to Constance.

John: It's because I shrewdly suspect that you have some very unpleasant thing to say about me that I am prepared reluctantly to neglect the call of duty and listen to you with my own ears.

Constance: She's been exercising miracles of restraint for the last three months, John. I think she has a right to let herself go now.

John: If she's suffering from suppressed desires she's come to the wrong establishment. She ought to go to a psycho-analyst.

Martha: I've only got one thing to say, John, and I'm perfectly willing that you should hear it. [*To* **Constance**] I don't know what your reasons were for shielding that abominable woman. I can only suppose you wanted to avoid more scandal than was necessary . . .

Mrs Culver [*interrupting*]: Before you go any further, my dear, you must let me put my word in. [*To* **Constance**] My dear child, I beg you not to decide anything in a hurry. We must all think things over. First of all you must listen to what John has to say for himself.

Martha: What can he have to say for himself?

Constance [*ironically*]: What indeed?

John: Not the right thing anyway. I've seen too much of married life.

Constance [*interrupting, with a smile*]: Let us be just. Other people's rather than your own.

John [*going on*]: To imagine that even the Archangel Gabriel could say the right thing.

Constance: I've no reason, however, to suppose that the Archangel Gabriel could ever find himself in such a predicament.

John: I'm for it and I'm prepared to take what's coming to me.

Constance [*to the world in general*]: No man could say handsomer than that.

John: I'm expecting you to make a scene, Constance. It's your right and your privilege. I'm willing to bear it. Give me hell. I deserve it. Drag me up and down the room by the hair of the head. Kick me in the face. Stamp on me. I'll grovel. I'll eat the dust. My name is mud. Mud.

Constance: My poor John, what is there to make a scene about?

John: I know how badly I've treated you. I had a wife who was good, loving, and faithful, devoted to my interests, a perfect mother and an excellent housekeeper. A woman ten times too good for me. If I'd had the smallest spark of decency I couldn't have treated you like this. I haven't a word to say for myself.

Martha [*interrupting him*]: You've humiliated her to all her friends.

John: I've behaved neither like a gentleman nor a sportsman.

Martha: Your conduct is inexcusable.

John: I haven't a leg to stand on.

Martha: Even if you didn't love her, you might have treated her with respect.

John: I've been as heartless as a crocodile and as unscrupulous as a typhoid bacillus.

Constance: Between you, of course, you're leaving me very little to say.

Martha: There *is* nothing to say. You're quite right. This is the sort of occasion when it's beneath a woman's dignity to make a scene. It just shows how little John knows women to think that you could demean yourself to vulgar abuse. [*To* **John**] I suppose you'll have the decency to put no obstacle in the way of Constance's getting her freedom.

Mrs Culver: Oh, Constance, you're not going to divorce him?

Martha: Mother, you're so weak. How can she go on

living with a man for whom she has no respect? What would her life be with this creature whom she can only mistrust and despise? Besides, you have to think of their child. How can Constance allow her daughter to be contaminated by the society of a person of this character?

Constance: John has always been an excellent father. Let us give the devil his due.

Mrs Culver: Don't be too hard, darling. I can understand that at the moment you feel bitter, but it would be very sad if you let your bitterness warp your judgement.

Constance: I don't feel in the least bitter. I wish I looked as sweet as I feel.

Mrs Culver: You can't deceive a mother, my dear. I know the angry resentment that you feel. Under the unfortunate circumstances it's only too natural.

Constance: When I look into my heart I can't find a trace of resentment, except perhaps for John's being so stupid as to let himself be found out.

John: Let me say this in justification for myself, Constance. I did my little best to prevent it. Angels could do no more.

Constance: And angels presumably have not the pernicious habit of smoking straight-cut cigarettes.

John: When you once get the taste for them, you prefer them to gippies.

Mrs Culver: Don't be cynical, darling. That is the worst way to ease an aching heart. Come to your mother's arms, my dear, and let us have a good cry together. And then you'll feel better.

Constance: It's sweet of you, Mother, but honestly I couldn't squeeze a tear out of my eyes if my life depended on it.

Mrs Culver: And don't be too hard. Of course John is to blame. I admit that. He's been very, very naughty. But men are weak and women are so unscrupulous. I'm sure he's sorry for all the pain he's caused you.

Martha: What puzzles me is that you didn't do something

the moment you discovered that John was having an affair.

Constance: To tell you the truth, I thought it no business of mine.

Martha [*indignantly*]: Aren't you his wife?

Constance: John and I are very lucky people. Our marriage has been ideal.

Martha: How can you say that?

Constance: For five years we adored each other. That's much longer than most people do. Our honeymoon lasted five years and then we had a most extraordinary stroke of luck: we ceased to be in love with one another simultaneously.

John: I protest, Constance. I've never ceased to be absolutely devoted to you.

Constance: I never said you had, darling. I'm convinced of it. I've never ceased to be devoted to you. We've shared one another's interests, we've loved to be together, I've exulted in your success, and you've trembled in my illness. We've laughed at the same jokes and sighed over the same worries. I don't know any couple that's been bound together by a more genuine affection. But honestly, for the last ten years have you been in love with me?

John: You can't expect a man who's been married for fifteen years . . .

Constance: My dear, I'm not asking for excuses. I'm only asking for a plain answer.

John: In the long run I enjoy your society much more than anybody else's. There's no one I like so much as you. You're the prettiest woman I've ever known and I shall say the same when you're a hundred.

Constance: But does your heart leap into your mouth when you hear my footstep on the stairs, and, when I come into the room, is your first impulse to catch me in your manly arms? I haven't noticed it.

John: I don't want to make a fool of myself.

Constance: Then I think you've answered my question. You're no more in love with me than I am with you.

John: You never said a word of this before.

Constance: I think most married couples tell one another far too much. There are some things that two people may know very well, but which it's much more tactful for them to pretend they don't.

John: How did you find out?

Constance: I'll tell you. One night as we were dancing together, all at once I noticed that we weren't keeping such good step as we generally did. It was because my mind was wandering. I was thinking how it would suit me to do my hair like a woman who was dancing alongside of us. Then I looked at you and I saw you were thinking what pretty legs she'd got. I suddenly realized that you weren't in love with me any more and at the same moment I realized that it was a relief because I wasn't in love with you.

John: I must say it never occurred to me for a moment.

Constance: I know. A man thinks it quite natural that he should fall out of love with a woman, but it never strikes him for a moment that a woman can do anything so unnatural as to fall out of love with him. Don't be upset at that, darling, that is one of the charming limitations of your sex.

Martha: Do you mean Mother and me to understand that since then John has been having one affair after another and you haven't turned a hair?

Constance: Since this is the first time he's been found out, let us give him the benefit of the doubt and hope that till now he has never strayed from the strict and narrow path. You're not angry with me, John?

John: No, darling, not angry. But I am a little taken aback. I think you've been making rather a damned fool of me. It never struck me that your feelings for me had changed so much. You can't expect me to like it.

Constance: Oh, come now, you must be reasonable. You surely wouldn't wish me to have languished for all these years in a hopeless passion for you when you had nothing to give me in return but friendship and affection. Think what a bore it is to have someone in love with you whom you're not in love with.

John: I can't conceive of your ever being a bore, Constance.

Constance [*kissing her hand to him*]: Don't you realize that we must thank our lucky stars? We are the favoured of the gods. I shall never forget those five years of exquisite happiness you gave me when I loved you, and I shall never cease to be grateful to you, not because you loved me, but because you inspired me with love. Our love never degenerated into weariness. Because we ceased loving one another at the very same moment we never had to put up with quarrels and reproaches, recriminations and all the other paraphernalia of a passion that has ceased on one side and is still alive and eager on the other. Our love was like a crossword puzzle in which we both hit upon the last word at the same moment. That is why our lives since have been so happy; that is why ours is a perfect marriage.

Martha: Do you mean to say that it meant nothing to you when you found out that John was carrying on with Marie-Louise?

Constance: Human nature is very imperfect. I'm afraid I must admit that at the first moment I was vexed. But only at the first moment. Then I reflected that it was most unreasonable to be angry with John for giving to another something that I had no use for. That would be too much like a dog in the manger. And then I was fond enough of John to be willing that he should be happy in his own way. And if he was going to indulge in an intrigue ... Isn't that the proper phrase, John?

John: I have not yet made up my mind whether it really is an indulgence.

Constance: Then it was much better that the object of his affections should be so intimate a friend of mine that I could keep a maternal eye on him.

John: Really, Constance.

Constance: Marie-Louise is very pretty so that my self-esteem was not offended, and so rich that it was certain John would have no reason to squander money on her to the inconvenience of myself. She's not clever enough to acquire any ascendancy over him, and so long as I kept his heart I was quite willing that she should have his senses. If you wanted to deceive me, John, I couldn't have chosen anyone with whom I would more willingly be deceived than Marie-Louise.

John: I don't gather that you have been very grossly deceived, darling. You have such penetration that when you look at me I feel as though I were shivering without a stitch of clothing on.

Mrs Culver: I don't approve of your attitude, Constance. In my day when a young wife discovered that her husband had been deceiving her, she burst into a flood of tears and went to stay with her mother for three weeks, not returning to her husband till he had been brought to a proper state of abjection and repentance.

Martha: Are we to understand, then, that you are not going to divorce John?

Constance: You know, I can never see why a woman should give up a comfortable home, a considerable part of her income and the advantage of having a man about to do all the tiresome and disagreeable things for her, because he has been unfaithful to her. She's merely cutting off her nose to spite her face.

Martha: I am at a loss for words. I cannot conceive how a woman of any spirit can sit down and allow her husband to make a perfect damned fool of her.

Constance: You've been very stupid, my poor John. In the ordinary affairs of life stupidity is much more tiresome than wickedness. You can mend the vicious, but what in Heaven's name are you to do with the foolish?

John: I've been a fool, Constance. I know it, but I'm capable of learning by experience, so I can't be a damned fool.

The Constant Wife

Constance: You mean that in the future you'll be more careful to cover your tracks?

Mrs Culver: Oh, no, Constance, he means that this has been a lesson to him, and that in the future you'll have no cause for complaint.

Constance: I've always been given to understand that men only abandon their vices when advancing years have made them a burden rather than a pleasure. John, I'm happy to say, is still in the flower of his age. I suppose you give yourself another fifteen years, John, don't you?

John: Really, Constance, I don't know what you mean. The things you say sometimes are positively embarrassing.

Constance: I think at all events we may take it that Marie-Louise will have more than one successor.

John: Constance, I give you my word of honour . . .

Constance [*interrupting*]: That is the only gift you can make for which I can find no use. You see, so long as I was able to pretend a blissful ignorance of your goings-on we could all be perfectly happy. You were enjoying yourself and I received a lot of sympathy as the outraged wife. But now I do see that the position is very difficult. You have put me in a position that is neither elegant nor dignified.

John: I'm awfully sorry, Constance.

Martha: You're going to leave him?

Constance: No, I'm not going to leave him. John, you remember that Barbara offered to take me into her business? I refused. Well, I've changed my mind and I'm going to accept.

John: But why? I don't see your point.

Constance: I'm not prepared any more to be entirely dependent upon you, John.

John: But, my dear, everything I earn is at your disposal. It's a pleasure for me to provide for your wants. Heaven knows, they're not very great.

Constance: I know. Come, John, I've been very reason-

able, haven't I? Don't try and thwart me when I want
to do something on which I've set my heart.

[*There is an instant's pause.*]

John: I don't understand. But if you put it like that, I
haven't a word to say. Of course, you must do exactly
as you wish.

Constance: That's a dear. Now go back to your patients
or else I shall have to keep you as well as myself.

John: Will you give me a kiss?

Constance: Why not?

John [*kissing her*]: It's peace between us?

Constance: Peace and goodwill.

[**John** *goes out.*]

He is rather sweet, isn't he?

Mrs Culver: What have you got on your mind, Constance?

Constance: I, Mother? [*Teasing her*] What do you suspect?

Mrs Culver: I don't like the look of you.

Constance: I'm sorry for that. Most people find me far
from plain.

Mrs Culver: You've got some devilry in mind, but for the
life of me I can't guess it.

Martha: I can't see what you expect to get out of working
with Barbara.

Constance: Between a thousand and fifteen hundred a
year, I believe.

Martha: I wasn't thinking of the money, and you know
it.

Constance: I'm tired of being the modern wife.

Martha: What do you mean by the modern wife?

Constance: A prostitute who doesn't deliver the goods.

Mrs Culver: My dear, what would your father say if he
heard you say such things?

Constance: Darling, need we conjecture the remarks of a
gentleman who's been dead for five and twenty years?
Had he any gift for repartee?

Mrs Culver: None whatever. He was good, but he was
stupid. That is why the gods loved him and he died
young.

The Constant Wife

[**Bernard Kersal** *opens the door and looks in.*]

Bernard: May I come in?

Constance: Oh, there you are. I wondered what had become of you.

Bernard: When Marie-Louise saw my car at the door she asked me to drive her. I couldn't very well refuse.

Constance: So you took her home.

Bernard: No, she said she was in such a state she must have her hair washed. I drove her to a place in Bond Street.

Constance: And what did she say to you?

Bernard: She said, I don't know what you must think of me.

Constance: That is what most women say to a man when his opinion doesn't matter two straws to them. And what did you answer?

Bernard: Well, I said, I prefer not to offer an opinion on a matter which is no business of mine.

Constance: Dear Bernard, one of the things I like most in you is that you always remain so perfectly in character. If the heavens fell you would still remain the perfect English gentleman.

Bernard: I thought it the most tactful thing to say.

Constance: Well, Mother, I won't detain you any longer. I know that you and Martha have a thousand things to do.

Mrs Culver: I'm glad you reminded me. Come, Martha. Good-bye, darling. Good-bye, Mr Kersal.

Bernard: Good-bye.

Constance [*to Martha*]: Good-bye, dear. Thank you for all your sympathy. You've been a great help in my hour of need.

Martha: I don't understand and it's no good saying I do.

Constance: Bless you.

[**Mrs Culver** *and* **Martha** *go out.* **Bernard** *closes the door after them.*]

Shall we be very late?

Bernard: So late that it doesn't matter if we're a little later. I have something important to say to you.

Constance [*teasing him a' little*]: Important to me or important to you?

Bernard: I can't tell you how distressed I was at that terrible scene.

Constance: Oh, didn't you think it had its lighter moments?

Bernard: It's only this afternoon I learned the truth, and then I never imagined for a moment that you knew it, too. I can't tell you how brave I think it of you to have borne all this torture with a smiling face. If I admired you before, I admire you ten times more now.

Constance: You're very sweet, Bernard.

Bernard: My heart bleeds when I think of what you've gone through.

Constance: It's not a very good plan to take other people's misfortunes too much to heart.

Bernard: Hardly an hour ago I told you that if ever you wanted me I was only too anxious to do anything in the world for you. I little thought then that the time would come so soon. There's no reason now why I shouldn't tell you of the love that consumes me. Oh, Constance, come to me. You know that if things were as I thought they were between you and John nothing would have induced me to say a word. But now he has no longer any claims on you. He doesn't love you. Why should you go on wasting your life with a man who is capable of exposing you to all this humiliation? You know how long and tenderly I've loved you. You can trust yourself to me. I'll give my whole life to making you forget the anguish you've endured. Will you marry me, Constance?

Constance: My dear, John may have behaved very badly, but he's still my husband.

Bernard: Only in name. You've done everything in your power to save a scandal and now if you ask him to let himself be divorced he's bound to consent.

The Constant Wife

Constance: Do you really think John has behaved so very badly to me?

Bernard [*astonished*]: You don't mean to say that you have any doubts in your mind about his relationship with Maria-Louise?

Constance: None.

Bernard: Then what in God's name do you mean?

Constance: My dear Bernard, have you ever considered what marriage is among well-to-do people? In the working classes a woman cooks her husband's dinner, washes for him, and darns his socks. She looks after the children and makes their clothes. She gives good value for the money she costs. But what is a wife in our class? Her house is managed by servants, nurses look after her children, if she has resigned herself to having any, and as soon as they are old enough she packs them off to school. Let us face it, she is no more than the mistress of a man of whose desire she has taken advantage to insist on a legal ceremony that will prevent him from discarding her when his desire has ceased.

Bernard: She's also his companion and his helpmate.

Constance: My dear, any sensible man would sooner play bridge at his club than with his wife, and he'd always rather play golf with a man than with a woman. A paid secretary is a far better helpmate than a loving spouse. When all is said and done, the modern wife is nothing but a parasite.

Bernard: I don't agree with you.

Constance: You see, my poor friend, you are in love and your judgement is confused.

Bernard: I don't understand what you mean.

Constance: John gives me board and lodging, money for my clothes and my amusements, a car to drive in, and a certain position in the world. He's bound to do all that because fifteen years ago he was madly in love with me, and he undertook it; though, if you'd asked him, he would certainly have acknowledged that nothing is so fleeting as that particular form of madness called love. It was either very generous of him or very imprudent. Don't you think it would be rather shabby of me to take advantage now of his generosity or his want of foresight?

Bernard: In what way?

Constance: He paid a very high price for something that he couldn't get cheaper. He no longer wants that. Why should I resent it? I know as well as anybody else that desire is fleeting. It comes and goes and no man can understand why. The only thing that's certain is that when it's gone it's gone forever. So long as John continues to provide for me what right have I to complain that he is unfaithful to me? He bought a toy, and if he no longer wants to play with it, why should he? He paid for it.

Bernard: That might be all right if a man had only to think about himself. What about the woman?

Constance: I don't think you need waste too much sympathy on her. Like ninety-nine girls out of a hundred, when I married I looked upon it as the only easy, honourable, and lucrative calling open to me. When the average woman who has been married for fifteen years discovers her husband's infidelity it is not her heart that is wounded but her vanity. If she had any sense, she would regard it merely as one of the necessary inconveniences of an otherwise pleasant profession.

Bernard: Then the long and short of it is that you don't love me.

Constance: You think that my principles are all moonshine?

Bernard: I don't think they would have much influence if you were as crazy about me as I am about you. Do you still love John?

Constance: I'm very fond of him, he makes me laugh, and we get on together like a house on fire, but I'm not in love with him.

Bernard: And is that enough for you? Isn't the future sometimes a trifle desolate? Don't you want love?

[*A pause. She gives him a long reflective look.*]

Constance [*charmingly*]: If I did I should come to you for it, Bernard.

Bernard: Constance, what do you mean? Is it possible that you could ever care for me? Oh, my darling, I worship the ground you tread on.

[*He seizes her in his arms and kisses her passionately.*]

Constance [*releasing herself*]: Oh, my dear, don't be so sudden. I should despise myself entirely if I were unfaithful to John so long as I am entirely dependent on him.

Bernard: But if you love me?

Constance: I never said I did. But even if I did, so long as John provides me with all the necessities of existence I wouldn't be unfaithful. It all comes down to the economic situation. He has bought my fidelity and I should be worse than a harlot if I took the price he paid and did not deliver the goods.

Bernard: Do you mean to say there's no hope for me at all?

Constance: The only hope before you at the moment is to start for Ranelagh before the game is over.

Bernard: Do you still want to go?

Constance: Yes.

Bernard: Very well. [*With a burst of passion*] I love you.

Constance: Then go down and start up the car, put a spot of oil in the radiator or something, and I'll join you in a minute. I want to telephone.

Bernard: Very well.

[*He goes out.* **Constance** *takes up the telephone.*]

Constance: Mayfair 2646 ... Barbara? It's Constance. That offer you made me a fortnight ago – is it still open? Well, I want to accept it ... No, no, nothing has happened. John is very well. He's always sweet, you know. It's only that I want to earn my own living. When can I start? The sooner the better.

Act Three

The scene is still the same. A year has passed. It is afternoon.

[**Constance** *is seated at a desk writing letters.* **Bentley** *shows in* **Barbara Fawcett** *and* **Martha**.]

Bentley: Mrs Fawcett and Miss Culver.

[*Exit* **Bentley**.]

Constance: Oh! Sit down, I'm just finishing a note.

Barbara: We met on the doorstep.

Martha: I thought I'd just look round and see if there was anything I could do to help you before you start.

Constance: That's very nice of you, Martha. I really don't think there is. I'm packed and ready, and for once I don't believe I've forgotten one of the things I shan't want.

Barbara: I felt I must run in to say goodbye to you.

Constance: Now, my dear, you mustn't neglect your work the moment my back is turned.

Barbara: Well, it's partly the work that's brought me. An order has just come in for a new house and they want an Italian room.

Constance: I don't like that look in your beady eye, Barbara.

Barbara: Well, it struck me that as you're going to Italy you might go round the shops and buy any nice pieces that you can find.

Constance: Perish the thought. I've worked like a dog for a year and last night at six o'clock I downed tools. I stripped off my grimy overalls, wrung the sweat from my honest brow, and scrubbed my horny hands. You said I could take six weeks' holiday.

Barbara: I admit that you've thoroughly earned it.

Constance: When I closed the shop-door behind me, I ceased to be a British working-man and resumed the position of a perfect English lady.

Martha: I never saw you in such spirits.

Constance: Something accomplished, something done. But what I was coming to was this: for the next six weeks I refuse to give a moment's thought to bathrooms or wallpapers, kitchen sinks, scullery floors, curtains, cushions, and refrigerators.

Barbara: I wasn't asking you to. I only wanted you to get some of that painted Italian furniture and a few mirrors.

Constance: No, I've worked hard and I've enjoyed my work, and now I'm going to enjoy a perfect holiday.

Barbara: Oh, well, have it your own way.

Martha: Constance dear, I think there's something you ought to know.

Constance: I should have thought you had discovered by now that I generally know the things I ought to know.

Martha: You'll never guess whom I saw in Bond Street this morning.

Constance: Yes, I shall. Marie-Louise.

Martha: Oh!

Constance: I'm sorry to disappoint you, darling. She rang me up an hour ago.

Martha: But I thought she wasn't coming back for another month. She was going to stay away a year.

Constance: She arrived last night and I'm expecting her every minute.

Martha: Here?

Constance: Yes. She said she simply must run in and see me before I left.

Martha: I wonder what she wants.

Constance: Perhaps to pass the time of day. I think it's rather sweet of her, considering how busy she must be on getting back after so long.

Barbara: She's been all over the place, hasn't she?

Constance: Yes, she's been in Malaya; Mortimer has

interests there, you know, and in China, and now they've just come from India.

Martha: I often wondered if it was at your suggestion that they set off on that long tour immediately after that unfortunate scene.

Constance: Which, you must confess, no one enjoyed more than you, darling.

Barbara: It was certainly the most sensible thing they could do.

Martha: Of course you know your own business best, darling, but don't you think it's a little unfortunate that you should be going away for six weeks just as she comes back?

Constance: We working-women have to take our holidays when we can.

Barbara: Surely John has had his lesson. He's not going to make a fool of himself a second time.

Martha: Do you think he has really got over his infatuation, Constance?

Constance: I don't know at all. But here he is, you'd better ask him.

[*As she says these words,* **John** *enters.*]

John: Ask him what?

Martha [*not at all at a loss*]: I was just wondering what you'd do with yourself during Constance's absence.

John: I've got a lot of work, you know, and I shall go to the club a good deal.

Martha: It seems a pity that you weren't able to arrange things so that you and Constance should take your holidays together.

Barbara: Don't blame me for that. I was quite willing to make my arrangements to suit Constance.

Constance: You see, I wanted to go to Italy and the only places John likes on the Continent are those in which it's only by an effort of the imagination that you can tell you're not in England.

Martha: What about Helen?

Constance: We've taken a house at Henley for August.

John can play golf and go on the river, and I shall be able to come up to town every day to look after the business.

Barbara: Well, dear, I'll leave you. I hope you'll have a wonderful holiday. You've deserved it. Do you know, I think I'm a very clever woman, John, to have persuaded Constance to work. She's been absolutely invaluable to me.

John: I never liked the idea and I'm not going to say I did.

Barbara: Haven't you forgiven me yet?

John: She insisted on it and I had to make the best of a bad job.

Barbara: Goodbye.

Constance [*kissing her*]: Goodbye, dear. Take care of yourself.

Martha: I'll come with you, Barbara. Mother said she'd look in for a minute to say goodbye to you.

Constance: Oh, all right. Goodbye.

[*She kisses the two and accompanies them to the door. They go out.*]

John: I say, Constance, I thought you had to go now because Barbara couldn't possibly get away.

Constance: Did I say that?

John: Certainly.

Constance: Oh!

John: If I'd dreamt that you could just as easily take your holiday when I take mine . . .

Constance [*interrupting*]: Don't you think it's a mistake for husbands and wives to take their holidays together? The only reason one takes a holiday is for rest and change and recreation. Do you think a man really gets that when he goes away with his wife?

John: It depends on the wife.

Constance: I know nothing more depressing than the sight of all those couples in a hotel dining-room, one little couple to one little table, sitting opposite to one another without a word to say.

John: Oh, nonsense. You often see couples who are very jolly and cheerful.

Constance: Yes, I know, but look closely at the lady's wedding ring and you'll see that it rests uneasily on the hand it adorns.

John: We always get on like a house on fire and when I slipped a wedding ring on your finger a bishop supervised the process. You're not going to tell me that I bore *you*.

Constance: On the contrary, you tickle me to death. It's that unhappy modesty of mine: I was afraid that you could have too much of my society. I thought it would refresh you if I left you to your own devices for a few weeks.

John: If you go on pulling my leg so persistently I shall be permanently deformed.

Constance: Anyhow, it's too late now. My bags are packed, my farewells made, and nothing bores people so much as to see you tomorrow when they've made up their minds to get on without you for a month.

John: H'm. Eyewash ... Look here, Constance, there's something I want to say to you.

Constance: Yes?

John: Do you know that Marie-Louise has come back?

Constance: Yes. She said she'd try and look in to say how do you do before I started. It'll be nice to see her again after so long.

John: I want you to do something for me, Constance.

Constance: What is it?

John: Well, you've been a perfect brick to me, and hang it all, I can't take advantage of your good nature. I must do the square thing.

Constance: I'm afraid I don't quite understand.

John: I haven't seen Marie-Louise since that day when Mortimer came here and made such a fool of himself. She's been away for nearly a year and taking all things into consideration I think it would be a mistake to resume the relations that we were on then.

339

Constance: What makes you think she wishes to?

John: The fact that she rang you up the moment she arrived looks ominous to me.

Constance: Ominous? You know some women can't see a telephone without taking the receiver off and then, when the operator says, 'Number, please,' they have to say something. I dare say ours was the first that occurred to Marie-Louise.

John: It's no good blinking the fact that Marie-Louise was madly in love with me.

Constance: Well, we can neither of us blame her for that.

John: I don't want to be unkind, but after all, circumstances have forced a break upon us and I think we had better look upon it as permanent.

Constance: Of course you must please yourself.

John: I'm not thinking of myself, Constance. I'm thinking partly of course of Marie-Louise's good, but, I confess, chiefly of you. I could never look you in the face again if everything between Marie-Louise and me were not definitely finished.

Constance: I should hate you to lose so harmless and inexpensive a pleasure.

John: Of course it'll be painful, but if one's made up one's mind to do a thing I think it's much better to do it quickly.

Constance: I think you're quite right. I'll tell you what I'll do, as soon as Marie-Louise comes I'll make an excuse and leave you alone with her.

John: That wasn't exactly my idea.

Constance: Oh?

John: It's the kind of thing that a woman can do so much better than a man. It struck me that it would come better from you than from me.

Constance: Oh, did it?

John: It's a little awkward for me, but it would be quite easy for you to say . . . well, you know the sort of thing, that you have your self-respect to think of and to cut a long story short, she must either give me up or you'll raise hell.

Constance: But you know what a soft heart I have. If she bursts into tears and says she can't live without you I shall feel so sorry for her that I shall say, Well, damn it all, keep him.

John: You wouldn't do me a dirty trick like that, Constance.

Constance: You know that your happiness is my chief interest in life.

John [*after a moment's hesitation*]: Constance, I will be perfectly frank with you. I'm fed up with Marie-Louise.

Constance: Darling, why didn't you say that at once?

John: Be a sport, Constance. You know that's not the kind of thing one can say to a woman.

Constance: I admit it's not the kind of thing she's apt to take very well.

John: Women are funny. When they're tired of you they tell you so without a moment's hesitation and if you don't like it you can lump it. But if you're tired of them you're a brute and a beast and boiling oil's too good for you.

Constance: Very well, leave it to me. I'll do it.

John: You're a perfect brick. But you'll let her down gently, won't you? I wouldn't hurt her feelings for the world. She's a nice little thing, Constance.

Constance: Sweet.

John: And it's hard luck on her.

Constance: Rotten.

John: Make her understand that I'm more sinned against than sinning. I don't want her to think too badly of me.

Constance: Of course not.

John: But be quite sure it's definite.

Constance: Leave it to me.

John: You're a ripper, Constance. By George, no man could want a better wife.

[*The* **Butler** *introduces* **Marie-Louise.**]

Butler: Mrs Durham.

The Constant Wife

[*The two women embrace warmly*.]

Marie-Louise: Darling, how perfectly divine to see you again. It's too, too wonderful.

Constance: My dear, how well you're looking. Are those the new pearls?

Marie-Louise: Aren't they sweet? But Mortimer bought me the most heavenly emeralds when we were in India. Oh, John, how are you?

John: Oh, I'm all right, thanks.

Marie-Louise: Aren't you a little fatter than when I saw you last?

John: Certainly not.

Marie-Louise: I've lost pounds. [*To* **Constance**] I'm so glad I caught you. I should have been so disappointed to miss you. [*To* **John**] Where are you going?

John: Nowhere. Constance is going alone.

Marie-Louise: Is she? How perfectly divine. I suppose you can't get away. Are you making pots of money?

John: I get along. Will you forgive me if I leave you? I've got to be off.

Marie-Louise: Of course. You're always busy, aren't you?

John: Goodbye.

Marie-Louise: I hope we shall see something of you while Constance is away.

John: Thank you very much.

Marie-Louise: Mortimer's golf has improved. He'd love to play with you.

John: Oh, yes, I should love it.

[*He goes out.*]

Marie-Louise: I did so hope to find you alone. Constance, I've got heaps and heaps to tell you. Isn't it tactful of John to leave us? First of all I want to tell you how splendidly everything has turned out. You know you were quite right. I'm so glad I took your advice and made Mortimer take me away for a year.

Constance: Mortimer is no fool.

Marie-Louise: Oh, no, for a man he's really quite clever. I gave him hell, you know, for ever having suspected me, and at last he was just eating out of my hand. But I could see he wasn't quite sure of me. You know what men are – when they once get an idea in their heads it's dreadfully difficult for them to get it out again. But the journey was an inspiration; I was absolutely angelic all the time, and he made a lot of money, so everything in the garden was rosy.

Constance: I'm very glad.

Marie-Louise: I owe it all to you, Constance. I made Mortimer buy you a perfectly divine star sapphire in Ceylon. I told him he owed you some sort of reparation for the insult he'd put upon you. It cost a hundred and twenty pounds, darling, and we're taking it to Cartier's to have it set.

Constance: How thrilling.

Marie-Louise: You mustn't think I'm ungrateful. Now listen, Constance, I want to tell you at once that you needn't distress yourself about me and John.

Constance: I never did.

Marie-Louise: I know I behaved like a little beast, but I never thought you'd find out. If I had, well, you know me well enough to be positive that nothing would have induced me to have anything to do with him.

Constance: You're very kind.

Marie-Louise: I want you to do something for me, Constance. Will you?

Constance: I'm always eager to oblige a friend.

Marie-Louise: Well, you know what John is. Of course he's a dear and all that kind of thing, but the thing's over and it's best that he should realize it at once.

Constance: Over?

Marie-Louise: Of course I know he's head over heels in love with me still. I saw that the moment I came into the room. One can't blame him for that, can one?

Constance: Men do find you fascinating.

Marie-Louise: But one has to think of oneself sometimes in this world. He must see that it could never be the same after we discovered that you knew all about it.

343

Constance: I kept it from you as long as I could.

Marie-Louise: One couldn't help feeling then that you were rather making fools of us. It seemed to take the romance away, if you see what I mean.

Constance: Dimly.

Marie-Louise: You know, I wouldn't hurt John's feelings for the world, but it's no good beating about the bush and I'm quite determined to have the thing finished and done with before you go.

Constance: This is very sudden. I'm afraid it'll be an awful shock to John.

Marie-Louise: I've quite made up my mind.

Constance: There isn't much time for a very long and moving scene, but I'll see if John is in still. Could you manage it in ten minutes?

Marie-Louise: Oh, but I can't see him. I want you to tell him.

Constance: Me!

Marie-Louise: You know him so well, you know just the sort of things to say to him. It's not very nice telling a man who adores you that you don't care for him in that way any more. It's so much easier for a third party.

Constance: Do you really think so?

Marie-Louise: I'm positive of it. You see, you can say that for your sake I've made up my mind that from now on we can be nothing but friends. You've been so wonderful to both of us, it would be dreadful if we didn't play the game now. Say that I shall always think of him tenderly and that he's the only man I've ever really loved, but that we must part.

Constance: But if he insists on seeing you?

Marie-Louise: It's no good, Constance, I can't see him. I shall only cry and get my eyes all bunged up. You will do it for me, darling. Please.

Constance: I will.

Marie-Louise: I got the most divine evening frock in pale green satin on my way through Paris, and it would look too sweet on you. Would you like me to give it to you? I've only worn it once.

Constance: Now tell me the real reason why you're so determined to get rid of John without a moment's delay.

[**Marie-Louise** *looks at her and gives a little roguish smile.*]

Marie-Louise: Swear you won't tell.

Constance: On my honour.

Marie-Louise: Well, my dear, we met a perfectly divine young man in India. He was A.D.C. to one of the governors and he came home on the same boat with us. He simply adores me.

Constance: And of course you adore him.

Marie-Louise: My dear, I'm absolutely mad about him. I don't know what's going to happen.

Constance: I think we can both give a pretty shrewd guess.

Marie-Louise: It's simply awful to have a temperament like mine. Of course you can't understand, you're cold.

Constance [*very calmly*]: You're an immoral little beast, Marie-Louise.

Marie-Louise: Oh, I'm not. I have affairs – but I'm not promiscuous.

Constance: I should respect you more if you were an honest prostitute. She at least does what she does to earn her bread and butter. You take everything from your husband and give him nothing that he pays for. You are no better than a vulgar cheat.

Marie-Louise [*surprised and really hurt*]: Constance, how can you say such things to me? I think it's terribly unkind of you. I thought you liked me.

Constance: I do. I think you a liar, a humbug, and a parasite, but I like you.

Marie-Louise: You can't if you think such dreadful things about me.

Constance: I do. You're good-tempered and generous and

The Constant Wife

sometimes amusing. I even have a certain affection for
you.

Marie-Louise [*smiling*]: I don't believe you mean a word
you say. You know how devoted I am to you.

Constance: I take people as they are and I dare say that
in another twenty years you'll be the pink of propriety.

Marie-Louise: Darling, I knew you didn't mean it, but
you will have your little joke.

Constance: Now run along, darling, and I'll break the
news to John.

Marie-Louise: Well, goodbye, and be gentle with him.
There is no reason why we shouldn't spare him as
much as possible. [*She turns to go and at the door –
stops.*] Of course I've often wondered why with your
looks you don't have more success than you do. I know
now.

Constance: Tell me.

Marie-Louise: You see – you're a humourist and that
always puts men off.

  [*She goes out. In a moment the door is cautiously
  opened and* **John** *puts his head in.*]

John: Has she gone?

Constance: Come in. A fine night and all's well.

John [*entering*]: I heard the door bang. You broke it to
her?

Constance: I broke it.

John: Was she awfully upset?

Constance: Of course it was a shock, but she kept a stiff
upper lip.

John: Did she cry?

Constance: No. Not exactly. To tell you the truth I think
she was stunned by the blow. But of course when she
gets home and realizes the full extent of her loss, she'll
cry like anything.

John: I hate to see a woman cry.

Constance: It is painful, isn't it? But of course it's a relief
to the nerves.

John: I think you're rather cool about it, Constance. I am

346

not feeling any too comfortable. I shouldn't like her to think I'd treated her badly.

Constance: I think she quite understands that you're doing it for my sake. She knows that you have still a very great regard for her.

John: But you made it quite definite, didn't you?

Constance: Oh, quite.

John: I'm really very much obliged to you, Constance.

Constance: Not at all.

John: At all events I'm glad to think that you'll be able to set out on your holiday with a perfectly easy mind. By the way, do you want any money? I'll write you a cheque at once.

Constance: Oh, no, thank you. I've got plenty. I've earned fourteen hundred pounds during this year that I've been working.

John: Have you, by Jove? That's a very considerable sum.

Constance: I'm taking two hundred of it for my holiday. I've spent two hundred on my clothes and on odds and ends and the remaining thousand I've paid into your account this morning for my board and lodging during the last twelve months.

John: Nonsense, darling. I won't hear of such a thing. I don't want you to pay for your board and lodging.

Constance: I insist.

John: Don't you love me any more?

Constance: What has that to do with it? Oh, you think a woman can only love a man if he keeps her. Isn't that rating your powers of fascination too modestly? What about your charm and good humour?

John: Don't be absurd, Constance. I can perfectly well afford to support you in your proper station. To offer me a thousand pounds for your board and lodging is almost insulting.

Constance: Don't you think it's the kind of insult you could bring yourself to swallow? One can do a lot of amusing things with a thousand pounds.

John: I wouldn't dream of taking it. I never liked the idea

of your going into business. I thought you had quite
enough to do looking after the house and so forth.

Constance: Have you been less comfortable since I began
working?

John: No, I can't say I have.

Constance: You can take my word for it, a lot of
incompetent women talk a great deal of nonsense about
housekeeping. If you know your job and have good
servants it can be done in ten minutes a day.

John: Anyhow, you wanted to work and I yielded. I
thought in point of fact it would be a very pleasant
occupation for you, but heaven knows I wasn't expecting to profit financially by it.

Constance: No, I'm sure you weren't.

John: Constance, I could never help thinking that your
determination had something to do with Marie-Louise.
[*There is a moment's pause and when* **Constance**
speaks it is not without seriousness.]

Constance: Haven't you wondered why I never reproached you for your affair with Marie-Louise?

John: Yes. I could only ascribe it to your unfathomable
goodness.

Constance: You were wrong. I felt I hadn't the right to
reproach you.

John: What do you mean, Constance? You had every
right. We behaved like a couple of swine. I may be a
dirty dog, but, thank God, I know I'm a dirty dog.

Constance: You no longer desired me. How could I blame
you for that? But if you didn't desire me, what use was
I to you? You've seen how small a share I take in
providing you with the comfort of a well-ordered home.

John: You were the mother of my child.

Constance: Let us not exaggerate the importance of that,
John. I performed a natural and healthy function of my
sex. And all the tiresome part of looking after the child
when she was born I placed in the hands of much more
competent persons. Let us face it, I was only a parasite
in your house. You had entered into legal obligations

that prevented you from turning me adrift, but I owe you a debt of gratitude for never letting me see by word or gesture that I was no more than a costly and at times inconvenient ornament.

John: I never looked upon you as an inconvenient ornament. And I don't know what you mean by being a parasite. Have I ever in any way suggested that I grudged a penny that I spent on you?

Constance [*with mock amazement*]: Do you mean to say that I ascribed to your beautiful manners what was only due to your stupidity? Are you as great a fool as the average man who falls for the average woman's stupendous bluff that just because he's married her he must provide for her wants and her luxuries, sacrifice his pleasures and comfort and convenience, and that he must look upon it as a privilege that she allows him to be her slave and bondman? Come, come, John, pull yourself together. You're a hundred years behind the times. Now that women have broken down the walls of the harem they must take the rough and tumble of the street.

John: You forget all sorts of things. Don't you think a man may have gratitude to a woman for the love he has had for her in the past?

Constance: I think gratitude is often very strong in men so long as it demands from them no particular sacrifices.

John: Well, it's a curious way of looking at things, but obviously I have reason to be thankful for it. But after all you knew what was going on long before it came out. What happened then that made you make up your mind to go into business?

Constance: I am naturally a lazy woman. So long as appearances were saved I was prepared to take all I could get and give nothing in return. I was a parasite, but I knew it. But when we reached a situation where only your politeness or your lack of intelligence prevented you from throwing the fact in my teeth, I changed my mind. I thought that I should very much like to be in a position where, if I felt inclined to, I could tell you, with calm and courtesy, but with determination – to go to hell.

John: And are you in that position now?

Constance: Precisely. I owe you nothing. I am able to keep myself. For the last year I have paid my way. There is only one freedom that is really important and that is economic freedom, for in the long run the man who pays the piper calls the tune. Well, I have that freedom, and upon my soul it's the most enjoyable sensation I can remember since I ate my first strawberry ice.

John: You know, I would sooner you had made me scenes for a month on end like any ordinary woman and nagged my life out than that you should harbour this cold rancour against me.

Constance: My poor darling, what are you talking about? Have you known me for fifteen years and do you think me capable of the commonness of insincerity? I harbour no rancour. Why, my dear, I'm devoted to you.

John: Do you mean to tell me that you've done all this without any intention of making me feel a perfect cad?

Constance: On my honour. If I look in my heart I can only find in it affection for you and the most kindly and charitable feelings. Don't you believe me?

[*He looks at her for a moment and then makes a little gesture of bewilderment.*]

John: Yes, oddly enough, I do. You are a remarkable woman, Constance.

Constance: I know, but keep it to yourself. You don't want to give a dog a bad name.

John [*with an affectionate smile*]: I wish I could get away. I don't half like the idea of your travelling by yourself.

Constance: Oh, but I'm not. Didn't I tell you?

John: No.

Constance: I meant to. I'm going with Bernard.

John: Oh! You never said so. Who else?

Constance: Nobody.

John: Oh! [*He is rather taken aback at the news.*] Isn't that rather odd?

Constance: No. Why?

John [*not knowing at all how to take it*]: Well, it's not usual for a young woman to take a six weeks' holiday with a man who can hardly be described as old enough to be her father.

Constance: Bernard's just about the same age as you.

John: Don't you think it'll make people gossip a bit?

Constance: I haven't gone out of my way to spread the news. In fact, now I come to think of it, I haven't told anyone but you, and you, I am sure, will be discreet.

[*John suddenly feels that his collar is a little too tight for him, and with his fingers he tries to loosen it.*]

John: You're pretty certain to be seen by someone who knows you and they're bound to talk.

Constance: Oh, I don't think so. You see we're motoring all the way and we neither of us care for frequented places. One of the advantages of having really nice friends like ours is that you can always be certain of finding them at the fashionable resorts at the very moment when everybody you know is there.

John: Of course I am not so silly as to think that because a man and a woman go away together it is necessary to believe the worst about them, but you can't deny that it is rather unconventional. I wouldn't for a moment suggest that there'll be anything between you, but it's inevitable that ordinary persons should think there was.

Constance [*as cool as a cucumber*]: I've always thought that ordinary persons had more sense than the clever ones are ready to credit them with.

John [*deliberately*]: What on earth do you mean?

Constance: Why, of course we're going as man and wife, John.

The Constant Wife

John: Don't be a fool, Constance. You don't know what you're talking about. That's not funny at all.

Constance: But, my poor John, whom do you take us for? Am I so unattractive that what I'm telling you is incredible? Why else should I go with Bernard? If I merely wanted a companion I'd go with a woman. We could have headaches together and have our hair washed at the same place and copy one another's nightdresses. A woman's a much better travelling companion than a man.

John: I may be very stupid, but I don't seem to be able to understand what you're saying. Do you really mean me to believe that Bernard Kersal is your lover?

Constance: Certainly not.

John: Then what *are* you talking about?

Constance: My dear, I can't put it any plainer. I'm going away for six weeks' holiday and Bernard has very kindly offered to come with me.

John: And where do I come in?

Constance: You don't come in. You stay at home and look after your patients.

John [*trying his best to control himself*]: I flatter myself I'm a sensible man. I'm not going to fly into a passion. Many men would stamp and rave or break the furniture. I have no intention of being melodramatic, but you must allow me to say that what you've just told me is very surprising.

Constance: Just for a moment, perhaps, but I'm sure you have only to familiarize yourself with the notion in order to become reconciled to it.

John: I'm doubtful whether I shall have time to do that, for I feel uncommonly as though 1 were about to have an apoplectic stroke.

Constance: Undo your collar then. Now I come to look at you I confess that you are more than usually red in the face.

John: What makes you think that I am going to allow you to go?

Constance [*good-humouredly*]: Chiefly the fact that you can't prevent me.

John: I can't bring myself to believe that you mean what you say. I don't know what ever put such an idea into your head.

Constance [*casually*]: I thought a change might do me good.

John: Nonsense.

Constance: Why? You did. Don't you remember? You were getting rather flat and stale. Then you had an affair with Marie-Louise and you were quite another man. Gay and amusing, full of life, and much more agreeable to live with. The moral effect on you was quite remarkable.

John: It's different for a man than for a woman.

Constance: Are you thinking of the possible consequences? We have long passed the Victorian Era when asterisks were followed after a certain interval by a baby.

John: That never occurred to me. What I meant was that if a man's unfaithful to his wife she's an object of sympathy, whereas if a woman's unfaithful to her husband he's merely an object of ridicule.

Constance: That is one of those conventional prejudices that sensible people must strive to ignore.

John: Do you expect me to sit still and let this man take my wife away from under my very nose? I wonder you don't ask me to shake hands with him and wish him good luck.

Constance: That's just what I am going to do. He's coming here in a few minutes to say goodbye to you.

John: I shall knock him down.

Constance: I wouldn't take any risks in your place. He's pretty hefty and I'm under the impression that he's very nippy with his left.

John: I shall have great pleasure in telling him exactly what I think of him.

Constance: Why? Have you forgotten that I was charming

353

to Marie-Louise? We were the best of friends. She never bought a hat without asking me to go and help her choose it.

John: I have red blood in my veins.

Constance: I'm more concerned at the moment with the grey matter in your brain.

John: Is he in love with you?

Constance: Madly. Didn't you know?

John: I? How should I?

Constance: He's been here a great deal during the last year. Were you under the impression that he only came to see you?

John: I never paid any attention to him. I thought him rather dull.

Constance: He is rather dull. But he's very sweet.

John: What sort of a man is it who eats a fellow's food and drinks his wine and then makes love to his wife behind his back?

Constance: A man very like you, John, I should say.

John: Not at all. Mortimer is the sort of man who was born to be made a fool of.

Constance: None of us know for certain the designs of Providence.

John: I see you're bent on driving me to desperation. I shall break something in a minute.

Constance: There's that blue-and-white bowl that your Uncle Henry gave us as a wedding present. Break that, it's only a modern imitation.

[*He takes the bowl and hurls it on the floor so that it is shattered.*]

John: There.

Constance: Do you feel better?

John: Not a bit.

Constance: It's a pity you broke it then. You might have given it away as a wedding present to one of your colleagues at the hospital.

[**Bentley** *shows in* **Mrs Culver**.]

Bentley: Mrs Culver.

354

Constance: Oh, Mother, how sweet of you to come. I was so hoping I'd see you before I left.

Mrs Culver: Oh, you've had an accident.

Constance: No, John's in a temper and he thought it would relieve him if he broke something.

Mrs Culver: Nonsense, John's never in a temper.

John: That's what you think, Mrs Culver. Yes, I am in a temper. I'm in a filthy temper. Are you a party to this plan of Constance's?

Constance: No, Mother doesn't know.

John: Can't you do something to stop it? You have some influence over her. You must see that the thing's preposterous.

Mrs Culver: My dear boy, I haven't the ghost of an idea what you're talking about.

John: She's going to Italy with Bernard Kersal. Alone.

Mrs Culver [*with a stare*]: It's not true; how d'you know?

John: She's just told me so, as bold as brass, out of a blue sky. She mentioned it in the course of conversation as if she were saying, Darling, your coat wants brushing.

Mrs Culver: Is it true, Constance?

Constance: Quite.

Mrs Culver: But haven't you been getting on with John? I always thought you two were as happy as the day is long.

John: So did I. We've never had the shadow of a quarrel. We've always got on.

Mrs Culver: Don't you love John any more, darling?

Constance: Yes, I'm devoted to him.

John: How can you be devoted to a man when you're going to do him the greatest injury that a woman can do to a man?

Constance: Don't be idiotic, John. I'm going to do you no more injury than you did me a year ago.

John [*striding up to her, thinking quite erroneously that he sees light*]: Are you doing this in order to pay me out for Marie-Louise?

The Constant Wife

Constance: Don't be such a fool, John. Nothing is further from my thoughts.

Mrs Culver: The circumstances are entirely different. It was very naughty of John to deceive you, but he's sorry for what he did and he's been punished for it. It was all very dreadful and caused us a great deal of pain. But a man's a man and you expect that kind of thing from him. There are excuses for him. There are none for a woman. Men are naturally polygamous and sensible women have always made allowances for their occasional lapse from a condition which modern civilization has forced on them. Women are monogamous. They do not naturally desire more than one man and that is why the common sense of the world has heaped obloquy upon them when they have overstepped the natural limitations of their sex.

Constance [*smiling*]: It seems rather hard that what is sauce for the gander shouldn't also be sauce for the goose.

Mrs Culver: We all know that unchastity has no moral effect on men. They can be perfectly promiscuous and remain upright, industrious, and reliable. It's quite different with women. It ruins their character. They become untruthful and dissipated, lazy, shiftless, and dishonest. That is why the experience of ten thousand years has demanded chastity in women. Because it has learnt that this virtue is the key to all others.

Constance: They were dishonest because they were giving away something that wasn't theirs to give. They had sold themselves for board, lodging, and protection. They were chattel. They were dependent on their husbands and when they were unfaithful to them they were liars and thieves. I'm not dependent on John. I am economically independent and therefore I claim my sexual independence. I have this afternoon paid into John's account one thousand pounds for my year's keep.

John: I refuse to take it.

Constance: Well, you'll damned well have to.

Mrs Culver: There's no object in losing your temper.

Constance: I have mine under perfect control.

John: If you think what they call free love is fun you're mistaken. Believe me, it's the most overrated amusement that was ever invented.

Constance: In that case, I wonder why people continue to indulge in it.

John: I ought to know what I'm talking about, hang it all. It has all the inconveniences of marriage and none of its advantages. I assure you, my dear, the game is not worth the candle.

Constance: You may be right, but you know how hard it is to profit by anybody's experience. I think I'd like to see for myself.

Mrs Culver: Are you in love with Bernard?

Constance: To tell you the truth I haven't quite made up my mind. How does one know if one's in love?

Mrs Culver: My dear, I only know one test. Could you use his tooth-brush?

Constance: No.

Mrs Culver: Then you're not in love with him.

Constance: He's adored me for fifteen years. There's something in that long devotion which gives me a funny little feeling in my heart. I should like to do something to show him that I'm not ungrateful. You see, in six weeks he goes back to Japan. There is no chance of his coming to England again for seven years. I'm thirty-six now and he adores me; in seven years I shall be forty-three. A woman of forty-three is often charming, but it's seldom that a man of fifty-five is crazy about her. I came to the conclusion that it must be now or never and so I asked him if he'd like me to spend these last six weeks with him in Italy. When I wave my handkerchief to him as the ship that takes him sails out of the harbour at Naples I hope that he will feel that all those years of unselfish love have been well worth the while.

John: Six weeks. Do you intend to leave him at the end of six weeks?

Constance: Oh, yes, of course. It's because I'm putting a limit to our love that I think it may achieve the perfection of something that is beautiful and transitory. Why, John, what is it that makes a rose so lovely but that its petals fall as soon as it is full blown?

John: It's all come as such a shock and a surprise that I hardly know what to say. You've got me at a complete disadvantage.

[**Mrs Culver**, *who has been standing at the window, gives a little cry.*]

Constance: What is it?

Mrs Culver: Here is Bernard. He's just driven up to the door.

John: Do you expect me to receive him as if I were blissfully unconscious of your plans?

Constance: It would be more comfortable. It would be stupid to make a scene and it wouldn't prevent my going on this little jaunt with him.

John: I have my dignity to think of.

Constance: One often preserves that best by putting it in one's pocket. It would be kind of you, John, to treat him just as pleasantly as I treated Marie-Louise when I knew she was your mistress.

John: Does he know that I know?

Constance: Of course not. He's a little conventional, you know, and he couldn't happily deceive a friend if he thought there was no deception.

Mrs Culver: Constance, is there nothing I can say to make you reconsider you decision?

Constance: Nothing, darling.

Mrs Culver: Then I may just as well save my breath. I'll slip away before he comes.

Constance: Oh, all right. Goodbye, Mother. I'll send you a lot of picture postcards.

Mrs Culver: I don't approve of you, Constance, and I can't pretend that I do. No good will come of it. Men were meant by nature to be wicked and delightful and deceive their wives, and women were meant to be

virtuous and forgiving and to suffer verbosely. That was
ordained from all eternity and none of your new-fangled
notions can alter the decrees of Providence.

[**Bentley** enters, followed by **Bernard**.]

Bentley: Mr Kersal.

Mrs Culver: How do you do, Bernard, and goodbye. I'm
just going.

Bernard: Oh, I'm sorry. Goodbye.

[She goes out.]

Constance [to **Bernard**]: How d'you do? Just one moment.
[To **Bentley**] Oh, Bentley, get my things downstairs and
put them in a taxi, will you?

Bentley: Very good, madam.

Bernard: Are you just starting? It's lucky I came when I
did. I should have hated to miss you.

Constance: And let me know when the taxi's here.

Bentley: Yes, madam.

Constance: Now I can attend to you.

[**Bentley** goes out.]

Bernard: Are you looking forward to your holiday?

Constance: Immensely. I've never gone on a jaunt like
this before, and I'm really quite excited.

Bernard: You're going alone, aren't you?

Constance: Oh, yes, quite alone.

Bernard: It's rotten for you not to be able to get away, old
man.

John: Rotten.

Bernard: I suppose these are the penalties of greatness. I
can quite understand that you have to think of your
patients first.

John: Quite.

Constance: Of course John doesn't very much care for
Italy.

Bernard: Oh, are you going to Italy? I thought you said
Spain.

John: No, she always said Italy.

Bernard: Oh, well, that's hardly your mark, is it, old boy?

Though I believe there are some sporting links on the Lake of Como.

John: Are there?

Bernard: I suppose there's no chance of your being anywhere near Naples towards the end of July?

Constance: I don't really know. My plans are quite vague.

Bernard: I was only asking because I'm sailing from Naples. It would be fun if we met there.

John: Great fun.

Constance: I hope you'll see a lot of John while I'm away. I'm afraid he'll be a trifle lonely, poor darling. Why don't you dine together one day next week?

Bernard: I'm terribly sorry, but you know I'm going away.

Constance: Oh, are you? I thought you were going to stay in London till you had to start for Japan.

Bernard: I meant to, but my doctor has ordered me to go and do a cure.

John: What sort of a cure?

Bernard: Oh, just a cure. He says I want bucking up.

John: Oh, does he? What's the name of your doctor?

Bernard: No one you ever heard of. A man I used to know in the war.

John: Oh!

Bernard: So I'm afraid this is goodbye. Of course, it's a wrench leaving London, especially as I don't expect to be in Europe again for some years, but I always think it rather silly not to take a man's advice when you've asked for it.

John: More especially when he's charged you three guineas.

Constance: I'm sorry. I was counting on you to keep John out of mischief during my absence.

Bernard: I'm not sure if I could guarantee to do that. But we might have done a few theatres together and had a game of golf or two.

Constance: It would have been jolly, wouldn't it, John?

John: Very jolly.

[**Bentley** *comes in.*]

Bentley: The taxi's waiting, madam.

Constance: Thank you.

[Bentley *goes out.*]

Bernard: I'll take myself off. In case I don't see you again I'd like to thank you now for all your kindness to me during the year I've spent in London.

Constance: It's been very nice to see you.

Bernard: You and John have been most awfully good to me. I never imagined I was going to have such a wonderful time.

Constance: We shall miss you terribly. It's been a great comfort to John to think that there was someone to take me out when he had to be away on one of his operations. Hasn't it, darling?

John: Yes, darling.

Constance: When he knew I was with you he never worried. Did you, darling?

John: No, darling.

Bernard: I'm awfully glad if I've been able to make myself useful. Don't forget me entirely, will you?

Constance: We're not likely to do that, are we, darling?

John: No, darling.

Bernard: And if you ever have a moment to spare you will write to me, won't you? You don't know how much it means to us exiles.

Constance: Of course we will. We'll both write. Won't we, darling?

John: Yes, darling.

Constance: John writes such a good letter. So chatty, you know, and amusing.

Bernard: That's a promise. Well, goodbye, old boy. Have a good time.

John: Thanks, old bean.

Bernard: Goodbye, Constance. There's so much I want to say to you that I don't know where to begin.

John: I don't want to hurry you, but the taxi is just ticking its head off.

The Constant Wife

Bernard: John is so matter-of-fact. Well, I'll say nothing then but God bless you.

Constance: *Au revoir*.

Bernard: If you do go to Naples you will let me know, won't you? If you send a line to my club, it'll be forwarded at once.

Constance: Oh, all right.

Bernard: Goodbye.

> [*He gives them both a friendly nod and goes out.* **Constance** *begins to giggle and soon is seized with uncontrollable laughter.*]

John: Will you kindly tell me what there is to laugh at? If you think it amuses me to stand here like patience on a monument and have my leg pulled you're mistaken. What did you mean by all that balderdash about meeting you by chance in Naples?

Constance: He was throwing you off the scent.

John: The man's a drivelling idiot.

Constance: D'you think so? I thought he was rather ingenious. Considering he hasn't had very much practice in this sort of thing I thought he did very well.

John: Of course if you're determined to find him a pattern of perfection it's useless for me to attempt to argue. But honestly, speaking without prejudice for or against, I'm sorry to think of you throwing yourself away on a man like that.

Constance: Perhaps it's natural that a man and his wife should differ in their estimate of her prospective lover.

John: You're not going to tell me he's better-looking than I am.

Constance: No. You have always been my ideal of manly beauty.

John: He's no better dressed than I am.

Constance: He could hardly expect to be. He goes to the same tailor.

John: I don't think you can honestly say he's more amusing than I am.

Constance: No, I honestly can't.

John: Then in Heaven's name why do you want to go away with him?

Constance: Shall I tell you? Once more before it's too late I want to feel about me the arms of a man who adores the ground I walk on. I want to see his face light up when I enter the room. I want to feel the pressure of his hand when we look at the moon together and the pleasantly tickling sensation when his arm tremulously steals around my waist. I want to let my head fall on his shoulder and feel his lips softly touch my hair.

John: The operation is automatically impossible, the poor devil would get such a crick in the neck he wouldn't know what to do.

Constance: I want to walk along country lanes and I want to be called by absurd pet names. I want to talk baby-talk by the hour together.

John: Oh, God.

Constance: I want to know that I'm eloquent and witty when I'm dead silent. For ten years I've been very happy in your affection, John, we've been the best and dearest friends, but now just for a little while I hanker for something else. Do you grudge it me? I want to be loved.

John: But, my dear, I'll love you. I've been a brute, I've neglected you, it's not too late, and you're the only woman I've ever really cared for. I'll chuck everything and we'll go away together.

Constance: The prospect does not thrill me.

John: Come, darling, have a heart. I gave up Marie-Louise. Surely you can give up Bernard.

Constance: But you gave up Marie-Louise to please yourself, not to please me.

John: Don't be a little beast, Constance. Come away with me. We'll have such a lark.

Constance: Oh, my poor John, I didn't work so hard to gain my economic independence in order to go on a honeymoon with my own husband.

The Constant Wife

John: Do you think I can't be a lover as well as a husband?

Constance: My dear, no one can make yesterday's cold mutton into tomorrow's lamb cutlets.

John: You know what you're doing. I was determined in future to be a model husband and you're driving me right into the arms of Marie-Louise. I give you my word of honour that the moment you leave this house I shall drive straight to her door.

Constance: I should hate you to have a fruitless journey. I'm afraid you won't find her at home. She has a new young man and she says he's too divine.

John: What!

Constance: He's the A.D.C. of a Colonial Governor. She came here today to ask me to break the news to you that henceforth everything was over between you.

John: I hope you told her first that I was firmly resolved to terminate a connexion that could only cause you pain.

Constance: I couldn't. She was in such a blooming hurry to give me her message.

John: Really, Constance, for your own pride I should have thought you wouldn't like her to make a perfect fool of me. Any other woman would have said, 'What a strange coincidence. Why it's only half an hour since John told me he had made up his mind never to see you again.' But of course you don't care two straws for me any more, that's quite evident.

Constance: Oh, don't be unjust, darling. I shall always care for you. I may be unfaithful, but I am constant. I always think that's my most endearing quality.

[Bentley *opens the door.*]

John [*irritably*]: What is it?

Bentley: I thought madam had forgotten that the taxi was at the door.

John: Go to hell.

Bentley: Very good, sir.

[*He goes out.*]

Constance: I don't see why you should be rude to him.

Bernard will pay the taxi. Anyhow I must go now or he'll begin to think I'm not coming. Goodbye, darling. I hope you'll get on all right in my absence. Just give the cook her head and you'll have no trouble. Won't you say goodbye to me?

John: Go to the devil.

Constance: All right. I shall be back in six weeks.

John: Back? Where?

Constance: Here.

John: Here? Here? Do you think I'm going to take you back?

Constance: I don't see why not. When you've had time to reflect you'll realize that you have no reason to blame me. After all, I'm taking from you nothing that you want.

John: Are you aware that I can divorce you for this?

Constance: Quite. But I married very prudently. I took the precaution to marry a gentleman and I know that you could never bring yourself to divorce me for doing no more than you did yourself.

John: I wouldn't divorce you. I wouldn't expose my worst enemy to the risk of marrying a woman who's capable of treating her husband as you're treating me.

Constance [*at the door*]: Well, then, shall I come back?

John [*after a moment's hesitation*]: You are the most maddening, wilful, capricious, wrong-headed, delightful, and enchanting woman man was ever cursed with having for a wife. Yes, damn you, come back.

[*She lightly kisses her hand to him and slips out, slamming the door behind her.*]

Our Betters

A COMEDY IN THREE ACTS

Characters

Elizabeth Saunders
Pole, *the butler*
Lady Grayston
Fleming Harvey
Thornton Clay
Duchesse De Surennes
Anthony Paxton
Princess Della Cercola
Lord Bleane
Ernest
Arthur Fenwick

The action of the play takes place at Lady Grayston's house in Grosvenor Street, Mayfair, and at her husband's place in Suffolk, Abbots Kenton.

Act One

Scene: the drawing-room at Lady Grayston's house in Grosvenor Street, Mayfair. It is a sumptuous double room, of the period of George II, decorated in green and gold with a coromandel screen and lacquer cabinets; but the coverings of the chairs, the sofas, and cushions, show the influence of Bakst and the Russian Ballet; they offer an agreeable mixture of rich plum, emerald green, canary, and ultra-marine. On the floor is a Chinese carpet, and here and there are pieces of Ming pottery.

It is about half past four, early in the season, and a fine day.

[*When the curtain rises, from the street below is heard the melancholy chant of the lavender man:*

> Won't you buy my sweet lavender?
> Sixteen blue branches for a penny.
> If you buy it once,
> You'll buy it twice,
> For it makes your clothes
> Smell very nice –
> Sweet-scented lavender.

Bessie Saunders *comes in. She is a very pretty American girl of twenty-two, with fair hair and blue eyes. She is dressed in the latest mode. She wears a hat and gloves, and carries a bag. She has just come in from the street. She has in her hand a telephone message, and going over to the telephone she takes up the receiver.*]

Bessie: Gerrard 4321. Is that the Berkeley? Put me through to Mr Harvey, please. Fleming Harvey, that's right. [*She listens and smiles.*] Yes. Who d'you think it is? [*She laughs.*] I've just got your telephone message.

Where have you sprung from? That's fine. How long are you staying in London? I see. I want to see you at once. Nonsense. This very minute. Now just jump into a taxi and come right away. Pearl will be in presently. Ring off, Fleming. No, I will not ring off first. [*A pause.*] Are you there? How tiresome you are. You might be half-way here by now. Well, hustle.

[*She puts down the receiver and begins to take off her gloves.* **Pole,** *the butler, comes in with a bunch of roses.*]

Pole: These flowers have just come for you, miss.

Bessie: Oh! Thank you. Aren't they lovely? You must give me something to put them in, Pole.

Pole: I'll bring a vase, miss.

[*He goes out. She buries her face in the flowers and inhales their fragrance.* **Pole** *enters with a bowl filled with water.*]

Bessie: Thank you. You're sure they are for me? There's no label.

Pole: Yes, miss. The person who brought them said they was for you, miss. I asked if there wasn't a card, and he said no, miss.

Bessie [*with a faint smile*]: I think I know who they're from. [*She begins to arrange the flowers.*] Her ladyship hasn't come in yet, has she?

Pole: Not yet, miss.

Bessie: D'you know if anyone is coming in to tea?

Pole: Her ladyship didn't say, miss.

Bessie: You'd better prepare for fifteen, then.

Pole: Very good, miss.

Bessie: I was being funny, Pole.

Pole: Yes, miss? Shall I take the paper away, miss?

Bessie [*with a sigh of resignation*] : Yes, do, will you? [*The telephone bell rings.*] Oh, I forgot, I switched the telephone on here. See who it is.

[**Pole** *takes up the receiver and listens, then puts his hand over its mouth.*]

Pole: Will you speak to Lord Bleane, miss?

Bessie: Say I'm not at home.

Pole: Miss Saunders hasn't come in yet. I beg pardon, my lord. I didn't recognize your lordship's voice. [*A pause.*] Well, my lord, I did hear them say there was a private view they thought of going to at the Grosvenor. You might find Miss Saunders there.

Bessie: You needn't elaborate, Pole.

Pole: I was only making it more convincing, miss. [*Listening*] I think so, my lord. Of course, I couldn't say for certain, my lord, they might have gone out to Ranelagh.

Bessie: Really, Pole!

Pole: Very good, my lord. [*He puts down the receiver.*] His lordship asked if you was expected in to tea, miss. Is there anything else, miss?

Bessie: No, Pole, thank you.

[*He goes out. She finishes arranging the flowers. The door is flung open and* **Lady Grayston** *comes in, followed by* **Fleming Harvey**. *Pearl* – **Lady Grayston** – *is a handsome, dashing creature, a woman of thirty-four, with red hair, and a face outrageously painted. She is dressed in a Paris frock, but of greater daring both in colour and cut than a French woman would wear.* **Fleming** *is a nice-looking young American in clothes that were obviously made in New York.*]

Pearl: My dear Bessie, I've found an entirely strange young man on the doorstep who says he is a cousin.

Bessie [*giving him her hands enthusiastically*]: Fleming.

Fleming: I introduced myself to Lady Grayston. She drove up just as they were opening the door. Please reassure your sister, Bessie. She looks upon me with suspicion.

Bessie: You must remember Fleming Harvey, Pearl.

Pearl: I've never set eyes on him in my life. But he looks quite – nice.

Bessie: He is.

Pearl: He's apparently come to see you.

Fleming: I rang up five minutes ago and Bessie ordered me to come round right away.

Pearl: Well, make him stop to tea. I've got to telephone.

I've suddenly remembered that I've asked twelve people to dinner.

Bessie: Does George know?

Pearl: Who is George?

Bessie: Don't be absurd, Pearl. George – your husband.

Pearl: Oh! I couldn't make out who you meant. No, he doesn't know. But what's much more important, the cook doesn't know either. I'd forgotten George was in London.

[*She goes out.*]

Bessie: George generally dines out when Pearl is giving a party, because he doesn't like people he doesn't know, and he seldom dines at home when we're alone, because it bores him.

Fleming: It doesn't sound as if Sir George enjoyed many of the benefits of home life.

Bessie: Now let's sit down and make ourselves comfortable. You are going to stay to tea, aren't you?

Fleming: It's not a beverage that I'm in the habit of imbibing.

Bessie: When you've been in England a month you won't be able to do without it. When did you land?

Fleming: This morning. You see, I've lost no time in coming to see you.

Bessie: I should think not. It *is* good to see someone straight from home.

Fleming: Have you been having a good time, Bessie?

Bessie: Wonderful! Since the beginning of the season, except when Pearl has had people here, I've been out to lunch and dinner every day, and I've been to a ball every night, generally two and sometimes three.

Fleming: Gee!

Bessie: If I stopped now I'd drop down dead.

Fleming: D'you like England?

Bessie: I adore it. I think it's too bad of Dad never to have let me come over to London before. Rome and Paris are nothing. We're just trippers there, but here we're at home.

Fleming: Don't get too much at home, Bessie.

Bessie: Oh, Fleming, I never thanked you for sending me the roses. It was perfectly sweet of you.

Fleming [*with a smile*]: I didn't send you any roses.

Bessie: Didn't you? Well, why didn't you?

Fleming: I hadn't time. But I will.

Bessie: It's too late now. I naturally thought they were from you, because Englishmen don't send flowers in the same way as American boys do.

Fleming: Is that so?

> [*There is a slight pause.* **Bessie** *gives him a quick look.*]

Bessie: Fleming, I want to thank you for that charming letter you wrote me.

Fleming: There's no occasion to do that, Bessie.

Bessie: I was afraid you might feel badly about it. But we'll always be the greatest friends, won't we?

Fleming: Always.

Bessie: After all, you were eighteen when you asked me to marry you, and I was sixteen. It wasn't a very serious engagement. I don't know why we didn't break it off before.

Fleming: I suppose it never occurred to us.

Bessie: I'd almost forgotten it, but when I came over here I thought I'd better make everything quite clear.

Fleming [*with a smile*]: Bessie, I believe you're in love.

Bessie: No, I'm not. I tell you I'm having a wonderful time.

Fleming: Well, who sent you the roses?

Bessie: I don't know. Lord Bleane.

Fleming: You're not going to marry a lord, Bessie?

Bessie: Have you any objection?

Fleming: Well, on first principles, I think American girls had better marry American men, but then I happen to be an American man.

> [**Bessie** *looks at him for a moment.*]

Bessie: Pearl gave a dinner party last night. I was taken in by a cabinet minister, and on the other side of me I had an ambassador. Just opposite was a man who'd been Viceroy in India. Madame Angelotti dined with us, and she sang afterwards, and a lot of people came on from an official dinner in their stars and ribands. Pearl looked superb. She's a wonderful hostess, you know. Several people told me they would rather come here than to any house in London. Before Pearl married George Grayston she was engaged to a boy who was in business in Portland, Oregon.

Fleming [*smiling*]: I see you're quite determined to marry a lord.

Bessie: No, I'm not. I'm keeping an open mind on the subject.

Fleming: What d'you mean by that?

Bessie: Well, Fleming, it hasn't escaped my notice that a certain noble lord is not unwilling to lay his beautiful coronet at my feet.

Fleming: Don't talk like a novelette, Bessie.

Bessie: But it feels just like a novelette. The poor dear is trying to propose to me every time he sees me, and I'm doing all I can to prevent him.

Fleming: Why?

Bessie: I don't want to refuse him, and then wish I hadn't.

Fleming: You could easily make him ask you again. Women find that so simple.

Bessie: Ah, but supposing he went right away to shoot big game in Africa. It's what they do, you know, in novelettes.

Fleming: I'm reassured about one thing. You're not in the least in love with him.

Bessie: I told you I wasn't. You don't mind my saying all this to you, Fleming?

Fleming: Gracious, no; why should I?

Bessie: You're sure you don't feel sore at my throwing you over?

Fleming [*cheerfully*]: Not a bit.

Bessie: I am glad, because then I can tell you all about the noble lord.

374

Fleming: Has it occurred to you that he wants to marry you for your money?

Bessie: You can put it more prettily. You can say that he wants to marry me with my money.

Fleming: And is that a prospect that allures you?

Bessie: Poor dear, what else can he do? He's got a large place to keep up, and he simply hasn't a cent.

Fleming: Really, Bessie, you amaze me.

Bessie: I shan't when you've been here a month.
[**Pearl** *comes in.*]

Pearl: Now, Bessie, tell me all about this strange young man.

Bessie: He's quite capable of telling you about himself.

Pearl [*to* **Fleming**]: How long are you staying?

Fleming: A couple of months. I want to see something of English life.

Pearl: I see. D'you want to improve your mind or d'you want to go into society?

Fleming: I suppose I couldn't combine the two?

Pearl: Are you rich?

Fleming: Not at all.

Pearl: It doesn't matter, you're good-looking. If one wants to be a success in London one must either have looks, wit, or a bank-balance. You know Arthur Fenwick, don't you?

Fleming: Only by reputation.

Pearl: How superciliously you say that!

Fleming: He provides bad food to the working classes of the United States at an exorbitant price. I have no doubt he makes a lot of money.

Bessie: He's a great friend of Pearl's.

Pearl: When he first came over because they turned up their noses at him in New York, I said to him: My dear Mr Fenwick, you're not good-looking, you're not amusing, you're not well-bred, you're only rich. If you want to get into society you must spend money.

Fleming: It was evidently in the nature of a straight talk.

Bessie: We must do what we can for Fleming, Pearl.

Our Betters

Pearl [*with a chuckle*]: We'll introduce him to Minnie Surennes.

Fleming: Who in the world is she?

Pearl: The Duchesse de Surennes. Don't you remember? She was a Miss Hodgson. Chicago people. Of course, they're nobody in America, but that doesn't matter over here. She adores good-looking boys, and I daresay she's getting rather tired of Tony. [*To* **Bessie**] By the way, they're coming in this afternoon.

Bessie: I don't like Tony.

Pearl: Why not? I think he's charming. He's the most unprincipled ruffian I ever met.

Fleming: Is Tony the duke?

Pearl: What duke? Her husband? Oh no, she divorced him years ago.

Bessie: I think Fleming would like the Princess much better.

Pearl: Oh, well, he'll meet her here today, too.

Bessie: She was a Miss van Hoog, Fleming.

Fleming: Is she divorced too?

Pearl: Oh no, her husband's an Italian. It's very difficult to get a divorce in Italy. She's only separated. She's quite nice. She's one of my greatest friends. She bores me a little.

[**Pole** *comes in to announce* **Thornton Clay** *and then goes out.* **Thornton Clay** *is a stout American with a bald head and an effusive manner. He is somewhat overdressed. He speaks with a marked American accent.*]

Pole: Mr Thornton Clay.

Clay: How d'you do?

Pearl: You're the very person we want, Thornton. An entirely strange young man has suddenly appeared on my doorstep, and says he's my cousin.

Clay: My dear Pearl, that is a calamity which we Americans must always be prepared for.

Bessie: I won't have you say such things, Mr Clay.

Fleming is not only our cousin, but he's my very oldest friend. Aren't you, Fleming?

Pearl: Bessie has a charming nature. She really thinks that friendship puts one under an obligation.

Fleming: Since you're talking of me, won't you introduce me to Mr Clay?

Pearl: How American you are!

Fleming [*smiling*]: It's not unnatural, is it?

Pearl: Over here we haven't the passion that you have in America for introducing people. My dear Thornton, allow me to present to you my long-lost cousin, Mr Fleming Harvey.

Clay: It's so long since I was in America that I almost forget, but I believe the proper answer to that is: Mr Fleming Harvey, I'm pleased to make your acquaintance.

Fleming: Aren't you an American, Mr Clay?

Clay: I won't deny that I was born in Virginia.

Fleming: I beg your pardon, I thought from the way you spoke . . .

Clay [*interrupting*]: But, of course, my home is London.

Pearl: Nonsense, Thornton, your home is wherever there's a first-class hotel.

Clay: I went to America seven years ago. My father died and I had to go and settle up his affairs. Everyone took me for an Englishman.

Fleming: That must have gratified you very much, Mr Clay.

Clay: Of course, I haven't a trace of an American accent. I suppose that was the reason. And then my clothes.
[*He looks at them with satisfaction.*]

Pearl: Fleming wants to see life in London, Thornton. He can't do better than put himself under your wing.

Clay: I know everyone who's worth knowing. I can't deny that.

Pearl: Thornton calls more countesses by their Christian names than any man in town.

Clay: I'll get him cards for some good balls, and I'll see that he's asked to one or two of the right parties.

Pearl: He's good-looking, and I'm sure he dances well. He'll be a credit to you, Thornton.

Clay [*to* **Fleming**]: But, of course, there's really nothing I *can* do for you. At Lady Grayston's you are in the very hub of society. I don't mean the stuffy, old-fashioned society, that goes about in barouches and bores itself stiff but the society that counts, the society that figures in the newspapers. Pearl is the most wonderful hostess in London.

Pearl: What *do* you want, Thornton?

Clay: In this house, sooner or later, you'll meet every remarkable man in England except one. That is George Grayston. And 'he's only remarkable because he's her husband.

Pearl [*with a chuckle*]: I might have known you were only saying a pleasant thing in order to make the next one more disagreeable.

Clay: Of course, I can't make out why you never ask George to your parties. Personally I like him.

Pearl: That's all the nicer of you, Thornton, since he always speaks of you as that damned snob.

Clay [*with a shrug of the shoulders*]: Poor George, he has such a limited vocabulary. I met Flora della Cercola at luncheon today. She told me she was coming to tea with you.

Pearl: She's getting up a concert in aid of something or other, and she wants me to help her.

Clay: Poor Flora, with her good works! She takes philanthropy as a drug to allay the pangs of unrequited love.

Pearl: I always tell her she'd do much better to take a lover.

Clay: You'll shock Mr Harvey.

Pearl: It won't hurt him. It'll do him good.

Clay: Did you ever know her husband?

Pearl: Oh yes, I met him. Just the ordinary little Dago. I

cannot imagine why she should ever have been in love
with him. She's an extraordinary creature. D'you know,
I'm convinced that she's never had an affair.

Clay: Some of these American women are strangely
sexless.

Fleming: I have an idea that some of them are even
virtuous.

Pearl [*with a smile*]: It takes all sorts to make a world.
[**Pole** *enters to announce the* **Duchesse de Surennes**,
and then goes out.]

Pole: The Duchesse de Surennes.
[*The* **Duchesse** *is a large, dark woman of forty-five
with scarlet lips and painted cheeks, a woman of
opulent form, bold, self-assured and outrageously
sensual. She suggests a drawing of a Roman Emperor
by Aubrey Beardsley. She is gowned with a certain
dashing magnificence, and wears a long string of
large pearls round her neck. During the conversation*
Pole *and two footmen bring in tea, and place it in
the back drawing-room.*]

Pearl: My dear, how nice of you to come.

Duchesse: Isn't Tony here?

Pearl: No.

Duchesse: He said he was coming straight here.

Pearl: I dare say he's been delayed.

Duchesse: I can't understand it. He telephoned a quarter
of an hour ago that he was starting at once.

Pearl [*reassuringly*]: He'll be here presently.

Duchesse [*with an effort over herself*]: How pretty you're
looking, Bessie. No wonder all the men I meet rave
about you.

Bessie: Englishmen are so shy. Why don't they rave *to*
me?

Duchesse: They'll never let you go back to America.

Pearl: Of course, she's never going back. I'm determined
that she shall marry an Englishman.

Clay: She'll make a charming addition to our American
peeresses.

Pearl: And there'll be another that you can call by her Christian name, Thornton.

Bessie: I wish you wouldn't talk as if I hadn't a word to say in the matter.

Clay: Of course you've got a word to say, Bessie – a very important one.

Bessie: Yes, I suppose?

Clay: Exactly.

Pearl: Pour out the tea, darling, will you?

Bessie: Surely. [*To* **Clay**] I know you don't share Fleming's contempt for tea, Mr Clay.

Clay: I couldn't live a day without it. Why, I never travel without a tea basket.

Fleming [ironically]: Is that so?

Clay: You Americans who live in America . . .

Fleming [*under his breath*]: So queer of us.

Clay: . . . despise the delectable habit of drinking tea because you are still partly barbarous. The hour that we spend over it is the most delightful of the day. We do not make a business of eating as at luncheon or dinner. We are at ease with ourselves. We toy with pretty cakes as an excuse for conversation. We discuss the abstract, our souls, our morals; we play delicately with the concrete, our neighbour's new bonnet or her latest lover. We drink tea because we are a highly civilized nation.

Fleming: I must be very stupid, but I don't follow.

Clay: My dear fellow, the degree of a nation's civilization is marked by its disregard for the necessities of existence. You have gone so far as to waste money, but we have gone farther; we waste what is infinitely more precious, more transitory, more irreparable – we waste time.

Duchesse: My dear Thornton, you fill me with despair. Compton Edwardes has put me off my tea. I thought he was only depriving me of a luxury, now I see he's depriving me also of a religious rite.

Fleming: Who in heaven's name is Compton Edwardes, that he should have such influence?

Pearl: My dear Fleming, he's the most powerful man in London. He's the great reducer.

Fleming: Gracious! What does he reduce?

Pearl: Fat.

Duchesse: He's a perfect marvel, that man. Do you know, the Duchess of Arlington told me he'd taken nine pounds off her.

Pearl: My dear, that's nothing. Why, Clara Hollington gave me her word of honour she'd lost over a stone.

Bessie [*from the tea-table*]: Anyone who wants tea must come and fetch it.

[*The men saunter over to the next room, while* **Pearl** *and the* **Duchesse** *go on with their conversation.*]

Duchesse: Who is that nice-looking young man, Pearl?

Pearl: Oh, he's a young American. He pretends to be a cousin of mine. He's come to see Bessie.

Duchesse: Does he want to marry her?

Pearl: Good heavens, I hope not. He's only an old friend. You know the funny ways they have in America.

Duchesse: I suppose nothing is really settled about Harry Bleane?

Pearl: No. But I shouldn't be surprised if you saw an announcement in the *Morning Post* one day.

Duchesse: Has she enough money for him?

Pearl: She has a million.

Duchesse: Not pounds?

Pearl: Oh, no, dollars.

Duchesse: That's only eight thousand a year. I shouldn't have thought he'd be satisfied with that.

Pearl: People can't expect so much nowadays. There won't be any more enormous heiresses as there were in your time. Besides, Harry Bleane isn't such a catch as all that. Of course, it's better to be an English baron than an Italian count, but that's about all you can say for it.

Duchesse: Of course, she'll accept him?

Pearl: Oh yes, she's crazy to live in England. And, as I tell her, it's quite pleasant to be a peeress even now.

Duchesse: What on earth can have happened to Tony?

Pearl: My dear, he's not likely to have been run over by a motor-bus.

Duchesse: I'm not afraid of motor-buses running over him; I'm afraid of him running after Gaiety girls.

Pearl [*dryly*]: I should have thought you kept a very sharp eye on him.

Duchesse: You see, he hasn't got anything to do from morning till night.

Pearl: Why doesn't he get a job?

Duchesse: I've been trying to get him something, but it's so difficult. You've got such a lot of influence, Pearl. Can't you do something? I should be so grateful.

Pearl: What can he do?

Duchesse: Anything. And as you know he's very good-looking.

Pearl: Does he know French and German?

Duchesse: No, he has no gift for languages.

Pearl: Can he type and write shorthand?

Duchesse: Oh, no. Poor dear, you can hardly expect that.

Pearl: Can he do accounts?

Duchesse: No, he has no head for figures.

Pearl [*reflectively*]: Well, the only thing I can see that he'd do for is a government office.

Duchesse: Oh, my dear, if you could manage that. You can't think what a comfort it would be for me to know that he couldn't get into mischief at least from ten to four every day.

[**Pole** *announces* **Tony Paxton. Tony** *is a handsome youth of twenty-five, in beautiful clothes, with engaging manners and a charming smile.*]

Pole: Mr Paxton.

Pearl: Well, Tony, how is life?

Tony: Rotten. I haven't backed a winner or won a rubber this week.

Pearl: Ah well, that's the advantage of not having money, you can afford to lose it.

Duchesse [*bursting in*]: Where have you been, Tony?

Tony: I? Nowhere.

Duchesse: You said you were coming straight here. It doesn't take twenty-five minutes to get here from Dover Street.

Tony: I thought there wasn't any hurry. I was just hanging about the club.

Duchesse: I rang up the club again, and they said you'd gone.

Tony [*after a very slight pause*]: I was downstairs having a shave, and I suppose they never thought of looking for me in the barber's shop.

Duchesse: What on earth did you want to be shaved for at half past four in the afternoon?

Tony: I thought you'd like me to look nice and clean.

Pearl: Go and get Bessie to give you some tea, Tony; I'm sure you want it after the strenuous day you've had.

[*He nods and walks into the inner room.*]

Pearl: Minnie, how can you be so silly? You can't expect to keep a man if you treat him like that.

Duchesse: I know he's lying to me, there's not a word of truth in anything he says: but he's so slim I can never catch him out. Oh, I'm so jealous.

Pearl: Are you really in love with him?

Duchesse: He's everything in the world to me.

Pearl: You shouldn't let yourself be carried away like this.

Duchesse: I'm not cold-blooded like you.

Pearl: You seem to have a passion for rotters, and they always treat you badly.

Duchesse: Oh, I don't care about the others. Tony is the only one I've ever really loved.

Pearl: Nonsense! You were just as much in love with Jack Harris. You did everything in the world for him. You taught him to wear his clothes. You got him into society. And the moment he could do without you he chucked you. Tony will do just the same.

Duchesse: I'm not going to be such a fool this time. I'm going to take care he can't do without me.

Pearl: I can't imagine what you see in him. You must know that . . .

Duchesse [*interrupting*]: There's very little I don't know. He's a liar, a gambler, an idler, a spendthrift, but in his way he is fond of me. [*Appealingly*] You can see he's fond of me, can't you?

Pearl: He's so much younger than you, Minnie.

Duchesse: I can't help it. I love him.

Pearl: Oh, well, I suppose it's no good talking. As long as he makes you happy.

Duchesse: He doesn't. He makes me miserable. But I love him. . . . He wants me to marry him, Pearl.

Pearl: You're not going to?

Duchesse: No, I won't be such a fool as that. If I married him I'd have no hold over him at all.

[*Enter* **Pole** *to announce the* **Princess della Cercola**. *She is a tall, thin woman of thirty-five, with a pale, haggard face and great dark eyes. She is a gentle, kind creature, but there is something pathetic, almost tragic, in her appearance. She is dressed though very well, and obviously by a Paris dress-maker, more quietly than the* **Duchesse** *or* **Pearl**. *She has not only wealth, but distinction.*]

Pole: Princess della Cercola.

[*Exit* **Pole**. **Pearl** *gets up to receive her. They kiss.*]

Pearl: Darling!

Princess: D'you hate me for coming to bother you? I ran up because I know how difficult you are to catch. [*Kissing the Duchesse*] How are you, Minnie?

Duchesse: Don't ask me for a subscription, Flora. I'm so poor.

Princess [*smiling*]: Wait till I tell you what it's for, and then you'll remember that you had a father called Spencer Hodgson.

Duchesse [*with a little groan*]: As if I wanted to be reminded of it!

Pearl: You're so absurd, Minnie. You should make a joke of the pork. I always tell people about Father's hardware store, and when I haven't got a funny story to tell about it, I invent one.

Princess: You've made your father quite a character in London.

Pearl: That's why I never let him come over. He couldn't possibly live up to his reputation.

[**Fleming Harvey** comes forward from the inner room.]

Fleming: I'm going to say good-bye to you.

Pearl: You mustn't go before I've introduced you to Flora. Flora, this is Mr Fleming Harvey. He's just come from America. He probably carries a six-shooter in his hip-pocket.

Fleming: I'm told I mayn't say I'm pleased to make your acquaintance, Princess.

Princess: When did you land?

Fleming: This morning.

Princess: I envy you.

Fleming: Because I landed this morning?

Princess: No, because a week ago you were in America.

Duchesse: Flora!

Fleming: I was beginning to think it was something to be rather ashamed of.

Princess: Oh, you mustn't pay any attention to Pearl and the Duchesse. They're so much more English than the English.

Pearl: I notice you show your devotion to the country of your birth by staying away from it, Flora.

Princess: Last time I was in America it made me so unhappy that I vowed I'd never go there again.

Duchesse: I was there ten years ago, when I was divorcing Gaston. I hadn't been in America since my marriage, and I'd forgotten what it was like. Oh, it was so crude. Oh, it was so provincial. You don't mind my saying so, Mr Harvey?

Fleming: Not at all. You're just as American as I am, and there's no reason why among ourselves we shouldn't abuse the mother that bore us.

Duchesse: Oh, but I don't look upon myself as American. I'm French. After all, I haven't a trace of an American accent. To show you how it got on my nerves, I almost didn't divorce Gaston because I thought I couldn't bring myself to stay in America long enough.

Princess: It's not because it was crude and provincial that I was unhappy in America. I was unhappy because after all it was home, the only real home I've ever had, and I was a stranger.

Pearl: My dear Flora, you're being very sentimental.

Princess [*Smiling*]: I'm sorry; I apologize. You're a New Yorker, Mr Harvey?

Fleming: I'm proud of it, madam.

Princess: New York's wonderful, isn't it? It has something that no other city in the world has got. I like to think of Fifth Avenue on a spring day. The pretty girls in their smart frocks and neat shoes, who trip along so gaily, and all the good-looking boys.

Duchesse: I grant you that; some of the boys are too lovely for words.

Princess: Everyone is so strong and confident. There's such an exaltation in the air. You feel in the passers-by a serene and unshakeable belief in the future. Oh, it's very good to be alive in Fifth Avenue on a sunny day in April.

Fleming: It's good for an American to hear another American say such pleasant things about his country.

Princess: You must come and see me, and you shall tell me all the news of home.

Pearl: How high the newest building is, and how much money the latest millionaire has got.

Fleming: Good-bye.

Pearl: Have you made friends with Thornton Clay?

Fleming: I hope so.

Pearl: You must get him to give you the address of his tailor.

Fleming: Aren't you pleased with my clothes?

Pearl: They're very American, you know.

Fleming: So am I.

[**Thornton Clay** *comes forward. The* **Duchesse** *strolls over to the inner room and is seen talking with* **Bessie** *and* **Tony Paxton**.]

Pearl: Thornton, I was just telling Mr Harvey that you'd take him to your tailor.

Clay: I was going to suggest it.

Fleming: My clothes are not at all a success.

Pearl: Who d'you go to? Stultz?

Clay: Of course. He's the only tailor in London. [*To* **Fleming**] Of course he's a German, but art has no nationality.

Fleming: I'm pleased at all events to think that it's a German tailor who's going to make me look like an Englishman.

[*He goes out.* **Thornton** *makes his farewells.*]

Clay: Good-bye, Pearl.

Pearl: Are you going? Don't forget you're coming down to Kenton on Saturday.

Clay: I won't, indeed. I adore your week-end parties, Pearl. I'm so exhausted by Monday morning that I'm fit for nothing for the rest of the week. Good-bye.

[*He shakes hands and goes out. As he is going,* **Pole** *opens the door to announce* **Lord Bleane**. *He is a young man, very English in appearance, pleasant, clean and well-groomed.*]

Pole: Lord Bleane.

[*Exit* **Pole**.]

Pearl: Dear Harry, how nice of you to come.

Bleane: I'm in absolute despair.

Pearl: Good heavens, why?

Bleane: They're sending a mission to Romania to hand the Garter to some bigwig and I've got to go with it.

Pearl: Oh, but that'll be very interesting.

Bleane: Yes, but we start tomorrow, and I shan't be able to come down to Kenton on Saturday.

Our Betters

Pearl: When do you come back?

Bleane: In four weeks.

Pearl: Then come down to Kenton the Saturday after that.

Bleane: May I?

Pearl: You must go and break the news to Bessie. She was so looking forward to your visit.

Bleane: D'you think she'll give me some tea?

Pearl: I have no doubt, if you ask her nicely.

[*He goes over to the inner room.*]

Princess: Now I've got you to myself for two minutes. You will help me with my concert, won't you? .

Pearl: Of course. What do you want me to do? I'll make Arthur Fenwick take any number of tickets. You know how charitable he is.

Princess: It's for a very good cause.

Pearl: I'm sure it is. But don't harrow me with revolting stories of starving children. I'm not interested in the poor.

Princess [*smiling*]: How can you say that?

Pearl: Are you? I often wonder if your philanthropy isn't an elaborate pose. You don't mind my saying that, do you?

Princess [*good-humouredly*] Not at all. You have no heart, and you can't imagine that anyone else should have.

Pearl: I have plenty of heart, but it beats for people of my own class.

Princess: I've only found one thing really worth doing with all this money I have, and that is to help a little those who need help.

Pearl [*with a shrug*]: So long as it makes you happy.

Princess: It doesn't, but it prevents me from being utterly miserable.

Pearl: You make me so impatient, Flora. You've got more money than you know what to do with. You're a princess. You've practically got rid of your husband. I cannot imagine what more you want. I wish I could get rid of mine.

Princess [*smiling*]: I don't know what you've got to complain of in George.

Pearl: That's just it. I shouldn't mind if he beat me or made love to chorus girls. I could divorce him then. Oh, my dear, thank your stars that you had a husband who was grossly unfaithful to you. Mine wants me to live nine months of the year in the country and have a baby every five minutes. I didn't marry an Englishman for that.

Princess: Why *did* you marry him?

Pearl: I made a mistake. I'd lived all my life in New York. I was very ignorant. I thought if you were a baronet you must be in society.

Princess: I often wonder if you're happy, Pearl.

Pearl: Do you? Of course I'm happy.

Princess: An ambassador told me the other day that you were the most powerful woman in London. It's very wonderful how you've made your way. You had nothing very much to help you.

Pearl: Shall I tell you how it was done? By force of character, wit, unscrupulousness, and push.

Princess [*smiling*]: You're very frank.

Pearl: That has always been my pose.

Princess: I sometimes think there's positive genius in the way you've ignored the snubs of the great.

Pearl [*with a chuckle*]: You're being very unpleasant, Flora.

Princess: And there's something very like heroism in the callousness with which you've dropped people when they've served your turn.

Pearl: You're driving me to the conclusion that you don't altogether approve of me.

Princess: On the other hand I can't help admiring you. You've brought all the determination, insight, vigour, strength, which have made our countrymen turn America into what it is, to get what you wanted. In a way your life has been a work of art. And what makes it

389

more complete is that what you've aimed at is trivial, transitory and worthless.

Pearl: My dear Flora, people don't hunt in order to catch a fox.

Princess: Sometimes, doesn't it make you rather nervous, when you're sitting on the top of your ladder, in case anyone should give it a kick as he passes?

Pearl: It'll want more than a kick to topple my ladder over. D'you remember when that silly woman made such a fuss because her husband was in love with me? It wasn't till I only just escaped the divorce court that the duchesses really took me up.

[*The* **Duchesse** *comes forward with* **Tony Paxton**.]

Duchesse: We really must be going, Pearl. I expect my masseur at six. Compton Edwardes told me about him. He's wonderful, but he's so run after, if you keep him waiting a moment he goes away.

Pearl: My dear, do be careful. Fanny Hallam got herself down to a mere nothing, but it made her look a hundred.

Duchesse: Oh, I know, but Compton Edwardes has recommended to me a wonderful woman who comes every morning to do my face.

Pearl: You are coming to my ball, aren't you?

Duchesse: Of course we're coming. Yours are almost the only parties in London where one amuses oneself as much as at a night club.

Pearl: I'm having Ernest to come in and dance.

Duchesse: I thought of having him one evening. How much does he charge for coming in socially?

Pearl: Twenty guineas.

Duchesse: Good heavens, I could never afford that.

Pearl: What nonsense! You're far richer than I am.

Duchesse: I'm not so clever, darling. I can't think how you do so much on your income.

Pearl [*amused*]: I'm a very good manager.

Duchesse: One would never think it. Good-bye, dear. Are you coming, Tony?

Tony: Yes.

[*She goes out.*]

Tony [*shaking hands with* **Pearl**]: I've not had a word with you today.

Pearl [*chaffing him*]: What are we to do about it?

Princess: I *must* get Minnie to go to my concert. Minnie.

[*She goes out.* **Tony** *is left face to face with* **Pearl**.]

Tony: You're looking perfectly divine today. I don't know what there is about you.

Pearl [*amused but not disconcerted*]: It is nice of you to say so.

Tony: I simply haven't been able to take my eyes off you.

Pearl: Are you making love to me?

Tony: That's nothing new, is it?

Pearl: You'll get into trouble.

Tony: Don't be disagreeable, Pearl.

Pearl: I don't remember that I ever told you you might call me Pearl.

Tony: It's how I think of you. You can't prevent me from doing that.

Pearl: Well, I think it's very familiar.

Tony: I don't know what you've done to me. I think of you all day long.

Pearl: I don't believe it for a minute. You're an unprincipled ruffian, Tony.

Tony: Do you mind?

Pearl [*with a chuckle*]: Shameless creature. I wonder what it is that Minnie sees in you.

Tony: I have all sorts of merits.

Pearl: I'm glad you think so. I can only discover one.

Tony: What is that?

Pearl: You're somebody else's property.

Tony: Oh!

Pearl [*holding out her hand*]: Good-bye.

[*He kisses her wrist. His lips linger. She looks at him from under her eyelashes.*]

Pearl: It doesn't make you irresistible, you know.

Tony: There's always the future.

Pearl: The future's everybody's property.

Tony [*in an undertone*]: Pearl.

Pearl: Be quick and go. Minnie will be wondering why you don't come.

[*He goes out.* **Pearl** *turns away with a smile.* **Bessie** *and* **Lord Bleane** *advance into the room.*]

Pearl: Has Harry broken the news to you that he can't come down to us on Saturday?

[*The* **Princess** *comes in.*]

Princess: I've got my subscription.

Pearl: I kept Tony up here as long as I could so as to give you a chance.

Princess [*with a laugh*]: That was really tactful.

Pearl: Poor Minnie, she's as mean as cat's meat. [*With a glance at* **Bessie** *and* **Lord Bleane**] If you'd like to come down to the morning-room we can go through my visitors' book and see who'll be useful to you.

Princess: Oh, that would be kind of you.

Pearl [*to* **Bleane**]: Don't go till I come back, will you? I haven't had a word with you yet.

Bleane: All right.

[**Pearl** *and the* **Princess** *go out.*]

Bessie: I wonder if you sent me these flowers, Lord Bleane?

Bleane: I did. I thought you wouldn't mind.

Bessie: It was very kind of you.

[*She takes two of the roses and puts them in her dress.* **Bleane** *is overcome with shyness. He does not know how to begin.*]

Bleane: D'you mind if I light a cigarette?

Bessie: Not at all.

Bleane [*as he lights it*]: D'you know, this is the first time I've ever been alone with you. It was very tactful of Lady Grayston to leave us.

Bessies I'm not sure if it wasn't a trifle too tactful.

Bleane: I was hoping most awfully to have the chance of getting a talk with you.

[*The song of the lavender is heard again in the street.*
Bessie *welcomes the diversion.*]

Bessie: Oh, listen, there's the lavender man come back
again. [*She goes to the window and listens.*] Throw him
down a shilling, will you?

Bleane: All right.

[*He takes a coin from his pocket and throws it into
the street.*]

Bessie: I seem to feel all the charm of England in that
funny little tune. It suggests cottage gardens, and
hedges, and winding roads.

Bleane: My mother grows lavender at home. When we
were kids we were made to pick it, and my mother
used to put it in little muslin bags and tie them up
with pink ribbon. And she used to put them under the
pillows of one's bed and in all the drawers. Shall I ask
her to send you some?

Bessie: Oh, that would be such a bother for her.

Bleane: It wouldn't. She'd like to. And you know, it's not
like the lavender you buy. It knocks spots off anything
you can get in shops.

Bessie: You must hate leaving London at this time of
year.

Bleane: Oh, I'm not very keen on London. [*Making a dash
for it*] I hate leaving you.

Bessie [*with comic desperation*]: Let's not talk about me,
Lord Bleane.

Bleane: But that's the only topic that occurs to me.

Bessie: There's always the weather in England.

Bleane: You see, I'm off tomorrow.

Bessie: I never saw anyone so obstinate.

Bleane: I shan't see you again for nearly a month. We
haven't known one another very long, and if I hadn't
been going away I expect I'd have thought it better to
wait a bit.

Bessie [*clasping her hands*]: Lord Bleane, don't propose to
me.

Bleane: Why not?

Bessie: Because I shall refuse you.

Bleane: Oh!

Bessie: Tell me about the part of the country you live in. I don't know Kent at all. Is it pretty?

Bleane: I don't know. It's home.

Bessie: I love those old Elizabethan houses that you have in England with all their chimneys.

Bleane: Oh, ours isn't a show-place, you know. It's just a rather ugly yellow brick house that looks like a box, and it's got a great big stucco portico in front of it. I think the garden's rather jolly.

Bessie: Pearl hates Abbots Kenton. She'd sell it if George would. She's only really happy in London.

Bleane: I don't know that I was so particularly struck on Bleane till I was over in France. When I was in hospital at Boulogne there didn't seem much to do but to think about things . . . It didn't seem as if I *could* get well. I knew I should if they'd only let me come home, but they wouldn't; they said I couldn't be moved . . . It's rather bleak in our part of the country. We've got an east wind that people find a bit trying, but if you've been used to it all your life it bucks you up wonderfully. In summer it can be awfully hot down there, but there's always something fresh and salt in the air. You see, we're so near the . . . It was only just across the water, and it seemed such an awful long way off. I ain't boring you, am I?

Bessie: No. I want you to tell me.

Bleane: It's a funny sort of country. There are a lot of green fields and elm trees, and the roads wind about – it's rotten for motoring; and then you have the marshes, with dykes in them – we used to jump them when we were boys, and fall in mostly; and then there's the sea. It doesn't sound much, but I felt it was the most ripping thing I knew. And then there are hop-fields – I forgot them – and the oast-houses. They're rather picturesque, I suppose. I expect it's like the lavender to you. To me it's just England.

[**Bessie** *gets up and walks towards the window. In
the distance is heard the melancholy cry of the lavender man.*]

Bleane: What are you thinking about?

Bessie: It must be very wonderful to feel like that about
one's home. I've never known anything but a red stone
house in Nineteenth Street. As soon as Dad can get a
decent offer for it we're going to move further up town.
Mother has a fancy for Seventy-Second Street, I don't
know why.

Bleane: Of course, I know it couldn't mean the same to
a girl that it means to me. I shouldn't expect anyone
to live there always. I can be quite happy in London.

Bessie [*with a smile*]: You're determined to do it?

Bleane: If you *could* bring yourself to marry me, I'd try
and give you a good time.

Bessie: Well I suppose that's a proposal.

Bleane: I've never made one before, and it makes me a
bit nervous.

Bessie: You haven't said anything that I can answer yes
or no to.

Bleane: I don't want to say anything that you can answer
no to.

Bessie [*with a chuckle*]: Let me say that I'll think it over,
may I?

Bleane: I'm going away tomorrow.

Bessie: I'll give you an answer when you come back.

Bleane: But that won't be for four weeks.

Bessie: It'll give us both a chance to make up our minds.
After all, it is rather a serious step. You may come to
the conclusion that you don't really want to marry me.

Bleane: There's no fear of that.

Bessie: You're coming down to Kenton for the week-end
after you get back. If you change your mind send Pearl
a wire putting yourself off. I shall understand, and I
shan't be in the least hurt or offended.

Bleane: Then it's good-bye till then.

Bessie: Yes. And thank you very much for wishing to marry me.

Bleane: Thank you very much for not refusing me outright.

[*They shake hands and he goes out. She walks over to the window to look at him, glances at the watch on her wrist, and then leaves the room. In a moment* **Pole** *shows in* **Arthur Fenwick**. *He is a tall, elderly man with a red face and grey hair.*]

Pole: I'll tell her ladyship you're here, sir.

Fenwick: That'll be very good of you.

[**Pole** *goes out.* **Fenwick** *takes a cigar from his case, and the evening paper from a table, and settles himself down comfortably to read and smoke. He makes himself very much at home.* **Pearl** *comes in.*]

Pearl: Aren't Bessie and Harry Bleane here?

Fenwick: No.

Pearl: That's very strange. I wonder what can have happened.

Fenwick: Never mind about Bessie and Harry Bleane. Give me your attention now.

Pearl: You're very late.

Fenwick: I like to come when I stand a chance of finding you alone, girlie.

Pearl: I wish you wouldn't call me girlie, Arthur. I do hate it.

Fenwick: That's how I think of you. When I'm present at one of your big set-outs, and watch you like a queen among all those lords and ambassadors and bigwigs, I just say to myself, She's my girlie, and I feel warm all over. I'm so proud of you then. You've got there, girlie, you've got there.

Pearl [*smiling*]: You've been very kind to me, Arthur.

Fenwick: You've got brains, girlie, that's how you've done it. It's brains. Underneath your flighty ways and that casual air of yours, so that one might think you were just enjoying yourself and nothing more, I see you thinking it all out, pulling a string here and a string there;

you've got them in the hollow of your hand all the time. You leave nothing to chance, Pearl, you're a great woman.

Pearl: Not great enough to make you obey your doctor's orders.

Fenwick [*taking the cigar out of his mouth*]: You're not going to ask me to throw away the first cigar I've had today?

Pearl: To please me, Arthur. They're so bad for you.

Fenwick: If you put it like that I must give in.

Pearl: I don't want you to be ill.

Fenwick: You've got a great heart, girlie. The world just thinks you're a smart, fashionable woman, clear, brilliant, beautiful, a leader of fashion, but I know different. I know you've got a heart of gold.

Pearl: You're a romantic old thing, Arthur.

Fenwick: My love for you is the most precious thing I have in the world. You're my guiding star, you're my ideal. You stand to me for all that's pure and noble and clean in womanhood. God bless you, girlie. I don't know what I should do if you failed me. I don't believe I could live if I ever found out that you weren't what I think you.

Pearl [*with her tongue in her cheek*]: You shan't, if I can help it.

Fenwick: You do care for me a little, girlie?

Pearl: Of course I do.

Fenwick: I'm an old man, girlie.

Pearl: What nonsense! I look upon you as a mere boy.

Fenwick [*flattered*]: Well, I expect a good many young men would be glad to have my physique. I can work fourteen hours on end and feel as fresh as a daisy at the end of it.

Pearl: Your vitality is wonderful.

Fenwick: I sometimes wonder what it is that first drew you to me, girlie.

Pearl: I don't know. I suppose it was the impression of strength you give.

Fenwick: Yes, I've often been told that. It's very difficult for people to be with me long without realizing that – well, that I'm not just the man in the street.

Pearl: I always feel I can rely on you.

Fenwick: You couldn't have said anything to please me better. I want you to rely on me. I know you. I'm the only man who's ever understood you. I know that, deep down in that big, beating, human heart of yours, you're a timid, helpless little thing, with the innocence of a child, and you want a man like me to stand between you and the world. My God, how I love you, girlie!

Pearl: Take care, there's the butler.

Fenwick: Oh, damn it, there's always the butler.

[**Pole** *comes in with a telegram and a parcel of books.*]

Pearl [*taking the telegram and glancing at the parcel*]: What's that, Pole?

Pole: They're books, my lady. They've just come from Hatchard's.

Pearl: Oh, I know. Undo them, will you? [**Pole** *cuts open the parcel and takes out a bundle of four or five books.* **Pearl** *opens the telegram.*] Oh, bother! There's no answer, Pole.

Pole: Very good, my lady.

[*Exit* **Pole**.]

Fenwick: Is anything the matter?

Pearl: That fool Sturrey was dining here tonight, and he's just wired to say he can't come. I do hate having my parties upset. I'd asked ten people to meet him.

Fenwick: That's too bad.

Pearl: Pompous owl. He's refused invitation after invitation. I asked him six weeks ago this time, and he hadn't the face to say he was engaged.

Fenwick: Well, I'm afraid you must give him up. I daresay you can do without him.

Pearl: Don't be a fool, Arthur. I'll get hold of him somehow. He may be Prime Minister one of these days. [*She reflects a moment.*] I wonder what his telephone number is. [*She gets up and looks in a book, then sits down at the telephone.*] Gerrard 7035. If he comes once because I force him to he'll come again because he likes it. This house is like the kingdom of heaven: I have to compel them to come in . . . Is Lord Sturrey in? Lady Grayston. I'll hold the line. [*Making her voice sweet and charming*] Is that you, Lord Sturrey? It's Pearl Grayston speaking. I just rang up to say it doesn't matter a bit about tonight. Of course, I'm disappointed you can't come. But you must come another day, will you? That's very nice of you. How about this day week? Oh, I'm sorry. Would Thursday suit you? Oh! Well, how about Friday? You're engaged every evening next week? You are in demand. Well, I'll tell you what, get your book and tell me what day you are free.

Fenwick: You're the goods, girlie. You'll get there.

Pearl: Tuesday fortnight. Yes, that'll suit me beautifully. 8.30. I'm so glad you chose that day, because I'm having Kreisler in to play. I shall look forward to seeing you. Good-bye. [*She puts down the receiver.*] This time I've got him. The ape thinks he understands music.

Fenwick: Have you got Kreisler for Tuesday fortnight?

Pearl: No.

Fenwick: Are you sure you can get him?

Pearl: No, but I'm sure you can.

Fenwick: You shall have him, girlie.

[*She takes the books that* **Pole** *brought in and puts them about the room. One she places face downwards, open.*]

What are you doing that for?

Pearl: They're Richard Twining's books. He's coming to dinner tonight.

Fenwick: Why d'you trouble about authors, girlie?

Pearl: London isn't like New York, you know. People like to meet them over here.

Fenwick: I should have thought your position was quite strong enough to do without them.

Pearl: We live in a democratic age. They take the place

in society of the fools whom kings kept about their courts in the Middle Ages. They have the advantage that they don't presume on their position to tell one home truths. They're cheap. A dinner and a little flattery is all they want. And they provide their own clothes.

Fenwick: You litter up your house with their rotten books.

Pearl: Oh, but I don't keep them. These are on approval. I shall send them all back to the bookseller tomorrow morning.

Fenwick: Pearl, you're a little wonder. When you want to go into business you come to me and I'll take you into partner-ship.

Pearl: How is business?

Fenwick: Fine! I'm opening two new branches next week. They laughed at me when I first came over here. They said I'd go bankrupt. I've turned their silly old methods upside down. He laughs longest who laughs last.

Pearl [*reflectively*]: Ah, I can't help thinking that's what my dressmaker said when she sent me in my bill.

[*He gives a slight start and looks at her shrewdly. He sees her blandly smiling.*]

Fenwick: Girlie, you promised me you wouldn't run up any more bills.

Pearl: That's like promising to love, honour, and obey one's husband, the kind of undertaking no one is really expected to carry out.

Fenwick: You naughty little thing.

Pearl: It's Suzanne – you know, the dressmaker in the Place Vendôme. The war has dislocated her business and she wants to get her money in. It isn't very convenient for me to pay just at present. It's rather a large sum.

[*She gives him a sheaf of typewritten documents.*]

Fenwick: This looks more like a five-act play than a bill.

Pearl: Clothes are expensive, aren't they? I wish I could dress in fig-leaves. It would be cheap, and I believe it would suit me.

Fenwick [*putting the bill in his pocket*]: Well, I'll see what I can do about it.

Pearl: You are a duck, Arthur ... Would you like me to come and lunch with you tomorrow?

Fenwick: Why, sure.

Pearl: All right. Now you must go, as I want to lie down before I dress for dinner.

Fenwick: That's right. Take care of yourself, girlie, you're very precious to me.

Pearl: Good-bye, dear old thing.

Fenwick: Good-bye, girlie.

[*He goes out. As he goes to the door the telephone rings.* **Pearl** *takes up the receiver.*]

Pearl: You're speaking to Lady Grayston. Tony! Of course I knew your voice. Well, what is it? I'm not at all stern. I'm making my voice as pleasant as I can. I'm sorry you find it disagreeable [*She gives a chuckle.*] No, I'm afraid I couldn't come to tea tomorrow. I shall be engaged all the afternoon. What is the day after tomorrow? [*Smiling.*] Well, I must ask Bessie. I don't know if she's free. Of course I'm not coming alone. It would be most compromising. A nice looking young man like you. What would Minnie say? Oh, I know all about that ... I didn't promise anything. I merely said the future was everybody's property. A sleepless night. Fancy! Well, goodbye ... Tony, do you know the most enchanting word in the English language? Perhaps.

[*She puts down the telephone quickly, and the curtain falls.*]

Act Two

The scene is a morning-room at Abbots Kenton, the Graystons' place in the country. It has an old-fashioned, comfortable look; nothing is very new; the chintzes are faded. Three long french windows lead on to a terrace.

It is after dinner, a fine night, and the windows are open.

> [*The women of the party are sitting down, waiting for the men; they are* **Pearl** *and* **Bessie**, *the* **Duchesse de Surennes**, *and the* **Princess Della Cercola**.]

Princess: You must be exhausted after all the tennis you played this afternoon, Minnie.

Duchesse: Not a bit. I only played four sets.

Princess: You played so vigorously. It made me quite hot to look at you.

Duchesse: If I didn't take exercise I should be enormous. Oh, Flora, how I envy you! You can eat anything you choose and it has no effect on you. And what makes it so unfair is that you don't care about food. I am a lazy and a greedy woman. I never eat any of the things I like, and I never miss a day without taking at least an hour's exercise.

Princess [*smiling*]: If mortification is the first step in sanctity, I'm sure you must be on the high road to it.

Pearl: One of these days you'll give up the struggle, Minnie, and, like Flora, take to good works.

Duchesse [*with immense decision*]: Never! I shall lie on my death-bed with my hair waved and a little rouge on my cheeks, and with my last breath murmur: Not gruel, it's so fattening.

Pearl: Well, you'll have more serious tennis tomorrow. Harry Bleane plays much better than Thornton.

Duchesse: It was very tiresome of him not to come till it was just time to dress.

Pearl: He only got back from Romania yesterday, and he had to go down to see his mother. [*With an amused glance at her sister*] Bessie asked me not to put him next to her at dinner.

Bessie: Pearl, you are a cat! I do think it's hateful the way you discuss my private affairs with all and sundry.

Duchesse: My dear Bessie, they've long ceased to be your private affairs.

Pearl: I'm afraid Bessie misses her opportunities. Just before he went to Romania I left them alone together, and nothing happened. All my tact was wasted.

Bessie: Your tact was too obvious, Pearl.

Duchesse: Well, do be quick and bring him to the scratch, my dear. I'm growing tired of people asking me, Is he going to propose or is he not?

Bessie: Don't they ever ask, Is she going to accept him or is she not?

Duchesse: Of course, you'll accept him.

Bessie: I'm not so sure.

Princess [*smiling*]: Perhaps it depends on the way he asks.

Pearl: For heaven's sake, don't expect too much romance. Englishmen aren't romantic. It makes them feel absurd. George proposed to me when he was in New York for the Horse Show. I wasn't very well that day, and I was lying down. I was looking a perfect fright. He told me all about a mare he had, and he told me all about her father and her mother and her uncles and her aunts, and then he said: [*imitating him*] Look here, you'd better marry me.

Princess: How very sudden.

Pearl: Oh, I said, why didn't you tell me you were going to propose? I'd have had my hair waved. Poor George, he asked *Why!*

Duchesse: The French are the only nation who know how to make love. When Gaston proposed to me he went down on his knees, and he took my hand, and he said

403

he couldn't live without me. Of course I knew that, because he hadn't a cent, but still it thrilled me. He said I was his guiding star and his guardian angel – oh, I don't know what! It was beautiful! I knew he'd been haggling with papa for a fortnight about having his debts paid; but it was beautiful.

Princess: Were you quite indifferent to him?

Duchesse: Oh, quite. I'd made up my mind to marry a foreigner. People weren't very nice to us in Chicago. My cousin Mary had married the Count de Moret, and mother couldn't bear Aunt Alice. She said, If Alice has got hold of a Count for Mary, I'm determined that you shall have a Duke.

Pearl: And you did.

Duchesse: I wish you could have seen the fuss those Chicago people made of me when I went over last. It was hard to realize that I used to cry my eyes out because I wasn't asked to the balls I wanted to go to.

Princess: Still, I hope Bessie won't marry any man she doesn't care for.

Pearl: My dear, don't put ideas in the child's head. The French are a much more civilized nation than we are, and they've come to the conclusion long ago that marriage is an affair of convenience rather than of sentiment. Think of the people you know who've married for love. After five years do they care for one another any more than the people who've married for money?

Princess: They have the recollection.

Pearl: Nonsense! As if anyone remembered an emotion when he no longer felt it!

Duchesse: It's true. I've been in love a dozen times, desperately, and when I've got over it and look back, though I remember I was in love, I can't for the life of me remember my love. It always seems to me so odd.

Pearl: Believe me, Bessie, the flourishing state of father's hardware store is a much sounder basis for matrimonial happiness than any amount of passion.

Act Two

Bessie: Oh, Pearl, what is this you've been telling people about Dad selling bananas?

Pearl: Bananas? Oh, I remember. They were saying that Mrs Hanley used to wash the miners' clothes in California. That and her pearls are taking her everywhere. I wasn't going to be outdone, so I said Father used to sell bananas in the streets of New York.

Bessie: He never did anything of the kind.

Pearl: I know he didn't, but I thought people were getting rather tired of the hardware store, and I made a perfectly killing story out of it. I had a new Callot frock on and I thought I could manage the bananas.

Duchesse: A most unpleasant vegetable. So fattening.
[*The men come in.* **Thornton Clay, Arthur Fenwick,** *and* **Fleming. Pearl** *and* **Bessie** *get up.*]

Bessie: You've been a long time.

Duchesse: Where is Tony?

Clay: He and Bleane are finishing their cigars.

Duchesse: Well, Mr Harvey, are you still enjoying life in London?

Clay: He should be. I've got him invitations to all the nicest parties. But he will waste his time in sightseeing. The other day – Thursday, wasn't it? – I wanted to take him to Hurlingham, and he insisted on going to the National Gallery instead.

Pearl [*smiling*]: What an outrageous proceeding!

Fleming: I don't see that it was any more outrageous for me than for you. I saw you coming in just as I was going out.

Pearl: I had a reason to go. Arthur Fenwick had just bought a Bronzino, and I wanted to see those in the National Gallery.

Duchesse: I think it's much more likely that you had an assignation. I've always heard it's a wonderful place for that. You never meet any of your friends, and if you do they're there for the same purpose, and pretend not to see you.

Fleming: I certainly only went to see the pictures.

Clay: But, good heavens, if you want to do that there's Christie's, and there you *will* meet your friends.

Fleming: I'm afraid you'll never make a man of fashion out of me, Thornton.

Clay: I'm beginning to despair. You have a natural instinct for doing the wrong thing. D'you know, the other day I caught him in the act of delivering half a bag full of letters of introduction ? I implored him to put them in the waste-paper basket.

Fleming: I thought as people had taken the trouble to give them to me, it was only polite to make use of them.

Clay: Americans give letters so carelessly. Before you know where you are you'll know all the wrong people. And, believe me, the wrong people are very difficult to shake off.

Fleming [*amused*]: Perhaps some of my letters are to the right people.

Clay: Then they'll take no notice of them.

Fleming: It looks as though the wrong people had better manners than the right ones.

Clay: The right people *are* rude. They can afford to be. I was a very young man when I first came to London, and I made mistakes. All of us Americans make mistakes. It wanted a good deal of character to cut people who'd taken me about, asked me to dine, stay with them in the country, and heaven knows what, when I found they weren't the sort of people one ought to know.

Pearl: Of course, one has to do it.

Duchesse: Of course. It shows that you have a nice nature, Thornton, to worry yourself about it.

Clay: I'm curiously sentimental. Another of our American faults. I remember when I'd been in London two or three years. I knew pretty well everyone that was worth knowing, but I'd never been asked to Hereford House. The duchess doesn't like Americans anyway, and she'd been very disagreeable about me in particular. But I was determined to go to her ball. I felt it wasn't the sort of function I could afford to be left out of.

Pearl: They're very dull balls.

Clay: I know, but they're almost the only ones you can't go to without an invitation. Well, I found out that the duchess had a widowed sister who lived in the country with her two daughters. Lady Helen Blair. My dear, she was a very stuffy, dowdy woman of fifty-five, and her two daughters were stuffier and dowdier still, and, if possible, older. They were in the habit of coming up to London for the season. I got introduced to them, and I laid myself out. I took them to the play, I showed them round the Academy, I stood them luncheons, I gave them cards for private views, for a month I worked like a Trojan. Then the duchess sent out her invitations, and the Blair girls had half a dozen cards for their young men. I received one, and, by George, I'd earned it. Of course, as soon as I got my invitation I dropped them, but you know I felt quite badly about it.

Duchesse: I expect they're used to that.

Clay: A strangely tactless woman, Lady Helen Blair. She wrote and asked me if I was offended about anything because I never went near them.

Pearl: I wish those men would come, and then we could dance.

Duchesse: Oh, that'll be charming! It's such good exercise, isn't it? I'm told that you dance divinely, Mr Harvey.

Fleming: I don't know about that. I dance.

Duchesse [*to the* **Princess**]: Oh, my dear, who d'you think I danced with the other night? [*Impressively*] Ernest.

Princess: Oh!

Duchesse: My dear, don't say, Oh! like that. Don't you know who Ernest is?

Pearl: Ernest is the most sought after man in London.

Princess: You don't mean the dancing-master?

Duchesse: Oh, my dear, you mustn't call him that. He'd be furious. He isn't a professional. He gives lessons at ten guineas an hour, but only to oblige. He's invited to all the best dances.

Fleming: One of the things that rather surprised me at balls was to see all these dancing-masters. Do English girls like to be pawed about by Greeks, Dagos, and Bowery toughs?

Clay: You Americans who live in America, you're so prudish.

Duchesse: Believe me, I would go to *any* dance where there was the remotest chance of meeting Ernest. It's a perfect dream to dance with him. He showed me a new step, and I can't get it quite right. I don't know what I shall do if I don't run across him again very soon.

Princess: But why don't you let him give you a lesson?

Duchesse: My dear, ten guineas an hour! I couldn't possibly afford that. I'm sure to meet him at a dance in a day or two, and I shall get a lesson for nothing.

Pearl: You ought to make him fall in love with you.

Duchesse: Oh, my dear, if he only would! But he's so run after.

[**Bleane** *and* **Tony Paxton** *come in from the terrace.*]

Duchesse: At last!

Tony: We've been taking a stroll in the garden.

Pearl: I hope you showed him my tea-house.

Bessie: It's Pearl's new toy. You must be sure to admire it.

Pearl: I'm very proud of it. You know, George won't let me do anything here. He says it's his house, and he isn't going to have any of my muck. He won't even have new chintzes. Well, there was an old summer-house just over there, and it was all worm-eaten and horrid and tumble-down, what they call picturesque, but it was rather a nice place to go and have tea in as it had a really charming view; I wanted to pull it down and put up a smart Japanese tea-house instead, but George wouldn't hear of it, because, if you please, his mother – a peculiarly plain woman – used to sit and sew there. Well, I bided my time, and the other day, when George was in London, I pulled down the old summer-house, got my Japanese tea-house down from town, put it up, and had everything finished by the time George came back twenty-four hours later. He very nearly had an apoplectic stroke. If he had I should have killed two birds with one stone.

Bessie: Pearl!

Princess: I don't know why you've furnished it so elaborately.

Pearl: Well, I thought in the hot weather I'd sleep there sometimes. It'll be just like sleeping in the open air.

Fenwick: These young people want to start dancing, Pearl.

Pearl: Where would you like to dance, in here with the gramophone, or in the drawing-room with the pianola?

Bessie: Oh, in the drawing-room.

Pearl: Let's go there then.

Bessie [to **Clay**]: Come and help me get the rolls out.

Clay: Right you are.

[*They go out, followed by the* **Duchesse** *and* **Pearl,** **Tony, Fenwick,** *and* **Bleane.**]

Fleming [*to the* **Princess**]: Aren't you coming?

Princess: No, I think I'll stay here for the present. But don't bother about me. You must go and dance.

Fleming: There are enough men without me. I'm sure Thornton Clay is a host in himself.

Princess: You don't like Thornton?

Fleming: He's been very kind to me since I came to London.

Princess: I was watching your face when he told that story about the Hereford ball. You must learn to conceal your feelings better.

Fleming: Didn't you think it was horrible?

Princess: I've known Thornton for ten years. I'm used to him. And, as you say yourself, he's very kind.

Fleming: That's what makes life so difficult. People don't seem to be good or bad as the squares on a chessboard are black or white. Even the worthless ones have got good traits, and it makes it so hard to know how to deal with them.

Princess [*smiling a little*]: You don't approve of poor Thornton?

Fleming: What do you expect me to think of a man who's proud of having forced his way into a house where he knew he wasn't wanted? He reckons success by the number of invitations he receives. He holds himself up to me as an example. He tells me that if I want to get into society, I must work for it. What do they think of a man like Thornton Clay in England? Don't they despise him?

Princess: Everywhere, in New York just as much as in London, there are masses of people struggling to get into society. It's so common a sight that one loses the sense of there being anything disgraceful in it. Pearl would tell you that English society is a little pompous; they welcome a man who can make them laugh. Thornton is very useful. He has high spirits, he's amusing, he makes a party go.

Fleming: I should have thought a man could find some better use for his life than that.

Princess: Thornton has plenty of money. Do you think there is any point in his spending his life making more? I sometimes think there's too much money in America already.

Fleming: There are things a man can do beside making money.

Princess: You know, American wealth has reached a pitch when it was bound to give rise to a leisured class. Thornton is one of the first members of it. Perhaps he doesn't play the part very well, but remember he hasn't had the time to learn it that they've had in Europe.

Fleming [*smiling*]: I'm afraid you don't think me very charitable.

Princess: You're young. It's a real pleasure to me to know a nice clean American boy. And I'm so glad that you're not going to be dazzled by this English life that dazzles so many of our countrymen. Amuse yourself, learn what you can from it, take all the good it offers you and go back to America.

Fleming: I shall be glad to go back. Perhaps I ought never to have come.

Princess: I'm afraid you're not very happy.

Fleming: I don't know what makes you think that.

Princess: It's not very hard to see that you're in love with Bessie.

Fleming: Did you know that I was engaged to her?

Princess [*surprised*]: No.

Fleming: I was engaged to her before I went to Harvard. I was eighteen then, and she was sixteen.

Princess: How very early in life you young people settle things in America!

Fleming: Perhaps it was rather silly and childish. But when she wrote and told me that she thought we'd better break it off I discovered I cared more than I thought.

Princess: What did you say to her?

Fleming: I couldn't try to hold her to a promise she gave when she was a schoolgirl. I answered that I sympathized and understood.

Princess: When did this happen?

Fleming: A couple of months ago. Then I got the chance to go over to Europe and I thought I'd come to see what was going on. It didn't take me long to tumble.

Princess: You're bearing it very well.

Fleming: Oh, the only thing I could do was to be pleasant. I should only have bored her if I'd made love to her. She took our engagement as an amusing joke, and there wasn't anything for me to do but accept her view of it. She was having the time of her life. At first I thought perhaps she'd grow tired of all these balls and parties, and then if I was on the spot I might persuade her to come back to America with me.

Princess: You may still.

Fleming: No, I haven't a chance. The first day I arrived she told me how wonderful she thought this English life. She thinks it full and varied. She thinks it has beauty.

Princess: That sounds rather satirical.

Fleming: Pearl has been very nice to me. She's taken me about, I've driven with her constantly, I've sat in her box at the opera, I'm her guest at the moment. If I had any decency I'd hold my tongue.

Princess: Well?

Fleming [*bursting out impetuously*]: There's something in these surroundings that makes me feel terribly uncomfortable. Under the brilliant surface I suspect all kinds of ugly and shameful secrets that everyone knows and pretends not to. This is a strange house in which the husband is never seen and Arthur Fenwick, a vulgar sensualist, acts as host; and it's an attractive spectacle, this painted duchess devouring with her eyes a boy young enough to be her son. And the conversation – I don't want to seem a prude, I dare say people over here talk more freely than the people I've known; but surely there are women who don't have lovers, there are such things as honour and decency and self-restraint. If Bessie is going to remain over here I wish to God she'd marry her lord at once and get out of it quickly.

Princess: D'you think she'll be happy?

Fleming: Are they any of them happy? How can they expect to be happy when they marry for ... [*The* **Princess** *gives a sudden start, and* **Fleming** *stops short.*] I beg your pardon. I was forgetting. Please forgive me. You see, you're so different.

Princess: I'm sorry I interrupted you. What were you going to say?

Fleming: It wasn't of any importance. You see, I've been thinking it over so much that it's rather got on my nerves. And I haven't been able to tell anyone what I was thinking about. I'm dreadfully sorry.

Princess: You were going to say, how can they expect to be happy when they marry for a trumpery title? You

thought, they're snobs, vulgar snobs, and the misery of
their lives is the proper punishment for their ignoble
desires.

Fleming [*very apologetically*]: Princess.

Princess [*ironically*]: Princess.

Fleming: Believe me, I hadn't the smallest intention of
saying anything to wound you.

Princess: You haven't. It's too true. Most of us who marry
foreigners are merely snobs. But I wonder if it's all our
fault. We're not shown a better way of life. No one has
even hinted to us that we have any duty towards our
own country. We're blamed because we marry
foreigners, but columns are written about us in the
papers, and our photographs are in all the magazines.
Our friends are excited and envious. After all, we are
human. At first, when people addressed me as Princess,
I couldn't help feeling thrilled. Of course it was snobbishness.

Fleming: You make me feel a terrible cad.

Princess: But sometimes there've been other motives, too.
Has it ever occurred to you that snobbishness is the
spirit of romance in a reach-me-down? I was only
twenty when I married Marino. I didn't see him as a
fortune-hunting Dago, but as the successor of a long
line of statesmen and warriors. There'd been a pope in
his family, and a dozen cardinals, one of his ancestors
had been painted by Titian; for centuries they'd been
men of war, with power of life and death; I'd seen the
great feudal castle, with its hundred rooms, where they
had ruled as independent sovereigns. When Marino
came and asked me to marry him it was romance that
stood in his shoes and beckoned to me. I thought of
the palace in Rome, which I had visited as a tripper,
and where I might reign as mistress. I thought it was
splendid to take my place after all those great ladies,
Orsinis, Colonnas, Gaetanis, Aldobrandinis. I loved
him.

Fleming: But there's no need to tell me that you could never do anything from an unworthy motive.

Princess: My husband's family had been ruined by speculation. He was obliged to sell himself. He sold himself for five million dollars. And I loved him. You can imagine the rest. First he was indifferent to me, then I bored him; and at last he hated me. Oh, the humiliation I endured. When my child died I couldn't bear it any longer; I left him. I went back to America. I found myself a stranger. I was out of place, the life had become foreign to me; I couldn't live at home. I settled in England; and here we're strangers too. I've paid very heavily for being a romantic girl.

[**Bessie** *comes in.*]

Bessie: Really, Fleming, it's too bad of you to sit in here and flirt with the Princess. We want you to come and dance.

[*The* **Princess**, *agitated, gets up and goes out into the garden.*]

Bessie [*looking after her*]: Is anything the matter?

Fleming: No.

Bessie: Are you coming to dance, or are you not?

Fleming: I had quite a talk with Lord Bleane after dinner, Bessie.

Bessie [*smiling*]: Well?

Fleming: Are you going to accept the coronet that he's dangling before your eyes?

Bessie: It would be more to the point if you asked whether I'm going to accept the coronet that he's laying at my feet.

Fleming: He's a very nice fellow, Bessie.

Bessie: I know that.

Fleming: I wanted to dislike him.

Bessie: Why?

Fleming: Well, I don't think much of these English lords who run after American girls for their money. I expected him to be a brainless loafer, with just enough cunning to know his market value, but he's a modest, unassuming fellow. To tell you the truth, I'm puzzled.

Bessie [*chaffing him*]: Fancy that!

Fleming: I think it's a low-down thing that he's doing, and yet he doesn't seem a low-down fellow.

Bessie: He might be in love with me, you know.

Fleming: Is he?

Bessie: No.

Fleming: Are you going to marry him?

Bessie: I don't know.

Fleming: I suppose he's come here to ask you?

Bessie [*after a short pause*]: He asked me a month ago. I promised to give him an answer when he came back from Romania ... I'm in a panic. He's waiting to get me alone. I was able to be quite flippant about it when I had a month before me, but now, when I've got to say yes or no, I'm so jumpy I don't know what to do with myself.

Fleming: Don't marry him, Bessie.

Bessie: Why not?

Fleming: Well, first, you're no more in love with him than he is with you.

Bessie: And then?

Fleming: Isn't that enough?

Bessie: I wonder if you realize what he offers me. Do you know what the position of an English peeress is?

Fleming: Does it mean so much to be called Your Ladyship by tradesmen?

Bessie: You donkey, Fleming. If I marry an American boy my life will be over; if I marry Harry Bleane it will be only just beginning. Look at Pearl. I could do what she's done; I could do more, because George Grayston isn't ambitious. I could make Harry do anything I liked. He would go into politics, and I should have a salon. Why, I could do anything.

Fleming [*dryly*]: I don't know why you should be in a panic. You've evidently made up your mind. You'll have a brilliant marriage with crowds outside the

church, your photograph will be in all the papers, you'll
go away for your honeymoon, and you'll come back.
What will you do then?

Bessie: Why, settle down.

Fleming: Will you break your heart like the Princess
because your husband has taken a mistress, or will you
take lovers like the Duchesse de Surennes, or will you
bore yourself to death like Pearl because your husband
is virtuous, and wants you to do your duty?

Bessie: Fleming, you've got no right to say things like
that to me.

Fleming: I'm sorry if I've made you angry. I had to say it.

Bessie: Are you quite sure that it's for my sake you don't
want me to marry Lord Bleane?

Fleming: Yes, I think it is. When you broke off our engagement I didn't blame you. You wouldn't have done it if
you'd cared for me, and it wasn't your fault if you
didn't. When I came over I saw that I could expect
nothing but friendship from you. You must do me the
justice to acknowledge that during this month I haven't
given the smallest sign that I wanted anything else.

Bessie: Oh, you've been charming. You always were the
best friend I've had.

Fleming: If in a corner of my heart I kept my love for
you, that is entirely my affair. I don't know that it puts
you to any inconvenience, and it pleases me. I'm quite
sure that I'm only thinking now of your happiness. Go
back to America, and fall in love with some nice fellow,
and marry him. You'll have all my best wishes. Perhaps
your life won't be so brilliant or so exciting, but it will
be simpler and wholesomer, and more becoming.

Bessie: You're a dear, Fleming, and if I said anything
disagreeable just now, forgive me. I didn't mean it. I
shall always want you to be my dearest friend.

[**Lord Bleane** *enters from the terrace.*]

Bleane: I was looking for you everywhere. I wondered
where you'd got to.

[*There is a moment's pause.* **Fleming Harvey** *looks from* **Bessie** *to* **Bleane**.]

Fleming: I really must go and dance with the Duchesse or she'll never forgive me.

Bleane: I've just been dancing with her. My dear fellow, it's the most violent form of exercise I've ever taken.

Fleming: I'm in very good condition.

[*He goes out.*]

Bleane: Blessings on him.

Bessie: Why?

Bleane: Because he's left us alone. Ask me another.

Bessie: I don't think I will.

Bleane: Then I'll ask you one.

Bessie: Please don't. Tell me all about Romania.

Bleane: Romania is a Balkan State. Its capital is Bucharest. It has long been known for its mineral springs.

Bessie: You're in very high spirits tonight.

Bleane: You may well wonder. Everything has conspired to depress them.

Bessie: Oh, what nonsense!

Bleane: First I was in England thirty-six hours before I had a chance of seeing you; secondly, when I arrived you'd already gone up to dress; then, when I was expecting to sit next to you at dinner, I was put between Lady Grayston and the Princess; and, lastly, you made me pound away at that beastly pianola when I wanted to dance with you.

Bessie: Well, you've survived it all.

Bleane: What I want to point out to you is that if notwithstanding I'm in high spirits, I must have a most engaging nature.

Bessie: I never dreamt of denying it.

Bleane: So much to the good.

Bessie: The man's going to propose to me.

Bleane: No, I'm not.

Bessie: I beg your pardon. My mistake.

Bleane: I did that a month ago.

Bessie: There's been a change of moon since then, and no proposal holds good after the new moon.

Bleane: I never knew that.

Bessie: You've been down to see your mother.

Bleane: She sends you her love.

Bessie: Have you told her?

Bleane: I told her a month ago.

[**Bessie** *does not speak for a moment, when she answers it is more gravely.*]

Bessie: You know, I want to be frank with you. You won't think it disagreeable of me, will you? I'm not in love with you.

Bleane: I know. But you don't positively dislike me?

Bessie: No. I like you very much.

Bleane: Won't you risk it then?

Bessie [*almost tragically*]: I can't make up my mind.

Bleane: I'll do all I can to make you happy. I'll try not to make a nuisance of myself.

Bessie: I know quite well that I wouldn't marry you if you weren't who you are, and I'm afraid I know that you wouldn't marry me if I hadn't a certain amount of money.

Bleane: Oh, yes, I would.

Bessie: It's nice of you to say so

Bleane: Don't you believe it?

Bessie: I suppose I'm a perfect fool. I ought to play the game prettily. You see, I know that you can't afford to marry a girl who isn't well-to-do. Everyone knows what I have. Pearl has taken good care that they should. You wouldn't ever have thought of me otherwise. We're arranging a deal. You give your title and your position, and I give my money. It's a commonplace enough thing, but somehow it sticks in my throat.

[**Bleane** *hesitates a moment, and walks up and down thinking.*]

Bleane: You make me feel an awful swine. The worst of it is that some part of what you say is true. I'm not such a fool that I didn't see your sister was throwing us together. I don't want to seem a conceited ass, but a fellow in my sort of position can't help knowing that many people think him rather a catch. Mothers of marriageable daughters are very transparent sometimes, you know, and if they don't marry their daughters they're determined it shan't be for want of trying.

Bessie: Oh, I can quite believe that. I have noticed it in American mothers, too.

Bleane: I knew it would be a good thing if I married you. I don't suppose I should have thought about you if I hadn't been told you were pretty well off. It's beastly now, saying all that.

Bessie: I don't see why.

Bleane: Because after a bit I found out I'd fallen in love with you. And then I didn't care if you hadn't got a bob. I wanted to marry you because — because I didn't know what to do without you.

Bessie: Harry!

Bleane: Do believe me. I swear it's true. I don't care a hang about the money. After all, we could get along without it. And I love you.

Bessie: It's very good to hear you say that. I'm so absurdly pleased and flattered.

Bleane: You do believe it, don't you?

Bessie: Yes.

Bleane: And will you marry me?

Bessie: If you like.

Blean: Of course I like.

[*He takes her in his arms and kisses her.*]

Bessie: Take care, someone might come in.

Bleane [*smiling and happy*]: Come into the garden with me.

[*He stretches out his hand, she hesitates a moment, smiles, takes it, and together they go out on to the terrace.*

For a moment the music of a one-step is heard more loudly, and then the **Duchesse** *and* **Tony Paxton** *come in. She sinks into a chair fanning herself and he goes over to a table, takes a cigarette, and lights it.*]

Duchesse: Did you see? That was Harry Bleane and Bessie. I wondered where they were.

Tony: You've got eyes like a lynx.

Duchesse: I'm positive they were hand in hand.

Tony: It looks as if she'd worked it at last.

Duchesse: I don't know about that. It looks as if he'd worked it.

Tony: She's not such a catch as all that. If I were a peer I'd sell myself for a damned sight more than eight thousand a year.

Duchesse: Don't stand so far away, Tony. Come and sit on the sofa by me.

Tony [*going over to her*]: I say, I've been talking to Bleane about two-seaters.

Duchesse [*very coldly*]: Oh!

Tony [*giving her a look out of the corner of his eye*]: He says I can't do better than get a Talbot.

Duchesse: I don't see why you want a car of your own. You can always use one of mine.

Tony: That's not the same thing. After all, it won't cost much. I can get a ripper for just over twelve hundred pounds, with a really smart body.

Duchesse: You talk as though twelve hundred pounds were nothing at all.

Tony: Hang it all, it isn't anything to you.

Duchesse: What with the income tax and one thing and another, I'm not so terribly flush just now. No one knows the claims I have on me. Because one has a certain amount of money one's supposed to be made of it. They don't realise that if one spends it in one way one can't spend it in another. It cost me seven thousand pounds to have my house redecorated.

Tony [*sulkily*]: You said I could buy myself a car.

Duchesse: I said I'd think about it. I wasn't under the impression that you'd go and order one right away.

Tony: I've practically committed myself now.

Duchesse: You only want a car so that you can be independent of me.

Tony: Well, hang it all, you can't expect me to be tied to your apron-strings always. It's a bit thick if whenever I want to take a man down to play golf I have to ring up and ask if I can have one of your cars. It makes me look such an ass.

Duchesse: If it's only to play golf you want it, I'm sure anyone would rather go down to the links in a comfortable Rolls-Royce than in a two-seater.

[*A silence.*]

Tony: If you don't want to give me a car, why on earth did you say you would?

Duchesse [*putting her hand on him*]: Tony.

Tony: For goodness' sake don't touch me.

Duchesse [*hurt and mortified*]: Tony!

Tony: I don't want to force you to make me presents. I can quite well do without a two-seater. I can go about in omnibuses if it comes to that.

Duchesse: Don't you love me?

Tony: I wish you wouldn't constantly ask me if I love you. It is maddening.

Duchesse: Oh, how can you be so cruel to me!

Tony [*exasperated*]: D'you think this is quite the best place to choose to make a scene?

Duchesse: I love you with all my heart. I've never loved anybody as much as I love you.

Tony: No man could stand being loved so much. D'you think it's jolly for me to feel that your eyes are glued on me whatever I'm doing? I can never put my hand out without finding yours there ready to press it.

Duchesse: I can't help it if I love you. That's my temperament.

Tony: Yes, but you needn't show it so much. Why don't you leave me to do the love-making?

Duchesse: If I did that there wouldn't be any love-making.

Tony: You make me look such a fool.

Our Betters

Duchesse: Don't you know there's nothing in the world I wouldn't do for you?

Tony [*quickly*]: Well, why don't you marry me?

Duchesse [*with a gasp*]: I can't do that. You know that I can't do that.

Tony: Why not? You could still call yourself Duchesse de Surennes.

Duchesse: No; I've always told you nothing would induce me to marry.

Tony: That shows how much you love me.

Duchesse: Marriage is so middle-class. It takes away all the romance of love.

Tony: You simply want to have your freedom and keep me bound hand and foot. D'you think it's jolly for me to know what people say about me? After all, I have got some pride.

Duchesse: I'm sure we shall be able to get you a job soon, and then no one will be able to say anything.

Tony: I'm getting fed up with the whole business; I tell you that straight. I'd just as soon chuck it.

Duchesse: Tony, you don't mean to say you want to leave me. I'll kill myself if you do. I couldn't bear it, I couldn't bear it. I'll kill myself.

Tony: For God's sake, don't make such a row.

Duchesse: Say you don't mean it, Tony. I shall scream.

Tony: After all, I've got my self-respect to think of. It seems to me the best thing would be if we put a stop to the whole thing now.

Duchesse: Oh, I can't lose you. I can't.

Tony: No one can say I'm mercenary, but hang it all, one has to think of one's future. I shan't be twenty-five for ever. I ought to be settling down.

Duchesse: Don't you care for me any more?

Tony: Of course I care for you. If I didn't, d'you think I'd have let you do all you have for me?

Duchesse: Then why d'you make me so unhappy?

Tony: I don't want to make you unhappy, but really sometimes you are unreasonable.

Duchesse: You mean about the car?

Tony: I wasn't thinking about the car then.

Duchesse: You can have it if you like.

Tony: I don't want it now.

Duchesse: Tony, don't be unkind.

Tony: I'm not going to take any more presents from you.

Duchesse: I didn't mean to be unreasonable. I'd like you to have the car, Tony. I'll give you a cheque for it tomorrow. [*Coaxingly*] Tell me what the body's like.

Tony [*sulkily*]: Oh, it's a torpedo body.

Duchesse: You'll take me for drives in it sometimes?

[*He turns round and looks at her, she puts out her hand, he thaws, and smiles engagingly.*]

Tony: I say, you are awfully kind to me.

Duchesse: You do like me a little, don't you?

Tony: Of course I do.

Duchesse: You have a good heart, Tony. Kiss me.

Tony [*kissing her, pleased and excited*]: I saw an awfully jolly body in a shop in Trafalgar Square the day before yesterday. I've got half a mind to get the people who made your body to copy it.

Duchesse: Why don't you get it at the shop you saw it at? My people are terribly expensive, and they aren't any better than anybody else.

Tony: Well, you see, I don't know anything about the firm. I just happened to catch sight of it as I was passing.

Duchesse: What on earth were you doing in Trafalgar Square on Thursday? I thought you were going to Ranelagh.

Tony: I was put off. I hadn't got anything to do, so I thought I'd just slope round the National Gallery for half an hour.

Duchesse: That's the last place I should have expected you to go to.

Tony: I don't mind having a look at pictures now and then.

[*A sudden suspicion comes to the* **Duchesse** *that he*

was there with **Pearl,** *but she makes no sign that he can see.*]

Duchesse [*blandly*]: Did you look at the Bronzinos?

Tony [*falling into the trap*]: Yes. Arthur Fenwick bought one the other day at Christie's. He paid a devil of a price for it too.

Duchesse [*clenching her hand in the effort to hide her agitation*]: Oh?

Tony: I do think it's rot, the prices people pay for old masters. I'm blowed if I'd give ten thousand pounds for a picture.

Duchesse: We'll go to the National Gallery together one of these days, shall we?

Tony: I don't know that I want to make a habit of it, you know.

[**Pearl** *and* **Thornton Clay** *come in. During the conversation the* **Duchesse** *surreptitiously watches* **Pearl** *and* **Tony** *for signs of an intelligence between them.*]

Pearl: I've got great news for you. Bessie and Harry Bleane are engaged.

Duchesse: Oh, my dear, I'm so glad. How gratified you must be.

Pearl: Yes, I'm delighted. You must come and congratulate them.

Clay: Above all we must congratulate one another. We've all worked for it, Pearl.

Tony: He hadn't much chance, poor blighter, had he?

Pearl: We're going to have one more dance, and then Arthur wants to play poker. You must come.

Clay [*to the* **Duchesse**]: Will you dance this with me, Minnie?

Duchesse: I'd like to.

[**Clay** *gives her his arm. She throws* **Tony** *and* **Pearl** *a glance, and purses her lips. She goes out with* **Clay.**]

Pearl: You haven't danced with me yet, Tony. You should really pay some attention to your hostess.

Tony: I say, don't go.

Pearl: Why not?

Tony: Because I want to talk to you.

Pearl [*flippantly*]: If you want to whisper soft nothings in my ear, you'll find the one-step exactly convenient.

Tony: You're a little beast, Pearl.

Pearl: You've been having a long talk with Minnie.

Tony: Oh, she's been making me a hell of a scene.

Pearl: Poor thing, she can't help it. She adores you.

Tony: I wish she didn't, and you did.

Pearl [*with a chuckle*]: My dear, it's your only attraction for me that she adores you. Come and dance with me.

Tony: You've got a piece of hair out of place.

Pearl: Have I?

[*She takes a small glass out of her bag and looks at herself. As she does so Tony steps behind her and kisses her neck.*]

You fool, don't do that. Anyone might see us.

Tony: I don't care.

Pearl: I do. Arthur's as jealous as cats' meat.

Tony: Arthur's playing the pianola.

Pearl: There's nothing wrong with my hair.

Tony: Of course there isn't. You're perfectly divine tonight. I don't know what there is about you.

Pearl: You're a foolish creature, Tony.

Tony: Let's go in the garden.

Pearl: No, they'll be wondering where we are.

Tony: Hang it all, it's not so extraordinary to take a stroll instead of dancing.

Pearl: I don't want to take a stroll.

Tony: Pearl.

Pearl: Yes?

[*She looks at him. For a moment they stare at one another in silence. A hot flame of passion leaps up suddenly between them, and envelops them, so that they forget everything but that they are man and woman. The air seems all at once heavy to breathe. Pearl, like a bird in a net, struggles to escape; their*] *voices sink, and unconsciously they speak in whispers.]*

Pearl: Don't be a fool, Tony.

Tony [*hoarsely*]: Let's go down to the tea-house.

Pearl: No, I won't.

Tony: We shall be quite safe there.

Pearl: I daren't. It's too risky.

Tony: Oh, damn the risk!

Pearl [*agitated*]: I can't!

Tony: I'll go down there and wait.

Pearl [*breathlessly*]: But – if they wonder where I am.

Tony: They'll think you've gone up to your room.

Pearl: I won't come, Tony.

Tony: I'll wait for you.

[*As he goes out,* **Arthur Fenwick** *comes in.* **Pearl** *gives a slight start, but quickly recovers herself.*]

Fenwick: Look here, I'm not going on pounding away at that wretched pianola unless you come and dance, Pearl.

Pearl [*exhausted*]: I'm tired, I don't want to dance any more.

Fenwick: Poor child, you look quite pale.

Pearl: Do I? I thought I'd put plenty of rouge on. Am I looking revolting?

Fenwick: You always look adorable. You're wonderful. I can't think what you see in an old fellow like me.

Pearl: You're the youngest man I've ever known.

Fenwick: How well you know the thing to say to please me!

[*He is just going to take her in his arms, but instinctively she draws back.*]

Pearl: Let's play poker now, shall we?

Fenwick: Not if you're tired, darling.

Pearl: I'm never too tired for that.

Fenwick: You don't know how I adore you. It's a privilege to be allowed to love you.

Pearl [*sure of herself again*]: Oh, what nonsense! You'll make me vain if you say things like that.

Fenwick: You do love me a little, don't you? I want your love so badly.

Pearl: Why, I dote on you, you silly old thing.

[*She takes his face in her hands and kisses him, avoids his arms that seek to encircle her, and goes towards the door.*]

Fenwick: Where are you going?

Pearl: I'm just going to my room to arrange my face.

Fenwick: My God, how I love you, girlie! There's nothing in the world I wouldn't do for you.

Pearl: Really?

Fenwick: Nothing.

Pearl: Then ring for Pole and tell him to set out the card-table and bring the counters.

Fenwick: And I was prepared to give you a sable coat or a diamond tiara.

Pearl: I much prefer chinchilla and emeralds.

Fenwick [*taking her hand*]: Must you really go and arrange your face?

Pearl: Really!

Fenwick: Be quick then. I can hardly bear you out of my sight.

[*He kisses her hand.*]

Pearl [*looking at him tenderly*]: Dear Arthur.

[*She goes out. **Fenwick** rings the bell. Then he goes on the terrace and calls out.*]

Fenwick: Thornton, we're going to play poker. Get them to come along, will you?

Clay [*outside*]: Right-ho!

[***Pole** comes in.*]

Fenwick: Oh, Pole, get the card-table ready.

Pole: Very good, sir.

Fenwick: And we shall want the counters. Let's have those mother-o'-pearl ones that I brought down last time I was here.

Pole: Very good, sir.

[*The **Princess** comes in. **Pole** proceeds to bring a card-table into the centre of the room and unfolds it. He*]

427

gets a box of counters out of a drawer, and puts them on the table.]

Fenwick: Pearl has just gone to her room. She'll be here in one minute.

Princess [*looking at the preparations*]: This looks like more dissipation.

Fenwick: We were going to have a little game of poker. I don't think we ought to play very long. Pearl is looking terribly tired.

Princess: I don't wonder. She's so energetic.

Fenwick: She does too much. Just now when I came in she was quite white. I'm really very uneasy about her. You see, she never spares herself.

Princess: Fortunately she's extremely strong.

Fenwick: She has a constitution of iron. She's a very wonderful woman. It's very seldom you meet a woman like Pearl. She's got a remarkable brain. I've frequently discussed business with her, and I've been amazed at her clear grasp of complicated matters. I owe a great deal to her. And she's good, Princess, she's good. She's got a heart of gold.

Princess: I'm sure she has.

Fenwick: She'll always do a good turn to anybody. She's the most generous, the most open-handed woman I've ever met.

[*The Duchesse comes in as he says these words.*]

Duchesse: Who is this?

Fenwick: We were talking of our hostess.

Duchesse: I see.

[*She has her bag in her hand; when the others are not looking she hides it behind a sofa.*]

Fenwick: I have no hesitation in saying that Pearl is the most remarkable woman in England. Why, she's got half the Cabinet in her pocket. She's very powerful.

Duchesse: I have often thought that if she'd lived in the reign of Charles II she would have been a duchess in her own right.

Fenwick [*innocently*]: Maybe. She would adorn any

sphere. She's got everything – tact, brains, energy, beauty.

Duchesse: Virtue.

Fenwick: If I were the British people, I'd make her Prime Minister.

Princess [*smiling*]: You're an excellent friend, Mr Fenwick.

Fenwick: Of course, you've heard of her hostel for young women alone in London?

Duchesse [*sweetly*]: Yes, there was a great deal about it in the papers, wasn't there?

Fenwick: That's a thing I've always admired in Pearl. She has a thoroughly modern understanding of the value of advertisement.

Duchesse: Yes, she has, hasn't she?

Fenwick: Well, believe me, she conceived the idea of that hostel, built it, endowed it, organized it, all on her own. It cost twenty thousand pounds.

Duchesse: But surely, Mr Fenwick, you paid the twenty thousand pounds? Pearl hasn't got sums like that to throw away on charity.

Fenwick: I gave the money, but the money isn't the important thing. The idea, the organization, the success, are all due to Pearl.

Duchesse: It has certainly been one of the best-advertized of recent philanthropic schemes.

[**Thornton Clay, Bessie, Bleane,** *and* **Fleming** *come in.*]

Clay: We're all dying to play poker.

Fenwick: The table is ready.

Bessie: Where is Pearl?

Fenwick: She's gone to her room. She'll be back in a minute. [*They gather round the table and sit down.*]

Bessie: You're going to play, Princess?

Princess: Oh, I don't think so, I'll look on. I'm going to bed in a minute.

Bessie: Oh, you must play.

Our Betters

[*The* **Princess** *smiles, shrugs her shoulders, and approaches the table.*]

Fenwick: Leave a place for Pearl.

Duchesse: You must leave one for Tony, too.

Clay: What's he doing?

Duchesse: He'll be here presently.

Fenwick: Shall I give out the counters? What would you like to play for?

Princess: Don't let it be too high.

Duchesse: How tiresome of you, Flora! I think I'm in luck tonight.

Fenwick: We don't want to ruin anyone. Shilling antes. Will that suit you?

Princess: Very well.

Fenwick [*to* **Clay**]: The whites are a shilling, Thornton, reds two, and blues five bob. Mr Harvey, you might count some out, will you?

Fleming: Sure.

[*The three of them start counting out the counters.*]

Duchesse: Oh, how stupid of me, I haven't got my bag.

Fenwick: Never mind, we'll trust you.

Duchesse: Oh, I'd rather pay at once. It saves so much bother. Besides, I hate not having my bag.

Princess: One always wants to powder one's nose if one hasn't got it.

Duchesse: Bessie dear, I left it in Pearl's new tea-house. Do run and fetch it for me.

Bessie: Certainly.

Bleane: No, I'll go.

Bessie: You don't know the way. I can go through the bushes. It's only twenty yards. You stop and count out the counters.

[*She goes out.*]

Fenwick: There's five pounds here. Will you take them, Princess?

Princess: Thank you. Here's my money.

Duchesse: I'll give you my fiver as soon as Bessie brings my bag.

Clay: How on earth came you to leave it in the tea-house?

Duchesse: I'm so careless. I'm always leaving my bag about.

Fleming: Here's another five pounds.

Princess: What beautiful counters they are!

Fenwick: I'm glad you like them. I gave them to Pearl. They've got her initials on them.

Clay: Let's have a hand before Pearl comes. Lowest deals.
[*They all cut.*]

Fleming: Table stakes, I suppose?

Fenwick: Oh yes, it makes it a much better game.

Clay: Your deal, Fenwick.

Fenwick: Ante up, Princess.

Princess: I beg your pardon.
[*She pushes forward a counter.* **Fenwick** *deals. The others take up their cards.*]

Fenwick: Two shillings to come in.

Fleming: I'm coming in.

Bleane: I always come in.

Fenwick: I oughtn't to, but I shall all the same. Are you going to make good your ante, Princess?

Princess: I may just as well, mayn't I?

Fenwick: That's how I've made a fortune. By throwing good money after bad. Would you like a card?

Princess: I'll have three.
[**Fenwick** *gives them to her.*]

Clay: The Princess has got a pair of deuces.

Fleming: I'll have one.
[**Fenwick** *gives it to him.*]

Bleane: One never gets that straight, Harvey. I'll take five.

Fenwick: That's what I call a real sport.

Clay: Nonsense. It just means he can't play.

Bleane: It would be rather a sell for you if I got a flush.

Clay: It would, but you haven't.
[**Fenwick** *has given him cards and* **Bleane** *looks at them.*]

Bleane: You're quite right. I haven't.

[*He flings them down. Through the next speeches the business with the cards follows the dialogue.*]

Fenwick: Don't you want any cards, Duchesse?

Duchesse: No, I'm out of it.

Clay: I'll have three. I thought you were in luck.

Duchesse: Wait a minute. You'll be surprised.

Fenwick: Dealer takes two.

Clay: Who bets?

Princess: I'm out of it.

Clay: I said it was a pair of deuces.

Fleming: I'll bet five shillings.

Clay: I'll take it and raise five shillings.

Fenwick: I suppose I must risk my money. What have I got to put down? Ten shillings?

Fleming: There's five shillings, and I'll raise you five more.

Clay: No, I've had enough.

Fenwick: I'll take you and raise you again.

Fleming: Very well. And once more.

Fenwick: I'll see you.

[**Bessie** *comes in. The* **Duchesse** *has been watching for her. Bessie is extremely disturbed.*]

Duchesse: Ah, there's Bessie.

Fenwick [*to* **Fleming**]: What have you got?

Duchesse: Did you find my bag?

Bessie [*with a gasp*] : No, it wasn't there.

Duchesse: Oh, but I remember distinctly leaving it there. I'll go and look for it myself. Mr Fenwick, will you come with me?

Bessie: No, don't – you can't go into the tea-house.

Princess [*surprised*]: Bessie, is anything the matter?

Bessie [*in a strained voice*]: The door of the tea-house is locked.

Duchesse: Oh, it can't be. I saw Pearl and Tony go in there just now.

[**Bessie** *suddenly hides her face and bursts into a flood of tears.*]

Princess [*starting to her feet*]: Minnie, you devil! What have you been doing?

Duchesse: Don't ask what I've been doing.

Fenwick: You must be mistaken. Pearl went up to her room.

Duchesse: Go and look for her . . .

[**Fenwick** *is about to start from his chair. The* **Princess** *puts her hand on his shoulders.*]

Princess: Where are you going?

Duchesse: I saw her.

[*For a moment there is a pause.*]

Clay [*in an embarrassed way*]: Well, we'd better go on with our game, hadn't we?

[*The* **Princess** *and* **Bleane** *are bending over* **Bessie**, *trying to get her to control herself.*]

Fleming: That was your money, Mr Fenwick.

Fenwick [*staring in front of him, with a red face and blood-shot eyes, under his breath*]: The slut. The slut.

[*The* **Duchesse** *takes her bag from behind the cushion, gets out the stick for her lips, and her mirror, and begins to paint them.*]

Clay: You'd better deal, Fleming. The Princess won't play, I expect.

Duchesse: Deal me cards. I want to play.

Clay: Bleane, come on. We'd better go on with our game. Take Bessie's chips.

[**Bleane** *comes forward.* **Fleming** *deals the cards. A stormy silence hangs over the party, broken only by the short speeches referring to the game; they play trying to relieve the tension. They are all anxiously awaiting* **Pearl**, *afraid she will come, knowing she must, and dreading the moment; they are nervous and constrained.*]

Clay: Your ante, Bleane.

[**Bleane** *puts forward a counter. The cards are dealt in silence.*]

Clay: I'm coming in.

[**Fenwick** *looks at his cards, puts forward a couple of*

Our Betters

counters, but does not speak. **Fleming** *puts forward counters.*]

Fleming: D'you want a card?

Bleane: Three, please.

Clay: Two.

Fenwick [*with an effort over himself*]: I'll have three.

[**Fleming** *deals them as they ask. Just as he has given* **Fenwick** *his,* **Pearl** *comes in, followed by* **Tony**. **Tony** *is smoking a cigarette.*]

Pearl: Oh, have you started already?

Fenwick [*violently*]: Where have you been?

Pearl: I? My head was aching a little and I went for a turn in the garden. I found Tony composing a sonnet to the moon.

Fenwick: You said you were going to your room.

Pearl: What are you talking about?

[*She looks round, sees the* **Duchesse's** *look of angry triumph, and gives a slight start.*]

Duchesse: Once too often, my dear, once too often.

[**Pearl** *takes no notice. She sees* **Bessie**. **Bessie** *has been staring at her with miserable eyes, and now she hides her face. Pearl realizes that everything is discovered. She turns coolly to* **Tony**.]

Pearl: You damned fool, I told you it was too risky.

Act Three

The scene is the same as in the last act, the morning-room at Kenton.

It is next day, Sunday, about three in the afternoon, and the sun is shining brightly.

[*The* **Princess**, **Thornton Clay**, *and* **Fleming** *are sitting down.* **Fleming** *lights another cigarette.*]

Princess: Is it good for you to smoke so many cigarettes?

Fleming: I shouldn't think so.

434

Clay: He must do something.

Princess: Perhaps you can get up a game of tennis later on.

Fleming: It's very hot for tennis.

Clay: Besides, who will play?

Princess: You two could have a single.

Clay: If we only had the Sunday papers it would be something.

Princess: You can hardly expect them in a place like this. I don't suppose there are many trains on Sunday.

Clay: I wonder if dinner is going to be as cheerful as luncheon was.

Fleming: Did Pearl send any explanation for not appearing at luncheon?

Princess: I haven't an idea.

Clay: I asked the butler where she was. He said she was lunching in bed. I wish I'd thought of that.

Princess: I'm afraid we were rather silent.

Clay: Silent! I shall never forget that luncheon. Minnie subdued – and silent. Tony sulky – and silent. Bessie frightened – and silent. Bleane embarrassed – and silent. Fenwick furious – and silent. I tried to be pleasant and chatty. It was like engaging the pyramids in small-talk. Both of you behaved very badly. You might have given me a little encouragement,

Fleming: I was afraid of saying the wrong thing. The Duchesse and Bessie looked as if they'd burst into tears on the smallest provocation.

Princess: I was thinking of Pearl. What a humiliation! What a horrible humiliation!

Fleming: What d'you think she'll do now?

Clay: That's what I'm asking myself. I have an idea that she won't appear again till we're all gone.

Princess: I hope she won't. She's always so sure of herself, I couldn't bear to see her pale and mortified.

Clay: She's got plenty of courage.

Princess: I know. She may force herself to face us. It would be a dreadful ordeal for all of us.

Fleming: D'you think she's feeling it very much?

Princess: She wouldn't be human if she weren't. I don't suppose she slept any better last night than the rest of us. Poor thing, she must be a wreck.

Fleming: It was a terrible scene.

Princess: I shall never forget it. The things that Minnie said. I couldn't have believed such language could issue from a woman's throat. Oh, it was horrible.

Clay: It was startling. I've never seen a woman so beside herself. And there was no stopping her.

Fleming: And with Bessie there.

Princess: She was crying so much, I doubt if she heard.

Clay: I was thankful when Minnie had the hysterics and we were able to fuss over her and dab her face and slap her hands. It was a very welcome diversion.

Fleming: Does she have attacks like that often?

Clay: I know she did when the young man before Tony married an heiress. I think she has one whenever there's a crisis in the affairs of her heart.

Fleming: For goodness' sake, Thornton, don't talk about it as if it were a joke.

Clay [*surprised*]: What's the matter, Fleming?

Fleming: I think it's abominable to treat the whole thing flippantly.

Clay: Why, I was very sympathetic. I wasn't flippant. Who got the sal volatile? I got the sal volatile.

Fleming [*with a shrug of the shoulders*]: I daresay my nerves are a bit on edge. You see, before, I only thought things were rather queer. It's come as, well, as a shock to discover exactly what the relations are between all these people. And what I can't very easily get over is to realize that I'm the only member of the party who doesn't take it as a matter of course.

Clay: We shall never make a man of the world of you, Fleming.

Fleming: I'm afraid that didn't sound very polite, **Princess**. I beg your pardon.

Princess: I should have few friends if I demanded the

standards that you do. I've learned not to judge my neighbours.

Fleming: Is it necessary to condone their vices?

Princess: You don't understand. It's not entirely their fault. It's the life they lead. They've got too much money and too few responsibilities. English women in our station have duties that are part of their birthright, but we, strangers in a strange land, have nothing to do but enjoy ourselves.

Fleming: Well, I thank God Bleane is a decent man, and he'll take Bessie out of all this.

[*The* **Duchesse** *comes in. Unlike the* **Princess**, *who is in a summer frock, suitable for the country, the* **Duchesse** *wears a town dress and a hat.*]

Princess: You've been changing your frock, Minnie.

Duchesse: Yes, I'm leaving this house in half an hour. I'd have gone this morning, if I'd been able to get away. I always thought it a detestable hole, but now that I've discovered there are only two trains on Sunday, one at nine, and the other at half past four, I have no words to express my opinion of it.

Clay: Yet you have an extensive vocabulary, Minnie.

Duchesse: I've been just as much a prisoner as if I'd been shut up with lock and key. I've been forced to eat that woman's food. I thought every mouthful would choke me.

Princess: Do keep calm, Minnie. You know how bad it is for you to upset yourself.

Duchesse: As soon as I found there wasn't a train I sent over to the garage and said I wanted to be taken to London at once. Would you believe it; I couldn't get a car.

Clay: Why not?

Duchesse: One of the cars went up to town early this morning, and the other is being overhauled. There's nothing but a luggage cart. I couldn't go to London in a luggage cart. As it is I shall have to go to the station in it. I shall look ridiculous.

Clay: Have you ordered it?

Duchesse: Yes. It's to be round at the door in a few minutes.

Clay: What on earth can Pearl have sent the car up to London for?

Duchesse: To show her spite.

Princess: That's not like her.

Duchesse: My dear, she's been my greatest friend for fifteen years. I know her through and through, and I tell you that she hasn't got a single redeeming quality. And why does she want to have the car overhauled today? When you're giving a party the least you can do is to see that your cars are in running order.

Princess: Oh, well, that was an accident. You can't blame her for that.

Duchesse: I only have one thing to be thankful for, and that is that she has had the decency to keep to her room. I will be just. It shows at least that she has some sense of shame.

Clay: You know, Minnie, Pearl has a good heart. She didn't mean to cause you pain.

Duchesse: Are you trying to excuse her, Thornton?

Clay: No, I think her conduct is inexcusable.

Duchesse: So do I. I mean to have nothing more to do with her. It's a judgement on me. I disliked her the first time I saw her. One should always trust one's first impressions. Now my eyes are opened. I will never speak to her again. I will cut her dead. I hope you'll tell her that, Thornton.

Clay: If that's a commission you're giving me, it's not a very pleasant one.

Princess: Will you let me have a word or two with Minnie?

Clay: Why, of course. Come along, Fleming.

[**Clay** *and* **Fleming Harvey** *go in to the garden.*]

Duchesse: My dear, if you're going to ask me to turn the other cheek, don't. Because I'm not going to. I'm going to do all I can to revenge myself on that woman. I'm going to expose her. I'm going to tell everyone how she's treated me. When I was her guest.

Princess: You must take care what you say for your own sake, Minnie.

Duchesse: I know quite enough about her to make her position in London impossible. I'm going to ruin her.

Princess: What about Tony?

Duchesse: Oh, I've finished with him. Ah! I'm not the kind of woman to stand that sort of treatment. I hope he'll end in the gutter.

Princess: Don't you care for him any more?

Duchesse: My dear, if he was starving, and went down on his bended knees to me for a piece of bread, I wouldn't give it to him. He revolts me.

Princess: Well, I'm very glad. It distressed me to see you on those terms with a boy like that. You're well rid of him.

Duchesse: My dear, you needn't tell me that. He's a thorough wrong 'un, and that's all there is about it. He hasn't even had the decency to try and excuse himself. He hasn't even made an attempt to see me.

Princess [*gives her a quick look*]: After all, he never really cared for you. Anyone could see that.

Duchesse [*her voice breaking*]: Oh, don't say that, Flora. I couldn't bear it. He loved me. Until that woman came between us I know he loved me. He couldn't help loving me. I did everything in the world for him. [*She bursts into tears.*]

Princess: Minnie. My dear, don't give way. You know what a worthless creature he is. Haven't you any self-respect?

Duchesse: He's the only man I've ever loved. I could hardly bear him out of my sight. What shall I do without him?

Princess: Take care, here he is.

[**Tony** *comes in. He is startled at seeing the* **Duchesse**. *She turns away and hurriedly dries her tears.*]

Tony: Oh, I beg your pardon. I didn't know anyone was here. I was looking for some cigarettes.

[*He stands there awkwardly, not knowing whether to go or stay. The* **Princess** *looks at him reflectively. There is a moment's silence. Then she shrugs her shoulders and goes out. He looks at the* **Duchesse** *who stands with her back to him. He hesitates a moment, then, almost on the tips of his toes, walks over to the cigarettes, fills his case, takes another look at the* **Duchesse,** *and is in the act of tiptoeing out of the room when she stops him with her question.*]

Duchesse: Where are you going?

Tony: Nowhere in particular.

Duchesse: Then you'd better stay here.

Tony: I thought you wished to be alone.

Duchesse: Is that why you've kept away from me all day? [*He sinks sulkily into an armchair. The* **Duchesse** *finally turns round and faces him.*]

Duchesse: Haven't you got anything to say for yourself at all?

Tony: What's the good of talking?

Duchesse: You might at least say you're sorry for the pain you've caused me. If you'd had any affection for me you wouldn't have done all you could to avoid me.

Tony: I knew you'd only make a scene.

Duchesse: Good heavens, you surely don't expect me not to make a scene?

Tony: The whole thing's very unfortunate.

Duchesse: Ha! Unfortunate. You break my heart and then you say it's unfortunate.

Tony: I didn't mean that. I meant it was unfortunate that you caught us out.

Duchesse: Oh, hold your stupid tongue. Every word you say is more unfortunate than the last.

Tony: It's because I knew you'd take offence at everything I said that I thought the best thing I could do was to keep out of the way.

Duchesse: You're heartless, heartless. If you'd had any decent feeling you couldn't have eaten the lunch you did. But you munched away, munched, munched, munched, till I could have killed you.

Tony: Well, I was hungry.

Duchesse: You oughtn't to have been hungry.

Tony: What are you going to do about it?

Duchesse: About your appetite? Pray to God your next mouthful chokes you.

Tony: No, about the other.

Duchesse: I'm going to leave this house this afternoon.

Tony: D'you want me to come, too?

Duchesse: What d'you suppose it matters to me whether you go or stay?

Tony: If you go I shall have to go, too.

Duchesse: You ought to start soon then. It's four miles to the station. I shall be obliged if you will not get in the same carriage as me.

Tony: I'm not going to walk. They can run me down in a car.

Duchesse: There's nothing but a luggage cart, and I'm going in that.

Tony: Isn't there room for me?

Duchesse: No.

Tony: When d'you want me to move out of my flat?

Duchesse: What has that got to do with me?

Tony: You know very well that *I* can't pay the rent.

Duchesse: That's your look-out.

Tony: I shall go to the colonies.

Duchesse: That's the very best thing you can do. I hope you'll have to break stones, and dig, and paint – with lead paint. I hope you're miserable.

Tony: Oh, well, it'll have its compensations.

Duchesse: Such as?

Tony: I shall be my own master. I was about fed up with this, I can tell you.

Duchesse: Yes, you can say that now.

Tony: D'you think it was all jam, never being able to call my soul my own? I was sick to death of it.

Duchesse: You cad.

Tony: Well, you may just as well know the truth.

Duchesse: D'you mean to say you never cared for me? Not even at the beginning?

[*He shrugs his shoulders, but does not answer. She speaks the next phrases in little gasps, gradually weakening as her emotion overcomes her. He stands before her in sulky silence.*]

Duchesse: Tony, I've done everything in the world for you. I've been like a mother to you. How can you be so ungrateful. You haven't got any heart. If you had you'd have asked me to forgive you. You'd have made some attempt to . . . Don't you want me to forgive you?

Tony: What d'you mean by that?

Duchesse: If you'd only asked me, if you'd only shown you were sorry, I'd have been angry with you, I wouldn't have spoken to you for a week, but I'd have forgiven you – I'd have forgiven you, Tony. But you never gave me a chance. It's cruel of you, cruel!

Tony: Well, anyhow, it's too late now.

Duchesse: Do you want it to be too late?

Tony: It's no good grousing about the past. The thing's over now.

Duchesse: Aren't you sorry?

Tony: I don't know. I suppose I am in a way. I don't want to make you unhappy.

Duchesse: If you wanted to be unfaithful to me, why didn't you prevent me from finding out? You didn't even trouble to take a little precaution.

Tony: I was a damned fool, I know that.

Duchesse: Are you in love with that woman?

Tony: No.

Duchesse: Then why did you? Oh, Tony, how could you?

Tony: If one felt about things at night as one does next morning, life would be a dashed sight easier.

Duchesse: If I said to you, Let's let bygones be bygones and start afresh, what would you say, Tony?

[*She looks away. He rests his eyes on her reflectively.*]

Tony: We've made a break now. We'd better leave it at that. I shall go out to the colonies.

Duchesse: Tony, you don't mean that seriously. You could never stand it. You know, you're not strong. You'll only die.

Tony: Oh, well, one can only die once.

Duchesse: I'm sorry for all I said just now, Tony. I didn't mean it.

Tony: It doesn't matter.

Duchesse: I can't live without you, Tony.

Tony: I've made up my mind. It's no good talking.

Duchesse: I'm sorry I was horrid to you, Tony. I'll never be again. Won't you forget it? Oh, Tony, won't you forgive me? I'll do anything in the world for you if only you won't leave me.

Tony: It's a rotten position I'm in. I must think of the future.

Duchesse: Oh, but Tony, I'll make it all right for you.

Tony: It's very kind of you, but it's not good enough. Let's part good friends, Minnie. If I've got to walk to the station, it's about time I was starting. [*He holds out his hand to her.*]

Duchesse: D'you mean to say it's good-bye? Good-bye for ever? Oh, how can you be so cruel!

Tony: When one's made up one's mind to do a thing, it's best to do it at once.

Duchesse: Oh, I can't bear it. I can't bear it. [*She begins to cry.*] Oh, what a fool I was! I ought to have pretended not to see anything. I wish I'd never known. Then you wouldn't have thought of leaving me.

Tony: Come, my dear, pull yourself together. You'll get over it.

Duchesse [*desperately*]: Tony, if you want to marry me – I'm willing to marry you.

[*A pause.*]

Tony: I should be just as dependent on you. D'you think it would be jolly for me having to come to you for every five pounds I wanted?

Duchesse: I'll settle something on you so that you'll be independent. A thousand a year. Will that do?

Tony: You are a good sort, Minnie. [*He goes over and sits down beside her.*]

Duchesse: You will be kind to me, won't you?

Tony: Rather! And look here, you needn't give me that two-seater. I shall be able to drive the Rolls-Royce.

Duchesse: You didn't want to go to the colonies, did you?

Tony: Not much.

Duchesse: Oh, Tony, I do love you so.

Tony: That's right.

Duchesse: We won't stay another minute in this house. Ring the bell, will you? You'll come with me in the luggage cart?

Tony [*touching the bell*]: I much prefer that to walking.

Duchesse: It's monstrous that there shouldn't be a motor to take luggage to the station. It's a most uncomfortable house to stay in.

Tony: Oh, beastly. D'you know that I didn't have a bathroom attached to my bedroom?

[**Pole** *comes in.*]

Duchesse: Is the luggage cart ready, Pole?

Pole: I'll inquire, your grace.

Duchesse: My maid is to follow in the morning with the luggage. Mr Paxton will come with me. [*To* **Tony**] What about your things?

Tony: Oh, they'll be all right. I brought my man with me.

Pole: Her ladyship is just coming downstairs, your grace.

Duchesse: Oh, is she? Thank you, that'll do, Pole.

Pole: Very good, your grace.

[*He goes out. As soon as he closes the door behind him the* **Duchesse** *springs to her feet.*]

Duchesse: I won't see her. Tony, see if Thornton is on the terrace.

Tony: All right. [*He goes to the french window.*] Yes, I'll call him, shall I? Clay, come here a minute, will you? [*He goes out.* **Thornton Clay** *comes in, followed immediately by the* **Princess** *and* **Fleming**.]

Duchesse: Thornton, I'm told Pearl is coming downstairs.

Clay: At last.

Duchesse: I won't see her. Nothing will induce me to see her.

Princess: My dear, what is to be done? We can't make her remain upstairs in her own house.

Duchesse: No, but Thornton can speak to her. She's evidently ashamed of herself. I only ask one thing, that she should keep out of the way till I'm gone.

Clay: I'll do my best.

Duchesse: I'm going to walk up and down till the luggage cart is ready. I haven't taken my exercise today. [*She goes out.*]

Clay: If Pearl is in a temper that's not a very pleasant message to give her.

Princess: You won't find her in a temper. If she's dreadfully upset, tell her what Minnie says gently.

Fleming: Here is Bessie. [*She comes in.*] It appears that Pearl is just coming downstairs.

Bessie: Is she?

Princess: Have you seen her this morning, Bessie?

Bessie: No. She sent her maid to ask me to go to her, but I had a headache and couldn't.

[*They look at her curiously. She is inclined to be abrupt and silent. It may be imagined that she has made up her mind to some course, but what that is the others cannot tell.* **Fleming** *goes over and sits beside her.*]

Fleming: I'm thinking of going back to America next Saturday, Bessie.

Bessie: Dear Fleming, I shall be sorry to lose you.

Fleming: I expect you'll be too busy to think about me. You'll have to see all kinds of people, and then there's your trousseau to get.

445

Bessie: I wish you could come over to Paris with me, Princess, and help me with it.

Princess: I? [*She gets an inkling of what* **Bessie** *means.*] Of course, if I could be of any help to you, dear child . . . [*She takes* **Bessie's** *hand and gives her a fond smile.* **Bessie** *turns away to hide a tear that for a moment obscures her eyes.*]

Perhaps it's a very good idea. We must talk about it. [**Pearl** *comes in. She is perfectly cool and collected, radiant in a wonderful audacious gown; she is looking her best and knows it. There is nothing in her manner to indicate the smallest recollection of the episode that took place on the preceding evening.*]

Pearl [*brightly*]: Good morning.

Clay: Good afternoon.

Pearl: I knew everyone would abuse me for coming down so late. It was such a lovely day I thought it was a pity to get up.

Clay: Don't be paradoxical, Pearl, it's too hot.

Pearl: The sun streamed into my room, and I said, It's a sin not to get up on a morning like this. And the more I said I ought to get up, the more delightful I found it to lie in bed. How is your head, Bessie?

Bessie: Oh, it's better, thank you.

Pearl: I was sorry to hear you weren't feeling up to the mark.

Bessie: I didn't sleep very well.

Pearl: What have you done with your young man?

Bessie: Harry? He's writing letters.

Pearl: Spreading the glad tidings, I suppose. You ought to write to his mother, Bessie. It would be a graceful attention. A charming, frank little letter, the sort of thing one would expect an *ingénue* to write. Straight from the heart.

Clay: I'm sure you'd love to write it yourself, Pearl.

Pearl: And we must think about sending an announcement to the *Morning Post*.

Fleming: You think of everything, Pearl.

Pearl: I take my duties as Bessie's chaperone very seriously. I've already got a brilliant idea for the gown I'm going to wear at the wedding.

Fleming: Gee!

Pearl: My dear Fleming, don't say Gee, it's so American. Say By Jove.

Fleming: I couldn't without laughing.

Pearl: Laffing. Why can't you say laughing?

Fleming: I don't want to.

Pearl: How obstinate you are. Of course, now that Bessie is going to marry an Englishman she'll have to take lessons. I know an excellent woman. She's taught all the American peeresses.

Fleming: You surprise me.

Pearl: She's got a wonderful method. She makes you read aloud. And she has long lists of words that you have to repeat twenty times a day – half instead of haf and barth instead of bath, and carnt instead of can't.

Fleming: By Jove instead of Gee?

Pearl: Peeresses don't say By Jove, Fleming. She teaches them to say Good heavens instead of Mercy.

Fleming: Does she make money by it?

Pearl: Pots. She's a lovely woman. Eleo Dorset had an accent that you could cut with a knife when she first came over, and in three months she hadn't got any more than I have.

Bessie [*getting up. To* **Fleming**]: D'you think it's too hot for a turn in the garden?

Fleming: Why, no.

Bessie: Shall we go then?

[*They go out together.*]

Pearl: What's the matter with Bessie? She must have swallowed a poker last night. No wonder she couldn't sleep. It's enough to give anyone indigestion.

Clay: You know that Minnie is going this afternoon, Pearl?

Pearl: Yes, so I heard. It's such a bore there are no cars to take her to the station. She'll have to go in the luggage cart.

Clay: She doesn't wish to see you.

Pearl: Oh, but I wish to see her.

Clay: I dare say.

Pearl: I must see her.

Clay: She asked me to tell you that she only wished you to do one thing, and that is to keep out of the way till she's gone.

Pearl: Then you can go and tell her that unless she sees me she shan't have the luggage cart.

Clay: Pearl!

Pearl: That's my ultimatum.

Clay: Can you see me taking a message like that to the Duchesse?

Pearl: It's four miles to the station, and there's not a scrap of shade all the way.

Clay: After all, it's not a very unreasonable request she's making.

Pearl: If she wants the luggage cart she must come and say good-bye to me like a lady.

Clay [to the **Princess**]: What am I to do? We used up all the sal volatile last night.

Princess: I'll tell her if you like. D'you really insist on seeing her, Pearl?

Pearl: Yes, it's very important.

[The **Princess** goes out. **Pearl** watches her go with a smile.]

I'm afraid Flora is shocked. She shouldn't know such people.

Clay: Really, Pearl, your behaviour is monstrous.

Pearl: Never mind about my behaviour. Tell me how luncheon went off.

Clay: My dear, it was like a gathering of relations who hate one another, after the funeral of a rich aunt who's left all her money to charity.

Pearl: It must have been priceless. I'd have given anything to be there.

Clay: Why weren't you?

Pearl: Oh, I knew there'd be scenes, and I'm never at my best in a scene before luncheon. One of the things I've learnt from the war is that a general should choose his own time for a battle.

Clay: Minnie moved heaven and earth to get away this morning.

Pearl: I knew she couldn't. I knew none of them could go till the afternoon.

Clay: The train service is atrocious.

Pearl: George says that is one of the advantages of the place. It keeps it rural. There's one at nine and another at half past four. I knew that not even the most violent disturbances would get people up at eight who never by any chance have breakfast till ten. As soon as I awoke I took the necessary steps.

Clay [*interrupting*]: You slept?

Pearl: Oh yes, I slept beautifully. There's nothing like a little excitement to give me a good night.

Clay: Well, you certainly had some excitement. I've rarely witnessed such a terrific scene.

Pearl: I sent out to the garage and gave instructions that the old Rolls-Royce was to be taken down at once and the other was to go to London.

Clay: What for?

Pearl: Never mind. You'll know presently. Then I did a little telephoning.

Clay: Why were you so anxious to prevent anybody from leaving the house?

Pearl: I couldn't have persuaded myself that my party was a success if half my guests had left me on Sunday morning. I thought they might change their minds by the afternoon.

Clay: If that's your only reason, I don't think it's a very good one.

Pearl: It isn't. I will be frank with you, Thornton. I can imagine that a very amusing story might be made out

449

of this episode. I never mind scandal, but I don't expose myself to ridicule if I can help it.

Clay: My dear Pearl, surely you can trust the discretion of your guests. Who do you think will give it away?

Pearl: You.

Clay: I? My dear Pearl, I give you my word of honour . . .

Pearl [calmly]: My dear Thornton, I don't care twopence about your word of honour. You're a professional entertainer, and you'll sacrifice everything to a good story. Why, don't you remember that killing story about your father's death? You dined out a whole season on it.

Clay: Well, it was a perfectly killing story. No one would have enjoyed it more than my poor old father.

Pearl: I'm not going to risk anything, Thornton. I think it's much better there should be no story to tell.

Clay: No one can move the clock backwards, Pearl. I couldn't help thinking at luncheon that there were the elements of a very good story indeed.

Pearl: And you'll tell it, Thornton. Then I shall say: My dear, does it sound probable? They all stayed quite happily till Monday morning; Sturrey and the Arlingtons dined on the Sunday night, and we had a very merry evening. Besides, I was lunching with Minnie only two days afterwards. And I shall say: Poor Thornton, he *is* such a liar, isn't he?

Clay: I confess that if you are reconciled with Minnie it will take a great deal of the point away from my story. What about Arthur Fenwick?

Pearl: He's a sensualist, and the sensual are always sentimental.

Clay: He scared me dreadfully at luncheon. He was eating a dressed crab, and his face grew every minute more purple. I was expecting him to have an apoplectic fit.

Pearl: It's not an unpleasant death, you know, Thornton, to have a stroke while you're eating your favourite dish.

Clay: You know, there are no excuses for you, Pearl.

Pearl: Human nature excuses so much, Thornton.

Clay: You really might have left Tony alone. This habit you have of snitching has got you into trouble before.

Pearl: People are so selfish. It just happens that I find no man so desirable as one that a friend of mine is in love with. I make allowances for the idiosyncrasies of my friends. Why shouldn't they make allowances for mine?

[*The* **Duchesse** *comes in, erect and haughty, with the air of Boadicea facing the Roman legions.* **Pearl** *turns to her with an ingratiating smile.*]

Pearl: Ah, Minnie.

Duchesse: I'm told the only way I can leave this house is by submitting to the odious necessity of seeing you.

Pearl: I wish you wouldn't go, Minnie. Lord Sturrey is coming over to dinner tonight, and so are the Arlingtons. I always take a lot of trouble to get the right people together, and I hate it when anybody fails me at the last minute.

Duchesse: D'you think anything would have induced me to stay so long if there'd been any possibility of getting away?

Pearl: It wouldn't have been nice to go without saying good-bye to me.

Duchesse: Don't talk nonsense, Pearl.

Pearl: D'you know that you behaved very badly last night, and I ought to be extremely angry with you?

Duchesse: I? Thornton, the woman's as mad as a hatter.

Pearl: You really oughtn't to have made a scene before Harry Bleane. And, you know, to tell Arthur wasn't playing the game. If you wanted to tell anyone, why didn't you tell George?

Duchesse: In the first place, he wasn't here. He never is.

Pearl: I know. He says that now society has taken to coming down to the country for week-ends he prefers London.

Duchesse: I'll never forgive you. Never. Never. Never. You'd got Arthur Fenwick. Why weren't you satisfied with him? If you wanted to have an affair with anyone, why didn't you take Thornton? He's almost the only

451

one of your friends with whom you haven't. The omission is becoming almost marked.

Pearl: Thornton never makes love to me except when other people are looking. He can be very passionate in the front seat of my box at the opera.

Clay: This conversation is growing excessively personal. I'll leave you.

[*He goes out.*]

Pearl: I'm sorry I had to insist on your seeing me, but I had something quite important to say to you.

Duchesse: Before you go any further, Pearl, I wish to tell you that I'm going to marry Tony.

Pearl [*aghast*]: Minnie! Oh, my dear, you're not doing it to spite me? You know, honestly, he doesn't interest me in the slightest. Oh, Minnie, do think carefully.

Duchesse: It's the only way I can keep him.

Pearl: D'you think you'll be happy?

Duchesse: What should you care if I'm happy?

Pearl: Of course I care. D'you think it's wise? You're giving yourself into his hands. Oh, my dear, how can you risk it?

Duchesse: He said he was going out to the colonies. I love him. . . . I believe you're really distressed. How strange you are, Pearl! Perhaps it's the best thing for me. He may settle down. I was very lonely sometimes, you know. Sometimes, when I had the blues, I almost wished I'd never left home.

Pearl: And I've been moving heaven and earth to get him a job. I've been on the telephone this morning to all the Cabinet Ministers I know, and at last I've done it. That's what I wanted to tell you. I thought you'd be so pleased. I suppose now he won't want it.

Duchesse: Oh, I'm sure he will. He's very proud, you know. That's one of the things I liked in him. He had to be dependent on me, and that's partly why he always wanted to marry me.

Pearl: Of course, you'll keep your title.

Duchesse: Oh yes, I shall do that.

Pearl [*going towards her as if to kiss her*]: Well, darling, you have my very, very best wishes.

Duchesse [*drawing back*]: I'm not going to forgive you, Pearl.

Pearl: But you've forgiven Tony.

Duchesse: I don't blame him. He was led away.

Pearl: Come, Minnie, don't be spiteful. You might let bygones be bygones.

Duchesse: Nothing will induce me to stay in this house another night.

Pearl: It's a very slow train, and you'll have to go without your tea.

Duchesse: I don't care.

Pearl: You won't arrive in London till half-past eight, and you'll have to dine in a restaurant.

Duchesse: I don't care.

Pearl: You'll be grubby and hot. Tony will be hungry and out of temper. And you'll look your age.

Duchesse: You promised me the luggage cart.

Pearl [*with a sigh*]: You shall have it; but you'll have to sit on the floor, because it hasn't got any seats.

Duchesse: Pearl, it's not going to break down on the way to the station?

Pearl: Oh, no. How can you suspect me of playing a trick like that on you ... [*With a tinge of regret*] It never occurred to me.

[**Thornton Clay** *comes in.*]

Clay: Pearl, I thought you'd like to know that Fenwick is coming to say good-bye to you.

Duchesse: I'll go and tell Tony about the job you've got him. By the way, what is it?

Pearl: Oh, it's something in the Education Office.

Duchesse: How very nice. What do they do there?

Pearl: Nothing. But it'll keep him busy from ten to four. [*The* **Duchesse** *goes out.*]

Pearl: She's going to marry him.

Clay: I know.

Pearl: I'm a wonderful matchmaker. First Bessie and

Harry Bleane, and now Minnie and Tony Paxton. I shall have to find someone for you, Thornton.

Clay: How on earth did you manage to appease her?

Pearl: I reasoned with her. After all, she should be glad the boy has sown his wild oats before he marries. And besides, if he were her husband, of course she wouldn't expect fidelity from him; it seems unnatural to expect it when he isn't.

Clay: But she's going all the same.

Pearl: I've got a quarter of an hour yet. Give me your handkerchief will you?

Clay [*handing it to her*]: You're not going to burst into tears?

Pearl [*she rubs her cheeks violently*]: I thought I ought to look a little wan and pale when Arthur comes in.

Clay: You'll never love me, Pearl. You tell me all your secrets.

Pearl: Shall I tell you what to do about it? Take the advice I give to Americans who come over to London and want to see the Tower: say you've been, and don't go.

Clay: D'you think you can bring Arthur round?

Pearl: I'm sure I could if he loved me.

Clay: My dear, he dotes on you.

Pearl: Don't be a fool, Thornton. He loves his love for me. That's quite a different thing. I've only got one chance. He sees himself as the man of iron. I'm going to play the dear little thing racket.

Clay: You're a most unscrupulous woman, Pearl.

Pearl: Not more than most. Please go. I think he ought to find me alone.

[**Clay** *goes out.* **Pearl** *seats herself in a pensive attitude and looks down at the carpet; in her hand she holds dejectedly an open volume of poetry. Presently* **Arthur Fenwick** *comes in. She pretends not to see him. He is the strong man, battered but not beaten, struggling with the emotion which he tries to master.*]

Fenwick: Pearl!

Pearl [*with a jump*]: Oh, how you startled me. I didn't hear you come in.

Fenwick: I dare say you're surprised to see me. I thought it was necessary that we should have a short conversation before I left this house.

Pearl [*looking away*]: I'm glad to see you once more.

Fenwick: You understand that everything is over between us.

Pearl: If you've made up your mind, there's nothing for me to say. I know that nothing can move you when you've once done that.

Fenwick [*drawing himself up a little*]: No. That has always been part of my power.

Pearl: I wouldn't have you otherwise.

Fenwick: I don't want to part from you in anger, Pearl. Last night I could have thrashed you within an inch of your life.

Pearl: Why didn't you? D'you think I'd have minded that from the man I loved?

Fenwick: You know I could never hit a woman.

Pearl: I thought of you all through the long hours of the night, Arthur.

Fenwick: I never slept a wink.

Pearl: One would never think it. You must be made of iron.

Fenwick: I think I am sometimes.

Pearl: Am I very pale?

Fenwick: A little.

Pearl: I feel a perfect wreck.

Fenwick: You must go and lie down. It's no good making yourself ill.

Pearl: Oh, don't bother about me, Arthur.

Fenwick: I've bothered about you so long. It's difficult for me to get out of the habit all at once.

Pearl: Every word you say stabs me to the heart.

Fenwick: I'll get done quickly with what I had to tell you and then go. It's merely this. Of course, I shall continue the allowance I've always made you.

455

Pearl: Oh, I couldn't take it. I couldn't take it.

Fenwick: You must be reasonable, Pearl. This is a matter of business.

Pearl: It's a question I refuse to discuss. Nothing would have induced me to accept your help if I hadn't loved you. Now that there can be nothing more between us – no, no, the thought outrages me.

Fenwick: I was afraid that you'd take up that attitude. Remember that you've only got eight thousand a year of your own. You can't live on that.

Pearl: I can starve.

Fenwick: I must insist, Pearl, for my own sake. You've adopted a style of living which you would never have done if you hadn't had me at the back of you. I'm morally responsible, and I must meet my obligations.

Pearl: We can only be friends in future, Arthur.

Fenwick: I haven't often asked you to do anything for me, Pearl.

Pearl: I shall return your presents. Let me give you my pearl necklace at once.

Fenwick: Girlie, you wouldn't do that.

Pearl [*pretending to try and take the necklace off*]: I can't undo the clasp. Please help me.

[*She goes up to him and turns her back so that he may get at it.*]

Fenwick: I won't. I won't.

Pearl: I'll tear it off my neck.

Fenwick: Pearl, you break my heart. Do you care for me so little that you can't bear to wear the trifling presents I gave you?

Pearl: If you talk to me like that I shall cry. Don't you see that I'm trying to keep my self-control?

Fenwick: This is dreadful. This is even more painful than I anticipated.

Pearl: You see, strength is easy to you. I'm weak. That's why I put myself in your hands. I felt your power instinctively.

Fenwick: I know, I know, and it was because I felt you

needed me that I loved you. I wanted to shelter you from the storms and buffets of the world.

Pearl: Why didn't you save me from myself, Arthur?

Fenwick: When I look at your poor, pale little face I wonder what you'll do without me, girlie.

Pearl [*her voice breaking*]: It'll be very hard. I've grown so used to depending on you. Whenever anything has gone wrong, I've come to you and you've put it right. I was begining to think there was nothing you couldn't do.

Fenwick: I've always welcomed obstacles. I like something to surmount. It excites me.

Pearl: You seemed to take all my strength from me. I felt strangely weak beside you.

Fenwick: It wasn't necessary that we should both be strong. I loved you because you were weak. I liked you to come to me in all your troubles. It made me feel so good to be able to put everything right for you.

Pearl: You've always been able to do the impossible.

Fenwick [*impressively*]: I have never found anything impossible.

Pearl [*deeply moved*]: Except to forgive.

Fenwick: Ah, I see you know me. I never forget. I never forgive.

Pearl: I suppose that's why people feel there's something strangely Napoleonic about you.

Fenwick: Maybe. And yet – though you're only a woman, you've broken me, Pearl, you've broken me.

Pearl: Oh no, don't say that. I couldn't bear that. I want you to go on being strong and ruthless.

Fenwick: Something has gone out of my life for ever. I almost think you've broken my heart. I was so proud of you. I took so much pleasure in your success. Why, whenever I saw your name in the society columns of the papers it used to give me a thrill of satisfaction. What's going to become of you now, girlie? What's going to become of you now?

Pearl: I don't know; I don't care.

Fenwick: This fellow, does he care for you? Will he make you happy?

Pearl: Tony? He's going to marry the Duchesse.

[**Fenwick** *represses a start.*]

I shall never see him again.

Fenwick: Then if I leave you, you'll have nobody but your husband.

Pearl: Nobody.

Fenwick: You'll be terribly lonely, girlie.

Pearl: You will think of me sometimes, Arthur, won't you?

Fenwick: I shall never forget you, girlie. I shall never forget how you used to leave your fine house in Mayfair and come and lunch with me down town.

Pearl: You used to give me such delicious things to eat.

Fenwick: It was a treat to see you in your beautiful clothes sharing a steak with me and a bottle of beer. I can order a steak, Pearl, can't I?

Pearl: And d'you remember those delicious little onions that we used to have? [*She seems to taste them.*] M . . . M . . . M . . . It makes my mouth water to think of them.

Fenwick: There are few women who enjoy food as much as you do, Pearl.

Pearl: D'you know, next time you dined with me, I'd made up my mind to give you an entirely English dinner. Scotch broth, herrings, mixed grill, saddle of lamb, and then enormous marrow bones.

[**Fenwick** *can hardly bear the thought, his face grows red, his eyes bulge, and he gasps.*]

Fenwick: Oh, girlie! [*With utter abandonment*] Let's have that dinner. [*He seizes her in his arms and kisses her.*] I can't leave you. You need me too much.

Pearl: Arthur, Arthur, can you forgive me?

Fenwick: To err is human, to forgive divine.

Pearl: Oh, how like you that is!

Fenwick: If you must deceive me, don't let me ever find out. I love you too much.

458

Pearl: I won't, Arthur, I promise you I won't.

Fenwick: Come and sit on the sofa and let me look at you. I seem to see you for the first time.

Pearl: You know, you wouldn't have liked the walk to the station. It's four miles in the sun. You're a vain old thing, and your boots are always a little too small for you.

[**Bessie** *comes in. She stops as she sees* **Pearl** *and* **Fenwick** *sitting hand in hand.*]

Pearl: Are you going out, Bessie?

Bessie: As soon as Harry has finished his letters, we're going for a walk.

Pearl [*to* **Fenwick**]: You mustn't squeeze my hand in Bessie's presence, Arthur.

Fenwick: You're a very lucky girl, Bessie, to have a sister like Pearl. She's the most wonderful woman in the world.

Pearl: You're talking nonsense, Arthur. Go and put some flannels on. It makes me quite hot to look at you in that suit. We'll try and get up a little tennis after tea.

Fenwick: Now, you mustn't tire yourself, Pearl. Remember those white cheeks of yours.

Pearl [*with a charming look at him*]: Oh, I shall soon get my colour back now.

[*She gives him her hand to kiss and he goes out. Pearl takes a little mirror out of her bag and looks at herself reflectively.*]

Pearl: Men are very trivial, foolish creatures. They have kind hearts. But their heads. Oh dear, oh dear, it's lamentable. And they're so vain, poor dears, they're so vain.

Bessie: Pearl, tomorrow, when we go back to London, I'm going away.

Pearl: Are you? Where?

Bessie: The Princess is going to take me over to Paris for a few days.

Pearl: Oh, is that all? Don't stay away too long. You ought to be in London just at present.

Bessie: On my return I'm proposing to stay with the Princess.

Pearl [*calmly*]: Nonsense.

Bessie: I wasn't asking your permission, Pearl. I was telling you my plans.

Pearl [*looks at her for a moment reflectively*]: Are you going to make me a scene, too? I've already gone through two this afternoon. I'm rather tired of them.

Bessie: Please don't be alarmed. I've got nothing more to say.

[*She makes as though to leave the room.*]

Pearl: Don't be a little fool, Bessie. You've been staying with me all the season. I can't allow you to leave my house and go and live with Flora. We don't want to go out of our way to make people gossip.

Bessie: Please don't argue with me, Pearl. It's not my business to reproach you for anything you do. But it isn't my business, either, to stand by and watch.

Pearl: You're no longer a child, Bessie.

Bessie: I've been blind and foolish. Because I was happy and having a good time, I never stopped to ask for explanations of this, that, and the other. I never thought ... The life was so gay and brilliant – it never struck me that underneath it all – Oh, Pearl, don't make me say what I have in my heart, but let me go quietly.

Pearl: Bessie, dear, you must be reasonable. Think what people would say if you suddenly left my house. They'd ask all sorts of questions, and heaven knows what explanations they'd invent. People aren't charitable, you know. I don't want to be hard on you, but I can't afford to let you do a thing like that.

Bessie: Now that I know what I do, I should never respect myself again if I stayed.

Pearl: I don't know how you can be so unkind.

Bessie: I don't want to be that, Pearl. But it's stronger than I am. I must go.

Pearl [*with emotion*]: I'm so fond of you, Bessie. You don't know how much I want you with me. After all, I've seen so little of you these last few years. It's been such a comfort to me to have you. You were so pretty and young and sweet, it was like a ray of April sunshine in the house.

Bessie: I'm afraid you think women are as trivial, foolish creatures as men, Pearl.

[Pearl *looks up and sees that* Bessie *is not in the least taken in by the pathetic attitude.*]

Pearl [*icily*]: Take care you don't go too far, Bessie.

Bessie: There's no need for us to quarrel. I've made up my mind, and there's the end of it.

Pearl: Flora's a fool. I shall tell her that I won't have her take you away from me. You'll stay with me until you're married.

Bessie: D'you want me to tell you that I can hardly bear to speak to you? You fill me with shame and disgust. I want never to see you again.

Pearl: Really, you drive me beyond endurance. I think I must be the most patient woman in the world to put up with all I've had to put up with today. After all, what have I done? I was a little silly and incautious. By the fuss you all make one would think no one had ever been incautious and silly before. Besides, it hasn't got anything to do with you. Why don't you mind your own business?

Bessie [*bitterly*]: You talk as though your relations with Arthur Fenwick were perfectly natural.

Pearl: Good heavens, you're not going to pretend you didn't know about Arthur. After all, I'm no worse than anybody else. Why, one of the reasons we Americans like London is that we can live our own lives and people accept things philosophically. Eleo Gloster, Sadie Twickenham, Maimie Hartlepool – you don't imagine they're faithful to their husbands? They didn't marry them for that.

Bessie: Oh, Pearl, how can you? How can you? Haven't you any sense of decency at all? When I came in just now and saw you sitting on the sofa with that gross, vulgar, sensual old man – oh! [*She makes a gesture of disgust.*] You can't love him. I could have understood if . . . but – oh, it's so disgraceful, it's so hideous. What can you see in him? He's nothing but rich . . . [*She pauses, and her face changes as a thought comes to her, and in coming horrifies her.*] It's not because he's rich? Pearl! Oh!

Pearl: Really, Bessie, you're very silly, and I'm tired of talking to you.

Bessie: Pearl, it's not that? Answer me. Answer me.

Pearl [*roughly*]: Mind your own business.

Bessie: He was right, then, last night, when he called you that. He was so right that you didn't even notice it. A few hours later you're sitting hand in hand with him. A slut. That's what he called you. A slut. A slut.

Pearl: How dare you! Hold your tongue. How dare you!

Bessie: A kept woman. That's what you are.

Pearl [*recovering herself*]: I'm a fool to lose my temper with you.

Bessie: Why should you? I'm saying nothing but the truth.

Pearl: You're a silly little person, Bessie. If Arthur helps me a little, that's his affair, and mine. He's got more money than he knows what to do with, and it amuses him to see me spend it. I could have twenty thousand a year from him if I chose.

Bessie: Haven't you got money of your own?

Pearl: You know exactly what I've got. Eight thousand a year. D'you think I could have got the position I have on that? You're not under the impression all the world comes to my house because of my charm, are you? I'm not. You don't think the English want us here? You don't think they like us marrying their men? Good heavens, when you've known England as long as I have you'll realize that in their hearts they still look upon us as savages and Red Indians. We have to force ourselves upon them. They come to me because I amuse them. Very early in my career I discovered that the English can never resist getting something for nothing.

If a dancer is the rage, they'll see her at my house. If a fiddler is in vogue, they'll hear him at my concert. I give them balls. I give them dinners. I've made myself the fashion, I've got power, I've got influence. But everything I've got — my success, my reputation, my notoriety — I've bought it, bought it, bought it.

Bessie: How humiliating!

Pearl: And, finally, I've bought you a husband.

Bessie: That's not true. He loves me.

Pearl: D'you think he'd have loved you if I hadn't shown you to him in these surroundings, if I hadn't dazzled him by the brilliant people among whom he found you? You don't know what love is made of. D'you think it's nothing that he should hear a Prime Minister pay you compliments? Of course I bought him.

Bessie [*aghast*]: It's horrible.

Pearl: You know the truth now. It'll be very useful to you in your married life. Run away and take your little walk with Harry Bleane. I'm going to arrange my face.

[*She goes out.* **Bessie** *is left ashamed and stunned.* **Bleane** *comes in.*]

Bleane: I'm afraid I've kept you waiting. I'm so sorry.

Bessie [*dully*]: It doesn't matter at all.

Bleane: Where shall we go? You know the way about these parts, and I don't.

Bessie: Harry, I want you to release me. I can't marry you.

Bleane [*aghast*]: Why?

Bessie: I want to go back to America. I'm frightened.

Bleane: Of me?

Bessie: Oh no, I know that you're a dear, good creature; I'm frightened of what I may become.

Bleane: But I love you, Bessie.

Bessie: Then that's all the more reason for me to go. I must tell you frankly. I'm not in love with you, I only like you. I would never have dreamt of marrying you if you hadn't been who you are. I wanted to have a title. That's why Pearl married her husband, and that's why the Duchess married. Let me go, Harry.

Bleane: I knew you didn't love me, but I thought you might come to in time. I thought if I tried I could make you love me.

Bessie: You didn't know that I was nothing but a self-seeking, heartless snob.

Bleane: I don't care what you say of yourself, I know that you can be nothing but what is true and charming.

Bessie: After what you've seen last night? After what you know of this house? Aren't you disgusted with all of us?

Bleane: You can't think I could class you with the Duchesse and . . . [*He stops.*]

Bessie: Pearl at my age was no different from what I am. It's the life.

Bleane: But perhaps you won't want to lead it. The set you've been living in here isn't the only set in England. It makes a stir because it's in the public eye. Its doings are announced in the papers. But it isn't a very good set, and there are plenty of people who don't very much admire it.

Bessie: You must let me try and say what I have in my heart. And be patient with me. You think I can make myself at home in your life. I've had a hint of it now and then. I've seen a glimpse of it through Pearl's laughter and the Duchesse's sneers. It's a life of dignity, of responsibilities, and of public duty.

Bleane [*with a rueful smile*]: You make it very strenuous.

Bessie: It comes naturally to the English girls of your class. They've known it all their lives, and they've been brought up to lead it. But we haven't. To us it's just tedious, and its dignity is irksome. We're bored, and we fall back on the only thing that offers, pleasure. You've spoken to me about your house. It means everything to you because it's associated with your childhood and all your people before you. It could only mean something to me if I loved you. And I don't.

Bleane: You've made me so wretched. I don't know what to say to you.

Bessie: If I make you wretched now, it's so that we may both be saved a great deal of unhappiness later on. I'm glad I don't care for you, for it would make it so much harder for me to go. And I've got to go. I can't marry you. I want to go home. If I marry ever I want to marry in my own country. That is my place.

Bleane: Don't you think you could wait a little before you decide finally?

Bessie: Don't put difficulties in my way. Don't you see that we're not strong enough for the life over here? It goes to our head; we lose our bearings; we put away our own code, and we can't adopt the code of the country we come to. We drift. There's nothing for us to do but amuse ourselves, and we fall to pieces. But in America we're safe. And perhaps America wants us. When we come over here we're like soldiers deserting our country in time of war. Oh, I'm homesick for America I didn't know how much it meant to me till now. Let me go back, Harry.

Bleane: If you don't want to marry me, of course, I'm not going to try and make you.

Bessie: Don't be angry, and be my friend always.

Bleane: Always.

Bessie: After all, three months ago you didn't know me. In three months more you will have forgotten me. Then marry some English girl, who can live your life and share your thoughts. And be happy.

[**Pearl** *comes in. She has rouged her cheeks, and has once more the healthy colour which is usual with her. She is evidently jubilant.*]

Pearl: The car has just come back from London. [*She goes to the french window and calls*] Minnie!

Bessie: I shall tell Pearl tomorrow.

Bleane: I won't post my letters then. I'll go and get them out of the box.

Bessie: Forgive me.

[*He goes out. The* **Duchesse** *and* **Clay** *appear at the window.*]

Duchesse: Did you call me?

Pearl: The car has just come back from London, so it can take you to the station.

Duchesse: That's a mercy. I didn't at all like the idea of going to the station in the luggage cart. Where is Flora? I must say good-bye to her.

Pearl: Oh, there's plenty of time now. The car will run you down in ten minutes.

[Tony *comes in, then the* **Princess** *and* **Fleming**.]

Duchesse: Tony, the car has returned, and is going to take us to the station.

Tony: Thank God for that! I should have looked a perfect fool in that luggage cart.

Clay: But what on earth did you send the car to London for, anyway?

Pearl: In one minute you'll see.

[**Arthur Fenwick** *comes in. He has changed into flannels.*]

Fenwick: Who is that gentleman that's just arrived, Pearl?

Pearl: The man of mystery.

[**Pole** *comes in, followed by* **Ernest**.]

Pole: Mr Ernest.

[*Exit* **Pole**.]

Duchesse: Ernest!

Clay: Ernest?

[*He is a little dark man, with large eyes, and long hair neatly plastered down. He is dressed like a tailor's dummy, in black coat, white gloves, silk hat, patent leather boots. He is a dancing master, and overwhelmingly gentlemanly. He speaks in mincing tones.*]

Ernest: Dear Lady Grayston.

Pearl [*shaking hands with him*]: I'm so glad you were able to come. [*To the others*] You were talking about Ernest last night, and I thought we would have nothing to do this evening and he would cheer and comfort us.

I sent the car up to London with orders to bring him back dead or alive.

Ernest: My dear Lady Grayston, I'm sure I'll get into no end of trouble. I had all sorts of calls to pay this afternoon, and I was dining out, and I'd promised to go to a little hop that the dear Duchess of Gloster was giving. But I felt I couldn't refuse you. You've always been such a good friend to me, dear Lady Grayston. You must excuse me coming in my town clothes, but your chauffeur said there wasn't a moment to lose, so I came just as I am.

Pearl: But you look a perfect picture.

Ernest: Oh, don't say that, dear Lady Grayston; I know this isn't the sort of thing one ought to wear in the country.

Pearl: You remember the Duchesse de Surennes?

Ernest: Oh, of course I remember the Duchesse.

Duchesse: Dear Ernest!

Ernest: Dear Duchesse!

Duchesse: I thought I was never going to see you again, Ernest.

Ernest: Oh, don't say that, it sounds too sad.

Pearl: It's such a pity you must go, Minnie. Ernest could have shown you all sorts of new steps.

Ernest: Oh, dear Duchesse, you're not going the very moment I come down? That is unkind of you.

Duchesse [*with an effort*]: I must go. I must go.

Ernest: Have you been practising that little step I showed you the other day? My dear friend, the Marchioness of Twickenham – not the *old* one, you know, the *new* one – is beginning to do it so well.

Duchesse [*struggling with herself*]: Have we time, Pearl? I should like Ernest to dance just one two-step with me.

Pearl: Of course there's time. Thornton, set the gramophone.

[**Thornton Clay** *at once starts it, and the notes of the two-step tinkle out.*]

Our Betters

Duchesse: You don't mind, Ernest, do you?

Ernest: I love dancing with you, Duchesse.

[They take up their positions.]

Duchesse: Just one moment. It always makes me so nervous to dance with you, Ernest.

Ernest: Oh, now, don't be silly, dear Duchesse.

[They begin to dance.]

Ernest: Now hold your shoulders like a lady. Arch your back, my dear, arch your back. Don't look like a sack of potatoes. If you put your foot there, I shall kick it.

Duchesse: Oh, Ernest, don't be cross with me.

Ernest: I shall be cross with you, Duchesse. You don't pay any attention to what I say. You must give your mind to it.

Duchesse: I do! I do!

Ernest: And don't dance like an old fish-wife. Put some vim into it. That's what I always say about these modern dances: you want two things, vim and nous.

Duchesse [*plaintively*]: Ernest!

Ernest: Now don't cry. I'm saying all this for your good, you know. What's wrong with you is that you've got no passion.

Duchesse: Oh, Ernest, how can you say such a thing. I've always looked upon myself as a very passionate woman.

Ernest: I don't know anything about that, dear Duchesse, but you don't get it into your dancing. That's what I said the other day to the dear Marchioness of Twickenham – not the *new* one, you know, the *old* one – You must put passion into it, I said. That's what these modern dances want – passion, passion.

Duchesse: I see exactly what you mean, Ernest.

Ernest: And you must dance with your eyes as well, you know. You must look as if you had a knife in your garter, and as if you'd kill me if I looked at another woman. Don't you see how I'm looking, I'm looking as though I meant, Curse her! how I love her. There!

[The music stops and they separate.]

468

Duchesse: I have improved, Ernest, haven't I?

Ernest: Yes, you've improved, dear Duchesse, but you want more practice.

Pearl: Minnie, why on earth don't you stay, and Ernest will give you a real lesson this evening.

Ernest: That's what you want, Duchesse.

[*The* **Duchesse** *wrestles with herself.*]

Duchesse: Tony, d'you think we can stop?

Tony: I didn't want to go away. It's rotten going up to town this evening. What on earth are we going to do with ourselves when we get there?

Duchesse: Very well, Pearl, if it'll please you, we'll stop.

Pearl: That is nice of you, Minnie.

Duchesse: You're very naughty sometimes, Pearl, but you have a good heart, and I can't help being fond of you.

Pearl [*with outstretched arms*]: Minnie!

Duchesse: Pearl!

[*They clasp one another and affectionately embrace.*]

Ernest: What an exquisite spectacle – two ladies of title kissing one another.

Bessie [*to* **Fleming**]: They're not worth making a fuss about. I'm sailing for America next Saturday!

THE HISTORY OF VINTAGE

The famous American publisher Alfred A. Knopf (1892–1984) founded Vintage Books in the United States in 1954 as a paperback home for the authors published by his company. Vintage was launched in the United Kingdom in 1990 and works independently from the American imprint although both are part of the international publishing group, Random House.

Vintage in the United Kingdom was initially created to publish paperback editions of books bought by the prestigious literary hardback imprints in the Random House Group such as Jonathan Cape, Chatto & Windus, Hutchinson and later William Heinemann, Secker & Warburg and The Harvill Press. There are many Booker and Nobel Prize-winning authors on the Vintage list and the imprint publishes a huge variety of fiction and non-fiction. Over the years Vintage has expanded and the list now includes both great authors of the past – who are published under the Vintage Classics imprint – as well as many of the most influential authors of the present. In 2012 Vintage Children's Classics was launched to include the much-loved authors of our youth.

penguin.co.uk/vintage-classics